Political issues in Britain today

Fifth edition
Revised and completely updated

edited by
Bill Jones

Manchester University Press

Manchester and New York

distributed exclusively in the USA by St. Martin's Press

First published by Manchester University Press 1985
Second edition published 1987
Third edition published 1989
Fourth edition published 1994

This edition published by Manchester University Press
Oxford Road, Manchester M13 9NR, UK
and Room 400, 175 Fifth Avenue, New York, NY 10010, USA
http://www.man.ac.uk/mup

Distributed exclusively in the USA by
St. Martin's Press, Inc., 175 Fifth Avenue, New York,
NY 10010, USA

Distributed exclusively in Canada by
UBC Press, University of British Columbia, 6344 Memorial Road,
Vancouver, BC, Canada V6T 1Z2

British Library Cataloguing-in-Publication Data
A catalogue record for this book is available from the British Library

Library of Congress Cataloging-in-Publication Data applied for

ISBN   0 7190 5431 1   *hardback*
       0 7190 5432 X   *paperback*

This edition first published 1999

05 04 03 02 01 00 99   10 9 8 7 6 5 4 3 2 1

Typeset by Ralph J. Footring, Derby
Printed in Great Britain by Biddles Ltd, Guildford and King's Lynn

Contents

Figures, tables and boxes

Contributors

Rob Baggott is Reader in Public Policy at De Montfort University.

David Coates is Professor of Labour History in the Department of Government at the University of Manchester.

Martin Durham is Senior Lecturer in Politics at the University of Wolverhampton.

The Right Honourable Lord Hurd of Westwell is former Home and Foreign Secretary in Conservative governments 1979–97 and is now a member of the House of Lords.

Bill Jones is Research Fellow in the Department of Government at the University of Manchester.

Geoff Lee is a senior consultant with ADC Limited, and an Associate Lecturer with the Open University Business School.

James Mitchell is Professor of Politics at the University of Sheffield.

Professor the Lord Norton of Louth is Professor of Government and Director of the Centre for Legislative Studies, Department of Politics, University of Hull.

Neill Nugent is Professor of Politics and Jean Monnet Professor of European Integration at Manchester Metropolitan University.

Lynton Robins is Principal Lecturer in Politics at De Montfort University.

Andrew Scott is Lecturer at the Europa Institute at the University of Edinburgh.

Graham P. Thomas is Lecturer in Politics at the Reading College of Technology.

Paul Wilding is Professor of Social Policy at the University of Manchester.

David Wilson is Professor of Public Administration at De Montfort University.

Bruce Wood is Dean of the Faculty of Economic and Social Studies and Senior Lecturer in Government at the University of Manchester.

Preface

It is almost a decade and a half since the first edition of *Political issues in Britain today* appeared. The spur for its publication was the dearth of short, accessible issue studies for students of politics at 'A' and undergraduate levels; those available tended to be too long and detailed and too theoretical for the readership.

Another consideration was that issues are intrinsically interesting. For example, Parliament with its procedures and labyrinthine committees can be somewhat dry and legalistic; issues like the environment, crime and Europe are the stuff of politics, things which move people to passion and occasionally to the streets to protest or demonstrate. Similarly, teachers of politics, eager to find common ground with their students, will find issues tend to provide it. Examination boards have generally agreed and in recent years a number have introduced a selection of issues as elements in their politics syllabuses. Throughout, the authors have tried to be objective but inevitably bias infiltrates, to a degree, the most even-handed of academic analyses.

As with other volumes in the Politics Today series, the aim is to provide a complement rather than a substitute for more comprehensive studies. We hope that the brief, clear introductions provided in the following chapters will interest students and help them enter more fully the fascinating, constantly changing world of the politically literate and well informed.

For this edition a number of topics have been dropped from the last, 1993 edition and a range of new ones introduced: for example, the monarchy, the political style of Tony Blair, reforming welfare, devolution, sleaze, Labour ideology and funding of political parties.

Thanks are due to Nicola Viinikka at Manchester University Press and all the contributors. Thanks are also due in no small measure to Ralph Footring for his laudably high standards of copy-editing. I hope readers will find the book stimulating, varied, readable and, if they are so embarked, useful for examination studies.

Bill Jones

Abbreviations

AMS	additional member system
AV	alternative vote
BA	British Airways
BAA	British Airports Authority
BAe	British Aerospace
BCS	British Crime Survey
BGC	British Gas Corporation
BL	British Leyland
BNFL	British Nuclear Fuels Limited
BR	British Rail
BSE	bovine spongiform encephalopathy
BT	British Telecom
C&W	Cable & Wireless
CAP	Common Agricultural Policy
CBI	Confederation of British Industry
CFCs	chorofluorocarbons
CFSP	common foreign and security policy
CLP	constituency Labour party
CND	Campaign for Nuclear Disarmament
DHA	district health authority
DTI	Department of Trade and Industry
EC	European Community
ECB	European Central Bank
ECU	European currency unit
EMI	European Monetary Institute
EMS	European Monetary System
EMU	economic and monetary union
EP	European Parliament
ERM	Exchange Rate Mechanism

ESCB	European System of Central Banks
EU	European Union
FOE	Friends of the Earth
FPTP	first past the post
GATT	General Agreement on Tariffs and Trade
GDP	gross domestic product
GM	genetically modified
GMB	General and Municipal Boilermakers and Allied Trades Union
GP	general practitioner
IGC	intergovernmental conference
JHA	justice and home affairs
LEA	local education authority
MMC	Monopolies and Mergers Commission
NALGO	National and Local Government Officers' Association
NATO	North Atlantic Treaty Organization
NHS	National Health Service
NUM	National Union of Mineworkers
NUPE	National Union of Public Employees
NUR	National Union of Railwaymen
OECD	Organization for Economic Cooperation and Development
PFI	Private Finance Initiative
POEU	Post Office and Engineering Union
PR	proportional representation
PSBR	public sector borrowing requirement
RPI	retail price index
RTZ	Rio Tinto Zinc
SATs	standard assessment tasks
SCAT	Services to Community Action and Tenants
SDP	Social Democratic Party
SEM	Single European Market
SERPS	state earnings-related pension scheme
SNP	Scottish National Party
STV	single transferable vote
TEU	Treaty on European Union
TGWU	Transport and General Workers' Union
TUC	Trades Union Congress
UN	United Nations

1

Tony Blair's style of government: an interim assessment

Bill Jones

Ever since its first edition, back in 1985, this book has opened with an assessment of the political style of the Prime Minister of the day. Such a topic may, at first sight, seem to be too slight to rank as a 'proper' political issue. This, however, is not the case. Margaret Thatcher's high-handed style was the talking point of Westminster and Fleet Street and contributed in no small measure, through her alienation of potential support, to her eventual downfall. John Major's style was totally different but there can be no doubt also that his appearance of being not quite in control of a shamblingly corrupt administration contributed substantially to Labour's landslide in May 1997.

So then we had Tony Blair, shining new leader, and, in the wake of his victory, with the political world at his feet. His approval ratings soared in the summer and autumn of 1997 to 93 per cent, exceeding those of any postwar Prime Minister; *The Economist* described him as 'Prince' of all he surveyed. Then things began slowly to cool and a more measured public view began to emerge in 1998. It is now much easier to track down people seriously concerned about Blair's stewardship of the nation's top job, many, indeed, in his own party.

In this chapter, following precedent, a number of critical propositions will be considered – points for and against – and a strictly interim overall judgement of this extraordinary man – the century's youngest Prime Minister – attempted. Prominent among the criticisms of Blair have been accusations of: betraying Labour values (wags have pointed out a part anagram of Tony Blair MP reads 'I'm a Tory'); arrogance; love of power; and ideas above his station as a democratic premier. These, and more, are considered below.

He has no ideas of his own but has merely hijacked Conservative ones

Opponents say...

Far from donating his own vision, Blair merely annexed existing Conservative or Thatcherite thinking and called it 'New' Labour policy. Blairism is therefore Thatcherism in disguise. The anatomy of this conjuring trick is as follows.

Law and order. Here Blair, as shadow Home Secretary, sought to end the perception of Labour as 'soft on crime'. He it was who introduced right-wing steel into the Party's message, summed up by his slogan 'Tough on crime – tough on the causes of crime'.

Employment. When shadowing this portfolio, he succeeded in ending his party's commitment to 'full employment' in 1990, when the document *Looking to the Future* talked instead of the 'highest possible levels of skilled and rewarding employment'.

Education. Blair sent his son Euan to the Oratory School, a grant-maintained school of the type Labour policy opposed (see Chapter 9). He received much criticism from the Tories for this ('Labour says one thing; it does another') and from former Labour deputy leader Roy Hattersley – who has long argued the case for comprehensive education – not to mention his own press secretary, Alastair Campbell. He later defended the right of Harriet Harman to send her son to St Olave's in Orpington, one of the country's 160 selective schools.

Union links. This was another aspect of his alleged closet Toryism. In his excellent, balanced biography of Blair, John Rentoul charts the details:

- In November 1989 he abandoned Labour's support for one of the unions' hallowed symbols – the closed shop – when shadow Employment Minister.
- As a member of the Union Links Group he reversed the emerging consensus to maintain the block vote, formalised as one member, one vote (OMOV), after an extended struggle at the 1993 conference in Brighton.
- At the 1997 conference he read the unions a humiliating lecture on how to pull together with management and not to expect any favours from him. Critics say he is more concerned with macho posturing to show 'Middle England' that he is not in the pocket of the unions than respecting the nexus out of which the Labour Party originally grew.
- Blair shows no desire to reverse Tory anti-union laws on employment and even boasted in the election campaign that Britain would retain under Labour one of the 'strictest' sets of employment laws.
- Blair has also declared himself very much in favour of 'flexible' employment laws which enable employers to hire and fire and limit the entitlements of part-timers.

Economy. Blair has accepted the Tory approach to the economy in every important respect:

- He accepted their spending plans for the first two years of his government.
- He has pledged not to increase the basic levels of income tax as fixed by the Conservatives after eighteen years in office.
- He has favoured big business people for a number of key appointments rather than more obviously Labour people (e.g. Lord Simon of BP as the Trade and Industry Minister, Martin Taylor of Barclays Bank, who is advising on benefits, and Geoffrey Robinson as a Treasury minister, ironically placed in charge of tax avoidance when he was revealed to have huge investments in offshore tax havens himself).
- He has accepted privatisation. The left-wing journalist Paul Foot has written that during the 1980s Labour pledged to renationalise every enterprise privatised by the Tories, but once Blair came to power each pledge was systematically abandoned, including, most shamefully for some, that of renationalising the railways.
- Blair abandoned any opposition to capitalism, the original source of socialism and the Labour Party, and regularly praised the 'dynamism' of free enterprise as well as accepting the existence of very rich people as legitimate.
- After he addressed the French parliament in French, on 25 March 1998, some present commented on the Thatcherite nature of his so-called 'third way'. Gaullist deputy Patrick Devedjian commented: 'Clearly it is very easy to make a mistake in English with the New Labour. It just means Conservative.'

Defenders say...

Blair has consistently identified core ideas ever since he was an undergraduate at Oxford. Rentoul even suggests his sense of mission, to 'make a difference', preceded this and is closely connected with his youthful religious leanings when he even considered, quite seriously, becoming a priest before swinging to 'politics as the vehicle for his moral commitment'. He was already a natural anti-establishment undergraduate, attracted to leftish politics but cautious and certainly no extremist.

Blair and his university friend Peter Thomson were strongly influenced by the ideas of John Macmurray, a Scottish philosopher writing in the 1930s. His central idea was that of 'community'. This sprung from the notion that human beings exist only in relation to others; Blair expressed it thus in 1993: 'We do not lose our identity in our relations with others; in part at least, we achieve our identity by those relations' (see Rentoul, 1996). The core of these relationships lay in the family. Macmurray argued we should all pursue the interests of the community in order to advance our own interests as a member of that community. The more closely society approximates to the family the more it realises its potential. Blair explained the impact of these ideas thus: 'It seemed to me a sensible explanation of the human condition. There seemed a coincidence between the philosophical theory of Christianity and left of centre politics. They were the influences which stayed with me.'

Blair was confirmed while at university and has been a devout churchgoer ever since. The strength of these influences can be clearly seen in all his speeches. He emphasises the primacy of caring for fellow citizens and being responsible for our local communities. He also stresses inclusivity, including everyone, especially the young and older people. These themes may chime in with Conservative ideas but what is beyond dispute is that their provenance in Blair was the result of the natural intellectual maturing of a highly intelligent young man and not crude opportunism once power beckoned.

The political writer Andrew Heywood perceives, through all the debate, a distinct Blairite project comprising:

- *Economic Thatcherism*. There should be no more state control, low public spending, flexible labour markets and a 'stake-holder' economy.
- *Liberal communitarianism*. Old Labour sought to alleviate via the benefits system while New Labour sees poverty as a reflection of a cultural deficit: poor people lack the resources to be self-reliant and employable. According to Blair the government has a moral responsibility to provide the skills for the individual in a global world where those without the resources live frugally or are excluded totally from society. The individual has the responsibility to acquire what is offered and has to accept a reciprocal moral responsibility to society to achieve self-reliance through working. It follows that education is the key interface whereby the government delivers its side of this bargain. Blairism is therefore a cultural project; it seeks to change the thinking of citizens, to make them actually think like citizens.
- *Constitutional radicalism*. Blair seeks to modernise the ramshackle constitution and in the process to entrench his social and political reforms, to make them irreversible, to make the twenty-first century a left-of-centre one, just as the twentieth century has been a Conservative one.

Blair did adapt the dominant political and economic philosophy of the day – but it has to be appreciated that:

- Four successive elections had been lost by Labour and as leader he had to redirect his party into a position from where it could realistically challenge for office; there is little point otherwise in being a political

party. A wealth of evidence showed that Labour's weakness was related
to: its perceived closeness to trade union sectional interests; its high
'tax and spend' policies; its predilection for government interference in
the economy, especially the discredited policy of nationalisation; and
its identification with 'losers' and regulation rather than 'winners' and
opportunity.

- The shrinkage of the working class meant Labour's natural voter base
  was disappearing following its heyday in the postwar years. In order
  to get into power Blair just had to appeal to middle-class voters too;
  Middle England values on law and order, low taxation and so forth
  therefore had to be addressed and incorporated into Labour thinking.
- Blair's son did actually go to a state school – albeit with overtones of
  selection in its admissions policy – and not a private one like the
  children of so many Conservative politicians.

In his address to the French parliament Blair was hugely praised for his
charisma and his clarity; reports confirm applause was won from left as
well as right by his tour de force performance.

'The third way' is the buzz word used to add, hopefully, some sharpness
to the Blairite project after just one year's accumulated fuzziness and
reinforced by a book of the same name by a Blairite guru, the sociologist
Tony Giddens. Blair himself authored a Fabian pamphlet (1998) so entitled,
and attended a seminar in Washington with Clinton and European leaders
on the same topic in late September 1998. What is apparently meant by
the term is a redefinition of the 'radical centre': a modernisation of
institutions to make them more democratic; governmental partnership with
capitalism to ensure business is confident and successful; an enthusing of
civil society to make it more participatory, with citizens having responsibilities
as well as rights, including the obligation to bring up children to be
competent, responsible citizens; the inclusion of what is becoming an
underclass in the mainstream; an approach to welfare which includes
personal involvement; and relatively low taxation.

Blair has betrayed the ideals of the Labour Party

Opponents say...

- *Clause 4.* Blair decided to abolish Clause 4 – the 'common ownership
  of the economy' clause of the Labour Party's constitution. Some Party
  members said this was like taking the 'salvation' out of the Salvation
  Army. Instead of the famous clause, formerly emblazoned on every
  Party member's card, a new form of words was substituted which
  embraced the idea of capitalism: amounting to a rejection of and the
  antithesis of socialism.

- *Unsympathetic to unions.* Blair has eschewed the traditional bond with the unions and embraced the idea of privatisation (see above).
- *Socialism ignored.* Blair has dropped the use of the word 'socialism' in manifestos and conference speeches.
- The fiercely right-wing think-tank the Adam Smith Institute undertook a review of Blair's first 200 days and, on a points system, awarded Labour 67.8 per cent – further evidence, say critics, that Blair had been implementing right-wing policies.

Defenders say...

- Some Continental socialist parties have adjusted their ideology to take account of modern circumstances. Labour's 'modernisation' process, instigated by Blair, has merely brought Britain's party in line with those like the German, which abandoned old-style socialism in 1959.
- Blair does have a vision for Britain which represents a consistent 'modernised' version of the principles underlying Labour's traditional message. At the 1997 conference he spelt out his vision, much of it confirming Heywood's analysis explained above:

I want this country to be nothing less than the model 21st century nation, a beacon to the world.... We can be the best; the best place to live, to bring up children, to lead a fulfilled life, to grow old.... [We have a responsibility] to be a government of high ideals and hard choices ... remembered for all time ... one of the great, radical reforming governments of our history.... Our goal ... to make Britain the best educated and most skilled country in the world. ... there is no place for militant trade unionism or uncaring management today.

In addition, he set a target of half a million extra students in higher and further education by 2002; more cash for school repairs and for children whose first language is not English; more support for families; the creation of ten health action zones (see Chapter 10); and a new hospital at Greenwich.

- The Adam Smith Institute has been right wing in its sympathies but praise from an opponent should be seen as a possible compliment as well as evidence that Blair's 'inclusive' strategy is working.

He is too concerned to woo the right-wing press, especially Rupert Murdoch

Opponents say...

In 1992 Labour had undertaken a one-year boycott of Murdoch's newspapers, after their move to Wapping, which had involved the dismissal of 5,000 print workers. In July 1995, Blair flew all the way to Hayman Island,

Australia, to address one of Murdoch's News International staff conferences. There a deal may have been struck: Murdoch's ruthlessness is legendary in wooing politicians who will ensure his business interests are protected. By March 1995, reported *The Independent* (11 February 1998), 'there were reports that Labour plans for cross media ownership would not force Murdoch to sell any of his empire'.

Blair received his reward when *The Sun* sensationally came out for Blair at the start of the election campaign, March 1997, despite its earlier rabid anti-Labour stance and stated opposition to key Labour policies at the time.

Murdoch received his reward on 10 February 1998, when Blair's office launched a passionate attack on critics who had helped pass an amendment to the Competition Bill which would rule out the 'predatory price setting' which Murdoch's *Times* was alleged to have pursued in order to make *The Independent* bankrupt. Ironically, Labour had sponsored a motion in July 1994 condemning newspaper price cutting by Murdoch 'with the intention of forcing rivals out of the market place'.

It is also rumoured that Blair has assured Murdoch his media empire will benefit from the forthcoming 'digitalisation' of the broadcast media process.

Instead of choosing Labour newspapers like *The Mirror* or Labour-leaning ones like *The Guardian*, Blair often issues key articles to the Conservative-supporting *Daily Mail*.

Blair's right-hand man and media expert Peter Mandelson is a friend of the tycoon's daughter, Elizabeth Murdoch, adding another element to the web binding Blair to the right-wing media.

In March 1998, it was reported Blair had intervened in Murdoch's attempt to buy a big stake in Mediaset, the company of Italian media mogul/politician Silvio Berlusconi. It was said he rang up Mr Prodi, the Italian Prime Minister, in an effort to broker the deal for Murdoch. As a result of learning Mr Prodi had advised an outside buyer would not be welcomed, Murdoch withdrew his £2 billion plus offer.

Andrew Neil, writing in *The Observer* (29 March 1998), gave testimony that his former boss courted politicians only for business reasons and dropped them as soon as they ceased to be useful.

Some, including Roy Hattersley (Channel 4, 19 April 1998), claim Labour has decided that the next election, which it is obsessed with winning, cannot be won without the support of the tabloids, giving Murdoch a virtual veto on anything Labour might seek to achieve.

Defenders say...

Blair has merely hit it off personally with the tycoon and seems to get on well with him.

The Sun's opposition in 1992 was said by some (including *The Sun* itself) to have won the election for the Conservatives. It was essential for Labour's leadership to build bridges with a pivotally important press influence if it hoped to win in 1997. By the time *The Sun* moved its support it had been rubbishing Major for months and most of its readers had decided to vote Labour in any case.

Mandelson is a very gregarious man and it is not surprising he makes friendships throughout the media, whatever the political colour.

The Lords' amendment to the Competition Bill was opposed by Blair because he genuinely felt, and argued the next day at Prime Minister's question time, the Bill was already strong enough to prevent 'predatory pricing' and that this was not the most effective way of tackling the problem.

Downing Street defended Blair's role in the Mediaset negotiations – including the allegation he met the tycoon to discuss the matter at Chequers – by saying: 'The Prime Minister has got to have private meetings, just as he is entitled to have private telephone calls ... if asked the Prime Minister would speak up for British firms. It would be odd if he did not.' (Murdoch's BSkyB is a British company though Murdoch is its biggest shareholder and a US citizen.) A row developed over the role of Alastair Campbell in March 1998 when he claimed all the press speculation about Blair's 'intervention' was 'crap'. (It later transpired his defence was based on the fact that Prodi had first rung Blair and not the other way around as alleged; the content of the conversation seemed to have been as reported: a clear example of being 'economical with the truth.')

He is bent on exercising supreme power

Opponents say...

Blair and Gordon Brown, in an act of arbitrary power, soon after the May election gave independence to the Bank of England even though it was not a manifesto pledge. Moreover, it took fifteen days for it to be announced to the House, earning a rebuke from the Speaker. Soon after, its supervisory powers over the City of London were removed.

Blair has imposed a tough disciplinary regime on his 419 MPs; on 7 May 1997 he lectured them on the need for strength, unity and discipline, and said he would not tolerate 'juvenile oppositionitis'.

Media engagements are being closely monitored from the centre, by a 'cabinet enforcer' and the press secretary. MP Gordon Prentice, writing in *The Observer* (11 October 1997), complained: 'Absolute loyalty is demanded on the grounds that we were elected New Labour and we must govern as New Labour – whatever that means.' Austin Mitchell joked New Labour MPs had a chip placed in their brains by Peter Mandelson to keep them 'on message'.

Blair announced without any consultation that Prime Minister's question time would be reduced from two fifteen-minute sessions per week to one of thirty minutes on Wednesdays, suggesting he wished to insulate himself from parliamentary criticism.

Despite his huge majority, Blair received only 43.2 per cent of the vote nationwide and seems to have forgotten the criticism he made of the Conservative's 'elective dictatorship' when he was leader of the opposition.

Further evidence of the centralisation of power under Blair is the new government's ministerial code. Paragraph 88 insists any speech, policy launch or media contact has first to be cleared with Downing Street. Ministers will also be scrutinised by a draconian new spending committee chaired by Gordon Brown.

He has ruthlessly centralised power, bringing in Mandelson, his trusted lackey, and later Cunningham to coordinate policy as well as Derry Irvine in a less defined way. While eschewing the lure of a Prime Minister's department, he has greatly strengthened the Cabinet Office to institutionalise the dominance of Number 10 in the machinery of government. To ensure his writ runs throughout the government, he has appointed, in the Fleet Street argot, an 'enforcer' – not Mandelson, as so many had predicted, but the likeable yet tough Geordie, Jack Cunningham.

More than one journalist has drawn parallels between Blair and the fascist leader Oswald Mosley. Francis Wheen points out Mosley was dismissive of the 'old politics' and was described by supporters as the 'New man for the New Britain'. He even formed a party called the New Party in 1930.

Finally, the opinion of Margaret Thatcher can be invoked. She has been known to admire Blair's drive and patriotism, but according to Peter Hennessy, at a conference in October 1998, she was overheard saying at a reception earlier in that year: 'That young man is getting terribly bossy.'

Defenders say...

The decision regarding the Bank of England's independence was taken quickly but in the interests of the economy, which has often been subject to financial speculation after Labour victories; Brown and Blair's decision was widely supported in the City and the financial press.

Media coordination is a sensible precaution for any government, as the damaging leaks emanating from the Major government revealed. Mandelson had an overall responsibility for policy coordination and monitoring.

Changes to Prime Minister's question time have been urged for years as the whole exercise had become like a kindergarten. Blair's confident style enables more questions in thirty minutes than used to be allowed in two fifteen-minute sessions. Blair has been keener on answering questions than engaging in party rhetoric and abuse. Paddy Ashdown has been given more time to feature in the weekly event.

At 43.2 per cent, Labour's share of the vote is substantial and it ill becomes the Conservatives to complain when they acted much more arbitrarily under Thatcher on a smaller share of the vote. Moreover, Blair has initiated steps to democratise the constitution via devolution and reform of the Lords: surely evidence of his democratic instincts?

There is no debate about Blair's approach to Party management: he is outspoken and honest, confronting opposition head on and winning the arguments with the help of Party members. But he is essentially a democratic politician, winning through advocacy and debate: he consulted 30,000 members over the repeal of Clause 4 and the draft manifesto in autumn 1996 was circulated to members for approval, which it won overwhelmingly.

Centralising power in a diffuse system like Britain's is no bad thing and placing tried and trusted people in charge is similarly sound political sense. A Prime Minister's department has been there in embryo for many years and it makes sense to make arrangements more explicit and formal in the form of a reformed Cabinet Office. Cunningham argues that Blair does not in any way need an enforcer:

> I can assure you the Prime Minister has authority and power and has had it from day one.... What he seeks is better 'joined up' government, better performance laterally between departments of state; he wants to see an end to turf wars, that will give colleagues an opportunity to work together in a collegiate way. The Prime Minister is in fact slightly moving back and leaving it more to ministers.

He is impressed by rich and powerful people and tends to defer to them

Opponents say...

Paul Foot makes the comparison between Blair and Ramsay MacDonald, the 'traitor' who split Labour by allying with the Conservatives in 1931. He quotes from and advises Blair to read an article which accused MacDonald of being 'ensnared in an aristocratic embrace', of shunning his own class and Labour voters and basking instead in the 'praise of the rich and powerful' (*The Guardian*, 15 December 1997).

Blair was a pushover for Murdoch when the media magnate set out to woo the likely next premier of Britain with newspaper support and invitations to Australia. He also sucked up to Richard Branson before the election and subsequently, and gave in to Bernie Ecclestone's blandishments over the exemption to the tobacco advertising ban (see Chapter 16).

In *The Guardian* (11 February 1998) Francis Wheen reported:

> Blair's colleagues have often told me that he has a boyish excitement at meeting famous or powerful people who treat him as an equal.... The people

who most impress him however are the billionaires. Only a few years ago Blair was distinctly sniffy about capitalism, but now he has the wide-eyed and credulous zeal of a convert.

In an ICM poll for *The Observer* (27 September 1998), 59 per cent of respondents felt 'Tony Blair pays too much attention to company bosses and not enough to ordinary working people'. Allied to this was a 54 per cent majority who felt 'rich people are buying influence with this government by giving Labour large amounts of money'.

Also, in *The Guardian* (5 March 1998), Roy Hattersley criticised Blair's government for being 'wonderfully tough towards the weak. But faced with either money or muscle, it rolls over on its back and kicks its legs in the air like a spaniel.'

Defenders say...

Blair is a very gregarious man who meets and likes an enormous range of people; as he comes from a public-school background it would be foolish to say he defers to members of the 'upper classes', as MacDonald clearly did.

Blair liked Murdoch and there was good personal chemistry (see above). His support also helped to win Labour's landslide.

Mosley was a flawed personality, obsessed by power and impatient with democracy, while Blair is the consummate constitutional moderate. However, there is a similarity between the two men in that they can both be seen as energetic reformers with original ideas to solve pressing modern problems. There the similarity ends.

Certainly, Blair enjoys meeting famous and talented people. Why should he not? But he is too well grounded in reality to allow his head to be turned by such minor perks of his office. Moreover, this enthusiasm is bound to diminish as he becomes used to power and a certain fame of his own. Francis Wheen is a witty and readable journalist but his negative opinions are worth little as he strives every week to find something to write about in his column.

Replying to Hattersley in *The Guardian* (6 March 1998), John Prescott, Deputy Prime Minister, refuted his accusations by pointing out how the government, among many other things: resisted the opposition of the utilities and pushed through its £5 billion windfall tax to fund the Welfare to Work programme; ignored business objections to the minimum wage; took on the gun lobby over handguns; and forced water companies to mend leaks.

While the ICM poll of 27 September reflected a majority opposed to Blair's apparent preference for company bosses, well over half of all polled were 'satisfied' with Blair's performance as premier and a big majority expressed Labour voting intentions.

He has diminished the importance of cabinet

Opponents say...

Blair has exploited his massive election victory either to push through his own demands to the exclusion of proper cabinet discussion, or to bypass such discussion via smaller decision-making groups. For example, the decision to exclude Formula One motor racing from the ban on tobacco advertising was taken after a small meeting with Bernie Ecclestone, Formula One's chief organiser, plus a few officials. Making it worse was the fact that the junior minister involved, Tessa Jowell, and her boss, Frank Dobson, also opposed this exclusion. Former permanent secretary Alan Bailey wrote that the episode 'shows the need to involve the relevant ministers in decision making, and to get back to proper Cabinet government which has been in decline for the last two decades' (*The Guardian*, 19 November 1997). The next day in the same newspaper Michael White wrote, 'The word is around that too many decisions are being taken bilaterally on Mr Blair's sofa with the big players being squared by phone instead of the forum of full Cabinet.' On 30 December 1997, that doyen of columnists, Hugo Young, wrote again in the same daily broadsheet that Blair was running the cabinet as:

> a personal fiefdom, consulting here, consulting there with selected colleagues, running the show through an inner cabinet ... which has taken further giant strides into the desert of irrelevance towards which Mrs Thatcher propelled it. Nobody these days talks of the cabinet as a centre of power.

Reflecting the ferment of comment and complaint, BBC Radio 4's *Analysis* programme on 15 January 1998 dealt with the charges. *Times* columnist Peter Riddell was a participant and agreed the process of centralisation of the premier's power had 'taken a noticeable step forward' under Blair. Tony King, another discussant, talked of a 'decline in collegiality', by which he meant Blair was neglecting to confer with colleagues:

> One of the things the Prime Ministers seem to forget is that those people sitting around the cabinet table are or should be politicians. Sure they ... can be very awkward as colleagues. But they can tell you in advance when things are going wrong.

Again in *The Guardian* (4 March 1998), Jonathon Freedland wrote:

> Blair prefers the Thatcher method: consulting one or two colleagues before delivering a fait accompli to the full cabinet on a Thursday morning ... [where] the whole business barely lasts more than half an hour. Political correspondents once grilled their contacts to find out what happened in Cabinet. These days they don't even bother.

In the same *Analysis* programme, journalist Peter Kellner identified tobacco sponsorship and the Millennium Dome as examples of how this governing style had produced severe problems. King chipped in by judging the 'government is backing into welfare reform in the most chaotic kind of way'. Riddell added that decisions about the single currency announced in the summer of 1997 had been made by Brown and Blair: 'The rest of the cabinet were not involved.' He discerned 'less of a sense of broader government loyalty ... I think that's quite a worry.'

Professor Peter Hennessy, someone much concerned by the drift of the Blair style, reports that an informant from Blair's staff told him even before the 1997 election to expect a change from a 'feudal to a Napoleonic system'. This change was clearly borne out, according to Hennessy, by the updatings of the ministerial 'bible' of dos and don'ts produced by the Cabinet Office, 'Questions of Procedure for Ministers'. Paragraph 88 of the revised document states:

> In order to ensure the effective presentation of government policy, all major interviews and media appearances, both in print and broadcast, should be agreed with the Number 10 Press Office before any commitments are entered into. The policy content of all major speeches, press releases and new policy initiatives should be cleared in good time with the Number 10 Private Office; the timing and form of announcements with the Press Office. Each department should keep a record of media contacts by both ministers and officials.

In the wake of this announcement, Peter Riddell, that wise observer of the government machine, wrote an article in *The Times* entitled 'Goodbye to Cabinet government, welcome to the Blair Presidency'.

Defenders say...

Centralisation of government power has been in train for many decades and Blair is merely advancing its evolution.

In the *Analysis* programme King qualified the over-centralisation claim by pointing out that many ministers – Straw, Blunkett, Cook – were 'doing their own thing'. In the same programme Lord Wakeham, a former cabinet minister, pointed out that cabinet had been changing for a 'very long time'; it was 'really like a holding company board where there are lots of subsidiaries carrying on business and it was therefore more a reporting body with perhaps discussions on particular issues'. Moreover, cabinet meetings were too short for discussion of most substantive issues and most discussion, in small gatherings, perforce preceded full meetings. Wakeham also insisted that 'the overwhelming bulk of issues for which there is a logical solution should never come anywhere near cabinet'. In addition, he observed, 'a new Prime Minister with a very large majority and a very big mandate is going to be in a very powerful position'. His judgement was that Blair was getting his way in cabinet simply because there had not, as yet, been a great deal of contention.

Speaking on the Radio 4 programme *The Matrix of Power*, Jack Straw, Home Secretary, agreed that his Prime Minister was comparable to the most dominant postwar Prime Ministers, but explained it thus:

> The similarity between Tony Blair and Margaret Thatcher is that both in part define their parties by their personalities. They are very dominant figures, they are popular figures in the country, they have a very clear sense of direction about where the country ought to go and that tends to give them a more dominant role inside the cabinet than other, more quiescent leaders, of whom the best contemporary example is John Major.

In the same programme, Linda Colley, the historian, addressed the allegation that he works via a small group of colleagues (the 'Tony's cronies' accusations). She argued that Prime Ministers have always sought to work via small groups of trusted advisers:

> Right from the beginning in the 1690s you've got Lord Sunderland saying 'we can't operate with a cabinet of fourteen, we really need a smaller core of ministers'. That's what Walpole constructed in the 1720s and '30s; that's what Pitt the Younger constructs in the late eighteenth century. And in the 1840s you have critics of Sir Robert Peel saying 'Peel hasn't really got a cabinet, he's got a set of dolls'.

Quoted in the *New Statesman* (18 February 1998) Clare Short, an outspoken cabinet member, responded to a suggestion that there was 'no serious discussion at Cabinet meetings' by saying, 'I can certainly speak my mind in Cabinet. The government has settled down. There was a period at the beginning when slightly odd things went on but it's settled down.' Short's analysis refutes Freedland's assertions and is supported by Professor George Jones, who, at a seminar on 6 March 1998, reported his intelligence that cabinet meetings were initially short as the government found its feet but after six months or so they became longer and more collegial.

He is too much in the hands of 'spin doctors'

Opponents say...

Blair is scrupulously polite and never descends into the mire of acrimony but he allows his spin doctors to do this for him. For example, Mandelson ran a dirty campaign in the Littleborough and Saddleworth by-election, unfairly calling the candidate 'soft on drugs'. Mandelson has contributed to Labour policy since the mid-1980s, always in a rightwards direction.

Blair consults his 'spinners' constantly, making presentation, marketing and public relations his government's top priorities. Polls and focus groups have informed most of what New Labour has offered. Even the apparently spontaneous reaction to Diana's death – 'the People's Princess' speech – was in fact the result of advice from his press secretary Alastair Campbell.

Blair is an excellent actor, who merely pretends to be sincere.

Blair's speeches are peppered with the buzz words which research with focus groups have validated, such as 'new' and 'modern'.

As soon as victory was won on 1 May 1997, Blair's Labour spinner, Dave Hill, announced the campaign for the second term had already started, revealing how much New Labour's approach depends on marketing and media manipulation.

In the autumn of 1997, a biography of Gordon Brown contested the version of history that Brown had voluntarily stood down as a candidate for the leadership following John Smith's death. It was Blair's chief spinner, Alastair Campbell, who briefed journalists that Brown had 'psychological flaws'. Clare Short claims that when she suggested the rich might pay more tax, Blair and Campbell played 'good cop, bad cop': 'he gave his emollient smile, while Campbell, with the Prime Minister's approval, did the dirty work' (Hattersley profile, *The Observer*, 22 February 1998). It is also alleged that, with Blair's passive approval, Campbell is allowed to rubbish the BBC and *The Guardian* while tabloids are assiduously courted (*ibid.*).

Blair won the election through skilful branding and marketing and already seeks to win the next through similar tactics – through tight Number 10 control of media presentation – causing the exit of a raft of information officers in late 1997 – and gimmicks like the Millennium Dome at Greenwich.

In March 1998 Alastair Campbell sent a memo – later leaked – to Frank Field and Harriet Harman at the Department of Social Security (neither was in place after the July cabinet reshuffle) ticking them off for 'congenital briefing about who is responsible for what'. Much criticism was voiced of Campbell's over-mighty (but Blair-backed) *modus operandi*, bullying, threatening and telling less than the whole truth.

Critics say the spinners are out of control and spin against each other (e.g. Campbell against Brown's press secretary, Charlie Whelan, and vice versa). Mandelson admitted (Channel 4, 19 April 1998) the Formula One debacle in the autumn of 1997 was the fault of the spinners messing it up.

Defenders say...

Every leading politician knows that, in a media age, presentation is paramount. Blair has merely absorbed this fact and done so better than his opponents. Alan Duncan, Hague's media adviser, was the one who advised an attack on Blair for 'annexing' Diana's death for party political reasons – a woeful judgement as it turned out.

Mandelson has finely attuned antennae, excellent contacts and a deep understanding of the media. He is right of centre politically but has realised this is the only electable position for a leftish party to take in modern-day Britain. But as Herbert Morrison's grandson he is steeped in the Labour Party and is committed to its ideals.

Blair is indeed a good actor – and was in school and university – but sincerity is hard to fake and over time such people are always found out and exposed.

Blair does use polls and focus groups a great deal but Old Labour was out of touch and democracy surely means being responsive to what people are thinking and wanting.

Preparing for the next election as soon as one has won the first is no bad thing and demonstrates a realistic attitude towards power, which was lost so quickly after Labour's landslides in 1945 and 1966.

Campbell vehemently denies he briefed against Brown, Clare Short has been publicly supported by Blair more than once and the BBC must accept it is not above criticism itself for 'trivialising' news and sometimes ignoring big stories favourable to the government.

Critics of Campbell should recall the role of Bernard Ingham, another unelected aide who came to exercise great power. The truth is the job is not for softies: the media have many difficult people in its ranks and an aggressive, outgoing personality deals with them more efficiently than a 'nicer' man like, for example, Gus O'Donnell, Major's last press secretary, widely judged not to have been especially effective.

Blair is too presidential

Opponents say...

As we saw above, Blair has allegedly reduced the power and role of the cabinet and already won the dubious accolade of 'presidential' in the minds of some commentators.

Blair has often expressed his admiration for Thatcher, the most presidential Prime Minister this century. As time goes by, say critics, buttressed by his huge majority, he will get worse as the corruption of power progresses.

He has assumed the trappings of power by flying Concorde to Denver, flying-in a hairdresser to the USA for his wife, Cherie, staying in a millionaire's villa in Italy and making champagne his regular tipple.

During the election campaign, Labour used 'imperial purple' as a background for Blair's press conferences.

By the autumn of his election year, Blair was so lauded in the media, especially after his 'speaking for the nation' after Diana's death, that *The Economist* wryly suggested, 'no publications are banned; yet self censorship achieves a near unanimity which would be the envy of many a totalitarian regime. It is not permitted to criticise the prime minister' (13 September 1997).

On 16 March 1998, *The Times* reported: 'Party managers are now so concerned about Mr Blair's "presidential" style that they are reviewing the whole structure of relations between the Prime Minister and his MPs.' The story detailed the alleged remoteness of the Prime Minister from key areas like the House of Commons tea-room. It seems the regular meetings with groups of MPs had been abandoned through lack of time and MPs were complaining of an aloof and inaccessible leader. Particular anger was directed at the Lord Chancellor, Lord Irvine, hugely unpopular because of his £650,000 renovation of his apartment; it was felt he enjoyed protected status as Blair's former boss as head of chambers.

Kenneth Clarke (Channel 4, 19 April 1998), admittedly biased but still a shrewd observer, reckoned Blair loves the 'glitter' and presidential glamour of the job.

Defenders say...

In the Radio 4 programme quoted above, Jack Straw argued that British government has a 'weak' centre and is essentially parliamentary, not presidential:

> Ministers may propose but Parliament disposes and the people who actually go to Parliament to make the propositions are not the Prime Minister but the Secretaries of State and their ministers and that does inevitably mean that the Prime Minister, however dominant, is still *primus inter pares*. So it's the minister who faces Parliament and this gives him some authority, some leverage. For all the guff about presidential government, the Prime Minister is running cabinet government. Yes, he appoints the people around the table, he can dismiss them, but he can't keep on dismissing them.

Blair is a strong leader with a clear vision and will naturally advance his views forcibly; his cabinet colleagues would expect nothing else but are no shrinking violets themselves.

Admiration of Thatcher does not imply imitation; he is not as vulnerable as she was to hubris and enjoying power for power's sake; he is unlikely, for instance, to use the royal 'we' as she famously did.

Labour experiments with a number of colours, like other parties, but still uses the traditional red as its official one.

Blair is a wealthy man with a wealthy wife; he should not be criticised for enjoying the benefits of a comfortable life, especially when he works so murderously hard – sixteen to eighteen hours a day.

Blair is a genuinely modest man who dislikes the attention he attracts and has a genuine desire to 'make a difference for the better'.

It is true the media loved Blair in the aftermath of the election but this was not manipulated – merely the dividend of his success and newness. Besides, as *The Economist* noted, 'Good government is not possible when government can no longer get a fair hearing, when every move is greeted with ridicule and contempt. Government had to recover some authority, which today comes only from a base of popular support. To that extent Mr Blair's success is not to be feared.'

Blair meets the parliamentary committee of the Party every Wednesday afternoon in a meeting chaired by Clive Soley and grievances are discussed and if possible rectified. Besides, every Prime Minister in modern times has been awfully pressed for time and this is no evidence necessarily of presidential remoteness.

He is subject to 'U' turns in office

Opponents say...

In opposition Labour promised a ban on all tobacco advertising, yet in office agreed an exemption for Formula One racing, which derives huge sums from such sponsorship. Following the announcement of the exemption, it became apparent that Bernie Ecclestone, impresario for the sport, had not only donated £1 million to Labour funds but had lobbied Blair himself at a key meeting on 16 October 1996.

In opposition Labour condemned the Conservative plan to reduce benefits for single mothers but in power they insisted on pushing it through in the autumn of 1997.

During the campaign Labour promised to improve welfare services yet in power have given only small extra amounts and resisted the major improvements for which welfare activists had called.

Labour's handling of the Competition Bill and the 'predatory pricing' of Murdoch newspapers provides another example.

Labour entered office committed to banning fox hunting but even though Michael Foster's bill won 411 to 151, the government refused to allow time for it to progress. Cynics said this was to pacify the Countryside Alliance, which crowded 120,000 people into Hyde Park in July 1997.

Connected with the above, Blair pandered to the countryside lobby on 25 February 1998 when he reneged on his pledge to provide ramblers with a 'statutory right to roam'. One disappointed minister commented: 'Tony has been panicked by the countryside campaign. The landowners got to him' (*The Guardian*, 26 February 1998).

In opposition Labour regularly used to protest against the increase in prescription charges. Harriet Harman condemned a 1996 increase as a 'tax on the sick' and lambasted the Conservatives for announcing the decision via a written answer, meaning there was no discussion on the floor of the House. She did, however, use the same tactic herself in announcing further increases in prescription charges.

At his spring 1998 conference Paddy Ashdown criticised Blair for talking about 'education, education, education' before the election and practising 'cuts, cuts, cuts' once in power. Stephen Byers, Education Minister, dismissed the attack, pointing out the extra cash which had been channelled into education since May 1997: over £1.5 billion.

Defenders say...

The Formula One decision was made on its merits after due consultation, revealing a commendable flexibility.

The single mothers' benefit reduction was taken for strictly financial reasons, to keep social security spending within limits.

Tony Blair explained at Prime Minister's questions that he thought the amendment to the Competition Bill was the wrong way to approach the problem. Murdoch, in any case, despite his media empire, has nowhere near a monopoly hold on a market boasting several flourishing daily newspapers.

Throughout the campaign Labour made it clear it would keep to the spending plans inherited from the Conservatives. In government it also made clear its view that the welfare services were no longer working (see Chapter 11): poverty was still increasing despite huge budgets; and the middle classes were no longer prepared to fund such an inefficient set of services via high taxation. Labour's plan is to reform the welfare state and make benefits a ladder to work, self-sufficiency and pride rather than passive dependency. In any case, the cut was reversed on 25 February when a new provision was introduced which more than compensated for the cut of lone mothers' benefit.

Polly Toynbee, an outspoken critic of the government, wrote in *The Guardian* (16 February 1998) that she could discern the outlines of a workable strategy to assist the poor:

> At first money will be poured into making work pay, creating what may be a very large difference between the quality of life for families on benefit and those in low paid jobs. With the minimum wage underpinning the bottom, on top of that will be a new higher tax credit, a new child care credit, a 10p Income Tax starting rate and far lower starting rates of National Insurance.... The package could mean a real change for the working poor.

The 1998 budget proved to be genuinely helpful to the poorer sections of society, delivering net income benefits to the poorest 50 per cent and only slightly disadvantaging the rest. In addition, the Welfare to Work theme of the government's social policy was reinforced by generous help regarding child care for women wishing to work.

Labour only ever promised a debate, not an Act on fox hunting and it is wise for governments to listen to dissenting voices from outside their traditional constituencies. Blair is reputed to have been impressed by Clinton's advice of 'never stop addressing the people who voted for you for the first time'. Blair, said *The Observer* (22 February 1998), 'is determined not to see his party corralled back into the inner cities.' (A MORI poll on 2 March revealed 80 per cent of the 120,000 marchers to be Conservative supporters.)

The 'right to roam' measure was not reversed; it was merely decided to pursue it via a voluntary agreement within a time limit of two years.

Written answers have been the standard means of announcing prescription charge increases for some time.

Overall judgement on Tony Blair

Personal considerations inevitably intrude into any judgements of this kind but even Margaret Thatcher has praised him as a 'patriot' and a book critical of Labour by Leo McKinstry (1996) concludes with a paean of praise for the Party's leader and the judgement that he would make an effective premier. Most commentators, even in the right-wing press, allow he is an extraordinary, dynamic and inspiring politician. His ability to communicate and persuade is better than that of any Labour politician this century, possibly ever.

His public-school, Oxford, barrister background make him attractive to the middle classes but has proved no barrier to support from his northern working-class constituents. He has no roots in Old Labour and the unions and while he indulges in visions of greatness for his country he is essentially pragmatic on policy, rather like Bill Clinton, preferring small, achievable goals to major projects likely to fail. It is true he has moved the Party substantially to the right but it had nowhere else to go if it wanted to regain power after eighteen years. Whether he has already betrayed its heritage of socialist principles it is too early to say but most commentators outside the Party, though not all those within it, are prepared to give him more time to prove the accusation wrong. He is certainly a powerful and decisive politician but that is no crime and arguably, after the drift of the Major years, such leadership is needed. All the evidence is that Blair is deeply committed to the democratic process and is unlikely to abuse his power in any arbitrary fashion.

He is very able and works constantly; as a younger man his papers and reports were always extremely impressive. Writing in *The Observer* (28 September 1997) Andy McSmith, a former Labour Party official, recalls his extraordinary acuity when a junior shadow spokesman. He seems to have to the intellectual skills needed of a premier and the energy as well as political skills to survive.

The Guardian has been perhaps more critical of Labour than some more right-wing papers but on 30 December 1997 Hugo Young was impressed overall with the government's performance:

Amazingly good so far ... I can't recall a precedent for its energy and calculated purpose ... Mr Blair has begun to do what he said he would do, including being more radical than anyone understood would be the case. He has been so damned active. There really will be a Scottish Parliament and a Welsh Assembly. There really will be a Freedom of Information Act and an incorporated Bill of Rights. No sooner does Mr Blair establish the priority, and have his people do the work, then the parliamentary majority will do the business.

Peter Riddell commented in *The Times* (October 1997) on the amazingly extended honeymoon Labour enjoyed after their victory. He judged voters wanted to give Blair a chance to show what it could do and still recorded deep disillusion with the Conservatives. Riddell reinforced his latter point in the same paper on 19 December when a MORI poll revealed more Conservative supporters liked Blair than liked William Hague, their own leader.

More remarkable perhaps was the finding of a Europe-wide poll reported on Radio 4's *Agenda*, 3 January 1998, which revealed over half of those interviewed thought Blair would make a good leader of their country.

It is true that Blair seems like a man in some kind of a hurry, but perhaps this is the urgency of a man of action, someone who knows what he wants and cannot wait to get it. Riddell makes a telling point when he observes he is impatient with the cabinet system: 'Blair thinks politically, not constitutionally; he responds to moods, not structures'.

Tony Blair seems a nice man and his relaxed accessibility is part of his charm; he seems to be what we see and this is reassuring to voters.

Andy McSmith reports he was always courteous but maybe a little remote: 'Nice, but not so very nice.... Like a lot of people who are good at imposing their own authority, he was only so-so at acknowledging others.' Maybe he is not an ideal team player and prefers to work more on his own or with small groups of colleagues and advisers. However, when McSmith lost his job at *The Mirror* Blair was genuinely concerned and arranged for his wife Cherie to give some of her extremely expensive 'employment-lawyer' time to advise him.

Graham Thomas (1998) argues that Blair is the most powerful premier this century, citing: his personal approval rating of 91 per cent in early 1998; his relatively united cabinet compared with Thatcher's 'wets' and 'dries'; his ability to enhance his power via reshuffles; his huge majority; his high international reputation in Europe and the USA; and his extraordinarily high media approval.

Moreover, his way of conducting cabinet seemed in the summer of 1998, contrary to the reassuring reports earlier in the year, to be even more premier dominated than under his female Conservative predecessor, at least according to *The Economist* (25 July), where its well informed 'Bagehot' columnist reported:

Agendas are vague, debate rare, dissent virtually unheard of. Typically, the prime minister simply recounts decisions already taken in more intimate gatherings. The full Cabinet had not met at all before the government announced its decision to free the Bank of England to set interest rates.

The article went on to identify an inner cabal comprising Blair, Brown, Mandelson and the unelected Campbell.

The comparison with Margaret Thatcher is compelling: not just Blair's economic ideas but his mode of operating as premier – highly personal, occasionally ruthless, relying on an accomplice press officer. However, Blair is keener to persuade and more willing than the famous lady to compromise. Perhaps it is Blair's persuasive skills which most set him apart from Thatcher. She was so imperious she ultimately had no time for dissent. Blair is the consummate politician, convinced he can win over the doubters; hence his missionary zeal to convert his party over Clause 4 and his welfare reforms. The Conservatives chose a long campaign in 1997 as they believed the inexperienced Blair would crack and indeed a few days into it Heseltine claimed he was fighting to retain his composure. However, Blair showed no signs of such a crack-up and his media performances consistently improved from good to brilliant as election day approached. One small anecdote reveals just how adept a politician he is. John Rentoul, his biographer, likes to tell the story of an interview in which Blair was asked if he approved of smacking children. He replied he had smacked his own kids when they were young but had always regretted it afterwards. The perfect answer is thus demonstrated: he was apparently honest and able to reveal human failings yet still essentially liberal and not politically incorrect. Right and left are thus both satisfied: next question?

If he has a defining characteristic as a premier it is that he is so intensely personal in his style. Rather like Clinton, perhaps, he seeks to reach out to people and makes them feel he understands and cares about them – and succeeds in doing so. In the wake of the row over single mothers' benefits, for example, he went on television and asked the nation to 'trust me'; to believe he would never deny benefits to those who really needed them. Indeed, 'Trust me politics' is a useful summary of the man's political style. So far it seems the country has acceded to his appeal.

He is, oddly for the cynics, a committed and religious man (some speculation did the rounds in March 1998 that he was considering a shift to Roman Catholicism) who really wants – the sincerity seems to shine through – to improve things for his country, rather than merely hold high office. Hugo Young believes Blair's 'abiding radical passion is', rather as Thatcher's was, only the reverse, 'to keep Conservatism out of power.... Observing it to be moving even further to the right, he's even more determined that Toryism's rival force, progressive modernity, under whatever guise, shall have the decades due to it' (*The Guardian*, 10 March 1998).

As 1998 drew to a close, Tony Blair was still the most recognised and the most popular of the party leaders. A 'State of the Nation' poll, published in *The Guardian* (7 July 1998), showed Labour twenty-five percentage points ahead of the Conservatives and a hefty set of majorities agreed with such statements as Britain is a 'good place in which to bring up children' and a 'good place in which to grow old'. However, these general questions perhaps masked the personal decline in Blair's ratings. Many commentators wondered whether his tendency to give in to powerful pressure groups, his tendency to preach – wickedly satirised in *Private Eye*'s St Albion Parish feature – and the less promising economic outlook had not eroded the image of the new wunderkind.

Part of the answer at least was delivered on 9 September in another 'State of the Nation' ICM/*Guardian* poll. The newspaper led with the dramatic headline 'Blair bubble bursts' and the details spelt out a perception of the Prime Minister which was, relatively, less than ecstatic. The lead article commented: 'The extraordinary bubble of popularity, which broke records in the aftermath of the election, has now burst'. Blair's ratings for 'honesty' and 'empathy with the voters' had plummeted compared with earlier polls and more closely resembled those for John Major than post-election assessments of the new Prime Minister. The article concluded, almost damningly, that the public now saw Blair as 'just another politician'. However, comfort could be derived from the ratings of William Hague, which showed no signs of taking off. At that time only one in ten believed the Conservatives could win the next election; the ICM poll of 27 September 1998 revealed that only 28 per cent were 'satisfied' with his performance, while 51 per cent were 'dissatisfied'.

Finally, and ICM focus group survey in four key marginal constituencies for *The Guardian* (28 September 1998) proved that surveys of popular opinion can be confusingly mixed. It revealed that despite disappointment with Labour's slow rate of progress, the groups were 'invariably ... impressed with what they regard as the strong Thatcherite style of Tony Blair'. Muddled messages maybe, but as long as Blair wins high personal ratings – 60 per cent satisfied (down from the 80 per cent of a year before but still high) to 28 per cent dissatisfied (27 September 1998) – Labour's most important 1997 election-winning instrument will remain its most potent of weapons and the one Conservatives should fear most.

Acknowledgements

Grateful thanks are due to Nicola Merrick, editor of BBC Radio 4's *Analysis*, who made available to me the transcript of the fascinating 'Heart of Government' documentary programme broadcast on 15 January 1998. Thanks are also due to Peter Hennessy, for permission to quote from his Politics Association lecture, 3

October 1998, and to Andrew Heywood, for his permission to quote from a lecture given in April 1998. Extra special thanks are offered to Graham Thomas, whose lectures at an April 1998 Politics Association conference were enlightening, as well as for his time and kind assistance in the writing of this chapter.

Reading

Adam Smith Institute (1997) *New Labour's 200 Days: A Hundred Ideas in Action*, ASI.

Blair, T. (1998) *The Third Way: New Politics for the New Century*, Fabian Society.

Giddens, A. (1998) *The Third Way: The Renewal of Social Democracy*, Polity Press.

Hennessy, P. (1998) *Re-engineering the State in Flight: A Year in the Life of the British Constitution*, Lloyd's Bank Public Affairs Department, 71 Lombard Street, London EC3P 3BS.

Hennessy, P. (1998) The Blair style of government: an historical perspective and internal audit, *Government and Opposition*, Vol. 33 (1).

McKinstry, L. (1996) *Fit to Govern?*, Bantam Press.

Rentoul, R. (1996) *Tony Blair*, Warner.

Seyd, P. (1998) 'Tony Blair and New Labour', in A. King (ed.), *New Labour Triumphs: Britain at the Polls*, Chatham House.

Thomas, G. (1998) *Prime Minister and Cabinet Today*, Manchester University Press.

2

The House of Commons:
the half empty bottle of reform

Philip Norton

At various times in its history, the House of Commons has undertaken dramatic reform and, more frequently, not so dramatic reform of its structures, practices and procedures. The reforms have not always kept pace with demands for change. Calls for reform have been especially strident in recent decades. Despite a number of important reforms, especially the introduction of departmental select committees in 1979, calls continue to be made for changes to the elected chamber of Britain's legislature. In both the 1992 and 1997 general elections, all the main political parties included proposals for some parliamentary reform in their manifestos. Given the reforms of recent decades, why is reform still on the political agenda? What changes are demanded? And what has been the response of MPs? Have they been receptive or resistant to calls for change?

Why reform?

The House of Commons has been the target of criticism by academics, journalists and some politicians for many years. A reform movement developed in the 1960s and has continued to press for reform – sometimes radical reform – since that time (Norton, 1981, pp. 203–8). Various books, tracts and pamphlets advocating reform have appeared. So too have various reports from the Select Committee on Procedure of the House of Commons recommending a number of changes to parliamentary structures and procedures. Some works have also appeared which have not so much advocated reform of the institution but rather dismissed it as irrelevant. According to two academic critics, 'the significance of Parliament ... is its very insignificance' (Richardson and Jordan, 1979, p. 121).

Despite such criticism, at the beginning of the 1990s the House of Commons was still well regarded by citizens; by the middle of the decade, however, it had lost much of its appeal. In a Gallup poll in 1991, 47 per cent of those questioned said they had a 'great deal' or 'quite a lot' of trust in Parliament; less than 10 per cent said they had no trust in Parliament at all. The same year, the MORI 'State of the Nation' poll found that most respondents believed that Parliament worked well: 5 per cent per cent thought it worked 'very well' and 54 per cent 'fairly well'. Only 16 per cent thought it worked badly. Four years later, the percentage believing it worked well had fallen by 16 per cent (see Table 2.1). In 1991, the gap between those thinking it worked well and those thinking it worked badly was 43 per cent. In 1995 the gap was down to 13 per cent. Though the figures do not suggest that public support has collapsed, they demonstrate clearly that Parliament does not enjoy high levels of public confidence.

Table 2.1. *Declining public support for Parliament (responses to the question 'Overall, how well or badly do you think Parliament works?' in MORI 'State of the Nation' polls)*

Response	1991 (%)	1995 (%)	Change
Very well	5	4	−1
Fairly well	54	39	−15
Neither well nor badly	21	22	+1
Fairly badly	12	19	+7
Very badly	4	11	+7
Don't know	4	6	+2
Combining figures:			
Well	59	43	−16
Badly	16	30	+14

Source: MORI, 'State of the Nation Polls', 1991 and 1995.

The result is that the House of Commons now enjoys low levels of support at elite and popular level. The combination means that the House has relatively few friends. However, the concerns of elite critics are not necessarily the same as those of the public. Although there is an overlap, the concerns of academics and other commentators are with the capacity of the House to fulfil the functions expected of it. Popular criticism has been directed more at the conduct of MPs.

Indeed, three levels of criticism can be identified and each, very roughly, can be attributed to a particular group. The three can be subsumed under three simple headings: scrutiny, convenience and conduct. The three groups to which these can be attributed are, respectively, academics, MPs and the public. The three are not mutually exclusive, with a substantial overlap occurring especially between academics and MPs.

Scrutiny

Legislatures are functionally adaptable institutions (Packenham, 1970; Norton, 1993, ch. 1). They fulfil a range of tasks, or functions, and those tasks can change over time. Traditionally, legislatures have been seen as law-making bodies but nowadays very few legislatures are actually involved in 'making' the law. Legislatures are now more frequently policy-influencing rather than policy-making bodies (Norton, 1984). They debate legislative proposals which are placed before them and they usually have to give their assent to those proposals if they are to become law – indeed, the giving of assent is what defines a legislature (Norton, 1990a, p. 1). Among their tasks – and central to those of the House of Commons – is that of scrutinising government, subjecting the actions and proposed measures of government to scrutiny (see Norton, 1981, 1993). If MPs are dissatisfied with the government's response, it is up to them to persuade or induce government – be it through argument, publicity, the threat of defeating the government, or actually denying the government a majority – to change course.

Many academics, critics and journalists have found the House of Commons deficient as a body of scrutiny and influence. The principal mechanisms of scrutiny – debate on the floor of the House, question time and standing committees for the consideration of bills – have come in for sustained criticism over several decades. With the growth throughout the twentieth century, and especially in the years since 1945, in government activity and the volume of public business, the floor of the House of Commons has increasingly been seen as inadequate as the forum in which to subject government to sustained scrutiny. In the 1960s and 1970s, for example, one question time every few weeks and one or two general debates a year were not seen as sufficient for the House to scrutinise foreign policy effectively. Question time was used for purposes other than eliciting information and keeping ministers responsive to parliamentary concerns: it was used increasingly as a tool of partisan conflict and for raising the profile of ambitious career politicians (see Franklin and Norton, 1993). Standing committees were anything but 'standing' – the membership of each committee changed for every bill – and were seen as inadequate tools of legislative scrutiny. They were appointed to consider the detail of bills, going through each bill clause by clause, but generally lacked the political will and the resources to fulfil their task. They had no power to take evidence and proceedings were largely a continuation of the partisan conflict in the chamber. As one submission to the Select Committee on Procedure noted in 1984, 'If at the end of the day the *committee* has actually improved (made "more generally acceptable") the contents of the bill – as opposed to approving the amendments introduced by the minister in charge of the bill – it is in all probability an unusual and unexpected benefit' (Select Committee on Procedure, 1984, p. 72).

One major reform, a product of this criticism by commentators and parliamentarians, was the appointment in 1979 of a series of departmental select committees. Fourteen were established but the number has grown, a consequence of some changes in the structure of government departments and of the creation of new committees to cover areas previously neglected. At the start of the 1997 Parliament, there were seventeen departmental select committees. They have proved extremely active bodies and appear to have achieved on occasion some change in government policy (see, generally, Drewry, 1989; Jogerst, 1993; Hawes, 1993). They have been characterised as the most radical change to the House of Commons in the twentieth century. However, they have also been criticised because they lack the time, resources, formal powers and links with the chamber to ensure that government departments are subjected to thorough scrutiny and made responsive to their recommendations (Norton, 1994a, pp. 29–33). Though the Select Committee on Procedure (1990) concluded that the committees had largely met the tasks expected of them, some academic commentators – as well as MPs – took a more pessimistic view, arguing for reform of the committees.

By the middle of the 1990s, there was a substantial body of informed opinion advocating reform of the House of Commons. On the legislative process, several proposals were advanced, including by the Hansard Society (1993; see also Norton, 1997a, 1997b). These included:

- *The regular use of special standing committees.* These committees can take evidence and provision for their use was introduced in 1981, but between then and 1997 only seven bills were sent to such committees. Feedback on the use of such committees was generally positive (see George and Evans, 1983, pp. 87–90).
- *The carry-over of bills from one session to another.* Bills fall at the end of the parliamentary year if they have not completed all their stages. As a result, bills are generally introduced early and go to committee at the same time, some having to be rushed at the end of the session in order to be enacted. Allowing bills to carry over from one year to the next would permit more structured and unhurried scrutiny.
- *The timetabling of bills.* Time in standing committee is often taken up by opposition members speaking at length on the opening clauses of a bill and with the government then introducing a guillotine (timetable motion) to limit debate on the rest of the bill; as a result, it is not uncommon for parts of bills not to be discussed at all. Having an automatic timetable for each bill would ensure that every part was allocated some time and the unproductive discussion on opening clauses dispensed with.
- *A permanent membership for committees.* The appointment of a new committee membership for every bill means that standing committees build up no collective memory, no membership built on subject specialisation,

no committee ethos, no positions of leadership specific to the committee, and no cross-party working relationships, all of which, it is argued, are necessary if committees are to exercise much independent judgement in the consideration of bills. Having members appointed to subject-specific standing committees for the lifetime of a Parliament would generate specialised and more discriminating committee scrutiny.

More radical proposals have included merging select and standing committees – creating committees of the sort that are common in other legislatures – and taking the committee stage of a bill before second reading, thus strengthening the position of the committees: they would not be tied by decisions already taken in the chamber.

Other proposals to strengthen the scrutinising capacity of the House extend beyond the legislative process. A number of recommendations to strengthen select committees have been made, including giving them their own budgets to commission research, giving them their own research staff, paying committee members (or giving them an extra allowance to hire staff) and introducing more time to debate committee reports on the floor of the House – including for motions to approve committee reports (see Norton, 1990b, pp. 139–46, 1997a, pp. 30–6). Other recommendations for reform include more rigorous scrutiny of delegated legislation, that is, secondary legislation introduced under powers conferred by the parent Act (Select Committee on Procedure, 1996), and European Union documents (Select Committee on European Legislation, 1996).

Convenience

Those pressing for an improvement in the scrutinising capacity of the House of Commons include many MPs (see, e.g., Garrett, 1992) as well as commentators. MPs are arguably even more noticeable in pressing for changes that will improve their own working conditions.

The resources available to MPs to carry out their jobs have improved enormously. In the early 1960s, few MPs had offices. Most had to content themselves with school-style lockers. They had no separate allowance to hire staff. They were poorly paid. Support facilities were limited. Many had difficulties coping. The situation has improved dramatically in recent decades: all MPs now have some office space and early in the new millennium each will have a dedicated office. Every MP has an office cost allowance, enabling each one to hire two or more staff. Resources, including library and technological resources, have expanded. Since the 1960s, there have been a number of increases in pay, on occasion voted for by MPs against the advice of government.

However, the resources have been criticised as falling short of what is needed. The office of an MP is not necessarily located close to where the

Member's secretary is located. Members' offices are scattered around the parliamentary estate and some, not least those in the Palace of Westminster, are sometimes cramped and lack natural light. Many MPs have difficulty coping with the demands made of them given limited secretarial and research support. Despite pay rises, MPs' salaries have lagged behind those in middle management and behind parliamentarians in comparable countries. Before 1996, the head teacher of a middle-sized secondary school was paid more than an MP.

Members have also criticised the working practices of the House. The business of the House has traditionally been announced only on the Thursday for the following week, thus creating problems for MPs wanting to plan ahead. Business – especially the report stage of bills – has sometimes necessitated late-night or all-night sittings: camp beds have been provided for those MPs involved in the proceedings so that they can take quick naps. The timing of recesses has also traditionally not been announced early, leaving Members unsure of when the House would rise for the summer, a problem especially for those with children and wanting to plan summer holidays.

A MORI poll of MPs in 1990 found that 58 per cent considered the House to be a very or fairly poor place in which to work. A committee appointed to consider the facilities reported that 'The MORI poll and our own findings reveal almost universal dissatisfaction about accommodation.... There is also criticism of office equipment and other facilities' (House of Commons Commission, 1990). A poll of new MPs at the start of the 1997 Parliament also tapped criticism of the facilities (Norton and Mitchell, 1997, pp. 10–13). Some were dissatisfied with the office arrangements. Almost half of those questioned (47 per cent) said they wanted to change various procedures of the House. Most found that they were not able to hire the number of staff they needed to do their jobs effectively. Most of those questioned (65 per cent) had no more than two members of staff: 73 per cent said that they wanted three or more.

Members of Parliament have variously sought a change in their working environment in order that they can operate more effectively and efficiently. The principal aim is arguably to make working life more tolerable for them. Rearranging the sitting time of the House may not necessarily improve its scrutinising capacity but it may make life easier for hard-pressed Members. At times there may even be a perceived tension between the two: giving MPs a longer summer recess, for example, may be to their convenience but may – certainly in the eyes of many members of the public – reduce the time they have to keep the government under scrutiny.

Among the various reforms proposed have been a fixed timetable (the dates of recesses being the same each year), changes in the sitting times of the House (including moving to morning sittings as standard), improvements in the working facilities of MPs (including in information technology), expanding office space, and increasing the office cost allowance. Some MPs would also like to see constituency offices provided for them.

Conduct

The conduct of MPs has often been the cause of public complaint and cynicism. Though constituents often have a high regard for their own particular MP (the evaluation of local MPs showed no decline in the MORI 'State of the Nation' polls in the 1990s) they take a negative view of politicians as a whole. A MORI poll in 1983 found that only 18 per cent of those questioned would generally trust politicians to tell the truth: only government ministers got a lower ranking. A Gallup poll in 1985 found that 46 per cent of respondents agreed with the statement that 'most MPs make a lot of money by using public office improperly'; only 31 per cent disagreed with the statement.

Public distrust of MPs increased as more stories appeared drawing attention to their outside interests. The 1980s saw a massive increase in the number of professional political lobbying firms (see Grantham and Seymour-Ure, 1990). A number of MPs were employed by these firms as consultants. Some Members themselves set up their own lobbying firms; others hired out their services as parliamentary advisers to companies and other bodies. Media stories about the activities of MPs serving as lobbyists served to undermine popular trust in MPs and the subject of lobbying was investigated by the Select Committee on Members' Interests. A number of proposals were made to strengthen requirements for the declaration of Members' interests, especially in the Register of Members' Interests (introduced in 1974), and for greater regulation of parliamentary lobbying.

The issue of MPs' conduct attracted widespread and negative publicity in 1994 when the *Sunday Times* revealed that a reporter posing as a businessman had offered twenty MPs £1,000 each to table a parliamentary question. Two Members (Graham Riddick and David Tredinnick) did not say no to the offer. The 'cash for questions' story attracted extensive coverage (see Chapter 15). Later in the year, *The Guardian* accused two ministers of accepting money – when backbenchers – to table questions; one of them (Tim Smith) admitted it and resigned as a minister; the other, Neil Hamilton, denied it but was subsequently forced to leave office.

The various accusations led the Prime Minister, John Major, to announce the setting up of a committee, the Committee on Standards in Public Life, under a judge, Lord Nolan, to 'examine current concerns about standards of conduct of all holders of public office ... and make recommendations as to any changes in present arrangements which might be required to ensure the highest standards of propriety in public life'. The Committee issued its first report in 1995.

The 'cash for questions' scandal, and the ensuing debate about the behaviour of MPs, further reduced public trust in MPs. A MORI poll in 1994 found that 64 per cent of those questioned believed that most MPs made a lot of money by using public office improperly – up from 46 per cent in 1985. Only 22 per cent disagreed. Only 28 per cent agreed that 'most MPs have a high personal moral code'. No less than 77 per cent agreed with the statement that 'Most MPs care more about special interests than they care about people like you' (Committee on Standards in Public Life, 1995, p. 108). When a Gallup poll was carried out to find out what people thought MPs should or should not accept, 95 per cent said it was not right to accept payment for tabling parliamentary questions, 92 per cent that it was not right to accept a free holiday abroad, and 85 per cent thought it was not right to take payment for giving advice about parliamentary matters. Almost half thought it was wrong to accept a free lunch at a restaurant or to accept bottles of wine or whisky at Christmas.

There was thus a clear clash between what citizens expected of their MPs and what MPs did and what parliamentary rules allowed them to do; although tabling questions for money was deemed a breach of privilege (Riddick and Tredinnick were briefly suspended from the service of the House), Members were allowed to accept hospitality and to give advice on parliamentary matters in return for payment as long as the hospitality and the relationship to those hiring them was declared in the Register of Members' Interests: there was no requirement to declare the amounts of money involved. There was popular pressure for a change in the rules.

What has been done?

Given these problems, what has been done? And is it sufficient to meet the criticisms levelled at the House and its Members?

The House of Commons has introduced a number of changes to its practices and procedures. Individually, they have not always been substantial, but in combination they have served to make the House a more specialised and a more professional body. The changes themselves can be seen as responses to the criticisms. In order to improve the scrutiny of government, greater emphasis has been placed on the committees and the House has agreed to changes in the legislative process. To enable Members to do their jobs better, and provide a more congenial working environment, the House has agreed to a change in the sitting hours (1994) and voted a significant increase in MPs' pay (1996). And in order to meet concerns about the links that MPs have with outside bodies, the House has introduced more rigorous regulations governing the conduct of Members. The overall effect has been a shift of emphasis away from the chamber to committee and the generation of a more professional body, that is, a body governed by more professional standards.

Scrutiny

The departmental select committees have been variously modified. Some new committees have been created, others have been merged or have disappeared as a consequence of changes in government departments. In the 1992–7 Parliament, a new committee on science and technology was introduced and the Select Committee on Public Service was created, taking over the civil service responsibilities of the Treasury and Civil Service Committee. The Select Committee on Deregulation was also appointed to examine proposals made by government under the 1994 Deregulation and Contracting Out Act. A committee covering the security services was also brought into being: a statutory rather than a parliamentary committee (that is, it was established by Act of Parliament), it nonetheless comprised senior parliamentarians. The bodies responsible for discussing matters affecting Scotland and Wales, the Scottish and Welsh Grand Committees, also had their powers strengthened: among the changes, each was given power to question ministers other than those from the territorial department. These various changes reflected the growing emphasis on parliamentary inquiry by committee.

The departmental select committees saw some further modest changes at the beginning of the 1997 Parliament. These included a greater use of subcommittees. The Environment and Transport Committee effectively became two committees in one, the committee having two chairmen, one to chair the environment subcommittee and the other to chair the transport subcommittee. The same arrangement existed with the Education and Employment Committee. These committees, along with one or two others, also saw some increase in the number of Members appointed to them, thus drawing even more MPs into the detailed committee work of the House.

At the beginning of the 1997 Parliament, other changes were also introduced. The Prime Minister announced that, in future, Prime Minister's question time would take the form of a single thirty-minute session each week, on a Wednesday, rather than two fifteen-minute sessions on Tuesdays and Thursdays. The House also appointed the Select Committee on the Modernisation of the House of Commons. The Committee began work by looking at the way the House dealt with legislation. It published its first report in July 1997 (Select Committee on Modernisation, 1997). It recommended, among other things:

- programming the passage of legislation, each standing committee to have the power to decide a programme for the bill it is considering;
- increasing the opportunity for pre-legislative scrutiny and consultation;
- greater use of special standing committees;
- allowing bills in certain circumstances to carry over from one session to another;

- allowing standing committees to have the same power as select committees to sit during recesses.

The Committee's report was debated by the House on 13 November 1997 and agreed to without a vote.

Convenience

Following pressure from Members on both sides of the House, a Select Committee on the Sittings of the House was appointed in 1991. The Committee moved quickly in order to produce a report before the end of the Parliament. It reported in 1992, shortly before the general election. It recognised the problems associated with late-night and all-night sittings and the uncertainty about dates of recesses. It recommended that the House should sit on Wednesday mornings, that when the House was in session there should be ten 'constituency' Fridays (ten Fridays when the House would not sit), that business should normally conclude at 10.00 p.m. and earlier if possible on Thursdays, and that bills should be timetabled. The report was eventually debated by the House at the end of 1994 and its recommendations approved: they took effect in 1995. (Rather than automatic timetabling of bills, the parties agreed to voluntary timetabling, which lasted to the end of that Parliament.) These changes, alongside the greater emphasis on committee work, facilitated a more specialised House of Commons, Members spending more and more time engaged in committee work and less in the chamber.

Members in 1996 also approved a recommendation from the Review Body on Senior Salaries that their annual salary be increased by 23 per cent, from £34,085 to £43,000 (Review Body on Senior Salaries, 1996). Over the years, parliamentary pay had slipped relative to that of comparable positions and was well below that of parliamentarians in other major western legislatures. To bring it up to the level that the Review Body considered appropriate required an increase that the government felt was not acceptable: it recommended a series of gradual increases. However, MPs decided to go for the 'big bang' approach, voting to introduce the increase in one go. The increase – though designed to make parliamentary service more attractive, not least to many outside the House who could not afford a pay cut to become MPs – was unpopular: over three-quarters of those interviewed in one survey opposed the pay increase. In future, pay increases will be determined by a formula, thus avoiding the need for parliamentary debate and vote.

A number of other change have also improved the working environment of Members. There has been an extension of office space, computer facilities have been improved and business is now usually announced, provisionally, two weeks ahead.

Conduct

The most highly visible, and most contested, changes were introduced as a consequence of public disquiet over Members' conduct. This is discussed more fully in Chapter 15. In brief, the Nolan Committee recommended that MPs be prohibited from being paid by lobbying firms with multiple clients, that agreements relating to parliamentary services be disclosed, that a code of conduct be introduced, that a new procedure for investigating complaints be introduced, and that a Commissioner for Parliamentary Standards be appointed (Committee on Standards in Public Life, 1995).

Some of the Committee's recommendations were acceptable to Members on both sides of the House, but those relating to disclosure and a ban on working for multi-client firms proved controversial. Many Conservative MPs objected to disclosing income, fearing it would discourage Members from taking on outside activities and lead to them leaving Parliament, and one even berated Lord Nolan in public. The House established a select committee to consider the Nolan report and, after two reports from the committee, it voted to implement the recommendations, some Conservative MPs joining with opposition Members to provide a majority. In one respect, the House went further than the Nolan recommendations: it voted to ban all paid advocacy by Members – in other words, an MP could advise an outside body for payment but could not raise an issue in the House on behalf of any body for payment. The House appointed Sir Gordon Downey as the new Commissioner for Parliamentary Standards and also established the Select Committee on Standards and Privileges, to replace the Privileges Committee and the Committee on Members' Interests.

The new Select Committee on Standards and Privileges held a number of widely publicised inquiries in 1996 and 1997. It took evidence in public and at the end of 1996 decided that in future it would take evidence from witnesses under oath, something which no other committee does. Its inquiry into the affair of Neil Hamilton, alleged to have accepted money – which he did not disclose – from Mohamed Al-Fayed in return for tabling parliamentary questions, attracted extensive coverage, though its final report was not issued until after the 1997 general election, in which Hamilton lost his seat.

These reforms – covering scrutiny, convenience, and conduct – have resulted in a very different House of Commons to that which existed at the beginning of the 1990s. New Members elected in 1997 faced very different structures, practices and rules than those first elected in 1987 or even in 1992.

Limitations of reform

Even though the House of Commons has undertaken such reforms in recent years, do they go far enough? And, if not, why not?

For many reformers, the changes of the 1990s do not go far enough. They represent the 'half full, half empty bottle' of reform. The reforms go so far – the bottle is half full – but they do not go far enough – the bottle is half empty. The limitations are clear when we look again at proposed reforms under the different headings.

Scrutiny

Though the introduction of select committees in 1979, their strengthening since, and the proposals of the Select Committee on Modernisation represent advances in parliamentary scrutiny of the executive, the select committees still lack extensive resources – they cannot commission research of their own – and they lack adequate links with the floor of the House. Governments remain free to ignore their reports and know that such action is not likely to attract parliamentary debate. The legislative process is still characterised by the use of committees appointed ad hoc. The recommendations of the Committee on Modernisation lack any means of locking the proposed changes into the system: the use of special standing committees may or may not become standard; some bills may or may not be carried over from one session to another. Scrutiny of government actions is better than it was before 1979 and the scrutiny of government bills looks like being better than it was before 1997, but neither is as effective as it could – and, for those wanting to see effective parliamentary scrutiny, should – be.

Convenience

Despite the major improvements in parliamentary pay and working conditions, the provisions for MPs to carry out the tasks expected of them remain modest. Support provision – in terms of staff and information technology – remain limited, and some Members still have to make do with small, cramped offices, sometimes some way from where their secretaries are located. (MPs' offices are allocated by the whips, secretaries' offices by the sergeant at arms.) Many Members have to supplement their paid staff with voluntary helpers, including student interns. Constituency provision is a particular problem, constituents not having a dedicated and neutral point of contact for their MP.

The burdens are especially great for those Members who have additional parliamentary responsibilities, such as service on a select committee – more so if that entails chairing the committee – or a front-bench position. Ministers are hard pressed to find the time to devote to constituency work – and are used to employing dictaphones during car journeys to dictate constituency correspondence – and members of the opposition front bench have difficulty coping with all the demands made of them. By the end of the 1992–7 Parliament, the staff of one member of the shadow cabinet were so busy that there was not time to file incoming material.

Conduct

Despite the implementation of the Nolan report, there is still a disparity between what the House of Commons has introduced and what the public regard as acceptable. As we have seen, over 85 per cent of those questioned in the 1994 Gallup poll believed that it was not right for MPs to accept money in connection with parliamentary duties: under the new rules, Members can still accept money as long as they disclose it (the disclosure being in terms of particular bands of income, not the precise amount). The investigations by the Select Committee on Standards and Privileges in 1996 and 1997 served to highlight cases of alleged abuse by MPs of parliamentary rules: though this showed that there was a new investigative system in action, the public focus was more on the misconduct rather than the form of the investigation. The report by the Committee on Neil Hamilton in 1997 also highlighted the fact that there was nothing it could recommend in terms of punishment, given that he was no longer an MP. There was also disagreement among Committee members as to whether evidence should have been taken from Hamilton's main accuser, Mohamed Al-Fayed, a disagreement that raised questions as to the capacity of the House to engage in fair and rigorous self-regulation.

Why not more?

The reforms of recent years thus did not go as far as those pressing for change wanted, and certainly not as far as radical reformers would wish. Why not? There are several explanations.

Government objections

Governments recognise the need for the opposition to have the right to criticise and to examine their proposals but at the same time emphasise their own right to get their measures through and to do so without too much delay. Ministers tend to favour reforms that achieve some balance and, on occasion, a balance that favours government. From a government's point of view, there is much to be said for framework legislation or a fast-track procedure for certain government bills but less to be said for increasing the powers and resources of Commons committees.

Backbenchers' objections

Not all backbenchers favour reform. Some have a principled objection, especially to proposals that shift the emphasis away from the floor of the House. For them, the chamber is the grand debating forum of the nation – the place where government proposals can be subjected to public scrutiny and competing ideas can be tested (see Powell, 1982). The use of committees detracts from the floor of the House, providing a means of keeping MPs busy looking at administrative matters rather than the big issues of the day. Though not large in number – only twelve MPs voted against the introduction of the departmental select committees in 1979 – they can be vocal. Enoch Powell (an MP until 1987) and Michael Foot (an MP until 1992) used to be notable opponents of reform. Among present-day supporters of the floor of the House is Labour MP Dennis Skinner.

Lack of interest

Those having a principled objection to change are buttressed by many backbenchers who are generally socialised into the practices of the House and do not give reform a high ranking in their priorities. Many quickly get used to the ways of the House. The survey of new MPs in 1997 found that no less than 71 per cent admitted that, on first arrival, their reaction was 'on the whole favourable' (Norton and Mitchell, 1997, p. 12). Few volunteered proposals for a significant change in the relationship between the House and government. For many MPs – those sitting on the government benches – there is little incentive to favour change. They want to support their party in government and may see themselves as future ministers. The 1997 general election also brought in many new Labour Members who won former Conservative seats. They were conscious of the need to give priority to constituency work in the hope of helping their chances of re-election. In the 1997 survey of new MPs, 86 per cent ranked being a 'good constituency Member' as their first priority. Less than 6 per cent of respondents listed 'checking the executive' as their highest priority.

Fear of being overwhelmed

For some Members, there is a fear of having too many staff, either for themselves or for committees of the House. They fear that experts will take over and be on top rather than on tap. Some admit they would not know what to do with researchers and some express concern that committee agendas would be driven by staff rather than Members. This view is fuelled by experience of the US Congress. Few Members appear to have extensive knowledge of other west European legislatures but do appear familiar with what happens in Congress, where – according to their perception – members leave a great deal to their staff and where committees are dependent on their large permanent staffs.

Competing demands

There are matters other than reform of the House competing for the time and attention of MPs. Letters from constituents and from pressure groups pour in as soon as an MP is elected. A new MP will probably be faced with a three-figure number of letters the moment the election result is announced and certainly before any staff have been appointed to help cope with the correspondence. Other issues tend to assume even greater priority as a Parliament progresses. The main window of opportunity for reform is at the beginning of a Parliament. After that, other business – especially the government's legislative programme – tends to crowd out Members' time. The daily demands become such that they do not have time to stand back and think about changing the institutional arrangements that impose such a burden on them.

Absence of leadership

Past experience, especially that of the introduction of the departmental select committees, suggests that for substantial reform to be introduced two conditions have to be met: there has to be an early window of opportunity, and there has to be leadership. That leadership needs to embody both a clear set of recommendations for change and a Leader of the House ready to promote them (Norton, 1994b). Those conditions existed in 1979 and, to some extent, in 1997, when the Committee on Modernisation, under Leader of the House Ann Taylor, moved quickly to produce its report, Taylor then ensuring that a debate took place reasonably promptly in order to approve its recommendations. However, such leadership is the exception rather than the norm, few clear sets of proposals from authoritative bodies (such as the Select Committee on Procedure) being available at the beginning of a Parliament and with few Leaders of the House willing to move quickly in support of radical reform: the preference tends to be to mould a consensus behind some modest reforms, as was the case with the report from the Select Committee on Sittings of the House.

Absence of agreement

Even if MPs agree that some change is necessary, that does not necessarily mean that they will agree on what the change should be. Proposals for a change in the sitting arrangements of the House generate disagreement between Members who sit for seats in or close to London and those who have to travel from far-flung constituencies: the former like to get home in the evenings, the latter cannot get home in the evenings and prefer a shorter working week. This was a problem facing the Select Committee on Sittings of the House.

As we have seen, Members were divided over the recommendations made by the Nolan Committee. There was a general recognition that something had to be done to meet public concern, but some Conservative MPs felt that the recommendations went too far. A number of commentators and some MPs felt that they did not go far enough, believing that external regulation – rather than self-regulation – of the House was now necessary.

If there is an absence of agreement, then there is a natural tendency for the Leader of the House to try to seek agreement, but that takes time and then runs the risk of falling foul of one of the other problems: the fact that MPs' time and attention are devoted to other issues. Some reform may be achieved, but it is not likely to be radical.

Conclusion

The House of Commons is going to be affected by changes to the constitutional framework of Britain. The Labour government elected in 1997 has introduced proposals for elected assemblies in Scotland and Wales, for the incorporation of the European Convention of Human Rights into British law, and established the commission to propose an alternative, proportional electoral system to the first-past-the-post system presently in use in parliamentary elections (see Chapter 3). All these proposals have implications for the powers and practices of the House of Commons; the implications of a new electoral system are potentially profound.

The House of Commons will thus change as a result of reforms taking place to the wider constitutional framework. Some changes are taking place within the House because of decisions taken by the House. However, those changes do not meet the demands made by those pressing for reform, at either an elite or a mass level. The bottle of parliamentary reform remains half empty or, in the eyes of some reformers, more than half empty. Wider constitutional change will add to the pressures for reform.

Reading

Committee on Standards in Public Life (1995) *Standards in Public Life: First Report from the Committee on Standards in Public Life, Vol. 1*, Cm 2850–1, HMSO.
Drewry, G. (ed.) (1989) *The New Select Committees* (revised edn), Clarendon Press.
Franklin, M. and Norton, P. (eds) (1993) *Parliamentary Questions*, Clarendon Press.
Garrett, J. (1992) *Westminster: Does Parliament Work?*, Victor Gollancz.
George, B. and Evans, B. (1983) 'Parliamentary reform – the internal view', in D. Judge (ed.), *The Politics of Parliamentary Reform*, Heinemann Educational Books.
Grantham, C. and Seymour-Ure, C. (1990) 'Political consultants', in M. Rush (ed.), *Parliament and Pressure Politics*, Clarendon Press.
Hansard Society (1993) *Making the Law: The Report of the Hansard Society Commission on the Legislative Process*, Hansard Society.
Hawes, D. (1993) *Power on the Back Benches?*, SAUS Publications.
House of Commons Commission (1990) *House of Commons Services: Report to the House of Commons Commission*, HMSO.
Jogerst, M. (1993) *Reform in the House of Commons*, University Press of Kentucky.
Norton, P. (1981) *The Commons in Perspective*, Martin Robertson.

Norton, P. (1984) 'Parliament and policy in Britain: the House of Commons as a policy influencer', *Teaching Politics*, Vol. 13 (2).

Norton, P. (1990a) 'General introduction', in P. Norton (ed.), *Legislatures*, Oxford University Press.

Norton, P. (1990b) 'Memorandum of evidence', in *The Working of the Select Committee System: Second Report from the Select Committee on Procedure, Session 1989–90, Vol. II: Minutes of Evidence*, HC 19–II, HMSO.

Norton, P. (1993) *Does Parliament Matter?*, Harvester Wheatsheaf.

Norton, P. (1994a) 'Select committees in the House of Commons: watchdogs or poodles?', *Politics Review*, Vol. 4 (2).

Norton, P. (1994b) 'Independence without entrenchment: the British House of Commons in the post-Thatcher era', *Talking Politics*, Vol. 6 (2).

Norton, P. (1997a) *'Think, Minister' ... Reinvigorating Government in the UK*, Centre for Policy Studies.

Norton, P. (1997b) 'Reforming the House of Commons', *House Magazine*, Vol. 23 (765), 9 June.

Norton, P. and Mitchell, A. (1997) 'Meet the new breed', *House Magazine*, Vol. 23 (779), 13 October.

Packenham, R. (1970) 'Legislatures and political development', in A. Kornberg and L. D. Musolf (eds), *Legislatures in Developmental Perspective*, Duke University Press.

Powell, J. E. (1982) 'Parliament and the question of reform', *Teaching Politics*, Vol. 11 (2).

Review Body on Senior Salaries (1996) *Review of Parliamentary Pay and Allowances, Vol. 1: Report*, Cm 3330–1, HMSO.

Richardson, J. and Jordan, A. G. (1979) *Governing Under Pressure*, Martin Robertson.

Select Committee on European Legislation (1996) *The Scrutiny of European Business: Twenty-Seventh Report from the Select Committee on European Legislation, Session 1995–96*, HC 51–xxxvi, HMSO.

Select Committee on Modernisation (1997) *The Legislative Process: Select Committee on Modernisation of the House of Commons, Session 1997–98*, HC 190, HMSO.

Select Committee on Procedure (1984) *Public Bill Procedure: Minutes of Evidence*, 18 December, HC 49–iv, HMSO.

Select Committee on Procedure (1990) *The Working of the Select Committee System: Second Report from the Select Committee on Procedure, Session 1989–90*, HC 19–1, HMSO.

Select Committee on Procedure (1996) *Delegated Legislation: Fourth Report from the Select Committee on Procedure, Session 1995–96*, HC 152, HMSO.

3

Reforming the electoral system

Bill Jones

The results of recent elections have strengthened calls for reform of the British electoral system. This chapter considers the arguments for and against such reform together with the two most likely alternatives: the single transferable vote (STV) system and the additional member system (AMS).

Introduction

When Prime Minister, the Duke of Wellington declared that the British constitution required no further improvement: it was already perfect. Lord Eldon had been even more specific on adducing the indivisibility of the system: 'Touch one atom of our glorious constitution,' he declared, 'and the whole is lost.' Shortly afterwards, in 1832, came the Great Reform Act and the subsequent transformation of the voting system from one involving one-quarter of a million voters to the present day, when forty-three million men and women aged over eighteen elect 659 MPs from single-member constituencies on the basis of a simple majority vote. In the wake of elections in the 1980s, not only Margaret Thatcher but also her vanquished opponents dismissed the idea of further electoral reform. Will history make their attitudes seem as short-sighted as those of Eldon and Wellington? If so, how long will it be before another Great Reform Act is passed?

The fact is that a growing consensus is emerging across the political spectrum in favour of electoral reform. In the nineteenth century, the first-past-the-post (FPTP) system was relatively advanced compared with the sundry authoritarian regimes in Europe, but many of those countries which went on to adopt the British system have since rejected it for proportional representation (PR). Why should this be and what are the arguments against our present system?

The case against first past the post

The core idea behind representative government is that it enables all sections of society to have a say in the formation and conduct of government. This fulfils a basic right which all are held to have and, we have good reason to believe, makes it more likely that government will be carried out in the interests of, and with the general consent of, the governed. Critics maintain that because our present system is insufficiently representative it offends against basic human rights and delivers the wrong kind of government.

1   *FPTP discriminates against smaller parties.* A party with thin national support might poll a substantial number of votes but win very few seats. Thus, in 1983, despite the fact that 26 per cent of votes cast went to the Social Democratic Party (SDP)–Liberal Alliance and that their candidates came second in 313 contests, they won only twenty-three contests outright: 3.5 per cent of the seats in the House of Commons. Over one-quarter of the voting population, therefore, received minimal representation. Under FPTP such parties struggle to win seats until they pass the threshold of about one-third of the poll, after which they begin to win seats in great numbers. Small parties face a virtually insuperable catch 22: they have to become big in order to stop being small!

2   *FPTP favours the three big parties disproportionately.* This criticism is the corollary of the last. In 1979 the Conservatives won 44 per cent of the votes yet 53.4 per cent of the seats; Labour 36.9 per cent of the vote yet 42.4 per cent of the seats. In 1983 the entry of the SDP helped split the non-Tory vote and the Conservatives were able to win 61 per cent of the seats on 42.4 per cent of the vote. Margaret Thatcher therefore gained some 100 seats compared with 1979, from a reduced vote.

3   *FPTP elects on minority votes.* In 1979, 203 candidates were elected on less than 50 per cent of the votes cast in their constituencies; in 1983 the figure rose to 334. Again, in 1987 over half of MPs were elected in contests where the majority of voters did not support them. At the national level, as already shown, the same applies. In October 1974 Labour formed a government on 39.3 per cent of votes cast. The Hansard Society Commission on Electoral Reform (1976) commented (p. 22), 'if fewer than 40% of voters (29% of electors) can impose their will on the other 60% or more, distortions are no longer a question of "fairness" but of elementary rights of citizens'.

4   *FPTP favours parties with concentrated regional support.* It follows under FPTP that even small parties with highly localised support (e.g. national-ist parties) will do relatively well – as they did in 1974. But Labour has its support concentrated in the north, where it duly wins the vast majority of its seats, and the Conservatives in the south, where they

do likewise. In 1987, excluding London, Labour won no seats south of a line joining the Bristol South, Oxford East and Norwich South constituencies. In Scotland, on the other hand, Labour won fifty seats to the Conservatives' ten. Moreover, can it be good that few Labour MPs represent rural constituencies or towns and cities with expanding new industries, while few Conservative MPs have first-hand experience, in their constituency surgeries, of decaying inner cities and the problems of obsolescent traditional industries? All this could change, say the reformers, if the system were changed.

5   *FPTP creates artificially large majorities.* Elections are decided by about 25 per cent of constituencies, mostly with mixed social composition, which are 'marginal': where majorities are such that the contest will be decided by small shifts in the voting either way. Psephologists calculate that a swing of 1 per cent from one of the large parties to the other will usually result, these days, in about ten marginal seats changing hands. A swing of only a few percentage points in voter preferences therefore can make the difference between defeat and victory, a small or a very large majority. Critics argue that such majorities, created by the vagaries of the voting system and the geography of class, are not true reflections of public opinion and provide a false mandate for the winning party's programme. When combined with a strong showing by a third party the results can be a gross distortion, as in 1983 and, to a slightly lesser extent, in 1987.

6   *FPTP produces 'wasted' votes.* Those votes which do not contribute directly to the election of a candidate are said by some to be wasted because they are not reflected in the House of Commons. Where the seat is safe these might comprise a substantial minority but, as we have seen, they might easily comprise the majority of voters in a constituency. It is also argued that the huge majorities piled up for some candidates are wasted votes which might be better used to reflect different and important shades of opinion. Small wonder, say reformers, that over 20 per cent of the electorate regularly fail to vote. By contrast, voters in marginal seats exercise a disproportionate influence over the outcome of elections: their votes can be infinitely 'more equal' than those in other constituencies.

7   *FPTP perpetuates the two-party system.* Because only the governing and opposition parties appear to have viable chances of gaining majorities in general elections, voters tend to withhold their support from small parties which more accurately reflect their beliefs and cast their vote for the main party they dislike least. For reformers this produces a number of evils. First, voter choice is limited to two rival philosophies which can be bitterly and irreconcilably antithetical, especially when radical voices win party arguments. Secondly, it encourages the maintenance of unwieldy political coalitions like the Labour Party, which

endeavoured throughout the 1970s and 1980s, for electoral benefit, to pretend it was united. Thirdly, it has in the past – for example, in 1951 when the Conservatives took over from Labour and 1974 when the reverse occurred – led to an 'adversary' style of politics whereby the winning party immediately sets about undoing a selection of the major measures of its predecessor. The end result when this happens is that millions of voters occupying the centre ground go unrepresented, the political process falls into disrepute and the uncertainty surrounding our political future deters proper economic planning and investment for both the private and public sectors.

8 *FPTP discriminates against women and ethnic minorities.* Women comprise over 50 per cent of the population but only 18 per cent of MPs (admittedly up from a paltry 10 per cent in 1992). Coloured ethnic minorities gained representation in 1987 for the first time for fifty-eight years, but nevertheless numbered only four. The simple reason for this is that candidates are chosen by local party selection committees who 'tend to choose a "safe" candidate who will be as near to an identikit model of an MP as it is possible to find. The candidate will be white, middle-aged and male' (Bogdanor, 1984, p. 113).

9 *FPTP leads to undemocratic government.* Exploiting the lack of constraint which Britain's unwritten constitution allows, it is argued that FPTP enables a modern political party, elected on a minority vote, to impose measures for which there is no popular approval. According to Professor Ridley, 'Britain seems to have the most powerful and least representative system of government in Western Europe' (*The Guardian*, 11 January 1989).

Reformers believe therefore that FPTP is inadequate when two parties dominate, farcical when a third party challenges strongly and inferior to certain of the PR systems used by other countries. Unsurprisingly, defenders of the present system will have none of this.

The case for first past the post

Understandably, proponents of FPTP are found within the ranks of those parties which benefit from it: Labour and Conservative. As they are defending the status quo – always the high ground in British politics – they do not need to elaborate their views with the enthusiasm and detail of their opponents but they do, in any case, have a substantial case to put forward. They maintain:

1 It is not the chief aim of government to be *representative* but to be *effective*. By creating administrations with healthy majorities FPTP, with

occasional exceptions, has provided strong, stable governments which have been able to fulfil most of their election promises.

2   The close personal relationship between MP and constituent is a valuable (and much admired) aspect of the present system.

3   By-elections enable sections of the public to register their views on the progress of a government between elections.

4   Adversarial politics is as much a reflection of a new volatile mood among the electorate as it is of the FPTP system.

5   Parties do have a chance to win seats once they pass a certain threshold; if smaller parties were to keep working for political success instead of pursuing a sour-grapes reformist campaign they might be able one day to enjoy the system's benefits.

6   In 1979 the Liberals asked the European Court of Human Rights in Strasbourg to judge whether FPTP was a violation of their democratic rights – the Court ruled that such rights had not been violated.

7   FPTP is well known and understood and has been in existence for some time. The disruption which a shift to another system would cause could scarcely be justified in terms of the movement for change, which is not widespread and intense but is confined to those parties with a vested interest in change, sundry pressure groups and individuals. As Angus Maude and John Szemery (1982) point out in *Why Electoral Change?*: 'It is not enough to assert that it [electoral change] might be better, or even that it must be better than what we have. It is necessary to show pretty conclusively that it would be better and could not in any circumstances make things worse.'

8   It is a mistake to think, as is often argued, that economic success is closely related to voting systems. It is the skill, energy and character of its people which make a country prosperous, not the way it elects its legislature.

9   FPTP may have disadvantages but they are not as grievous as those of its alternatives.

10 Ironically, just when Labour and Charter 88 seemed to be seeing the light at the end of the PR tunnel, Italy, in early 1993, voted in a referendum to scrap its own PR system, the progenitor and cause of so many short-term, corrupt administrations. Though, as David McKie pointed out in *The Guardian*, the system preferred by the Italians was not pure FPTP but a revised form of the German system.

Proposals for electoral reform in Britain

What are the alternatives on offer? The human mind seems particularly fecund in this respect: there are literally hundreds, but only a few have been seriously considered in the British context. Having said this, it sometimes comes as a surprise to British people that their government came close to changing our electoral system on two occasions. In 1910 the Royal Commission on Electoral Reform suggested that the alternative vote (AV) be adopted for parliamentary elections, with some experimental use of PR – the STV – at local level.

The AV is based upon the numbering by voters of candidates according to preference in single-member constituencies. Any candidate who receives over 50 per cent of first preferences is elected. If no one manages this, the candidate with the least votes is eliminated and second preferences distributed accordingly to the other candidates. This process is repeated until one candidate receives a majority and is declared the winner. The system is not proportional but gives more voter choice and reduces wasted votes.

In 1917 a Speaker's Conference on Electoral Reform unanimously recommended a combination of both AV and STV systems for parliamentary elections but the resultant Representation of the People Bill (1917) foundered on the Commons' preference for AV on its own and the Lords' for STV. The bill lapsed but, writes David Butler (1963), 'the survival of the existing system plainly expressed not so much an endorsement of its merits as a failure to agree upon the remedy for its faults' (p. 39).

The industrious Proportional Representation Society maintained the pressure, winning the support of several leading politicians. Following the hung Parliament of 1929, MacDonald's minority government – partly to appease their Liberal allies – set up another Speaker's conference. This time AV was favoured, but not without fierce opposition from advocates of PR and opponents of all electoral change. The Commons endorsed the reform by fifty votes but the Lords rejected it and the government fell before the upper chamber could be overruled (Butler, 1963, pp. 58–83).

Since then no serious legislative attempt has been made to reform the basis of the voting system. Indeed, during the period of two-party hegemony after the war the issues became the virtual preserve of small pressure groups and the Liberal Party. The 1974 election results, however – which in February gave the Liberals only fourteen seats from six million votes – put new fire into the reformers' cause. Their case had been already strengthened by the 1972 decision of the British government to introduce PR into non-parliamentary elections in Northern Ireland: if it was thought PR could help heal the divisions over there, then why not use it to counteract the increasingly intractable polarities on the mainland? PR now became part of the political atmosphere of the decade and the most favoured type of alternative system for Britain. It was recommended by many bodies and study groups for a reformed House of Lords, was used increasingly by professional bodies and, in its 'list' form, was the dominant electoral system used by Britain's new European Community partners. In 1979 Britain was conspicuous in refusing to use PR in elections to the European Parliament.

In 1981 electoral reform received the support of a whole new political party of converts in the shape of the SDP. Minority support also grew in the two big parties, but the results of the 1983 election elevated the issue into one of constant underlying importance. The Conservatives polled 42.4 per cent of the total vote yet won 61 per cent of the seats; Labour had 28.3 per cent and 32 per cent respectively, and the poor Alliance 26 per cent and a miserable 3.5 per cent. The small nationalist parties did relatively better on this measure – 1.5 and 0.5 per cent – than the Alliance, as their support was concentrated geographically rather than dispersed. But the pendulum swings the other way too; the result of the historic 1997 election was equally unfair proportionally. Labour won 43.2 per cent of the votes yet nearly two-thirds of the seats. Conservatives won 30.7 per cent of the poll but only 25 per cent of the seats. Furthermore, Tories won 17.5 per cent of the Scottish vote yet no seats whatsoever; nor did they win a single seat in Wales.

Supporters of FPTP accuse the reformers of having centrist moderate axes to grind and claim PR's dubious advantages are won at too great a cost. PR supporters, for their part, maintain such criticisms are either biased, ill informed, exaggerated or based on selective use of evidence. The major elements in the debate are explained below.

The case for and against proportional representation

Representation

Against   Opponents of PR, such as the late Enoch Powell, argue that it is not the purpose of Parliament to offer a perfect reflection of society: the existing system is held to give adequate representation of most important interests, regions and ideas.

For   Advocates of PR do not claim it will give a perfect reflection, merely a better one, which will give better representation to women, ethnic minorities and those views at present stifled by the simple majority system.

Professor Ridley pointed out (*The Guardian*, 11 January 1989) 'that the 1987 Conservative government was elected on a smaller proportion of the electorate than any other in Europe'.

Complexity

Against   The system is too complex for voters to understand.

For   A small number of ballot papers will always be spoiled or filled in unthinkingly but while some of the mathematics behind PR systems might be complex, filling in the ballot paper is invariably straightforward. Are we to assume that British voters are less able to cope than Irish, Italian or Belgian voters or the hundreds of thousands who fill in complicated football pools or bingo cards each week?

The MP–constituent connection

Against PR would destroy the traditionally close link which exists between MP and constituents and for the recognisable, single MP would substitute a group of members, none of whom would have the same feeling of responsibility for their vastly enlarged constituencies.

For The single-member seat is no sacred British institution: multi-member constituencies functioned right into the present century and local government district council wards are usually represented by three members. Moreover, the Irish STV system arguably strengthens the connection (see below) and some PR systems (e.g. in Germany) retain single-member seats.

By-elections

Against PR systems do not allow for this traditional means of testing public opinion between elections.

For This argument is exaggerated in that local elections and regular opinion polls provide barometers of public opinion and, again, under certain forms of PR, by-elections can be fought.

Extremism and proliferation of parties

Against PR lets small, extremist parties into the legislature (e.g. the Nazis under the Weimar Republic constitution) and causes the proliferation of small parties (e.g. in Denmark and Finland, which have nine each).

For Where – as in Israel – the whole country is one multi-member constituency, this can and does certainly happen, but by stating a specific threshold below which parties will not be awarded seats this problem can be minimised or eliminated: only five parties are represented in the Bundestag in Germany under its limit of 5 per cent.

Party power and selection of candidates

Against Under PR, political parties, not voters, determine the names which appear on the candidate lists, meaning that they are often of low calibre.

For Even under FPTP it is a small minority of the party faithful who choose candidates. Moreover, the German and Irish systems allow equal or more voter choice in candidate selection (see below).

Coalitions

Against PR increases the number of parties and hence the chances of an indecisive result, making coalition politics the order of the day. This in turn produces:

- indecisive government and political immobilism;
- long delays while coalitions are being constructed (e.g. anything up to six months in the Netherlands);
- regular crises when they break down and frequent changes in government;
- flagrant unfairness in that politicians in smoke-filled rooms decide the colour of governments, not the voter.

For   Indecisive results do occasionally happen under PR but it must be remembered that eight out of the past twenty-five elections in Britain have been indecisive. Moreover, coalitions under PR have produced stable governments in a number of countries including Sweden, Germany and Austria, and in Greece and Spain majority single-party governments.

Delays, crises and changes of government are exaggerated: between 1945 and 1975 Britain had more general elections and changed finance and foreign ministers to a greater degree than many PR countries, including Belgium, Austria, Ireland, Israel, Sweden, Switzerland and West Germany (Finer, 1975, p. 24). Some PR systems, like those in Ireland and Germany, give the voter a chance to express an opinion on proposed coalitions (see below).

Coalitions which reflect consensus might reduce the potential role of conviction politicians like Margaret Thatcher or Tony Benn in their heyday, but it can be powerfully argued that if the majority of voters desire centrist or moderate policies then it is the function of a democracy to deliver them. Moreover, governments which people want are more likely to be stable and unifying and, if Germany and Austria are anything to go by, encourage economic growth and development.

Criteria of acceptability

Clearly, advocates of PR are justified in complaining that their opponents seek to highlight those systems, of the many available examples of PR in practice, which display it to least possible advantage. However, this alone does not rebut the charge that PR will be bad for Britain; most reformers recognise that a British PR system should retain – as far as possible – the valued features of the present system:

- simplicity;
- strong and stable, preferably one-party, government;
- good constituency–MP links;
- a manageable number of minor parties.

It might already have become apparent that the systems employed in Germany and Ireland appear to go a long way towards meeting these criteria and, indeed, the German AMS together with the Irish STV system are the only two serious candidates offered by the reform lobby. Both systems are explained below and their merits debated.

The additional member system

AMS seeks to marry the advantages of FPTP with those of PR. Out of 669 overall seats in the German lower house (Bundestag), 328 are elected according to the British system from one-member constituencies; the remainder are elected proportionately through a regional list system of nominated party candidates. Voters make two crosses on their ballot papers: one for a constituency candidate and the other on an adjacent list of political parties. *It is the percentage of the vote gained by parties in the latter ballot which determines, usually within a few decimal points, the total number of seats finally allocated.* Seats allocated from the constituency ballot are 'topped up' to the requisite levels from the regional list section. For example, in the election held on 27 September 1998, the SDP gained 212 seats in the constituency section; the CDU 112; the PDS 4; and the other parties did not win a seat. However, in the second ballot, these parties received, respectively, 41, 35 and 5.1 per cent of the vote. In addition, the Greens got 6.7 per cent and the Free Democrats 6.3 per cent. When the topping up had finished, the allocation of seats was as follows: SDP 212 + 86 = 298; CDU 112 + 133 = 245; PDS 4 + 31 = 35; and the Greens 47 and the Free Democrats 44. Seat allocations are nearly but not quite proportional to votes because parties must gain at least 5 per cent of list votes or three constituency seats before they are allotted any list seats.

Most voters are politically consistent in their choice but some split their votes for a variety of reasons, for example: knowing that their constituency candidate has no chance, Green supporters might vote for the candidate they dislike least from the other parties, but cast their regional list votes for their own party; knowing that their party plans a coalition with the Free Democrats, Social Democrat voters might cast their regional list vote for the Free Democrats.

Advantages of the additional member system

- After Germany's total collapse in 1945, AMS (introduced in 1949) has helped provide stable coalition government, which has itself enabled old wounds to heal and the economy to recover. Two parties have dominated the legislature and since 1961 only three small ones have been represented in addition; in 1969 the far-right NPD just failed to reach the 5 per cent limit; in 1987 it scored only 0.6 per cent in the list section.

- It enables voters to express an opinion on proposed coalitions (traditionally declared by parties before elections).
- It retains the constituency link yet delivers a proportional result.
- With only two crosses required on the ballot paper it is simple to understand.

Criticisms of the additional member system

- Coalition government has produced a very crowded political centre ground in Germany, which discourages radical new initiatives.
- It has enabled a small party, the Free Democrats, to play a disproportionately big part in every government except one since 1961.
- It creates two 'classes' of MP: those popularly elected and the list representatives (in practice, though, this does not seem to matter in Germany).
- Constituencies are relatively large by British standards.
- Political parties determine candidatures in the regional lists (though electoral law insists that democratic selection procedures be adhered to) and it often occurs that candidates who fail to be elected in constituencies get into the Bundestag through their nomination in the regional list. Moreover, the whole idea of party lists is attacked on the grounds that the voter is asked to choose not between individual candidates with personalities of their own but faceless political parties. This last characteristic in particular seems to go against the grain of the Anglo-Saxon political tradition.

Some reformers have concluded that to be suitable for British political conditions, AMS needs to be modified. In 1976 the Hansard Society Commission on Electoral Reform accordingly offered its well considered thoughts.

The Hansard Society Commission's variation

The last mentioned criticism weighed particularly with the Commission, which felt it was of overriding importance that all candidates should be elected directly by voters (1976, paras 116–17). Their proposals were as follows:

- Of the 640 MPs then in the House of Commons, three-quarters (not half) should be directly elected by FPTP from constituencies which would be enlarged, but not doubled as under the German system.
- One hundred and sixty seats would be available to make up party strengths to accord with votes cast but they would not be allocated to party lists. Instead, they would be taken up by parties on a regional

basis according to the percentages gained by losing candidates. The 'top-up' seats therefore would go to the best losers and only one vote, not two, would be required.

- Parties gaining less than 5 per cent of the votes cast in any region would not gain any additional seats. *= prevent extremism,*

This variation of the AMS offers several advantages: it requires no change in existing voting procedure; it would give representation to parties with substantial but not majority support in certain regions of the country (e.g. Labour in the south, Conservatives in the north); it would retain the constituency connection; it requires all MPs to submit themselves to the voters.

However, the scheme has several disadvantages, as Bogdanor notes (1984, pp. 72–3): 'failed' candidates would be able to sit in the House; it could easily happen that some constituencies could gain an unfair two or even three MPs; 'best losers' will frequently be determined by the number of candidates fighting their constituencies; small parties will be encouraged to fight every constituency in order to make the 5 per cent threshold; the lack of a second vote would remove the possibility of indicating a preference for a coalition partner – PR after all would make coalitions much more likely, and disproportionality would often result if only 25 per cent of seats were available to add to constituency seats.

The single transferable vote

In Ireland voters are divided into multi-member constituencies and at elections register their preferences for candidates as 1, 2, 3, 4 or as far down as they wish or there are candidates. In a four-member constituency a quota is set of one-fifth of the votes cast plus one: a simple calculation will reveal that only four candidates can possibly reach this quota figure. The quota can be expressed thus:

$$\text{Quota} = \frac{\text{total valid votes cast}}{\text{total number of seats}} + 1$$

Any candidate who receives the quota number of first preferences is elected. However, in the likely event that not all the seats will be filled so straightforwardly, the person with the least votes is eliminated and their second preferences redistributed to the other candidates, some of whom may now make the quota.

The surplus votes gained by those who make the quota are also reallocated if necessary. This process continues until all the available quotas are reached.

Complexity

Against Even STV supporters allow that the sorting of preferences is highly complex: if voters cannot understand the principles which underlie their system this could lead to cynicism and distrust.

For The voter is asked to think – but not to the extent where confusion takes over: it is relatively easy to mark preferences on a ballot paper. In 1968, moreover, a referendum on the voting system in Ireland resoundingly endorsed it three to two.

Party control

Against It is likely that parties could still control candidate selection even under STV.

For It is possible, however, that voters would be able to choose between candidates from different wings of the same party; STV offers a virtual built-in 'primary' in this respect. The ability of individuals to attract personal followings would also help reduce party domination of the political system.

Coalitions

Against STV would almost certainly lead to coalition government, with all its attendant disadvantages.

For Voters are enabled under STV to register an opinion on proposed coalitions between parties.

Small parties

Against The smaller the number of seats per constituency, the larger is the quota required to become elected. By reducing the number of seats big parties can squeeze out or disadvantage smaller ones: both Fianna Fail and Fine Gael have tried to do this in the past.

For The quota system is a guarantee against small-party proliferation and since 1977 an impartial boundary commission has been set up in Ireland which has removed political influence from the process and which increased the number of five-member constituencies from six to fifteen; four-member constituencies from ten to thirteen; and reduced three-member constituencies – the minimum size allowed – from twenty-six to thirteen (Lakeman, 1982, pp. 91–2).

Proportionality

Against STV is not truly proportional – some say that it is not a PR system at all. For example, in 1969 Fianna Fail obtained 45.7 per cent of first preference votes but ended up with 51.7 per cent of the seats.

For   Anomalies notwithstanding, the overall result in Irish elections is usually pretty proportional and much more so than recent British election results. Further, as the Hansard Society Commission (1976) pointed out, strict proportionality is not that important, 'because the whole purpose of STV is to allow later preferences to have an effect' and these do not, of course, show up in first preference percentages. STV would, moreover, if adopted in Britain, give reasonable representation to Labour in the south, Conservatives in the north, the Liberal Democrats all over the country and the nationalists in their respective countries. STV would also allow women and ethnic minority candidates to stand with a good chance of election especially where, in the latter case, the constituency included substantial numbers of immigrant voters.   = would encourage more electoral participation.

MP–constituency link

Against   STV would produce cumbersome, unnatural constituencies of over 200,000 voters, where neither constituents nor their multiple members could develop a proper relationship.

For   Many existing constituencies are unnatural creations, having been chopped and changed about with great regularity and, where the seat is safe, MPs have little incentive to be good constituency MPs. Under STV, on the other hand, there are no safe seats; sitting MPs can quite easily be defeated by rival candidates from their own party. This would of course make it more desirable to be a local candidate but STV would in any case make it easier for candidates to stand in their locality rather than 'migrating' to areas where their parties had significant support. Moreover, under FPTP the majority of voters often have to seek the aid of an MP for whom they did not vote: under STV this would tend not to happen as a wider range of MPs would be available.

The barriers to change

Which of the two favoured systems suits Britain best? Both systems have their fervent advocates (STV remains the choice of the Liberal Democrats). It is obvious that each would gain us different things at differing costs, the balance of advantage depending upon the value one places upon these changes; indeed, what is a gain for one person might be a loss to another. It cannot be denied that reforming the system carries with it political risks. Those who think the present system, despite its faults, produces acceptably stable and effective government will be disinclined to take such risks. But those like Professor Finer who 'fear the discontinuities, the reversals, the extremism of the existing system and its contribution to our national decline' believe 'The time for change is now' (Finer, 1975, p. 32).

Labour and electoral reform

As the Conservatives, for most of this century government's sitting tenants, have always opposed voting reform and the Liberal Democrats, Britain's political Cinderella, have always supported it, it is the views on this topic of Labour, the only serious threat to Conservative hegemony, which have attracted real interest.

Left-wingers in the Party have tended to oppose voting reform as they preferred to take FPTP's chance of either winning or losing 'big'. Supporters, however, have been drawn from all sections of the Party, such as Austin Mitchell, Jeff Rooker and even, when he was a member, Arthur Scargill. Rooker used to argue in the early 1990s that voting reform was the only way to prevent Britain becoming a one-party Conservative state; the victory on 1 May 1997 caused something of a rethink.

The report of Lord Plant for the Labour Party on this subject was published in July 1991. It came out, somewhat confusingly, in favour of PR for elections other than those to Westminster, for which the 'supplementary vote' system was preferred. According to this, second preferences would come into play where candidates failed to gain an overall majority: all candidates would then be eliminated and the one with the most first and second preferences would be elected. One member of the Plant Commission, Jeff Rooker, preferred a modified AMS form in which regional list seats would top up constituency members. The Electoral Reform Society calculated this system would still have delivered a Conservative victory in 1992.

In July 1992 John Smith, the Party leader, decided to keep his options open and backed a referendum on the subject if Labour won the next election. The 1993 conference plumped for conservatism and voted to retain FPTP. Before the 1997 election Labour and the Liberal Democrats signed a deal – brokered by Robin Cook and Robert Maclennan – to set up an independent commission to propose a single 'proportional' alternative to FPTP, the idea being that voters would choose between the two in a referendum.

Once Labour was in power, reformers waited anxiously for some movement on the issue; cynics inevitably drew comparisons between Lord Hailsham's condemnation of Britain's 'elective dictatorship' in the 1970s and his complacent acceptance of it once his party regained power. However, many new Labour MPs believed, with their narrow majorities in former Tory seats, they could only be re-elected under a new system of voting. Stephen Twigg, for example, the young man who ousted Michael Portillo at Enfield–Southgate, is unlikely to be re-elected at the next election under the present system. They would like to see reform come quickly.

Blair, in the event, proved as good as his word, despite letting it be known he was 'unpersuaded' on PR. On 17 September 1997 Paddy Ashdown met with Blair and Cook in a joint cabinet committee on constitutional reform, with voting reform obviously high on its agenda. On 1 December Blair announced, after months of wrangling over terms of reference, the formation of a five-member commission to 'observe the requirement for broad proportionality, the need for stable government, an extension of voter choice and the maintenance of a link between MPs and geographical constituencies'. The commission comprised:

1   Lord Jenkins, former Labour cabinet minister and head of the SDP, confidant of the Prime Minister and leading elder statesman of the Liberal Democrats;
2   Lady (Joyce) Gould, a member of the Plant Commission who voted for STV;
3   David Lipsey, Labour adviser and author of *The Economist*'s excellent Bagehot column;
4   Lord Alexander of Weedon, barrister turned businessman and author of *Voice of the People*, which tentatively advocates a 'personal preference' for STV;
5   Sir John Chilcot, former permanent secretary in the civil service but his ostensible neutrality on reform might conceal a preference formed when he served in the Home Office in 1966 under the commission's chair, Lord Jenkins.

The commission's recommendation will be set against the present system in a referendum, the timing of which will be crucial. The government has made it clear the commission's result will not be binding and it will decide what is best at the time.

The wider debate

One little-considered element in the debate is the European consensus in favour of moving to a common voting system for the whole of the EU. According to paragraph 3 of Article 138 of the Maastricht Treaty, 'The European Parliament shall draw up proposals for elections by direct universal suffrage in accordance with a uniform procedure in all member states.' The choice of an acceptable system would make disputes over membership and finance seem mild and minor disagreements by comparison but the pressure from Europe to move in this direction will inevitably have some effect in Britain eventually.

What would be the principal aim of reforming the voting system? Reformers recite the mantra of 'fairness' but few believe this is a serious objective for power-hungry politicians: as Hugo Young put it (*The Guardian*, 2 December 1997), 'Fairness is not the prime self validating axiom of a good election system. Other abstractions such as clarity and stability have as high a claim to be considered.' He believes the Blair/Jenkins exercise is about power, 'to secure the base of his political project for years ahead.... It's the opportunity ... the centre left missed for most of this century: the chance to define it as a progressive rather than a conservative century.'

The field of voting reform is large. Euro-elections will use PR in 1999, but there was a battle over this, with reformers disappointed. On 9 March 1998 Jack Straw, a known sceptic on reform, rejected the so-called Belgian version of PR for the 1999 Euro-elections; his view was that it could not translate voter preference for individual candidates into a win for such candidates. As Michael White reported in *The Guardian* (10 March 1998) 'The 1999 Europoll will be held on a regional list system of PR ... but electoral reformers deplored Mr Straw's insistence on a "simple party list system" in which voters cannot vote for individuals as well as their preferred party.' Most Labour MEPs believe this system will help them as Labour is likely to be suffering a mid-term loss of support at that time.

Regional assemblies in Wales and Scotland will also use PR as will, according to Andrew Adonis (*The Observer*, 19 October 1998), the new London authority. Labour was keen to win the regional referendums and so eschewed any clearly unfair proposals on voting, despite the fact that the Conservatives are bound to win seats in areas where they currently have none in Westminster. So for devolution, a form of AMS has been adopted. If all goes according to plan, there will be elections for a 129-member Scottish Parliament and a sixty-member Welsh Assembly in 1999. Seventy-three Scottish members will be elected via FPTP with the remaining fifty-six selected from party lists; in Wales the numbers will be forty and twenty, respectively.

The local level is more problematic. Adonis asserts the need for PR at this level is 'urgent and unanswerable to banish the one party states disfiguring town halls nationwide. Glasgow (Lab 76, others 7), Hull (Lab 59, others 1) and Doncaster (Lab 58, others 5) are textbook cases of the evils of government without any opposition or any prospect of one.'

Of course, PR is already in use in Northern Ireland for all elections except those to Westminster. Whether it will spread to all local elections in the mainland will depend on the acceptability of such an approach to a culture which might find this 'Irish' system alien.

Labour, despite the bad publicity emanating from these local fiefdoms, is loath to abandon a system which delivers to them the vast majority of town halls. The Liberal Democrats, too, are reluctant to adopt PR in local elections, as FPTP has also been kind to heir council candidates in the south and south-west.

But it is at the national level that the real battle (at the time of writing in preparation) will be fought. The Liberal Democrats and many Labour supporters favour STV (which would have given Labour an overall majority of only twenty-five at the 1997 election) but as David Lipsey noted in *The*

Economist (17 October 1997), 'it is not going to happen. Nearly all MPs believe that it would ruin the quasi-mystical relationship between a member of Parliament and his or her individual constituency, which is the only thing voters like about the existing first past the post system.' All Conservatives and some influential ministers also dislike STV.

The AMS has its supporters and it will be in use for the devolved assemblies, but it would have left Labour short of an overall majority by twenty-seven seats in 1997. In contrast, the AV system, which Blair says he could 'live with', would have given Labour an even bigger majority – of 213 instead of 179. So which one will be chosen? Michael White, the wise political editor of *The Guardian*, comments, 'In reality a compromise is likely, such as a mixture of STV and AV'.

'AV could be part of solution,' said the Prime Minister's official spokesman on 1 December 1997.

The Jenkins report of October 1998

Michael White's analysis proved prescient indeed, as the unusually short and unusually well written report – some were amused by the consistently intense food imagery employed – came out at the end of October 1998. Its hybrid nature sought to combine the merits of AMS and FPTP and to balance the requirements given in the commission's remit of: broad proportionality, the need for stable government, the extension of voter choice and the maintenance of the link between MP and geographical constituencies. Jenkins recommended voters be given two votes in two different ways of electing MPs.

First, 80 per cent of MPs – 530–560 in number – would be elected from single-member constituencies. However, they would be elected via the AV system. All candidates would be ranked by voters according to preference and any receiving over 50 per cent would be elected. If no one made the grade, the candidate at the bottom of the poll would be eliminated and the second preferences of that candidate redistributed to the other candidates. If anyone then made the halfway mark, that candidate would be elected, but if not, the process would continue until someone did.

So, minority-based MPs would be a thing of the past. Jenkins defended his proposal by arguing: it would end 'wasted' votes; it would encourage candidates to appeal as widely as possible, to pick up high preference ratings from the weaker candidates' supporters; it would deter candidates from attacking each other personally, as all would have an interest in maximising their preference ratings; and it would encourage any coalition deals to be done before elections, not after them.

Second, there would be top-up seats to make the result more proportional. These would be taken by MPs elected from eighty regions comprising blocks

Table 3.1. *Actual numbers of seats won in general elections under FPTP and estimations of results under the Jenkins system*

| | Actual | | | | Jenkins estimation | | | |
	Conser-vative	Labour	Liberal Democrats[a]	Other	Conser-vative	Labour	Liberal Democrats[a]	Other
1997	165	418	46	30	165	384	78	32
1992	336	271	20	24	307	250	66	28
1987	376	229	22	23	332	204	88	26
1983	397	209	23	21	338	178	111	23
1979	339	269	11	16	334[b]	250[b]	38[b]	28[b]

[a]Liberal Party, 1979; Liberal–SDP Alliance, 1983–7.
[b]Calculated on 1983–92 boundaries.

of constituencies. The second vote would be cast essentially for a party, although individual names of candidates would appear on the ballot paper. Where a party found itself winning fewer seats than it should given its share of the vote, it would be awarded the top-up seat or seats.

Based on this system, Jenkins asserts that, in 1983 and 1987, the Conservatives would have had small but workable majorities (Table 3.1). In 1992, it would have produced a hung Parliament, but even a coalition might have been preferable to the indecisive rule of John Major over 1992–7. In 1997, the new system would have produced fewer Labour seats, but still a healthy overall majority. Jenkins acknowledged that the new system would create big problems for the Boundary Commission and that it would take some eight years to introduce such a radical constitutional innovation. He also advised the creation of independent electoral commissions, one to regulate elections and one to regulate referendums. Before the new scheme could be introduced, a major programme of public education would be necessary.

The arguments began immediately, not least in the Labour Party, where a majority of members had been polled in favour in PR, but a sizeable majority in the parliamentary party and the cabinet were opposed in the autumn of 1998.

Public opinion

What do the public think about voting reform? The message is mixed. A MORI poll for *The Economist* from 28 April 1997 showed 65 per cent either 'strongly supported' or ' tended to support' PR but in the same poll only 50 per cent of the combined two categories favoured 'holding a referendum on the voting system'.

Foreign experience

Foreign experience is varied regarding voting reform. In 1992 Italy decided to abandon its PR system as too unstable; the rapid turnover in coalition governments was legendary and the endemic corruption was also blamed on the voting system. Instead, Italy opted for a simple majority system so reviled by Britain's chattering classes.

In New Zealand a popular vote decided to move from FPTP to one of mixed-member plurality, an adapted form of the German AMS whereby sixty-five MPs are elected by constituencies and fifty-five from the top-up regional party lists to ensure a proportional result, with 5 per cent of the vote being the threshold below which parties could not qualify for any top-up seats. As Jones describes (1997), no party gained overall control in 1996 and it took an astonishing eight weeks for a coalition to be formed. Moreover, the leader of the New Zealand First party, Winston Peters, a maverick former National Party MP, courted both the big parties, Labour and National, to see who would give him the best deal in the resultant coalition. This experience seems to bear out the views of those who claim PR delivers power to party caucuses who wheel and deal for their own ends and often benefits small unrepresentative groupings, like the Free Democrats in Germany. No doubt this and similar foreign experiences will be cited in an extended debate on electoral reform in the wake of the Jenkins report: nothing less than the political colour of the next century is at stake.

Reading

Bogdanor, V. (1984) *What is Proportional Representation?*, Martin Robertson.
Butler, D. E. (1963) *The Electoral System in Britain since 1918*, Oxford University Press.
Finer, S. E. (1975) *Adversary Politics and Electoral Reform*, Wigram.
Hansard Society Commission on Electoral Reform (1976) *Report*, Hansard Society, 12 Gower St, London.
Jones, A. (1997) 'Electoral reform in New Zealand and the consequences', *Talking Politics*, spring, pp. 198–202.
Lakeman, E. (1982) *Power to Elect*, Heinemann.
Maude, A. and Szemery, J. (1982) *Why Electoral Change?*, Conservative Political Centre.
Plant Commission (1991) *Report*, Guardian Studies.

4

The present usefulness of the House of Commons

Douglas Hurd

Politicians, not just in Britain, but across the democratic world, are conscious that they are in disrepute. The paradox is that politicians are in worst repute when things are best. In a slump or a war, political leadership emerges and people respect and follow those political leaders. When things are reasonably good, when we have a reasonably good economy and a reasonably safe world, then people get fed up with politics and politicians. Politicians, being human beings, feel this and react. They react in different ways, mostly misguided. They react by hyperactivity, by claiming that they can do things by legislation which in fact are beyond the political scope – like preventing crime, making people good instead of bad, making teachers good instead of bad. These are not things which politicians can decide. They can affect them indirectly, but they do not actually decide.

The second, and particularly British, reaction is to make political discussion too adversarial. Matters which ought to be considered by the political body as a whole and decided on their merit after discussion are snatched by one part of the political body and used as a weapon to beat the other. This is true of criminal justice, but it is also true of constitutional matters. There is a danger in this country of too much hassling on matters which are not adversarial. In Continental countries, there is an opposite danger, that things get snuffed out because a political consensus is too easily reached, with too little discussion. We have the danger of pretending that there are only two possible versions of a particular incident, one held by one side of the rectangle of the House of Commons and one held by the other.

I have only been a Member of Parliament for twenty-two years, which is not very long in the sweep of things. But in that time I have seen a change, and as the son and a grandson of Members of Parliament, I had

This chapter was originally given as a talk to the Centre for Legislative Studies at the University of Hull in November 1996. Thanks are due to Philip Norton, editor, for permission to reproduce the paper from the *Journal of Legislative Studies* (1997), Vol. 3 (3), pp. 1–9.

glimpses of earlier periods. The change since the 1935 general election, which is the first one I remember taking part in, is substantial.

One can divide the role of the House of Commons into two parts: the legislative and the control of the executive. The quality of legislation coming from the House of Commons is poor. I am not talking about the policy content but about the ability of the people who draft and pass legislation to get it right for their purpose. Because there is too much legislation, the strain on the people who actually draft is great. They tend to receive instructions rather late, the purpose is not always clearly defined and as a result the quality of draft bills reaching the Commons or the Lords is lower than it used to be. There is a relatively simple test for this, which is to look at the government amendments which then follow. Of course, you can have government amendments which represent some new policy. But I am talking about the raft of government amendments which follow as civil servants and ministers realise that what they first drafted is not right, that they have missed out something.

The Firearms (Amendment) Bill in 1988 was a classic instance. Once you put forward measures, you learn on the ground from the people who will be affected by them that you have got the details wrong. Not that your policy is wrong, although they will certainly argue that too, but they tell you that you have got the facts of the matter wrong. A weapon which you described in one way is not that way. A category which you thought included a particular weapon does not do so and you just have to correct yourself. The quality of legislation reaching Parliament is poor and the quality of parliamentary discussion of it is poor. This is particularly true in the Commons. The second reading discusses the principle, then it goes upstairs to a standing committee, except in constitutional or exceptionally important measures, to be discussed by a couple of dozen (perhaps rather fewer) Members of Parliament who have posted an interest. But the adversarial aspect remains. The government managers, the whip and the minister have an interest in getting the bill through quickly and without change. Sometimes, in order to get the bill through quickly, the minister will make a concession. But my experience in getting legislation through is that governments are not anxious to make changes. The merits of the matter tend to get swept aside in the adversarial atmosphere. That is why the revising chamber is crucial.

Most of the improvements in legislation occur in the House of Lords. A bill can start in the Lords as you know, but wherever it starts, improvements are usually made in the Lords. There is a less adversarial atmosphere and a mass of cross-benchers who do not belong to any party. Those who intervene on a particular bill will tend to be life peers who have knowledge and experience of that particular subject. Then of course the Lords' amendments come to the Commons. If the Lords have frustrated an important part of government policy, the government will try to upset the

Lords' amendments. But there are many cases where the Lords have taken a swipe at or improved a secondary problem. I have sat very often in cabinet, and we have said, well okay, it is not worth a fight; let the Lords' amendments go through. In my experience, those Lords' amendments are improvements to the legislation. If one was marking the House of Commons for legislative efficiency, the mark nowadays would be very low.

The ways of improving that are not too difficult and are being considered. There is a system by which, before we actually begin to vote and discuss texts, you would listen to expert opinion from outside Parliament. Legislators, those actually on the standing committee dealing with the detail of the bill, should be exposed at first hand to experts from outside. They may disagree on a criminal justice bill with what the chief constables or representatives of the judiciary or the magistrates, the probation officers or the prison governors think, but they should have some opportunity to listen directly to those views. Of course, this holds the whole process up. For reasons which are usually not very good, most legislation is thought to be in a huge hurry. This procedure involves a delay but, on the whole, a healthy delay. This procedure is not used often. It is generally used on minor bills which the government does not greatly care about. It should also be used for important bills. The corollary is that you should allow bills to go over from one session to another. We should not be in a hurry to complete legislation; it should be allowed to take its time. If the consequence of that is that there is less legislation, then that is probably a good thing.

On the other hand, Parliament is rather better at influencing and controlling the executive than most people now suppose. The constitutional debate outside Parliament is very much a matter of fashion. Media commentators pick up the latest ideas. They write as if there was an overwhelming consensus when all they have done is read the article of one of their colleagues the previous Friday, so one article succeeds another. One has constantly to beware of the sweep of fashion when one is trying to discover what is sensible and important.

The control of the executive is better than is sometimes supposed. I speak as someone who has spent sixteen years on the trot as a minister. I never lost my wholesome respect, even fear, of the House of Commons. I felt it was always there behind my shoulder. Why? Not because of the stage-managed mini-drama of Prime Minister's question time, which is a disaster. It has achieved cult status in the USA from people who watch public service television. But, in serious parliamentary terms, it is a disaster. The Prime Minister and the leader of the opposition would concur. Nor really because of the formal debates in the chamber, where there has been definite deterioration. Until quite recently, Members of Parliament used to go along to debates to listen. Now, if you drop into the chamber to listen to a debate or watch it on closed-circuit television, the House is almost empty. There are Members who have spoken, because there is still a convention that one stays around after one has spoken, plus those who are about to speak. You cannot just go in at five o'clock and expect to catch the Speaker's eye. She is aware that you have not been there from the beginning. But people rarely go just to listen. Whereas, even when I started as an MP, the House was often reasonably full. We were there to listen and to learn, sometimes to make up our minds. All that has almost gone.

So why, in charge of three departments, the Northern Ireland Office, the Home Office and then the Foreign Office, did I always feel conscious of the House of Commons and often worry about that? Partly, my own question time. These departmental question times are of a much higher quality than Prime Minister's question time. They go on longer, lasting an hour in the case of the Home Office, three-quarters of an hour in the case of the Foreign Office, once a month, and you get pinned down. You get pinned down partly by people who are advocates of a particular cause, who are passionate Zionists or passionately pro-Palestinian, pro-Greek, pro-Turkish, pro-Pakistani, pro-Indian. You may not care very much for them, because they are one sided, but they know about that side. They will know exactly what has happened and who has said what, and they can be formidable. What you cannot afford to do is to ignore them.

On Home Office matters, you get people who are representing surges of opinion. Conservative Home Secretaries are particularly vulnerable to these people when they come from the right or the punitive part of the Conservative Party, which represents a strong viewpoint. They tend to make up in boldness and conviction what they sometimes lack in accurate knowledge of the facts. They can make your life very difficult. They are behind you. Technically, it is much more difficult to deal with criticism which comes from behind than from in front. You are very conscious of this and you spend a lot of time trying to pre-empt it. The fact that you can have a bad quarter of an hour during your question time in the House of Commons is very much something on your mind. You can spoil what you are trying to do for months ahead if you have had a really rotten question time.

The back-bench committee of your own supporters is a formidable instrument. You go to it from time to time, but even when you do not attend, you hear about its weekly meetings. People come to you from it to make representations. They are an important focus of influence. I am speaking about my experience as a Conservative minister. The Labour Party has different structures and I would not presume to describe them. I imagine that, broadly speaking, the same is true.

The select committees are public and vary hugely, but they are a formidable instrument also. The Foreign Affairs Select Committee under David Howell's chairmanship is an accomplished body. It has good clerks and it is always sensible and knowledgeable. You go in front of it, not for three-quarters of an hour, but for two hours and a half, in public. The

Foreign Secretary goes before the Foreign Affairs Select Committee before every European summit and is cross-examined in detail about every matter that could conceivably come up at that summit. Sometimes, if these matters are controversial, the radio and television are there, so the evidence is on air. But even if the evidence does not reach the media, it is a formative experience. There are other select committees which are rubbishy, though I have not actually come across them myself. But select committees are a very considerable asset in the control of the executive.

In all these things, I have not been talking about things you will see described or codified in textbooks. I have been looking at what it is actually like when you are a minister. The idea that ministers feel contemptuous of the House of Commons, that they do not need to worry about it, is nonsense. We come from it and, for the reasons I have described, we feel it over our shoulder the whole time.

I will now go on to say two things which challenge the orthodoxy and perhaps slightly overstate the case. The direction in which we are being steered by Lord Justice Scott and Lord Justice Nolan are both, on balance, harmful to the effectiveness of the House of Commons. These are the heresies.

The Scott report is a deeply inadequate document. I am not talking about the unfairness of the proceedings, although a lot of people thought they were unfair. I am talking about the basic mis-description of modern government. Scott started, of course, to examine a very serious allegation, which was that innocent men had been convicted because the government feared for its skin and sat on information which was available to them and would have secured their acquittal. That was a very serious charge and it was on that basis that an inquiry was set up. That charge disappeared in the course of the years. Instead, Scott fastened on two issues, one of which was public interest immunity certificates, which I do not propose to talk about. The other was the accusation that there had been an alteration in the guidelines, not the law, by which government departments would judge individual applications for export licences for Iraq and Iran. There had been an alteration, decided on by three junior ministers, about which the House of Commons should have been informed and was not. That was, as it were, the accusation to which he moved, the earlier dramatic one having collapsed completely.

On this point volumes were written and huge quantities of evidence taken. That particular decision taken by those three junior ministers was certainly incomplete and not fully codified. It was understood later and in recollection by different people in different ways as to whether it was a real alteration in the guidelines or a minor difference in interpretation. If you look at the evidence, there are endless different ways in which this was described by different people.

The point which Scott neglects is that this kind of decision is taken by a junior minister about half a dozen times a week. A cabinet minister takes decisions of this kind of magnitude about two or three times a night when he gets home to his boxes after his dinner. They were of that order. There is a flow through government of several dozen comparable decisions a week in any major department. These are decisions which actually have to be taken. There are ministers (I will not name them), who act as Lord Justice Scott in his report would wish them to act. They do not take the decision. They delay. They say 'Are we sure we have every possible bit of information which may be relevant? Are we sure we have had everything from the intelligence service which might be relevant? Are we sure everyone has been involved in the discussion who ought to be? Have we really combed through Whitehall to make sure in this decision everybody is on board?' There are ministers who behave in the way that Lord Scott recommends; they do not last long because they do not take the necessary decisions.

I am writing a novel about this at the present time because it is just not understood.[1] The pell-mell of government, the pace at which things move, the fact that you have to get on, to take the decision, even if not every 'i' has been dotted and every 't' crossed, is not understood. I tried to explain this to Lord Justice Scott. I really went through it. I sent him my memorandum. He smiled in his nice way, but it simply was and remained outside his care. I do not think the Scott report will have very much influence in the long run. I do not think it is a useful tool. Government is an art, an imperfect art, a hurried art. It always had been to some extent, is so now, certainly, and will remain so.

Sensible ministers know that in the modern world you get into more trouble if you try to conceal information than if you reveal it. Often, you have to decide whether or not to make a statement to the House of Commons about a relatively minor change. Usually, nowadays, you take the decision to make a statement, even though you might have a bit of trouble, but it is better to do that than to sit on it. This is part of the discretion that you have. People will say that is not good enough, because there is an absolute obligation. What is the purpose of the House of Commons? If you read the media and the fashionable commentators, they give what I would call a 'Whig' answer. Their interpretation is one which Macaulay would have given. The job of the House of Commons is to check, control and in general make life difficult for the executive power, because the great danger is that executive power will 'go Stuart', will become overweening, will become tyrannical, and the essential job of the House of Commons is to prevent that. That is the Whig view of the House of Commons. The media love it because they like challenges, they like clashes.

But I do not believe, as a Member of Parliament, that the voice of the newspapers in this respect is the voice of my constituents. Under our system

1   *The Shape of Ice* (1998).

Parliament is not set up against the executive. It is so in the US system after their experiences with George III, but not in ours. In our system, the government grows out of Parliament and is not separated from it. Part of the job of Parliament is to create and sustain the executive, to make its life possible. This is what one might call a Tory view of Parliament. The Duke of Wellington expressed it when he said 'the Queen's Government must be carried on'. The Duke changed his view on several matters. He ceased to obstruct Catholic emancipation and eventually even the Great Reform Bill, on the grounds that, at the end of the day, what was really important was that the government should carry on. That is the Tory view. I think it is entirely sustainable and what most people want. If you went into the streets of Witney or Woodstock and asked people what they wanted of Parliament, they would not want more argument, more control, more political challenges and argy-bargy. They want better decisions of government – maybe fewer – but better.

The instinct of the people is that they want the political class, whether in government or in Parliament (they do not really distinguish hugely between the two), to get on and do a good job in those areas which they have to deal with. They are not particularly interested in making life more difficult for government. They want fewer poll taxes and more successful industrial relations legislation. They want Parliament and government together to do a better job. In our system, Parliament and government should be together.

Now we come to Lord Justice Nolan. He produced a report which was well received. The whole question of sleaze got a bit out of hand and is now probably back in hand again. Two things got hopelessly confused which are of their nature quite different. Sexual sleaze is wholly exciting and for readers of *The Sun* newspaper it is much more interesting reading than politics. But the fact that it is discovered twenty years later that a girl had a baby on a man's initiative twenty years before when he was at university is not a reason why a minister should resign in any sane society. Yet we got to the point when that did happen. It got out of hand.

Financial sleaze is quite different. That is a serious impairment of the political system. They may be small examples; they obviously have been in this country. But right across the democratic world, financial sleaze is what destroyed the Italian party system, has done a lot of harm in Japan, a huge amount of harm in Belgium and does a certain amount, though lesser harm, here. So you have to be rigid and robust about financial sleaze. My worry about the answer which is being found is that it may create another difficulty. I think there is a real danger that the 'Nolan tendency' will lead to a narrowing of the political class, which is undesirable.

When I was at Cambridge, I was passionately interested in party politics. There happened to be two general elections when I was there. We had a lovely time careering round Cambridge constituencies making a nuisance of ourselves. I was very interested in, almost hypnotised by, national politics. But, there was no ladder, there was no way in which I could move from that kind of excitement to national politics. I could see the ladder, but its lowest rung was about fifteen years away. I had to do something else and then come back. But now, the rungs of the ladder are there, right in front of you. There are plenty of jobs. The Palace of Westminster is full of young men and women pouncing on you, asking you to give an interview for an undergraduate magazine or this and that. They are special advisers, members of think-tanks, executives of public relations firms specialising in politics. These are the people who go before selection committees for parliamentary seats and there is no interruption in the ladder up to heaven. Is this a good idea? I do not think it is. We will get and are already getting – you see it already in the House of Commons, in both main political parties – a narrowing of the reservoir from which people are taken. More people are being just professional politicians all their lives. There are fewer people with outside interests and outside activities, who think it possible, agreeable, or their duty, to go into politics. It is a big change.

After the war, there were plenty of people in the Commons who were primarily farmers, or industrialists or ex-soldiers, people who had and continued to draw experience from the outside world, not through a think-tank but actually through their daily lives. Those people now find politics unattractive. Nolan and the worry about outside interests make politics much less appealing. If you continue to earn in the City, or as a lawyer, or as a farmer, or as a businessman, you are now constantly faced with the accusation that you are only a part-time MP, that you are not doing the job properly. All the accent now is on attitudes which will stimulate a narrow political class and deter people from coming in from outside and doing it part time.

Constituency work has increased in volume and a Member of Parliament now has resources to deal with them. He has an allowance which enables him to employ a secretary and at least half a research assistant. I would reckon, although I have not researched this, that a Member of Parliament who is energetic and prepared to work evenings and Saturdays, can do his constituency job and pursue one substantial parliamentary interest in half the available time. That is to say, he can be a good constituency Member, do everything that could reasonably be expected of him, which is much more than it used to be, and follow foreign affairs or Treasury matters, and still have half his time free, if you are including evenings and Saturdays. If you are really energetic and prepared to go through those things, then you can have half your time free and still have time to be a complete parliamentarian, until, of course, you become a minister. But that division of time is now becoming unattractive. The overwhelming pressure, all the registers and declarations of transparency, will make people spend all their time in purely party political matters, fidgeting around the Palace of

Westminster. Is it the best use of their time? Would it not be better to have at least 100 or 200 Members who are active and transparently engaged in outside activities, bringing all the time that experience gives into the general debate? That is the big question. My own view is that you need both the part-timers and the full-timers but that at the moment the balance is tipping really strongly in a narrowing direction. I know people in their thirties who would love to be in the House of Commons, and would be very good, but would not now touch it with a barge pole. I also know people who are in the House of Commons who are skilled only in being rude to one another, which is a skill you learn after a political life. This is an impoverishment. We do need to encourage outside interests. Otherwise, we will find a growing and dangerous gap between the problems which a minister has to tackle and his qualifications for tackling them.

That is my worry. It is not the Nolan report or anything that he has said or done which worries me, but the whole tendency embodied in Nolan. The Nolan report may deal with sleaze and produce transparency, but the Nolan tendency may actually have a narrowing and impoverishing impact on the House of Commons.

5

Do we need the monarchy?

Bill Jones

In his book *On the Constitution*, Lord Hailsham (1992), veteran Conservative politician and occasionally maverick commentator on the political scene, said of the monarchy: 'I am wholly persuaded that of all our institutions this is the one with which I would be least inclined to meddle' (p. 23). As he had recommended devolution and a diet of reform which only Labour felt able to advocate (until 1998 when his own party began to catch up), this defence has to be seen as significant. It is doubtful, however, if even he would feel quite the same in the present day, having absorbed the continuing tale of scandal and woe from the Windsors, not to mention the tragic death of Princess Diana and the ensuing swingeing criticisms of the royal family from just about every quarter. Indeed, in the wake of her death republican arguments can be said to have entered the mainstream of debate for the first time in a hundred years. This chapter will seek to answer the question of whether we still need the monarchy via a number of themes: tradition, democracy, politics, cost, symbolism and moral authority.

Tradition

The British monarchy has been around a long time; it did not achieve countrywide authority until Alfred (849–99) and Athelstan (895–939). Political unity was not achieved until the Danish king Cnut (c. 994–1035). In those days kings were little more than tribal leaders and ruled according to custom; they tended to declare the laws of the land rather than utilise a legislative process but the germ of a parliament was there in the form of the witenagemot, an advisory council. The medieval period witnessed desperate struggles for the right of succession, which Shakespeare quarried so effectively for dramatic purposes. Kings depended for their power on feudal loyalties, military skill and their ability to exploit the wealth of royal estates as well as appropriate church lands. The emerging power of Parliament led to conflicts of power and resources which were resolved only by the Civil War (1642–9). For a short period the country was no longer a monarchy as Cromwell (1599–1658) ruled as Lord Protector supported by an elected single chamber. His rule and that of his son were not successful and in 1660 Charles II (1630–85) was restored. James II (1633–1701) tried to favour Catholicism and a group of seven prominent public men invited William of Orange (1650–1702) to invade the country. This he did successfully and ruled with his wife, James's daughter, Mary, though not until the Glorious Revolution, with its Declaration and Bill of Rights, had circumscribed their powers and made Parliament's will superior to the monarch's.

The eighteenth century was a story of historical accidents and incremental change of great significance to the English constitution. William and Mary's daughter, Anne (1665–1714), proved infertile and a new royal house was imported from Hanover. George I (1660–1727) proved hopeless at learning English and uninterested in affairs of state. The minister, namely First Lord of the Treasury, Robert Walpole (1676–1745), who chaired his committee of senior ministers, now called the cabinet, consequently gained great power and came to exercise himself many powers on his King's behalf. Despite a rearguard effort by George III (1738–1820) to win back royal power, the monarchy could not reverse the tide of history which, following the French Revolution, was on the side of democratic and representative government. After a period of resistance to reform, the monarchy had to accede to popular elections as arbiters of the colour of government.

From then on the institution, in the person of Queen Victoria (1819–1901), moved steadily out of the heated kitchen of political decision making into the more leisurely state rooms of symbolic head of state. All monarchs since her have inherited basically the same institution and have accepted its constraints with greater or lesser grace.

Some opponents of reform argue that the very longevity of the monarchy is evidence of its utility and a reason for its continuance; as Enoch Powell said of the Lords: 'it is there because, like Topsy, "it growed"; it is there because it has always been there; it is there because it has come to be there' (Powell, 1982, p. 168). Those who argue this line tend to favour tradition for tradition's sake and this is a dangerous road which would lead to the retention of every redundant stick of constitutional furniture long after it ceased to have any relevance to the present day; the monarch, for example, would still exercise near absolute powers.

According to this theme, the monarchy should be preserved for the sake of tradition, but in an efficient democracy the place for tradition should surely be in a museum: the yardsticks of efficiency and relevance should be rigorously applied and if an institution is found wanting appropriate steps taken.

Democracy

According to this theme the monarchy is relevant to our democracy for the functions it performs. Inevitably it rests on a contradiction as the monarchy, being hereditary and exclusive, can never be democratic. Moreover, the monarchy reinforces a divisive class system in Britain. It is the linchpin – supported by honours and private education – which locks the whole stratified scheme together; without the monarchy to validate it, it is hard to see how the aristocracy could survive for long. The Queen's personal staff are also drawn from the topmost stratum of society: Eton, Oxbridge, the Guards. The Queen's private secretaries since 1952, as Adonis notes, have been professional courtiers, with manifold links to the Palace through education and family. Michael Charteris – Eton, Sandhurst, grandson of an earl and a duke – was chosen to be the Queen's secretary when she was still a princess: 'Choosing me,' he charmingly admitted, 'was an act of pure nepotism' (Adonis and Pollard, 1997, p. 139). When he retired, as Adonis points out, he became Provost of Eton, where he could watch over the fortunes of Prince William. The Queen is thought to be very sympathetic to African rulers but there are few signs she pursues an equal-opportunities policy in relation to the ethnic complexion of her personal staff.

Against this it can be argued the monarchy actively helps to integrate classes. Adonis quotes Brian Harrison, who maintains the monarchy, itself foreign, helped to mediate between the middle classes and the aristocracy in Victorian and Edwardian times and to integrate working classes in the twentieth century. Edward VIII famously said 'something must be done' about mass unemployment in the 1930s and set up summer camps for working-class and public-school boys. Harrison also points to the garden parties in Buckingham Palace, the invitation lists of which now exceed 35,000 a year from a wide cross-section of social classes.

Added to this might be the empathy the royals have often felt for working-class people. The royals' favourite cabinet member in the Attlee era was the rough-hewn Ernie Bevin; the Queen's favourite premiers since the war have tended to be Labour – Wilson and Callaghan she liked a great deal but Heath and Thatcher not at all (see below). Moreover, she has always seen herself as a unifying influence, a queen of all the people. Consequently, she tended to favour the postwar consensus. Lord Charteris agrees: 'the Queen prefers a sort of consensus politics rather than a polarised one' (Hennessy, 1995, pp. 141–2). She was not attracted by Thatcher's policies, which seemed to favour the middle classes and show scant regard for those many thousands of unemployed and members of an emergent underclass who proved casualties of the lady's unfettered free enterprise policies.

But finally, it has to be said, the monarchy is still popular with the voters – whatever the failings of individual members of the royal family. Indeed, the reaction to the death of Diana revealed just how deeply that particularly flawed member of the dynasty had entered the hearts of the nation. That event is important in that it revealed for many the deeply undemocratic instincts of the royal family. Even a constitutionally con-servative academic, Philip Norton, pointed out that at garden parties the royals took tea in a tent separate from the rest of the guests. Rumours also abounded that the Queen, exasperated by Diana's behaviour and competition for public affection with her son, had banned the mention of her name in her presence. It was rumoured she denied permission for Diana's body to lie in anything but a public morgue and saw no reason to communicate any grief she might have felt personally to the nation. She also favoured a small private funeral instead of the national event the nation clearly desired. It was left to the Prime Minister, Tony Blair, to speak for the nation with his 'People's Princess' speech and to persuade the Queen of the need for a major funeral. The media abounded with stories of how the royal family had been dysfunctional, helping to produce an heir who was unable to express emotions and could not help Diana feel welcome and happy in its bosom.

To counter this widespread impression of being uncaring and distant, the Queen decided to make an unprecedented personal broadcast live to the nation, expressing her grief. To rub home the critical message Earl Spencer, Diana's brother, delivered a brilliantly conceived but accusatory tribute to her at her funeral in Westminster Abbey, in which he criticised the royals for their lack of feeling and humanity.

Finding a conclusion under this heading is not easy as there is a glaring paradox. The institution is in many ways the antithesis of democracy yet there is still massive support for it: in a poll appearing in *The Observer* (14 September 1997) there was reflected much criticism of the monarchy but still 74 per cent wanted it to continue in a modernised form; only 5 per cent favoured a republic (see Table 5.1). Up until the summer of 1997 the balance under this heading might have been roughly equal but since Diana's death there has been a feeling that the monarchy is distant, unfeeling and in dire need of Blair's favourite buzz word: 'modernisation'.

Politics

There has been much debate about the political role of the monarchy in recent years. As shown above, by the end of the nineteenth century the monarchy had eschewed any active political role in exchange for a revered symbolic one, above the noisy, partisan debates. However, this is not to say the monarchy is apolitical.

Constitutional power of choosing a Prime Minister

Peter Hennessy has expressed a belief that 'British historians since 1945 have very largely neglected the continuing political influence of the monarchy as practised by George VI and Elizabeth II' (1995, p. 53). Andrew Adonis also dismisses the myth that the 'monarchy is essentially unimportant, a distraction from the serious business of government and society' (Adonis and Pollard, 1997, p. 133). Both are at pains to remove the impression inherited from the great nineteenth-century political sage, Walter Bagehot, that the monarch – who 'alone possesses a continuous political experience' – has only 'the right to be consulted, the right to encourage, the right to warn' and that we had a 'disguised republic ... insinuated ... within the folds of a monarchy' (Bagehot, 1867). Consequently, he concluded, the monarchy was part of the 'dignified' as opposed 'efficient' and functioning elements of the state. Both experts pursue different lines of argument.

Adonis points out that any institution able to 'command the degree of popular obsession achieved by the monarchy ... could scarcely be "dignified" in the sense of inconsequential'. He continues:

> Add to its charismatic power the royal family's wealth, its influence over policy and government, its status at the head of the honours system and the hereditary aristocracy, and the monarchy looks every bit as 'efficient' as most departments of state. Indeed it is a department of state, for the Court and royal household are an enterprise as elaborate and relentless about self-promotion as any Whitehall ministry. (p. 134)

Hennessy concentrates on the influence of the monarchy over policy and government, discerning a substantial residual role for it. The received wisdom is that the monarch's 'reserve' or theoretical powers – like signing treaties or declaring war – are irrelevant as they have either fallen into disuse or are effectively performed by the Prime Minister of the day. These two examples fall into these categories perhaps but the powers to dissolve Parliament or appoint a Prime Minister are less clear. Hennessy's point is that these are 'anything but marginal activities'. He argues these powers are: still alive; exert substantial influence on politics from time to time; and could prove decisive in certain future scenarios.

To support the first point he delves into the guidelines which have informed political conduct in 'conditions of uncertainty' since 1945. He concludes the use of these powers has arisen in at least six real or threatened contingencies, such as October 1964, when it seemed either

major party might fail to achieve a majority, or in March 1974, when
Heath, having lost his majority in the House, sought a deal with the
Liberals. Hennessy argues that these examples prove the election of party
leaders after 1965 did not exorcise the ghost of uncertainty from whom
the monarch should invite to form a government. Moreover, the members
of the 'golden triangle' at the heart of the constitution – the Prime
Minister's principal private secretary, the Cabinet Secretary and the monarch's
private secretary – all consider these 'reserve powers' active when it comes
to calling elections and appointing Prime Ministers. All party leaders who
have contested power have accepted these rules and have acted within
them, seeking to avoid a situation in which the monarch might be either
embarrassed or politicised.

Hennessy also quotes Sir Kenneth Stowe, principal private secretary to
Wilson, Callaghan and Thatcher, who distils three principles whereby any
uncertainty can be resolved:

1   the Queen's government must be carried on;
2   the Prime Minister appointed by the sovereign must be able to command
     a majority in the House of Commons;
3   the Prime Minister must be confident of leading or commanding the
     support of the majority party in the House of Commons.

He adds there is an assumption that 'everybody will conduct themselves
in the same spirit': what Hennessy calls the 'good chap' theory of government
and which he invokes to argue that the powers still live and are important,
in unforeseen future contingencies. He points to electoral volatility, which
produced a 'two and a half party' situation in the 1980s and the prospect
of electoral reform, which would produce, if proportional representation
were introduced (see Chapter 3), the certainty of uncertainty whereby the
monarch's role might become crucial in choosing Prime Ministers.

Another leading commentator on British politics, Andrew Marr, agrees:
'The real muscle of the monarch only comes into play in the highly unusual
circumstances of there being no president mimicking figure resident at
Downing Street when illness, parliamentary putsch or an indecisive election
result give Buckingham Palace an umpiring role.' But he sees such 'real
power' as 'increasingly under threat', citing 1992 when the 'golden triangle'
sat considering the options in what was anticipated to be a close result
(Marr, 1995, pp. 230–5). On that occasion the opposition leader, Kinnock,
'was mistrustful enough' of established practice to seek a 'separate legal
opinion' (so much for the 'good chaps' theory?).

Pimlott feels Hennessy tends to exaggerate this aspect of the monarch's
role, arguing that if she did ever exercise her actual power in choosing a
first minister, it would almost certainly lead, and quite properly, to it being
dismantled: its only chance of surviving is if it is never used. Strangely

for those like Hennessy who favour removing this remaining unused piece of royal muscle, the public seem to regard it with nostalgia. In *The Economist* (5 May 1997) a MORI poll revealed only 19 per cent wishing to remove the 'constitutional powers of the monarchy', with 62 per cent opposing such a measure.

Advising Prime Ministers

The weekly audiences between Queen and Prime Minister, usually lasting an hour, are strictly confidential but it might be interesting to consult some of the biographies, notably Pimlott's study of the Queen (1996), to discover how the Queen has dealt with her successive Prime Ministers.

Churchill was her first premier and Pimlott presents their relationship as partly master–pupil, partly favourite uncle–favourite niece. He used to arrive, cherubic in a frock coat and top hat, and be in conclave for an increasing length of time with the young Queen. Gentle questioning of him, however, suggested topics of conversation seldom ranged far beyond racing and polo. But she held the grand old man in high regard and he thought she was 'splendid' (p. 194). Eden was not overly concerned with the monarchy, which he regarded as a 'distraction', but Macmillan was more on her wavelength. He came to look forward to the weekly audiences almost as if they were 'trysts'; he described them as one of the 'most agreeable aspects' of his job and in his memoirs ascribed considerable importance to the sovereign's advice, as well as seeking to strengthen her prerogative where possible. According to Pimlott, Tom Nairn suggested the wily old trouper had used the glamour of the monarchy to disguise Britain's rapid withdrawal from Empire. Alec Douglas-Home was another Prime Minister with whom the Queen could relax: they were, after all, from the same aristocratic class and shared the same values and interests. Douglas-Home stayed at Balmoral as a friend rather than the chief politician in the Queen's realm. Harold Wilson could not have offered a bigger contrast but, paradoxically perhaps, they got on famously. Pimlott says he treated her as an equal, a member of his cabinet. He enjoyed the company of confident women and was bowled over by the aura of the monarchy, its romance and pageantry. She seems to have found him very sympathetic and easy to talk to. As to her advice, Joe Haines reported Wilson 'thought her advice quite wise'. Despite the delight of courtiers at the Palace, her relationship with the surprise victor of the 1970 election was uneasy. Heath was of working-class provenance but, unlike Wilson, took no deferential delight in his powerful position regarding his social betters. The Queen liked to be treated with gallantry, says Pimlott, but this was scarcely Heath's style. Consequently, 'she was never comfortable with him'. James Callaghan proved a 'devoted monarchist'. Less cosy than Wilson, he nevertheless found his audiences both enjoyable and useful. She seldom stated disapproval but avoidance of the topic was one indication, as was a quotation of another's adverse view. Approval was always openly stated.

Margaret Thatcher was a different kind of politician altogether. She dismisses talk of two 'powerful women' clashing as press trivia; 'more nonsense was written about the so-called "feminine factor" during my time in office than almost anything else' (Thatcher, 1995, p. 18). Yet Pimlott asserts that the notion they did not enjoy each other's company was 'not imaginary'. Apparently the Queen spoke dismissively when the Prime Minister fainted at a Palace function: 'She's keeled over again', she said to fellow guests. Anthony Sampson wrote in 1992 that the relationship between Thatcher and the Queen was 'uneasy' and that she returned from her weekly audiences 'in urgent need of a drink' (p. 58). As she became more powerful, especially after the Falklands War, she gave herself airs, carrying herself in an imperial fashion, commandeering the royal 'we' and ensuring she upstaged any royal presence at scenes of disasters. Pimlott judges she regarded the monarchy as to some extent part of the consensual monument to be removed. Audiences were strictly businesslike and formal, with the Prime Minister sitting on the edge of her seat, in the view of an ex-minister: 'slightly nervous ... in awe of the position'. The view grew that the Queen 'had greater concern for the welfare and preservation of the Commonwealth ... than did her government.' The Queen has a sense of destiny about the Commonwealth, dating from her coronation oath, according to Lord Charteris: 'She accepts it, however bloody awful it may be.' And there seems to have been a clash over the issue of economic sanctions against apartheid South Africa, which Thatcher vehemently opposed and the Queen favoured.

Woodrow Wyatt's diaries reveal another perspective. According to him, the Queen Mother admired Margaret Thatcher enormously, though the Queen was less enamoured. He relates an occasion when the Queen loudly contradicted the Prime Minister on the subject of the Falklands, when she said, 'I don't agree with you at all.' According to Wyatt's source, Thatcher was highly embarrassed and blushed. In the same memoir, the Queen is alleged to have said Thatcher was 'all right' but that 'like all prime ministers, she won't listen' (*The Guardian*, 5 October 1998).

John Major was both younger than the Queen and a vastly different personality to his predecessor. Pimlott notes that in the years of his premiership, 'There had been no hint of the tension that was reported to exist between the Palace and Downing Street in the 1980s'.

About Tony Blair it is too soon to speak, but in the wake of Diana's death it was widely assumed he was the person, rather than the Queen, who encouraged, consulted and warned, regarding the nature of the funeral and the manner in which the monarchy was handling the public relations side of matters.

Conclusion

To seek a conclusion, does the monarch's advisory/consultant's role add up to much? The answer has to be 'not really'. Some premiers – Heath and Thatcher – have regarded the monarchy as an irritant, to be borne rather than utilised; others – Churchill, Wilson, Callaghan – revelled in the romantic intimacy of the audiences. But the overall judgement has to be that the Prime Minister does not lack for advisers and among them the monarch probably comes way down the list in terms of importance. It is only on relatively minor items that she is likely to exert influence. For example, in 1964 Tony Benn, Postmaster General, was affronted by the power of the monarch over national life and suggested the Queen's head be removed from stamps. He went to discuss the matter with her and believed he had gained her approval. Wilson doubted this and later it transpired the Queen had been dismayed by the proposal and had moved to prevent it. Perhaps this represents the limit of royal power in the postwar period.

Maybe the Queen's prosaic assessment of her own role should provide the last word on this matter: 'They unburden themselves if they have any problems ... occasionally one can put one's point of view and perhaps they hadn't seen it from that angle' (Pimlott, 1996, p. 547).

Head of armed forces

The Queen also performs a role as head of the armed forces and it has been argued the role is a useful preventative of any possible coup attempt. The royal family is well versed in military matters and most hold honorary ranks in various regiments; younger members often serve in them too, as in the case of Prince Andrew, who fought in the Falklands War. The loyalty of the armed forces to the Queen is remarkably strong and, as Norton observes:

> In the event of a military coup, the prevailing view ... is that the monarch would serve as the most effective bulwark to its realisation, the Queen being in the position to exercise the same role as that of King Juan Carlos of Spain in 1981, when he forestalled a rightwing military takeover by making a public appeal to the loyalty of army commanders. (Norton, 1997, p. 235)

Cost

The annual cost to the taxpayer of the monarchy in 1991 – including the civil list, upkeep of castles and the royal yacht, *Britannia* – was calculated at £57 million. The previous year a deal had been struck whereby, to

avoid annual disagreement, the civil list payment to the Queen was fixed
at £7.9 million per year. Calls for her to pay tax had gathered strength
in the 1980s; in 1988, 40 per cent of respondents in a poll had said the
monarchy 'cost too much'; another revealed three-quarters believing the
Queen should pay income tax.

In 1992 there were lurid stories about marriages on the rocks and then
Windsor Castle burnt down and public reaction to the government's intent
to fund the £50 million restoration was fiercely negative. A few days
afterwards Major announced the Queen had agreed: to be taxed; to remove
all family members from the civil list except for the Queen, the Duke of
Edinburgh and the Queen Mother. She would also open Buckingham Palace
to the public to help raise money for the restoration of Windsor Castle.
But criticism remained in that the Queen was still absorbing large amounts
of public cash and not using her own deep pocket to fund a luxurious
lifestyle. Michael Portillo's suggestion that *Britannia* should give way to a
£60 million replacement in January 1997 was not well received and when
Labour won the election no more was heard of it when the yacht was
officially retired, clearly much to the Queen's regret.

In February 1998 the Way Ahead Group – which comprises senior
members of the royal family and meets twice a year to plan royal diaries
and consider long-term issues – decided to abandon the 240-year-old civil
list in favour of a new arrangement which restricts financial rewards to
those regularly performing public duties. Instead of refunding the taxpayer,
as she had done since 1994, for the cost of eight 'minor royals' (e.g.
Andrew, Edward, Margaret, Alexandra and Alice), these will henceforward
have to support themselves; useful expensive perks like free travel in Britain
were also scheduled for the axe by the same meeting.

At the heart of the debate over the cost of the monarchy is the argument
that our 'splendid monarchy' is something the British people want and need
for it to fulfil its symbolic role. The 'cycling monarchs' of Scandinavia and
Holland are thought to be inappropriate for us. Moreover, argue royalists,
such a monarchy would not attract the tourists and the crowds on foreign
trips. Polls suggest the public is less wedded to the ideal of a splendid
monarchy and would settle for something less lavish.

Symbolism

Bagehot had much to say on the symbolism of the monarchy. He argued
that to the extent we have a 'disguised republic we must see too that the
classes for whom the disguise is necessary must be tenderly dealt with'.
By this he probably meant the masses needed a soothing and believable
set of symbols wrapped up in the form of the monarchy, the 'characteristic
of which', he wrote, 'is that it retains the feelings by which the heroic kings

governed in their rude age, and has added the feelings by which the constitutions of later Greece governed in more refined ages.' No great fan of the common man, he also believed:

> Royalty is a government in which the attention of the nation is concentrated on one person doing interesting actions. Accordingly, so long as the human heart is strong and the human reason weak, Royalty will be strong because it appeals to diffused feeling, and Republics weak because they appeal to understanding.

Women were judged to be especially weak in the reasoning department: 'Women – one half the human race at least – care fifty times more for a marriage than a ministry.' So for him the monarchy was part of the necessary obfuscation whereby wise men ruled foolish subjects.

Pimlott adds his own analysis of Queen Elizabeth in the 1950s: 'Love for Elizabeth, as for her father, was partly a product of the need for a focus above nation, in a fragile yet still functioning Empire. It was monitored by an Empire monitoring press which linked respect for the Crown with patriotism.' Pimlott discerned a problem, however, regarding the symbolism of the institution, in that the decline of its imperial role had already diminished its hold on the 'public imagination'. The monarchy is to some extent a mirror in which the nation sees itself and what it wants to see. Unless the monarchy provides believable images it will lose its appeal. Hence the role of ceremony.

The monarch has long been regarded as having special powers. From the time of Edward the Confessor to Queen Anne, it was widely believed that scrofula (tuberculosis of the lymphatic glands) could be cured by the touch of the sovereign. The coronation was a ceremony laden with religious and patriotic symbolism. The notion of the right of hereditary accession was connected with the ancient divine right of kings. At a dinner for Commonwealth premiers six days before Elizabeth II's coronation, Churchill spoke of its symbolism: continuity, duty and national unity. The service itself, preceded by a grand procession, comprised: an oath of duty to govern according to the 'laws and customs' of her subjects; an anointing, in which the Queen had to take off her robes and wear a simple white dress; and finally the crowning. Then the monarch processed back through the crowds accompanied by 13,000 troops, twenty-nine bands and twenty-seven carriages. It was a magnificent spectacle which the nation enjoyed enormously. In every town and village school children marched through the streets waving flags and receiving symbolic gifts (in the case of the author, then living in mid-Wales, an orange, a mug and sixpence).

Perhaps all nations, even the most advanced and politically sophisticated, need, at a fundamental emotional level, some formal ceremonies to legitimise their political institutions and processes. And contrary to Bagehot's elitist comments, it seems they appeal to all strata of society and not just the less well educated. Indeed, an analogy is the degree ceremony, which formalises the reward for a set period of study and the achievement of a given standard. Many undergraduates affect, in advance, to regard it as a waste of time but few miss it in practice and they usually end up enjoying it as much as their parents.

The idea of British government is that it is Her Majesty's government, that everything done by ministers and civil servants is for and on behalf of the Queen. This is, of course, a fiction, as the involvement of the monarch is tenuous indeed, as we have already seen. But it is a useful fiction for both the governed and the government. Anthony Eden described her views as 'quite simply the voice of our land' (Pimlott, 1996, p. 273) and in one tangible and publicly recognisable sense the Queen personifies the state itself in her public duties. For the public and ministers alike, she is the nation in symbolic form.

One problematic aspect of her role is a facet of this symbolic function: the place of the media. The connection goes back to the coronation, in that the debate as to whether it should be televised was complex. Initially, in March 1952, it was only to be the procession which would be covered and the religious parts not. The organising committee was unanimous about this, largely because the Queen herself was not keen to place even more pressure on herself. She was supported by the Prime Minister, the Archbishop of Canterbury and the Abbey clergy, who felt such coverage would 'detract from its dignity' and reduce the crowds on the street. However, as soon as this became known there was a fury of complaint expressed in the press and elsewhere at political level – as well as from that doyen of broadcasters Richard Dimbleby – and the decision was reversed. The result was day-long coverage of the ceremony and the beginnings of the revolution in the viewing behaviour of the nation. The numbers of licence holders doubled to three million; link-ups were made to Europe and film was taxied by plane to the USA. At least twenty-seven million people crowded into a television-owning home and watched the national event. They felt a new experience of their royal family, a closeness, almost as if they had been participants in the great day rather than mere observers.

From then on television grew as a leisure activity and a weapon of political persuasion. Yet the royals initially kept their distance. Anthony Sampson, in his first historic *Anatomy of Britain*, wrote that 'the palace, has succeeded in maintaining not only wealth and dignity but also secrecy'. Bagehot had perceptive and much-quoted things to say on this too: 'Above all things our royalty is to be reverenced, and if you begin to poke about in it you cannot reverence it.... Its mystery is its life. We must not let in daylight on magic.' The BBC was keen to comply with this tenet and provided no coverage of John Grigg's attack on the monarchy in 1957 – he criticised her accent and speaking style – nor the rumours of Prince Philip's infidelity current at that time.

Sir John Colville, the royal press secretary for twenty years, retired in 1967 and was replaced by William Heseltine. The newcomer was very different from his ultra-traditionalist predecessor, who had refused press requests for access almost automatically. He saw his job as to some extent selling the monarchy, and a new era dawned. The first major consequence was the 1969 television documentary *The Royal Family*, a fly-on-the-wall look at the everyday life of the royals, made by Richard Cawston. The idea was discussed with Prince Philip before being put to the Queen, who was initially cool towards it, but the royals soon became used to the presence of the cameras and the result was an unprecedented behind-the-scenes examination of the hitherto secretive and highly private Windsors. Never had light been shone so directly on the magic. The initial reactions were enthusiastic and the verdict favourable, but many believe the rot started with that film and that, instead of satisfying the curiosity of the press, it merely whetted it. After all, the family had merely used or manipulated the media to present a particular sanitised image and the press were keen to ask other questions, especially as reticence and deference had been virtually banished in the 1960s. Kenneth Rose commented, 'The sight of Prince Philip cooking sausages meant that after that people would want to see the dining room, the sitting room, then everything except the loo.'

The investiture of the Prince of Wales, also in 1969, was a successful if rather staged event and similar events followed to adorn the royal jubilee in 1977 and then the royal wedding in 1981, when Charles married Diana Spencer.

Television was easier to control, however, than the press, which began to take an approach which was not just disrespectful but aggressive towards the principal royals, especially Diana, who, with her beauty and vulnerability, attracted the intense interest of both cameras and the readers. Her concern to preserve her privacy prompted Michael Shea, the then press secretary, to summon all the principal media players in December 1982 to beg them to respect the privacy of the young couple. Significantly, Kelvin MacKenzie, editor of *The Sun*, did not attend. In February 1983 pictures appeared in the tabloids of Diana on a beach in the Bahamas, heavily pregnant. When the Queen expressed her displeasure *The Sun* and the *Daily Star* published the same pictures again, without apology. Tabloid rivalry was such that morality had been postponed until someone won. The Murdoch press was especially uncaring of royal sensibilities and the *Sunday Times* splashed the book by Andrew Morton, which alleged the Waleses were desperately unhappy. It was open season on the royals, especially Charles and Diana, though the media do not deserve all the blame as both protagonists used the press to leak information and, effectively, vie for the nation's sympathies. Similar stories appeared when Prince Andrew and Sarah Ferguson separated and 'Fergie' was alleged to be having affairs with various men, including a Texan businessman who was photographed sucking her toes. If the royals thought they could put the genie of publicity back in the bottle, they were proved wildly wrong.

Moral authority

It follows that the ability of ordinary citizens, as Bagehot had observed, to relate to a 'ruling family' brought with it some expectations of behaviour on behalf of that family. It was commonly assumed by members of the elite and the Church, not to mention the comfortable middle classes, that the royal family, the 'first family', would provide a model of propriety, of 'moral authority', which the rest of the nation could look up to and attempt to emulate. The Queen is head of the Church of England and so is expected by many to reflect the espousal of the whole package of Church morality. Royal events – weddings, funerals, christenings – are usually also religious events. So Archbishop Ramsay, in 1964, on the occasion of the birth of Prince Edward, expressed this notion of the model Christian family perfectly when said that it meant a great deal that at times when many suffered, 'there was around the throne a Christian family united, happy and setting an example to all of what the words "home and family" most truly meant'. Reading this thirty-five years on, it is hard not to hear a hollow laugh. So much has happened to damage the idea of the perfect family. Of course, no family can be perfect and over time the royals have had their scandals: the plenitude of royal mistresses going back to the early nineteenth century and before; abdication crisis in 1936; and the love affair between Princess Margaret and the divorcee Peter Townsend in the 1950s.

The last scandal reached its climax with an article by Sir William Haley, editor of *The Times*, in October 1954. He focused on the idea of the family and its moral role in the life of the nation and Commonwealth. For Haley the Queen was the 'universal representative' of national society and it was 'in her that people saw their better selves ideally reflected' (Pimlott, 1996, p. 237). The royal family existed as the 'symbol and guarantee of the unity of the British peoples.... If one of the family's members becomes a cause of division, the salt has lost its savour. There is no escape from the logic of this situation.' Confronted with these moral and religious imperatives, Margaret had to end the affair.

Few will deny that the public attitude towards divorce and separation changed radically in the decades following, but the behaviour of the royals – the Yorks and Waleses in particular – combined with a hypocritical and predatory tabloid press, exceeded the tolerance, not to say understanding, of much of the British public. 'Fergie' was represented and perceived as not worthy of living within the royal orbit and not just by the tabloids:

'vulgar, vulgar, vulgar!' was the description of her by Lord Charteris. Her behaviour in terms of her love life and financial dealings did little to dispel this impression. Diana was the divisive one, though. An international icon of beauty, altruism and personal vulnerability, she manipulated the press cleverly to win a strange kind of contest with her former husband and the Palace for public popularity. When she died, the repercussions were adverse for the royals: she was seen as a martyr, as the lost acceptable face of a redundant institution.

Writing in *The Guardian* (17 September 1997), columnist Jonathon Freedland saw the monarchy confirming 'ours as a semi feudal society'. He concluded, 'The monarchy cannot be reformed. It must go.' Responding to the impact of Diana's death, other voices echoed this view: Andrew Rawnsley in *The Observer* (14 September), for example, calling for a republic.

Public opinion reflected this collapse of royal moral authority. The poll in the same issue of *The Observer* – see Table 5.1 – showed a total collapse of faith between 1981 and 1997 in the way the key royals carried out their roles. Gallup polls also reveal a haemorrhage of support: in November 1993, 46 per cent of respondents answered their 'personal opinion' had 'gone down'; in the succeeding three years the figure was 54, 49 and 57; and this was before Diana's death. No longer a touchstone of moral behaviour or family values, the royal family faces a crisis of national role in the first decade of the new millennium.

The future

In his *Observer* piece (21 September 1997) Andrew Rawnsley reckoned, 'Even those who have been most devoted to the increasingly discredited fairytale of monarchy sense that this is its closing chapter. In future princesses will belong in children's books. So will kings and queens.'

The Observer poll of 14 September 1997 (see Table 5.1) tends to support a little of what Rawnsley says but its major findings and those of an August 1998 poll contradict him. While 12 per cent would be happy for the monarchy to continue 'in its present form', nearly three-quarters wish it to continue in a 'modernised' – that quintessentially Blairite term – form. Only 12 per cent wish to see it replaced by a republic, either immediately or after the Queen's death.

Supporters of the monarchy should not take refuge in complacency, however, as there was much in the poll to focus the minds of the February 1998 meeting of the Way Ahead Group. Had they considered the poll, members of the Group would have noted the huge majorities who: wished royalty to be more 'informal and less traditional'; thought it 'out of touch with ordinary people'; and should desist from 'field sports'. A MORI poll which they did consider, leaked to the *Sunday Times*, confirmed many of

Table 5.1. *The public's opinion of the royal family*

	Percentage of respondents

How many marks out of 10 would you give the Queen as Britain's head of state and Prince Charles as Prince of Wales for the way they carry out their roles (percentage giving 10 out of 10)

Queen	
1981	71
1997	10
Charles	
1981	58
1997	5

Which of these options would you prefer?

The monarchy should continue in its present form	12
The monarchy should continue but be modernised	74
The monarchy should be replaced with a republic when the Queen dies	5
The monarchy should be replaced with a republic as soon as possible	7

Assuming that the monarchy continues, do you agree or disagree with each of these statements?

The royal family should become much more informal
and less concerned with preserving their traditional ways

Agree	81
Disagree	15

The royal family is out of touch with ordinary people in Britain

Agree	79
Disagree	17

The royal family should not take part in field sports
such as fox hunting and grouse shooting

Agree	62
Disagree	23

The Queen should start to give interviews like other public figures

Agree	49
Disagree	39

The Queen should give up functions such as
signing new laws, opening Parliament and
formally appointing a Prime Minister and stick
to purely ceremonial duties

Agree	37
Disagree	57

If the monarchy does continue, when the Queen dies, do you think the crown should pass to Prince Charles or straight to Prince William

Charles	38
William	53

Source: *The Observer*, 14 September 1997.

the earlier poll's findings. The monarchy was seen as being: lacking in understanding, wasteful, not good value for money, out of touch, remote, badly advised and insincere. On the other hand, it was shown to be: trustworthy, an integral part of British society and good at performing its duties. Interestingly, the September poll showed a majority against the Queen becoming a purely ceremonial monarch and withdrawing from the constitutional duties regarding legislation, Parliament and appointing Prime Ministers, which Hennessy and others feel should possibly be removed. On 6 March 1998 the Way Ahead Group announced further modernisations of the monarchy: a reduction of the twenty-two people entitled to use the title HRH down possibly to only the sovereign and heir. In addition further relaxations were added to the archaic forms of curtseying, often seen as symbols of the antique nature of the institution. Most worrying for supporters of the monarchy, however, was the poll response to the proposal that the crown should pass directly to Prince William when the Queen dies. Over half agreed with the idea, with only 38 per cent favouring Charles as the recipient. Even this scenario might be fraught with intractabilities if stories in the tabloids on 1 March 1998 have any truth: that Prince William does not want to be king and yearns after a 'normal life'. Sadly, even if not king, he will be denied that, whatever the views of Lord Hailsham and his ilk.

However, while they may provide important information, polls are mere snapshots of opinion and by the following August the public's view, softened by the transparently genuine attempts of Charles to be a good father to his two sons, had changed for the better. An ICM poll published in *The Guardian* on 15 August showed 54 per cent thought he would make a 'good king' compared with only 40 per cent a year earlier. In October 1994, 70 per cent thought the country would be better off without a royal family while in August 1998 the figure was down to 52 per cent. Nonetheless, majorities agreed that the royal family was out of touch with ordinary people and that Charles should not marry Camilla Parker-Bowles. In August 1998 the think-tank Demos produced a report on the monarchy by Mark Leonard and Nick Hames. Its most important recommendations included: the abolition of the automatic right of succession with a public right to apply a veto through a referendum to an unacceptable monarch; the education of royals in state schools and treatment at National Health Service hospitals; loss of headship of the Church of England; the Speaker to take over from the monarch the responsibility of appointing the Prime Minister and dissolving Parliament; abolish the need for royal assent; and an Office of the Monarchy run by the civil service. Despite the closeness of Demos to Tony Blair, his office was quick to distance itself from these recommendations, although it seems likely that some at least will come to fruition in the early years of the new millennium.

Reading

Adonis, A. and Pollard, S. (1997) *A Class Act*, Hamish Hamilton.
Bagehot, W. (1867) *The English Constitution*, Fontana (1963 edition).
Hennessy, H. (1995) *The Hidden Wiring*, Gollancz.
Hennessy, H. (1996) *Muddling Through*, Gollancz.
Lord Hailsham (1992) *On the Constitution*, Harper Collins.
Marr, A. (1995) *Ruling Britannia*, Michael Joseph.
Norton, P. (1997) In Bill Jones *et al. Politics UK*, Prentice Hall.
Pimlott, B. (1992) *Harold Wilson*, Harper Collins.
Pimlott, B. (1996) *The Queen: A Biography of Queen Elizabeth*, Harper Collins.
Powell, E. (1982) 'Reforming Parliament', *Teaching Politics*, May, pp. 167–77.
Sampson, A. (1992) *The Essential Anatomy of Britain*, Hodder and Stoughton.
Thatcher, M. (1995) *The Downing Street Years*, HarperCollins.
Young, H. (1990) *One of Us*, Pan.

I am also grateful for points made to me personally by Ben Pimlott.

6

Leaders or led?
Senior ministers in British government
Philip Norton

There is a remarkable lacuna in the study of British government. There is a considerable literature, both political and academic, on the role of the Prime Minister and of the cabinet, and a considerable debate about the relationship between the two. That debate has continued but has been complemented in recent years by an academic discussion of policy communities, networks and core executives: the emphasis in this discussion is on interrelations and change.

Yet what is missing in all this is a literature that has as its specific focus the role of senior ministers *as* senior ministers. We read something about such ministers as members of the cabinet (and we take membership as defining senior ministers), as heads of departments, as part of the 'networks' in the policy process. Yet we rarely see literature that is devoted wholly to them and which looks at them in the round. Over the past thirty years, there have been only four major scholarly works devoted to the subject, and only three of these provide an overview of ministers as ministers. Bruce Headey's *British Cabinet Ministers* established itself as the authoritative work on the subject but was published in 1974. In 1987, Richard Rose published *Ministers and Ministries*, providing a functional analysis, and therefore more concerned with the offices than the individuals occupying them. Similarly, Rodney Brazier's *Ministers of the Crown*, published in 1997, focuses on the formal position of the office holder. Diana Woodhouse (1994) has looked at ministers, but specifically in relation to the doctrine of individual ministerial accountability to Parliament. These works have been supplemented by Kevin Theakston's short but thorough volume on junior ministers (Theakston, 1987). That exhausts the list of scholarly books devoted to a study of ministers *qua* ministers. If one were to confine the list to works published in paperback editions, the list would be empty.

Why have senior ministers received so little attention? Partly, I suspect, because senior ministers are fragmented and, as a collectivity, are visible only when meeting as the cabinet. The Prime Minister and the cabinet are politically visible. The doctrine of collective responsibility has stressed the centrality of the collective role of cabinet, and the relationship of government (that is, the collectivity of ministers) to Parliament has been central to the constitutional development of the British state. The roles of Prime Minister and cabinet have been central to the traditional institutional literature on British politics[1] and to constitutional law texts.

The growth of new schools of analysis in political science has shifted attention to policy and to processes. The literature on policy networks necessarily goes beyond ministers since it is concerned, by definition, with multiple and interconnecting relationships (Marsh and Rhodes, 1992; Rhodes, 1997). Attempts to resuscitate institutional analysis by focusing on the core executive are concerned with the mass of bodies within government (see Dunleavy and Rhodes, 1990); so, again, although ministers are not left out of this approach, the focus is broad rather than specific to ministers. Membership of the European Union (EU) and, even more fundamentally, globalisation of economic markets have consequences that have attracted the attention of a hard-pressed and relatively small discipline of political scientists.

The result is that ministers have largely been left out in the academic cold. The reasons I have suggested are plausible but not a total explanation. The Prime Minister and the cabinet may be politically visible, but they have no legal powers. Statutory powers are vested in individual ministers. The doctrine of individual ministerial responsibility makes ministers individually highly visible in relation to policy failures and in terms of answerability to Parliament. It could hardly be claimed that Michael Howard was not highly visible when he occupied the post of Home Secretary. Cabinet papers are generally kept secret for thirty years, yet we know much about what individual ministers have done in more recent years from a growing body of published memoirs and diaries. (The publication of memoirs and autobiographies by retired ministers is not new, but the number has grown in recent decades.) And developments such as membership of the EU have important implications for ministers and ministers themselves have a role to play in the law-making process of the EU. Thus we can identify some of the reasons why ministers as ministers have been neglected in the study of government but there appears no convincing explanation of why they have been neglected quite to the extent that they have.

My purpose is to help fill the gap in the scholarship on ministers in British government. My working hypothesis is that ministers as ministers are important in government but that this power is exercised predominantly

---

1   See, for example, the literature in the 1960s and 1970s on prime ministerial versus cabinet government. The material is summarised by Norton (1982, pp. 41–2).

within a particular policy space. Ministers can determine outcomes. They are able, in pluralist terms, to exercise power, both coercive and persuasive. That is, in coercive terms, they can ensure that a particular body does that which otherwise it would not do. In persuasive terms, they may get a body to choose to do that which otherwise it may not have done.

This power is exercised primarily within a particular policy space. What Rhodes (1995) has characterised as the segmented decision model of policy making in British government asserts that political actors operate in different policy spheres. I identify three broad policy spaces, those of high and low policy and the space between the two. High policy – policy that is fundamental to the peace and economic wellbeing of the nation – is the preserve largely of the Prime Minister and of a small coterie of senior ministers. Low policy – incremental policy adjustments usually affecting only particular interests – is the preserve of policy communities (civil servants and representatives of affected groups) (Jordan and Richardson, 1982). The policy space in between – middle-level policy – is the preserve primarily of ministers and accounts for most of the principal public policies announced by government. While the Prime Minister and Chancellor of the Exchequer may be meeting to discuss a particular item of high policy, other senior ministers will be working individually on their own middle-level policy initiatives.

My purpose in this chapter is to unpack the nature of ministerial power – to identify the variables that determine the place of ministers in policy making – and in so doing to offer a typology of ministers in British government. I shall be drawing on an analysis of existing literature (not least Headey's pioneering study), primary sources and a number interviews with former senior ministers.

Box 6.1. *The components of ministerial power*

The office
Powers of the office
Constraints of the office

The individual in the office
Purpose in taking office
Skills of the incumbent

External environment
The power situation
Climate of expectation
International developments

Ministerial power

James D. Barber argued in *The Presidential Character* (1972) that presidential power in the USA was determined by the interaction of three variables: the personality of the incumbent, the power situation and the climate of expectation. This is a useful but not exhaustive list. My thesis is that ministerial power is determined by the interaction of seven variables (Box 6.1). Two are specific to the office: the powers of the office and the constraints (responsibilities or limitations) of the office. Two are specific to the individual: the purpose of the incumbent in taking office and the skills of the incumbent. The last three are essentially external to the office: the power situation, the climate of expectation and international developments.

The office

Powers

Ministers are powerful by virtue of the doctrine of individual ministerial responsibility.[2] The doctrine confers important legal, departmental and even parliamentary powers.

Legal powers The legal dimension is central. No statutory powers are vested in the Prime Minister or cabinet. As Nevil Johnson (1980, p. 84) has written, 'the enduring effect of the doctrine of ministerial responsibility has been over the past century or so that the powers have been vested in ministers and on a relentlessly increasing scale'. Postwar years have seen a substantial increase in the volume of legislation passed by Parliament. Bills are not more numerous, but they are longer and more complex. It is common for bills to confer powers on ministers and to do so in broad terms. The 1988 Education Reform Act, for example, is replete with sections beginning, 'The Secretary of State may make regulations requiring...' and so on.

Departmental powers The doctrine confers important departmental powers in that it asserts ministerial line control. The focus of much of the writing on the doctrine has often been the culpability of ministers for the actions of their civil servants, but more importantly and more pervasively the doctrine establishes that civil servants are answerable to the minister and to no one else. Civil servants work in departments headed by ministers. They answer to the minister formally through the permanent secretary. The creation of 'Next Steps' agencies has not destroyed this basic relationship. Agency heads have some degree of autonomy but the agencies remain

2   I have developed this point in Norton (1997).

within government, under a sponsoring department, and the agency chief is responsible – answerable – to the minister in that department.

Parliamentary powers The doctrine may be deemed important also in that the minister is answerable to Parliament for the department. That may appear a limitation – in that the minister is the subject of parliamentary questioning and attack – but it is also a power in that the minister *alone* is answerable to Parliament. Civil servants are not. They cannot appear at the dispatch box. They may be summoned before a select committee but they have no independent voice before that committee.

Parliamentary powers also derive from being Her Majesty's ministers. Since the crown alone can request money, money resolutions can be moved only by a minister. Parliamentary rules also provide that certain other motions, such as the motion to suspend the ten o'clock rule (ending business at ten o'clock), can be moved only by ministers.

Ministers, then, enjoy considerable formal powers. They also enjoy some public visibility – itself a potential source of power – deriving from their position in government. A senior minister will have a greater chance of persuading a newspaper editor to come to dinner than will a member of the opposition front bench or a humble backbencher. A minister will be able to attract publicity by virtue of exercising the power of the office or by announcing an intention to exercise that power. Even if no formal power to act exists, a minister may attract publicity by making a statement. Thus, for example, Chris Smith, as National Heritage Secretary, within a matter of days of taking office in May 1997, was able to employ the media to criticise the directors of Camelot, running the National Lottery, for taking massive bonuses; and he used that publicity as a means of seeking to persuade them to give up their bonuses.

Senior ministers also have some power by virtue of their political position. That is, they will be drawn (by convention) from one of the two Houses of Parliament. Unlike members of some other executives, they retain a seat in the legislature. More importantly, though also subject to much greater variability, they may also enjoy a power base in Parliament. That may give them leverage in relation to other ministers and to their departments.

Constraints

Ministers, though, also labour under a number of constraints. The most important are constitutional, legal and managerial.

Constitutional constraints Ministers are constrained by the doctrine of collective ministerial responsibility. Major decisions have to percolate up for cabinet approval, which means, in practice, a committee of the cabinet (cabinet business is too extensive to be dealt with by the cabinet, and most is now handled by committees of the cabinet, comprising some cabinet ministers and sometimes non-cabinet ministers); and approval may not always be forthcoming. The constitutional power exercised by the Prime Minister to hire, fire and shuffle ministers may also be a powerful constraint on ministerial actions, and may be exercised in order to reflect the Prime Minister's policy preferences.

Ministers are also constrained to some extent by Parliament in that they have to defend themselves in what can be a demanding arena; indeed, the terminology is appropriate and the reputation of ministers may not always survive the ordeal in that arena. Ministers are also constrained not so much *by* Parliament but rather *within* Parliament by their own party; the parliamentary party, and party committees, may at times constitute an awkward audience for ministers and even prevent them proceeding with a desired policy (Norton, 1994).

Legal constraints These exist in that ministers may be limited by the powers conferred on them by Parliament. They have increasingly to be sensitive to the risk of acting *ultra vires*. A greater degree of judicial activism since the 1960s may be the product of a change of judicial culture (or of those who are affected by government being more prepared to seek judicial review) or a change in the nature of government; but whichever it is, the courts are more active nowadays in reviewing the legality of ministerial actions.

Ministers are also constrained by the conditions of membership of the EU. In some matters, they can no longer exercise power unilaterally but rather form part of a collective decision-making body (the Council of Ministers) in which they may be overruled. As their responsibilities have increased as a consequence of Britain's membership of the EU, so their capacity to affect outcomes has decreased.

Managerial constraints Responsibilities as members of the Council of Ministers also feed into the other principal constraint, which is best described as managerial. Ministers have a mass of responsibilities and duties: they are departmental ministers, they are members of the cabinet, they are members of the appropriate EU Council of Ministers, they are party and political figures (invited to attend and address a mass of meetings), they are ministers answerable to Parliament, they are (except for those ministers who are peers) constituency MPs, and they are party MPs, who have to attend Parliament to vote. Ministers have difficulty managing their time. Their evenings are taken up with their ministerial red boxes. Time spent travelling between meetings is often spent dictating constituency correspondence into a dictaphone. They are also public and political figures, driven increasingly by the demands of a twenty-four-hour news service.

These constraints are considerable. The most important, and of growing importance, are those I have mentioned last. To take a recent example: no sooner had Douglas Henderson been appointed Minister for Europe in May 1997 than he was on a plane to Brussels being briefed by officials. That was exceptional only because it attracted publicity.

What is perhaps most surprising is that the constitutional constraints –
in the form of Prime Minister and cabinet – are not as powerful as many
suppose. Prime Ministers also suffer from problems of organisation and time
management. They cannot attend to all the major issues of government;
they have neither the time nor the resources. Furthermore, they do not
attempt to direct policy through ministers to the extent that they could do,
or the extent that they are assumed to do. One of the most remarkable
findings of my interviews with a number of former cabinet ministers is that
when they were appointed to office by the Prime Minister, they rarely
discussed with the Prime Minister what was expected of them. I can find
little or no evidence of the Prime Minister telling a minister what the
minister was expected to do.[3] (The ministers I interviewed spanned primarily
two premierships – those of Margaret Thatcher and John Major.) This
applies to very senior posts and not just intermediate and junior ones.

Cabinet meets no more than once or twice a week when Parliament is
in session and rarely if at all during the summer. It is not geared to being,
and is not, a regular decision-making body. Most government policy is
determined by ministers in their departments, not by ministers sat at the
cabinet table. Most policy is approved at cabinet committee, with ministers
rarely having to go back and think again. Few issues are ever taken from
cabinet committee to cabinet.

The individual in the office

There are two dimensions to the individual in the office: purpose and skills.
A minister may have important powers as a minister, but knowing that
fact tells us little about how and why the power is exercised. For that, we
have to turn to the person in the office. Ministers become ministers for a
variety of reasons. Some simply want to be ministers. Some want to achieve
particular policy outcomes. Some want to be Prime Minister. What they
want will determine how they act.

I have identified essentially four types of senior minister – team player,
commanders, managers and agents – though two of these categories may
be further subdivided (see Box 6.2). The types relate to different locations
of decision-making power. With commanders and managers, decision-making
power is retained in the office but exercised in different ways. With team
players and agents, policy is made elsewhere, because ministers either
cannot prevent it or prefer to abdicate power to these locations.

3   The number of ministers interviewed (at the time of writing) constituted a small
    proportion of the total to have held office in the years from 1979 to 1997
    but the consistency in the answers is striking.

> Box 6.2. *Types of senior minister*
>
> *Team player*
>
> Commander
> Self-driven
> Ideologue
>
> *Manager*
>
> Agent
> Prime ministerial
> Civil service
> European Union

Team player

A team player is someone who believes in collective decision making and wants to be part of that team. This correlates more or less precisely with the conception of cabinet government. Proposals may be put by a minister to cabinet, but it is the cabinet that deliberates and decides on the policy. In practice, cabinet has difficulty fulfilling this role because of the managerial constraints already mentioned (it does not have the time). It is also constrained from fulfilling this role by the fact that few ministers want to be team players. None of those I interviewed offered responses that suggested this was their favoured role; only one claimed to be a team player and by that he meant that he did not want to cause problems. There is very little evidence to suggest that many senior ministers see themselves primarily as team players.

Commander: self-driven

The self-driven commanders are those who have very clear ideas of what they want to achieve and those ideas derive from their own personal preferences and goals. (Preferences should be taken to include ambition.) When they accept a particular office, they usually have some idea of what they want to achieve.

Individuals may not be consistent self-driven commanders throughout their ministerial career. They may have a very clear idea of what they want to achieve in one particular office but not in another. For example, one politician who held five cabinet posts during the Thatcher and Major premierships had a clear idea of what he wanted to achieve in three of them (one was the post he had always wanted); in another he had a general idea (even though it was a post he had not wanted) and in the other – a rather senior post – he had no clear perception of what he wanted to achieve. Rather he assumed one of the other roles: that of manager.

My research suggests that the self-driven commander type of minister is far more prevalent than is generally recognised. Initial evidence suggests that it may emerge as the largest single category over the past twenty years. Taking holders of one single cabinet post – that of Education Secretary – examples would include Kenneth Baker, Kenneth Clarke and John Patten.

Commander: ideologue

An ideologue as commander is someone who is driven by a clear, consistent philosophy. Thus, whatever office they occupy, the policies ideologue commanders pursue will derive from that philosophy. A minister who would seem to fit this role in the last Parliament was John Redwood; and, indeed, it may be thought that this type of minister would be fairly prevalent during the premiership of Margaret Thatcher. In fact, it was not. It is difficult to find many ministers, certainly at senior level, who occupy this category. (Of former Education Secretaries, the only obvious instance in the past twenty years is Sir Keith Joseph.) This, in part, reflects the fact that Prime Ministers have rarely appointed ministers on purely ideological grounds. When John Major complained about ideologues who were in his cabinet – though he used another term for them (reflecting on their parentage) – the only thing they really had in common was their stance on Europe, plus the fact that the Prime Minister could not risk sacking them. Margaret Thatcher never managed to craft a Thatcherite cabinet and left the appointment of junior ministerial posts to others (Norton, 1993, pp. 47–8).

Some ministers who may appear to be ideologues are not; rather their views in particular sectors coincide with those of a particular ideological strand. One minister who held office under Margaret Thatcher conceded that in one particular post he had what he described as 'Thatcherite priorities'; but when he occupied another, more senior post later, he was certainly not seen as a Thatcherite, but rather viewed by Thatcherites as having 'gone native'.

Managers

Here the minister takes the decisions, but is not driven by any particular ideology or personal world view. Rather the approach is pragmatic, sometimes

Oakeshottian:[4] that is, helping to keep the ship of state afloat and operating efficiently. Ministers may anticipate issues; more frequently they respond to them. They do not necessarily take the departmental line but decide it for themselves. When several competing demands are made of them, they act as brokers, listening and weighing the evidence and then taking a view. This category competes with that of the self-driven commander for the honour of being the most occupied category. Examples in terms of Education Secretaries would include Peter Brooke and John MacGregor. Examples among other senior ministers would include Douglas Hurd and John Major.

Agent

Here the minister essentially acts on behalf of another body. There are three types of agent: those of the Prime Minister, the civil service and the EU.

Prime ministerial Here the minister is appointed to ensure that the wishes of the Prime Minister are carried out. (This is distinct from an ideologue, who may share the Prime Minister's ideology but is an enthusiast for the ideology and will give that preference over the Prime Minister's wishes.) Prime ministerial agents are not as numerous as may be thought. Few if any ministers are given instructions or guidance when they are appointed. Occasionally, Prime Ministers may decide to be their own 'foreign secretary' or 'chancellor of the exchequer', though that depends on the willingness of the minister in question to comply: Margaret Thatcher had an easier time influencing economic policy with Geoffrey Howe as Chancellor than she did when it was Nigel Lawson. Prime ministerial agents are not that visible at the level of senior ministers. During the Thatcher era, it was assumed that some ministers were put in at middle-ranking level to act as the Prime Minister's eyes and ears in a department; but if so, it did not appear to have much effect.

Civil service Here the minister essentially adopts the departmental brief and does what the officials in the department want the minister to do. Ministers may adopt this role because they want a quiet life – some actually move up the 'greasy pole' of government despite being remarkably lazy – or because they do not have the personal will or intellect to resist the persuasive briefings of officials. Civil servants can be remarkably persuasive, and indeed devious (papers put in late, or among a mass of papers in the red box) as any viewers of *Yes, Minister* and *Yes, Prime Minister* are

4   Michael Oakeshott, a noted political philosopher, argued (1962, p. 127) that when people engage in political activity 'the enterprise is to keep afloat on an even keel; the sea is both friend and enemy; and the seamanship consists in using the resources of a traditional manner of behaviour in order to make a friend of every hostile occasion'.

aware – and one or two departments do have reputations for pursuing a particular departmental ideology. However, instances are rare of officials seeking to undermine ministers who take a strong line that is at variance with the established departmental view. The instances are not unknown but civil servants will usually carry out loyally the wishes of a minister. Once the minister has overruled their objections, they then find ways of ensuring that the minister's wishes are implemented. When a minister is determined on a particular policy, then the minister will get his or her way. On some issues, ministers do not take a stand – and, as Gerald Kaufman (1997) recounts in *How To Be a Minister*, will read out their departmental brief in cabinet committee – but they rarely do so consistently. The category of civil service agents is not a particularly large one.

European Union   Finally, and essentially for the record, ministers may be agents of the EU. By virtue of the office they hold, they have to fulfil certain policies to comply with Britain's treaty obligations. Some may do so willingly, others reluctantly. It is possible that some may serve as agents for the EU in the same way that some may serve as agents of the Prime Minister or their officials. They may not have the will or the expertise to resist their colleagues in the Council of Ministers, or the officials who liaise with the officials of the European Commission. This category, though, also appears not to be a crowded one.

From this brief review, what emerges is that two categories are more crowded than the others: self-driven commanders and the managers. In other words, the more minister-centred categories. As such, we have the basis for positing the existence of ministerial government, at least in respect of middle-level policy, in Britain. Ministers have important powers and they tend to want to exercise those powers. However, whether they do so successfully depends on their skills and the political environment they occupy.

Skills

In a study of prime ministerial power, published in *Teaching Politics* (Norton, 1987), I argued that the essential skills needed by a Prime Minister, in addition to those of selection, were those of leadership, anticipation and reaction, and that a number of strategic options were available to them to achieve the desired outcome (Figure 6.1). The strategic options were those of: command, persuasion, manipulation and hiding. These skills and options apply also to senior ministers.

Command   Ministers may have a clear intellectual view of what they want to achieve, but actually taking decisions to ensure that view is realised may be difficult. Sir Keith Joseph was notorious for having difficulty making decisions to achieve his ideological goals. Conversely, some ministers have

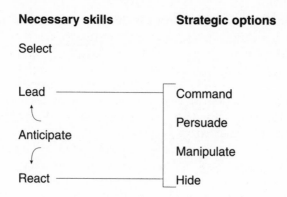

Figure 6.1. *Ministerial skills*

no difficulty making decisions: Kenneth Clarke would be a particularly good example.

Persuade   Some ministers may know what they want to achieve and take a clear view. However, unless they have the formal power to act unilaterally, they need to able to carry colleagues and others – MPs, outside organised interests, the public – with them. There are different devices that ministers may employ to bring the different actors on side: meetings with the relevant backbench committee, for example; a 'dear colleague' letter to the party's MPs; a press conference; private briefings for journalists; and – one of the most important devices mentioned by former ministers – 'keeping Number 10 briefed' ('Number 10' meaning principally the Prime Minister but also, on occasion, other actors in Downing Street, such as the head of the Number 10 Policy Unit or the relevant person in the Unit). Some ministers will also spend time meeting affected bodies, for example by making an effort to attend their annual conferences and accepting invitations to speak.

Manipulate   The Prime Minister is sometimes devious and the same applies to senior ministers. On occasion, one may have to play off one body against another. Manipulation may entail 'kite flying' in the media, feeding a misleading story that can be denied, and then using it as leverage to achieve a particular outcome. Manipulation may be met by manipulation. When a story leaked in December 1996 that the Prime Minister, John Major, was thinking of abandoning the government's 'negotiate and decide' policy on a single European currency, Deputy Prime Minister Michael Heseltine said publicly that there had been no change in government policy, and at the dispatch box in the afternoon John Major was forced to acknowledge that was the case, thus forcing him to stick with the policy he had apparently been hoping to abandon.

Hiding Ministers need to know when to avoid a particular problem. Sometimes it is better to keep one's head below the parapet rather than risk putting it above the parapet and getting shot at by the media and disgruntled MPs. One of the values of having junior ministers is that they can be made to take the flak. For example, when the Child Support Agency attracted enormous criticism in the first half of the 1990s, it was the relevant junior minister, rather than the Secretary of State, who appeared principally before the cameras to justify the government's position. When senior ministers decided on the evening of Black Wednesday in September 1992 to suspend British membership of the Exchange Rate Mechanism (ERM) they avoided giving television interviews and instead put up the party chairman – who was not even a minister – to respond.

These are strategic options. However, there are two other skills that ministers need in order to achieve their goals: they need to be good time managers and they need to understand how the system – and their particular department – works.

Effective time management Ministers have difficulty organising their time effectively. Some former cabinet ministers have admitted that they had difficulty prioritising their activities and saying 'no' to various activities. Some expressed admiration for their colleagues who managed to organise their time and stay on top of their departments: Michael Howard was one of those singled out in this capacity. One means of relieving some of the pressure is by delegation. Some ministers are good at delegating and making use of junior ministers. One cabinet minister in the 1980s gave his junior ministers particular responsibilities and then had them draw up a work programme for the next two years, and every three months had a meeting with each minister to discuss progress. Others are less organised and some have difficulty delegating tasks effectively.

Understanding the system Ministers need to know how the process works. Very occasionally some ministers are appointed without any experience of Parliament and the experience has rarely been a happy one, those involved displaying a lack of sensitivity to the needs of a parliamentary environment. One way to understand the system is by study. Before the 1997 general election, seminars were organised for shadow ministers on the workings of government. Another way – the more frequently used – is ministerial apprenticeship. Holding junior ministerial office is useful as a way of seeing how the system works from the inside. A point made by one former minister was that in order to be effective in achieving goals as a senior minister it helped, first, to have been a junior minister in the department that one was appointed to head; and, secondly, to have served in the whips' office. As a junior minister, one gets to know how the particular department works (departments differ enormously), and as a whip one gets to know how to handle MPs and to anticipate what is likely to cause trouble in the House. Understanding of a department may also derive from longevity in the office, but that is something largely beyond the control of the incumbent.

Without some (ideally, all) of these skills, ministers – however intelligent and self-driven – are not likely to succeed and may find their ministerial career stunted or destroyed altogether. Within a few months of the appointment of the new Labour government in May 1997, there were reports that some members of the cabinet would not last beyond the autumn of that year: the one most frequently mentioned was Gavin Strang, largely because he was indecisive and was poor at the dispatch box; in other words, he was poor at command and persuasion.

External environment

Ministers may be helped or hindered by the environment external to their department. This environment includes the power situation, the climate of expectation and international developments.

Power situation

The power situation overlaps with the powers and constraints of the office but provides a dynamic element. Power relationships are not static. And what the 'power situation' refers to is the relationship between different bodies in the immediate political environment. In terms of ministers, this covers Downing Street, cabinet, Parliament, the civil service, the media, the courts and, in a European context, the institutions of the EU and other member states.

A government with a large overall majority, for example, will face a power situation that is more favourable than a government having to cope with a small or non-existent majority. Ministers facing an activist judiciary will face a more fraught power situation than is the case when the judiciary is quiescent. The power situation may also be affected by particular events, such as the Falklands War and the Westland crisis.

Climate of expectation

The expectations of citizens change over time. It may be in reaction to a particular event, such as war or, more recently, in terms of attitudes towards the media and the royal family – for example the death in August 1997 of Diana, Princess of Wales. It may be in response to the economic situation or a more general perception of the state of the nation. The climate changes over time and sometimes rapidly. The Conservative Party was the beneficiary of a particular climate of expectation in 1979 and the victim of a very different climate in 1997. In terms of how it affects senior ministers, the climate may change with respect to particular issues: for example, dangerous dogs[5] or privacy.[6]

International developments

Ministers are constrained by what happens internationally, not least by virtue of treaty obligations (notably but not exclusively in the context of the EU), by virtue of what is an increasingly global market in capital and technology, and by particular events and opinion in other countries. Senior ministers could not stop market forces pushing the pound out of the ERM in September 1992. Ministers in 1996 and early 1997 had difficulty handling the BSE ('mad cow disease') crisis and the pressures for a change in the Common Fisheries Policy.

These variables help us understand ministerial power in Britain and provide us with the means of analysing particular ministerial failures and successes. Douglas Hogg, for example, was constrained as Agriculture Minister in 1996 by the powers vested in EU institutions and by his own failure to anticipate and to persuade and, indeed, by a negative power situation and climate of expectation. In the new Labour government, the International Development Minister, Clare Short, was blown off course (no pun intended) within months of taking office by an international event – an exploding volcano on a Caribbean island – and by a failure to hide and, in her relations with the Foreign Office, to manipulate.

Conclusion

Two principal conclusions can be drawn from this analysis. The first is that governments – and ministers – are increasingly constrained, not least as a consequence of treaty agreements and technology. Changes in the external environment mean that the capacity of government to affect outcomes is increasingly limited. That is hardly a revelation. Others have variously made this point. Within government, ministers are increasingly constrained by the competing demands made on them, not least by the responsibilities of EU membership and the development of a virtual twenty-four-hour news service.

5 In 1991, widely publicised cases of attacks on children by dogs, especially Rottweilers, resulted in pressure on ministers to take immediate action; the government rushed through Parliament the rapidly drafted Dangerous Dogs Bill.
6 For example, demands for greater protection of privacy became pronounced following the death in August 1997 of Diana, Princess of Wales, who was widely seen as victim of press intrusiveness.

However, insofar as government is still able to affect outcomes, then senior ministers are far more important actors – that, is acting individually – than has generally been conceded in the literature. Ministers vary enormously in terms of purpose and skill, and will be influenced by the ministry they occupy, but for those ministers who want to make a mark, the opportunity is there; what is not that well recognised by students of British government is the extent to which that opportunity is actually taken.

Reading

Barber, J. D. (1972) *The Presidential Character*, Prentice-Hall.

Brazier, R. (1997) *Ministers of the Crown*, Oxford University Press.

Dunleavy, P. and Rhodes, R. A. W. (1990) 'Core executive studies in Britain', *Public Administration*, Vol. 68 (1), pp. 3–28.

Headey, B. (1974) *British Cabinet Ministers*, George Allen and Unwin.

Johnson, N. (1980) *In Search of the Constitution*, Methuen.

Jordan, A. G. and Richardson, J. (1982) 'The British policy style or the logic of negotiation?', in J. Richardson (ed.), *Policy Styles in Western Europe*, George Allen and Unwin.

Kaufman, G. (1997) *How To Be A Minister*, Faber.

Marsh, D. and Rhodes, R. A. W. (eds) (1992) *Policy Networks in British Government*, Clarendon Press.

Norton, P. (1982) *The Constitution in Flux*, Blackwell.

Norton, P. (1987) 'Prime ministerial power: a framework for analysis', *Teaching Politics*, Vol. 16 (3), pp. 325–45.

Norton, P. (1993) 'The Conservative Party from Thatcher to Major', in A. King (ed.), *Britain at the Polls 1992*, Chatham House.

Norton, P. (1994) 'The parliamentary party and party committees', in A. Seldon and S. Ball (eds), *Conservative Century*, Oxford University Press.

Norton, P. (1997) 'Political leadership', in L. Robins and B. Jones (eds), *Half A Century in British Politics*, Manchester University Press.

Oakeshott, M. (1962) *Rationalism and Politics and Other Essays*, Methuen.

Rhodes, R. A. W. (1995) 'From prime ministerial power to core executive', in R. A. W. Rhodes and P. Dunleavy (eds), *Prime Minister, Cabinet and Core Executive*, Macmillan.

Rhodes, R. A. W. (1997) *Understanding Governance: Policy Networks, Governance, Reflexivity and Accountability*, Open University Press.

Rose, R. (1987) *Ministers and Ministries*, Clarendon Press.

Theakston, K. (1987) *Junior Ministers in British Government*, Blackwell.

Woodhouse, D. (1994) *Ministers and Parliament*, Clarendon Press.

7

Devolution

James Mitchell

Introduction: understanding the United Kingdom

Debate on how to govern beyond London is concerned with past experience and the sense of national and regional identities which exist within the UK. Though Parliament at Westminster is central to the politics of the UK, it could not operate without institutions in other parts of the state. Debate on what these institutions should be, to whom they should be accountable and how they should relate to London have persisted. Devolution has been proposed, in different forms, as a response to the need for government beyond London. What becomes evident when considering devolution are the variety of forms it can take.

The UK is a multinational state made up of England, Scotland, Wales and Northern Ireland. The government of the UK is conducted through institutions operating at different levels. The most important central institutions are Parliament at Westminster, the cabinet and the civil service in Whitehall. Local government exists throughout the state but its structure, powers and responsibilities differ in the UK's component nations. Local government in Northern Ireland is far less significant in the affairs of that part of the UK than it is elsewhere. Apart from local government, the UK has always had complex mechanisms for dealing with the distinct territories within it. Catering for Scottish, Welsh and (Northern) Irish distinctiveness within the UK has been a constant theme of politics.

The territorial dimension of UK politics is only one aspect of the changing nature of the state. The role of the state has changed dramatically over time. The 'night-watchman state' of the nineteenth century, when the state intervened to a very limited extent, gave way in the twentieth century to the establishment of state intervention, planning and the welfare state, particularly in the immediate postwar period, when Attlee's Labour government set up the National Health Service (NHS) and nationalised a number of key industries. The nature and extent of state intervention have changed

again over the last twenty years. The changing dimensions of state intervention have had territorial implications. Catering for national distinctiveness
within the UK has had to take account of these changes in the role of
the state.

The NHS, for example, could not operate entirely from the centre under
parliamentary control. There need to be doctors and nurses throughout the
country attending to the health needs of the population and that requires
some regional or local administration. This is true of most major activities
of government. The point was made by the Royal Commission on the
Constitution (Kilbrandon), which reported in 1973 in favour of devolution:

> The individual a hundred years ago hardly needed to know that the central
> government existed. His birth, marriage and death would be registered, and
> he might be conscious of the safeguards for his security provided by the forces
> of law and order and of imperial defence; but, except for the very limited
> provisions of the poor law and factory legislation, his welfare and progress
> were matters for which he alone bore the responsibility. By the turn of the
> century the position was not much changed. Today, however, the individual
> citizen submits himself to the guidance of the state at all times. His schooling
> is enforced; his physical well-being can be looked after in a comprehensive
> health service; he may be helped by government agencies to find and train
> for a job; he is obliged while in employment to insure against sickness,
> accident and unemployment; his house may be let to him by a public
> authority or he may be assisted in its purchase or improvement; he can avail
> himself of a wide range of government welfare allowances and services; and
> he draws a state pension on his retirement. In these and many other ways
> unknown to his counterpart of a century ago, he is brought into close and
> regular contact with government and its agencies. (p. 76, paras 232–3)

Even since that was written, there have been changes in the reach and
activities of the state. The abandonment of an active regional industrial
policy, the sale of nationalised industries and council houses, the increased
role of regulatory politics in the fields of the environment, for example,
have all had an impact on government beyond London.

As well as these economic pressures, there has also been a cultural
dimension to territorial politics in the UK. The fact that the UK is a
multinational state with people having a sense of Scottish, Welsh and other
national identities has been important in how the state has been organised.
Unlike in other parts of Europe, most notably France, there has never been
any attempt to create a single, all-encompassing UK national identity and
eradicate more local identities. Though cultural identity need not have a
political dimension, there has always been a significant political dimension
to the various identities which exist within the UK. Local, regional and
national identities have persisted over time, though the institutions through
which these identities have been articulated have often changed.

In Northern Ireland, religious identity continues to be central to territorial identities. Catholics tend to identify with Ireland as a whole and Protestants tend to identify primarily with Northern Ireland and with the UK as a whole. The Welsh language remains a key transmitter of national identity in Wales. In Scotland, a more diffuse yet stronger sense of Scottish nationalism exists. A variety of institutions and traditions have helped maintain a sense of Scottish identity over time – the Church of Scotland, education and the law, among others. What is most significant is that an exclusive sense of UK national identity does not exist. This is evident in the dual national identities commonly held (Scottish and British, for example, by most people living in Scotland). As Richard Rose maintained, there is no nation associated with the UK state: 'No one speaks of the "Ukes" as a nation' (Rose, 1982, p. 11).

Complicating matters further, the terms 'United Kingdom' and 'Britain' are often used interchangeably, though they are not synonymous. The correct name of the state is the 'United Kingdom of Great Britain and Northern Ireland', though 'Britain' is more often used. While Scots and Welsh often complain about the inability of people in England to distinguish between England and Britain, people in Scotland and Wales are as guilty of failing to distinguish between Britain and the UK. All of this merely draws attention to the manner in which the state came into being and has developed. The UK is an organic entity, formed incrementally over centuries. There is no founding constitution setting out principles and institutions for a rational constitutional order. The absence of an entrenched written constitution allows for the existence of apparent anomalies in the constitution. The British constitution is a set of anomalies held together by a series of unwritten conventions.

The sovereignty of 'the crown in Parliament' is the phrase used in legal textbooks to refer to the ultimate resting place of power and authority. The notion that the UK is a *unitary state* follows from this understanding of where power lies. All other institutions are thought to derive their authority, and even their existence, from the wishes of Parliament at Westminster. Westminster's suspension of Stormont, the Northern Ireland Parliament, in 1972 and the abolition of the Greater London Council and metropolitan councils in 1986 were striking examples of this power. It is in this sense that the UK is a unitary state.

An alternative view of the UK exists. In this view, the UK is seen as a *union state*, rather than a unitary state. Whereas the unitary state view sees the UK as having been 'built up around one unambiguous political centre which enjoys economic dominance and pursues a more or less undeviating policy of administrative standardisation', in the view of the UK as a union state, 'integration is less than perfect' (Rokkan and Urwin, 1982, p. 11). This latter view does not deny the importance of Parliament but acknowledges the importance of other institutions. As Rhodes has commented, the conventional view of the UK is of a 'unitary state with a single Parliament, government and civil service, deciding on policy for the whole country and applying it through the national territory' as if there are 'no local or other autonomous bodies which even compare in authority with national government' (Rhodes, 1985, p. 33). This, he stresses, is false. Though Westminster may have the power to abolish institutions below it, it is difficult to imagine Westminster and other central institutions operating without some local or other autonomous bodies.

The diverse nature of the UK is best captured in the union state view. The establishment of a Scottish Parliament, Assemblies in Northern Ireland and Wales, a London authority and directly elected London mayor and new regional bodies in England would suggest that in the years ahead the view of the UK as a unitary state will wither. The prospect of constitutional change of this magnitude is dramatic. But when it is appreciated that the UK has evolved, with a series of different institutions emerging, changing and disappearing over time, taking account of the state's territorial diversity, then these imminent constitutional reforms appear less radical.

Devolution in Northern Ireland

Ireland was the last component nation to join the UK. Though it had first come under English control as early as the twelfth century, it formally became part of the UK in 1801. The Irish Parliament, with no Catholic representation, decided to join the union in common with England, Wales and Scotland. But the UK, as thus defined, was to last for only just over a century. Relations between Ireland and the rest of the UK were always troubled and the 'Irish question' dominated much of that period.

Calls for independence or some measure of home rule were frequently heard and violence in pursuit of these goals was common. Many of the current debates on the status of Scotland and Wales had their equivalents in nineteenth-century Irish politics though there has been remarkably little violence in Scotland and Wales. The relationship between religion, national identity and territory complicated matters. The Irish were a minority within the UK but within Ireland a Protestant minority preferred to stay with the UK. There was a geographic concentration of this minority within a minority in the north. It was this minority within a minority, the Ulster Protestants, who most vehemently opposed Irish home rule or devolution, fearing the consequences of majority Catholic rule. Ironically, it was this community which eventually enjoyed the benefits of devolution within the UK.

Around the time of the First World War, attempts to meet the twin demands of Irish home rule and Ulster Protestant opposition resulted in proposals for 'home rule within home rule'. Ireland as a whole would be given home rule while the north would also be given some measure of home rule within Ireland or the chance to opt out altogether. The Government of Ireland Act 1920 made provision for home rule for Ireland and for six counties of Ulster (a further three Ulster counties were excluded as these were predominantly Catholic – this remains a matter of controversy). The provisions of the Act affecting Ireland as a whole were never implemented as events overtook the legislation, but a parliament for the six counties, in what became Northern Ireland, was established. Devolution, therefore, came to the one part of the UK which had been most opposed to it.

Under the provisions of the legislation, Parliament's authority would remain 'unaffected and undiminished over all persons, matters, and things in Ireland and every part thereof'. Westminster retained important 'override' powers which enabled it to veto legislation passed by the Northern Ireland Parliament. Legislation passed there had to be submitted to the Governor for approval. In other words, Westminster was not abandoning its full rights over Northern Ireland – it was not proposing to share sovereignty. The Northern Ireland Parliament was given power to make laws for the 'peace, order and good government' of the area, with a number of specified matters excluded. Ulster, or that part which was devolved (the name 'Ulster' still attracts controversy because of the three counties which were excluded), continued to return MPs to Westminster, though the number was reduced, while most domestic affairs were devolved to the Assembly.

Though power was retained at Westminster, Stormont (as the Assembly became known after it was housed there from 1932) was given a remarkable degree of autonomy. Indeed, Stormont extended its reach beyond the legislation which had created it shortly after it was established. It was able to do this because Westminster had no desire to involve itself in the affairs of Northern Ireland (Hadfield, 1992, p. 3). Stormont repealed provisions for proportional representation, which had been designed to ensure minority Catholic representation, in 1922 for local elections and in 1929 for elections to Stormont. The government of Northern Ireland had threatened to resign if London intervened to overrule the law abolishing proportional representation for local government. In effect, Northern Ireland had raised the stakes. London's choice was to impose direct rule from London or to accept the legislation abolishing proportional representation for local government. It accepted the abolition of proportional representation.

London's failure to veto the measure set the sectarian tone of Northern Irish politics for the next fifty years. In addition, the parameters of autonomy were set far more widely than the 1920 Act had suggested (Buckland, 1979, ch. 12). The episode 'unequivocally dictated the course of the relationship that was to develop over the ensuing decades between Westminster and Stormont' (Hadfield, 1989, p. 51).

The prospect of 'override' powers being used was raised on one further occasion. In 1970 the Governor was petitioned to intervene over the Public Order (Amendment) Bill (NI) – enacted to counter the (non-violent) civil rights movement – but failed to do so after consulting the Home Office. In effect, London's policy towards Northern Ireland was one of neglect. Until 1968 there was not a single civil servant in London concerned full time with the politics of Northern Ireland (Rose, 1976, p. 20).

The in-built majority held by the Protestant Unionists and Westminster's refusal to intervene created problems. Unionists won 66.9 per cent of the vote in the first elections in 1921 and 67.4 per cent in the last Stormont election in 1969. They normally had about three-quarters of the seats in the Assembly. Sir Basil Brooke, Northern Ireland Prime Minister from 1943 to 1963, often played the 'Orange card' and made anti-Catholic speeches. He made no attempt to build consensus within Northern Ireland. Terence O'Neill took office in 1963 and sought to pursue a new path of reconciliation between Protestants and Catholics. But the policy offered too little, too late.

Civil unrest and violence in the late 1960s forced London to intervene as the 'Troubles' escalated. British troops were sent to Northern Ireland to help restore public order in 1969. The original intention for central government intervention may have been to make the Stormont system work in an acceptable manner but by 1972 any hope of achieving this had diminished to such an extent that Westminster suspended Stormont. An attempt to transfer powers over law and order to Westminster was resisted by Stormont, forcing London's hand. The model adopted for direct rule was a version of the Scottish Office. A Secretary of State for Northern Ireland heading a Northern Ireland Office was appointed though, unlike the Scottish Office where all Scottish Secretaries have had Scottish connections (see below), none of the incumbents in the Northern Ireland Office has come from the area (see Table 7.1).

Table 7.1. *Secretaries of State for Northern Ireland and constituencies represented in the Commons*

Date of taking office	Holder	Constituency
24 April 1972	W. Whitelaw	Penrith and Border
2 December 1973	F. Pym	Cambridgeshire
5 March 1974	M. Rees	Leeds South
10 September 1976	R. Mason	Barnsley
5 May 1979	H. Atkins	Spelthorne
14 September 1981	J. Prior	Lowestoft
11 September 1984	D. Hogg	Grantham
3 September 1985	T. King	Bridgwater
24 July 1989	P. Brooke	City of London and Westminster South
15 April 1992	Sir P. Mayhew	Tunbridge Wells
3 May 1997	M. Mowlam	Redcar

Source: Butler and Butler (1994).

The principal aims of successive Northern Ireland Secretaries of State have been to restore peace and find an acceptable constitutional settlement for Northern Ireland. Conferences and meetings, often in private, have been held over the years in pursuit of these goals. For a brief period an experiment in sharing power, with participation from both communities, was attempted but failed after a Loyalist strike in 1974 forced the reintroduction of direct rule. A constitutional convention elected to consider the most appropriate form of government for Northern Ireland in 1975 produced a report which essentially amounted to the return of Stormont, which was unacceptable to Westminster and the Catholic minority. In the early 1980s, proposals for 'rolling devolution', the gradual re-establishment of a Northern Ireland Parliament, came to nothing when elections were boycotted by the Catholic community.

Alongside these, there have been attempts to find mechanisms through which the governments of the UK and the Irish Republic could reach agreement on the best system of government for Northern Ireland. In 1985, the governments of the two countries signed the Anglo-Irish Agreement and in 1993 the Downing Street Declaration was issued by both governments. Both statements angered hard-line Unionists and highlighted the complexities involved in debates on Northern Ireland. In comparable debates elsewhere in the UK, there has never been any suggestion that another country should be involved. It is this and the attendant violence that distinguishes debate on devolution of Northern Ireland from the debates in Scotland and Wales.

The arguments in favour of devolution to Northern Ireland since direct rule have been categorised as those with which everyone might agree and those which appeal to only a section of the community (Maguire, 1992, p. 17). The former, inclusive arguments concern greater accountability, more responsive government and the regeneration of the political process. While Stormont existed, each level of administration (central, regional and local) had its own political institutions (Westminster, Stormont and elected local authorities). The abolition of Stormont removed a level of accountability and created a system of government which, according to Peter Brooke, Secretary of State for Northern Ireland 1989–92, 'no-one would dream of inventing as a long term way of governing any sizeable community' (Maguire, 1992, p. 18). Other arguments made by supporters of devolution were that decision making would become speedier, based on a better understanding of issues and local needs and that political life in Northern Ireland operates in a vacuum without devolution (Maguire, 1992, pp. 17–20).

The second set of arguments for devolution are ones on which not all may agree. Support for devolution among Ulster Unionists is based on a belief that having institutions controlled by Unionists in Northern Ireland would help secure the union with the rest of the UK. Supporters of devolution in London see it as the only answer to the area's problems, anything else being seen as too risky. Nationalists in Northern Ireland who support devolution do so because they see it as a process which will lead to a united Ireland, as they believe it would accentuate the differences between Northern Ireland and Britain and give nationalists a role in its government (Maguire, 1992, pp. 20–4). The reason why one party supports devolution for Northern Ireland 'is the direct opposite of the reason why another seeks it' (Maguire, 1992, p. 25).

Devolution alone could never resolve the conflicts in Northern Ireland. When the IRA ceasefire was declared in 1994, followed by the Loyalist paramilitaries six weeks later, talks had been taking place which eventually resulted in the publication of the 'Belfast Agreement' in 1998, after much hesitancy and uncertainty. The 'peace process', as it became known, had a number of elements. The Belfast Agreement had three 'strands'. Democratic institutions in Northern Ireland with devolution as its central element was strand one. Strand two was a North/South Ministerial Council. A British–Irish Council and the British–Irish Intergovernmental Conference were strand three. In addition, it involved the decommissioning of weapons, release of prisoners, policing matters, safeguards for equal opportunities and civil rights, and a commitment to remove those articles of the Irish Republic's constitution which claimed sovereignty over Northern Ireland. In the language of the debates and documents, it was the intricate and complex 'totality of relationships' (within Northern Ireland; between North and South; and between Northern Ireland and other parts of the UK) which were important. Devolution in Northern Ireland was re-established in 1998 after a gap of twenty-six years, but it was a different sort and within a wholly different context. In essence, devolution had been restored and demoted simultaneously.

Scotland's century of administrative devolution

The expansion of government activities in the nineteenth century had its impact on how Scotland was governed. Much government activity in the period after 1707, when Scotland and England united to form Britain, until the mid-1800s was conducted at a local level. A series of local administrative arrangements had developed with fairly limited central control covering such disparate matters as poor law, education, police and public health. Parliament was then, as now, 'the centre' but in terms of day-to-day policy making it had a very limited role. The 'centre' in Scotland for much of the last century consisted of a series of patronage boards, largely made up of lawyers based in Edinburgh. Rules emanating from these guided the work of the local administration, but in a fairly unsystematic manner. These boards were the legacy of pre-union institutions and traditions – in Scots law and local administration – which persisted after Scotland and England united. They were distant from government in London geographically and politically.

The expansion of government activities changed all of this. Stronger central control allied with a more systematic pattern of government emerged as the state's role expanded. But the 'centre' remained ambiguous. Parliament may have passed more laws affecting the lives of its citizens, but much of this passed through the Scottish boards to the local level. Special legislation or Scottish clauses to English legislation were often added to take account of Scottish distinctiveness. The centre, from the perspective of ordinary Scots, was both London and Edinburgh. More legislation and more decisions being made by government ministers meant that London was becoming increasingly important in Scotland.

Out of this emerged an argument for a Scottish Minister in London, someone who would be part of the inner core of decision makers. In addition, the increased scope of activities was deemed to require a more professional and systematic government apparatus across the UK as a whole. Major reforms in the civil service in England did not immediately affect Scotland because of its distinct pattern of administrative boards. By the early 1880s, the case for a Scottish Minister had won the support of the Liberals and Conservatives, the two major parties of the day, and in 1885, after a number of failed attempts, the office of Secretary for Scotland was established. The Prime Minister at the time was Lord Salisbury. He invited the Duke of Richmond and Gordon to accept the post in a letter which gave away more about the nature of the office, and which remains valid today, than anything that was said in Parliament. The office existed, 'to redress the wounded dignities of the Scotch people – or a section of them – who think that enough is not made of Scotland' (Hanham, 1965, p. 230). This was not simply an example of the Prime Minister's notorious cynicism. It reflected the pressure which had been growing in Scotland for some new means of taking account of Scottish distinctiveness in a time when the centre in London was becoming increasingly important in people's lives.

The willingness, if grudging, to take account of Scottish distinctiveness reflects the almost perennial willingness of British Prime Ministers to accommodate and not assimilate Scotland within the union. The main role for the Scottish Secretary from its establishment was to articulate Scotland's interests at the highest levels of government. The Scottish Secretary would also have responsibility for the variety of boards in Edinburgh. In time, these would be completely subsumed under the office of Scottish Secretary and a Scottish Office would emerge which was comparable to other Whitehall government departments, except in its location – based in Edinburgh – and its wide remit.

As government activities expanded, so too did the role and activities of the Scottish Office. Education and local administration had been the chief administrative responsibilities of the Scottish Secretary in 1885. The scope of central government activity and central government expenditure in these areas grew dramatically over the course of the next century. In addition, other responsibilities were added to the Scottish Office's list. Agriculture in Scotland came under the Scottish Office in 1912, health and housing from 1919 and many matters relating to planning later, in the interwar period. In the era following the Second World War, the state's responsibilities grew even more as the welfare state was established and industries were nationalised. These, too, were almost invariably to take account of Scottish distinctiveness and in some cases came under the Scottish Office's remit.

What remained constant was London's willingness to cater for Scottish distinctiveness within the confines of one Parliament for the UK. Demands for a Scottish Parliament, constitutionally similar to Stormont, were made but never conceded. However, though legislative devolution as in Northern Ireland was not acceptable, the Scottish Office itself was felt to constitute a form of devolution – 'administrative devolution'. This was the term coined by a civil servant in the 1930s to describe the arrangements whereby Scotland had a minister in the cabinet with a wide and growing range of responsibilities and a civil service operating in Scotland implementing legislation, often specially designed to cater for Scottish distinctiveness. The term itself was a reaction to the demands at the time for a Scottish Parliament. Scotland, it was argued, did not need a Parliament as it was catered for with administrative devolution in the shape of the Scottish Office.

The welfare state and nationalised industries were typical of the ambiguity at the heart of government in Scotland. The *national* in the National Heath Service and in the nationalised industries was both British and Scottish. Parliament legislated for these major reforms and they were passed on the mandate given by the people of the UK as a whole in the 1945 general election. Yet, most elements of the welfare state had a distinctly Scottish dimension. Notably, it was the Conservative Party in Scotland, though it called itself the Scottish Unionist Party between 1912 and 1965 (itself a manifestation of Scottish distinctiveness), which argued most vociferously in favour of special concessions to take account of Scottish distinctiveness in the newly nationalised industries and welfare state which emerged after 1945 (Mitchell, 1990).

The great weakness of administrative devolution was that while it took account of Scottish distinctiveness, it failed to take account of Scottish democracy. It was headed by a Minister chosen by the Prime Minister from her or his own party, even if that party was in a minority in Scotland. Scotland's share of seats at Westminster exceeded its share of the population after the Irish settlement in the early 1920s but this still fell far short of giving Scottish MPs much hope of determining which party won a general election. There was always the possibility that the UK would be governed by a party which the Scots had rejected because England, its largest component, had voted for it. From 1959, every time the Conservatives won a general election in Britain (i.e. 1959, 1970, 1979, 1983, 1987, 1992), the Scottish Office was controlled by that party though Labour was Scotland's largest party. This created tensions especially during Margaret Thatcher's term as Prime Minister. There were few comparable examples of England having a party foisted on it by the Scots. Since 1945, only in the elections in 1964 and February and October 1974 did Labour win the election though the Conservatives won more votes in England.

The Scottish Office contributed to the sense that a separate political system existed north of the border (Kellas, 1989). While few Scots were aware of what it was, its work had a direct impact on their lives and much political debate in Scotland was framed by its existence. Pressure groups would lobby the Scottish Office and the Scottish Secretary would be appealed to on a wide range of matters. Media coverage of their work was extensive. Few people living in Scotland were unaffected by Scottish Office policies. Its very existence was an acknowledgement that Scotland was somehow different and lent legitimacy to claims for special treatment and self-government. It would prove difficult for opponents of a Scottish Parliament to argue that Scotland was just the same as any other part of the state. They had to argue either that it should be treated no differently – a very radical stance which would have involved the abolition of the Scottish Office, the eradication of Scots law and other distinct Scottish institutions – or that Scottish distinctiveness was well catered for with the existing arrangements. Few dared to argue the former, assimilationist position, though Margaret Thatcher was thought by many Scots to sympathise with it. Her memoirs suggested that they were not far wrong. The Scottish Office, which successive Conservative Prime Ministers had helped establish and develop, was seen by Thatcher as part of the problem in Scotland:

> The pride of the Scottish Office – whose very structure added a layer of bureaucracy, standing in the way of the reforms which were paying such dividends in England – was that public expenditure per head in Scotland was far higher than in England. (Thatcher, 1993, p. 627)

Public support for a Scottish Parliament of some description has been at around 70–75 per cent over the postwar period (Mitchell, 1996). But the issue did not become salient until the 1960s. The rise of the Scottish National Party (SNP) in the 1960s signalled the emergence of Scotland's constitutional status as a salient issue. Labour under Harold Wilson in the late 1960s set up the Royal Commission on the Constitution, which reported in 1973 in favour of devolution for various parts of the UK, but its members differed over the nature and extent of devolution in its different components. The Conservatives under Ted Heath came out in favour of an elected assembly in 1968, though Heath made no effort to do anything when he became Prime Minister in 1970. It was left to Labour, back in power in 1974, to legislate for devolution in the late 1970s. However, Labour was deeply divided on the issue and the government had no overall majority in the Commons for most of the Parliament.

As a concession to opponents on its own back benches, the Labour government agreed that there would be a referendum. This was held in 1979, at the tail-end of Labour's period in office, after a period of industrial discontent when Labour was unpopular and deeply divided on devolution. The result was only a narrow endorsement of devolution: 51.6 per cent voted in favour and 48.4 per cent against. Parliament had decided that a majority for devolution was not enough and that 40 per cent of the eligible electorate (i.e. everyone entitled to vote, including those who did not vote) had to vote for devolution. Only 33 per cent of those entitled to vote had supported the measure. Devolution then helped to bring down the government. Its failure to move the repeal order, as it knew the Labour Party in Parliament was disunited, provoked the SNP to support a motion of no confidence in the government, which united most opposition MPs and defeated the government. An election was held and the Conservatives under Margaret Thatcher came to power.

Devolution receded in importance as an issue after the 1979 election but over the 1980s came back to prominence. The Conservatives governed Scotland through the Scottish Office without a majority of seats in Scotland. Thatcher and her party came to be seen as anti-Scottish by a majority of the electorate in Scotland (Mitchell and Bennie, 1996). The introduction of the poll tax in Scotland a year ahead of the rest of Britain only fuelled perceptions of the Conservatives as an anti-Scottish party. This sparked off the constitutional debate once more. Scots came to see devolution as a way of safeguarding their interests. The issue became increasingly polarised as the Conservatives argued against devolution and Labour, Liberal Democrats and SNP argued in favour of some measure of home rule.

In 1988 the SNP launched its policy 'independence in Europe', arguing for Scottish independence within the European Community. The following year, Labour and the Liberal Democrats along with representatives of the churches, local government and others formed the Constitutional Convention to agree a scheme of devolution. The issue rarely receded far from the forefront of Scottish politics. For most of the period from the late 1980s, the debate in Scotland shifted from whether there should be a Scottish Parliament to whether Scotland should have independence or devolution. Ironically, given that they were in power, it was almost as if the Conservatives were not part of the debate. This changed dramatically in 1995 when Michael Forsyth was appointed Conservative Secretary of State for Scotland. Forsyth attacked the tax-varying powers of the scheme agreed by the Constitutional Convention, which he dubbed the 'tartan tax'. Though the

Table 7.2. *The 1997 Scottish referendum results*

	% of votes cast	% of electorate
Q1. *Support a Scottish parliament?*		
Yes	74.3	44.7
No	25.7	15.5
Q2. *Support tax-varying powers?*		
Yes	63.5	38.1
No	36.5	21.9
Turnout		60.2

tax-varying powers were modest, symbolically they were politically significant. Labour was determined to alter its image as a 'tax and spend' party but Michael Forsyth's 'tartan tax' campaign placed that aim in jeopardy. Labour's response was to propose a referendum in which Scots would be asked two questions: whether they wanted a Parliament and whether they wanted it to have tax-varying powers.

This removed the issue from the 1997 general election campaign but not for long. Despite the defeat of all Scottish Conservative MPs in 1997 and that every Scottish MP promised that a Scottish Parliament would be set up (even Tam Dalyell, maverick anti-devolution MP, included a commitment to devolution in his 1997 election manifesto), Labour was obliged to hold a referendum. The government issued a white paper, *Scotland's Parliament*, outlining its proposals in July 1997 and a referendum was held on 11 September. On this occasion, the Scots voted overwhelmingly in favour of devolution and for tax-varying powers (Table 7.2). Counting took place in each of Scotland's thirty-two local authority areas. Each area voted for the Parliament and all but two (Dumfries and Galloway, and Orkney) voted for tax-varying powers.

The first elections to the Scottish Parliament are scheduled to take place in spring 1999. It will have control over a wide range of matters, including health, education and training, local government, housing, social work, economic development, transport, the law and home affairs, the environment, including the natural and built heritage, agriculture, fisheries and forestry, sports and arts. Certain matters are defined as outwith the scope of devolution and retained at Westminster. These include the constitution of the UK, foreign policy, defence and national security, the stability of the UK's fiscal, economic and monetary system, common markets for UK goods and services, employment legislation, some health issues, including abortion, social security matters and most aspects of transport safety and regulation.

The bulk of the spending of the Parliament will be derived from a grant from Westminster, though a limited power to raise its own money will be available. The number of Scottish MPs at Westminster will be reduced. The new Parliament will have 129 members, seventy-three elected on a constituency basis plus fifty-six additional members (seven from each of the existing eight European constituencies) allocated proportionately. This will reduce the possibility of any single party having an overall majority. The office of Secretary of State for Scotland will continue to exist though its functions will be reduced.

The election of a Scottish Parliament is unlikely to resolve the issue of Scotland's constitutional status once and for all. Scotland's status within the UK has always undergone change. The context in which the Scottish Parliament operates, as well as changes elsewhere, notably in the scope and nature of government in London, will have an impact on the nature of the devolution settlement. In this sense, devolution is likely to be evolutionary, the final destination uncertain.

Welsh language and devolution

Wales has been both more and less distinct than Scotland within the UK. It has been more distinct in that there is a separate Welsh language spoken today by over half a million people in Wales, although this is under a fifth of the Welsh population. It is less distinct in that the sense of Welsh identity is weaker than Scottish identity and there are fewer distinctly Welsh institutions than there are Scottish institutions. In large measure this is accounted for by history. Wales entered a union with England earlier and was assimilated to a far greater extent. An Act of Parliament passed by Westminster in 1746 provided that legislative references to England would be taken to refer to Wales too. In effect, it stated that 'for England read England and Wales'. This remained in place until 1967. Nonetheless, a sense of Welsh identity has persisted.

Towards the end of the 1800s, special provision for the administration of Welsh secondary education was granted in legislation passed by Parliament and in the early part of the 1900s a Welsh department within the Department of Education was set up. This eventually led to the establishment of the Welsh Office, modelled on the Scottish Office, in 1964. Essentially Welsh administrative devolution came much later and developed much more slowly than Scottish administrative devolution. The precedent of the Scottish Office was frequently mentioned by advocates of a Welsh Office. Though Labour had been committed to establishing a Welsh Secretary at the election in 1945, this promise was not fulfilled. In 1946, the cabinet considered the case for a Welsh Office. Herbert Morrison, a noted centraliser, argued against, suggesting that Wales could not 'carry a cadre of officials of the highest calibre and the services of high English officials would no longer be available'. He argued that what Wales required was to be part of a 'single economic plan for the whole country' (Morgan, 1982, p. 377). Two years later the cabinet agreed to set up an advisory council drawn from local government, industry and the trade unions.

The Conservatives returned to power in 1951 and established a Ministry of Welsh Affairs. The Conservatives had few seats in Wales and a trend was set which was to have repercussions over thirty years later. The first Minister of Welsh Affairs was a Scot representing an English constituency. In 1959, a later Welsh Minister, who represented Hampstead in Parliament, provoked the hostility of many people in Wales with a decision to flood the Tryweryn valley in Merioneth to create a reservoir for Liverpool. The area was Welsh speaking and though an overwhelming majority of Welsh MPs opposed the bill to authorise the scheme, it went ahead (Osmond, 1977, p. 113).

Welsh nationalism has been at least as concerned with the preservation of the language as with the promotion of Welsh devolution and independence. In a famous radio broadcast in 1962, Saunders Lewis, a leading Welsh nationalist, argued for a more militant defence of the language and that the preservation of the language was more important than self-government. Lewis's broadcast led to the establishment of the Welsh Language Society, which campaigned vigorously in defence of the language. In 1967, the Welsh language was given official status. A more militant element had emerged in the 1960s, the Free Wales Army. Twenty years later the Sons of Glyndwr burned down holiday homes in Wales owned by English people. These were elements who were frustrated at the slow progress of the language and feared that assimilation would lead to the anglicisation of Wales.

Political nationalism in Wales has a voice in Plaid Cymru (the Party of Wales), established in 1925. Gwynfor Evans, its president for over thirty years from 1945, won Plaid's first parliamentary seat in a by-election in Carmarthen in 1966. But the association of Welsh nationalism with the Welsh language was to place a glass ceiling on the party's fortunes. It has proved difficult to break out of the Welsh-language heartland and make electoral headway into the larger and politically dominant English-speaking parts of Wales.

As in Scotland, the rise of political nationalism led to proposals for devolution in the 1970s and again the Labour Party was deeply divided on the issue. Neil Kinnock, future leader of the Party, made a name for himself opposing devolution in the 1970s and was one of the leading campaigners against devolution in the Welsh referendum held on St David's Day in 1979, the same day as the Scottish referendum. In Wales, the result was an emphatic rejection of devolution: 79.8 per cent voted against and 20.2 per cent in favour.

But devolution re-emerged in Wales over the ensuing years. As in Scotland, a perception that the Conservatives had no sympathy or under- standing of the local situation developed among people in Wales. The notion that Wales was a quango state governed by unelected, appointed bodies became part of the dominant critique of Welsh politics. Welsh devolution was proposed as a solution to this problem. In effect, support for a Welsh Assembly was taking on a new form. It was losing its strong association with the language and gaining a more inclusive association with Welsh identity. Politically, being Welsh meant more than speaking the language. It meant being opposed to the Conservatives and for an increasing number of people it meant supporting an Assembly.

In part, Wales was swept along with the Scottish tide. Nonetheless, the Welsh debate was distinct and the proposals for a Welsh Assembly put forward throughout the 1980s by the Labour Party were more modest than those for Scotland (the term 'Assembly' was used rather than 'Parliament' as in Scotland). The second Welsh devolution referendum was held in September 1997, a week after the one for Scotland. Supporters hoped that an emphatic endorsement by the Scots might bolster support in Wales. The result was extremely close. On a turnout of 50.12 per cent, Wales voted 50.3 per cent in favour of devolution and 49.7 per cent against.

The Welsh Assembly will be set up in 1999 and will have responsibility for the £7 billion budget of the Welsh Office. The overall amount will continue to be determined by Westminster. It will take over most of the responsibilities of the Welsh Secretary (see Box 7.1). It will have powers to make secondary legislation but not primary legislation, that is, Acts of Parliament will continue to be made by Westminster but, for example, the

---

Box 7.1. *List of responsibilities of the Secretary of State for Wales*

Economic development
Agriculture, forestry, fisheries and food
Industry and training
Education
Local government
Health and personal social services
Housing
Environment
Planning
Transport and roads
Arts, culture, the Welsh language
The built heritage
Sport and recreation

Source: Welsh Office (1997).

Assembly will be able to determine the details of the school curriculum. The Assembly will have sixty members, elected using a similar method to the Scottish Parliament. There will be forty constituency members plus an additional twenty members elected (four elected in each of the five Welsh Euro-constituencies). The latter will reflect the strength of the parties in each area (Welsh Office, 1997). It will be a much more limited form of devolution than that proposed for Scotland.

England and its regions

As the largest constituent nation of the UK, England presents the greatest challenge to devolutionists. It creates an anomaly if it is left out of the devolution process. Scottish and Welsh MPs at Westminster will continue to vote on English domestic affairs while these matters are devolved in Scotland and Wales. It was this anomaly which led the English legal theorist A. V. Dicey to oppose Irish home rule in the nineteenth century. In his book, *England's Case Against Home Rule* (1886), Dicey argued that devolution to any one part of the state is a 'plan for revolutionising the constitution of the whole United Kingdom'. It was the implications for the rest of the UK which worried Dicey. The same implications have been voiced by opponents of devolution in recent debates. Concern that parliamentary sovereignty will be undermined and that the asymmetrical anomalies inherent in devolution would lead to the break-up of the state have been the main arguments against devolution.

One alternative is to give England a Parliament of its own and create a federal or quasi-federal system of government in which each of the constituent units of the UK has its own domestic Parliament. One problem with this is that the English Parliament would be the largest and most powerful and might challenge the authority of Westminster. Disputes between any of the domestic Parliaments and Westminster would be likely but those between an English Parliament and Westminster could prove very troublesome. The alternative would be to create a number of domestic Parliaments in the English regions. This might create a workable and symmetrical system of devolution all round. However, difficulties arise in determining the number of and boundaries for English regional assemblies. While some support exists for devolution in the north of England there is little evidence of this elsewhere, especially in the Midlands and south-east.

The sense of regional identity in England around which regional government might emerge differs across the nation. Even where there is evidence of a strong sense of regional identity this does not always translate into support for regional devolution. The absence of debate on the subject suggests that regional devolution throughout England would probably have to be imposed from above. This does not mean that it would be unsuccessful.

Box 7.2. *'Declaration for the North'*

We declare that the massive potential of the people of this region has long been hindered by neglect and isolation from over-centralised government in London. Our inability to develop our political, economic and cultural agenda has historically been restrained by the absence of meaningful local power.

We welcome our Scottish neighbours' move towards their own democratic voice in order to have a greater say in their own affairs inside the British system of government. We support their move to devolution and feel a Regional Development Agency in the North East could be a positive contribution towards devolution in this region too.

We believe however that true decision-making here can only come through a Directly Elected Assembly representing the people of the North.

We believe that an historic opportunity to bring government down to the people is now in our reach within the lifetime of this Parliament.

We therefore ask government in London to prepare for a referendum of voters in our region at the earliest opportunity in order that the people here can endorse the call for an Assembly to take the North into the new Millennium and into a new democracy.

In other countries this approach has been adopted, most notably in the Federal Republic of Germany, where regions were created after 1945 which did not relate to any pre-existing boundaries or regional identities but which in time have come to win the loyalty of their citizens and are widely acknowledged to have been successful. Unlike in Scotland and Wales, therefore, the prospect of devolution in English regions will be a top-down rather than a bottom-up phenomenon.

In one sense, regional government already exists in England. For administrative purposes, regions have been created to administer a range of services, but these are neither elected nor are the boundaries of the various bodies contiguous. In 1994 ten regional offices of various Whitehall departments were brought together to administer a single integrated budget. The work of these offices covers a mixture of regeneration and economic programmes. Not all central government matters were included within these regional bodies but this was a substantial move towards creating a uniform tier of regional government in England.

The debate in England is still at an early stage though a new authority and directly elected mayor is promised for London. Labour's election manifesto in 1997 proposed to consider English regional government in an ad hoc manner. Each area would be treated individually, with no single model imposed from the centre. The possibility of regional assemblies emerging in time was not discounted, though Labour was careful not to suggest that it would happen. After London, the most active campaign for a regional assembly is to be found in the north of England. In November 1997, a 'Declaration for the North' was issued by a number of key political figures in favour of an assembly (Box 7.2).

Conclusion

Devolution has a number of meanings in UK politics. The Scottish Office was described as a form of 'administrative devolution'. Similar arrangements for Northern Ireland following the suspension of Stormont, a form of legislative devolution, was referred to as 'direct rule'. The Scottish Parliament will be a form of legislative devolution, similar in some respects to Stormont. It will differ from the Welsh Assembly not only in its name but in that it will be able to pass laws over a range of issues. The Welsh Assembly will be able to make only secondary legislation, that is, make decisions within the framework of laws still made in Parliament in London.

This diversity of forms devolution can take reflects the asymmetrical nature of territorial politics in the UK. The new institutions which will be established for the start of the new millennium will continue the tradition of treating the different parts of the UK in different ways. Devolution has an evolutionary quality. This would suggest that the new arrangements will not necessarily be the end of the story.

Reading

Buckland, P. (1979) *The Factory of Grievances: Devolved Government in Northern Ireland*, Gill and Macmillan.

Buckland, P. (1981) *A History of Northern Ireland*, Gill and Macmillan.

Butler, D. and Butler, G. (1994) *British Political Facts, 1900–1994* (7th edn), Macmillan.

Hadfield, B. (1989) *The Constitution of Northern Ireland*, SLS.

Hadfield, B. (ed.) (1992) *Northern Ireland: Politics and the Constitution*, Open University Press.

Hanham, H. J. (1965) 'The creation of the Scottish Office, 1881–87', *Juridical Review*, pp. 205–44.

Kellas, J. (1989) *Scottish Political System* (4th edn), Cambridge University Press.

Maguire, P. (1992) 'Why devolution?', in B. Hadfield (ed.), *Northern Ireland: Politics and the Constitution*, Open University Press.

Mitchell, J. (1990) *Conservatives and the Union*, Edinburgh University Press.

Mitchell, J. (1996) *Strategies for Self-Government*, Polygon.

Mitchell, J. and Bennie, L. (1996) 'Thatcherism and the Scottish question', in C. Rawlings *et al.* (eds), *British Elections and Parties Yearbook 1995*, Frank Cass.

Morgan, K. O. (1982) *Rebirth of a Nation: Wales 1880–1980*, Oxford University Press.

Osmond, J. (1977) *Creative Conflict: The Politics of Welsh Devolution*, Routledge and Kegan Paul.

Rhodes, R. A. W. (1985) 'Intergovernmental relations in the United Kingdom', in Y. Mény and V. Wright (eds), *Centre–Periphery Relations in Western Europe*, George Allen and Unwin.

Rokkan, S. and Urwin, D. (eds) (1982) *The Politics of Territorial Identity*, Sage.

Rose, R. (1976) *Northern Ireland: A Time of Choice*, Macmillan.

Rose, R. (1982) *Understanding the United Kingdom*, Longman.

Thatcher, M. (1993) *The Downing Street Years*, HarperCollins.

Welsh Office (1997) *A Voice for Wales: The Government's Proposals for a Welsh Assembly*, HMSO, Cm. 3718.

8

Who makes policy?
Policy making in local government
David Wilson

New Labour, new context

Following Labour's general election victory in May 1997 the new Prime Minister soon made it clear what was expected of local government. Writing in March 1998, Tony Blair observed:

> The government will not hesitate to intervene directly to secure improvements where services fall below acceptable standards. And, if necessary, it will look to other authorities and agencies to take on duties where an authority is manifestly incapable of providing an effective service and unwilling to take the necessary action to improve its performance. (Blair, 1998, p. 20)

Elected local authorities would, Blair warned, lose powers unless they operated efficiently and effectively. Policy making at local level needed to be rooted in the local community. The Labour government's consultation paper *Modernising Local Government: Local Democracy and Community Leadership* (February 1998) emphasised two imperatives for local authorities in the context of policy making:

1 'developing new ways in which councils can listen to their communities and involve local people in their decisions, and in their policy planning and review' – via new forms of local consultation;
2 'devising new ways of working for councils, giving them clearer political and management structures' – via piloting of measures such as executive committees, lead members, cabinets or directly elected mayors.

It was emphasised that change must be 'owned' by local authorities themselves – the government would lay down parameters, but the councils themselves must develop new ways of working (e.g. through 'piloting' directly elected mayors or executive cabinets). At the Labour Party local government conference in February 1998, Hilary Armstrong, Minister for Local Government and Housing, put it like this: 'Councils must cease to be prisoners of their past and become the masters of their destiny, driving change not just responding to it.' A similar 'modernisation' theme permeated the July 1998 white paper *Modern Local Government: In Touch with the People*.

The Labour government's stress upon local democracy as the *raison d'être* of local government was 'in stark contrast to the attempted "managerial-isation" of local politics under the Conservatives, which championed consumer choice and producer competition over party politics, local elections and public deliberation' (Lowndes, 1998, p. 12). Tony Blair (1998, p. 13) made the importance of local leadership very clear:

> At the heart of local government's new role is leadership. It will mean councils using their unique status and authority as directly elected bodies to develop a vision for their locality ... provide a focus for partnership [and] guarantee quality services for all.

New Labour has provided a new context for local policy making, one in which democratic renewal is perceived as being of central importance. All this has taken place against a backcloth of structural change.

Structural change and local governance

British local government has undergone massive change in recent years. Two changes have been particularly important: structural change and local governance.

Structural change has resulted in the number of major elected authorities in England, Scotland and Wales declining from 1,857 in 1970 to 521 in 1974 and to 441 in 1998. The slimming down of British local authorities in the 1990s as a result of the Local Government Review is set out in Table 8.1.

Those parts of Britain affected by 'reform' have lost between them almost a third of their former councillors, with Wales being particularly adversely affected (a 36 per cent reduction).

The second important change has been the rise of local *governance*. Elected local government is now but one element of what has become known as local governance, a term which emphasises the shift away from a system in which elected local authorities were the key actors in their localities, to one where decision-making authority and service provision are divided between a number of agencies. Put simply, government at the local level is not what it was. It has become fragmented, with the elected element increasingly marginalised as successive Conservative governments imposed non-elected bodies upon localities.

Table 8.1. The downward spiral: fewer and fewer elected authorities

Year	Shire districts	Shire counties	New unitary authorities	London boroughs/ metropolitan districts	Scottish	Welsh	Total
1994	296	39	0	69	65	45	514
1995	294	38	1	69	65	45	512
1996	274	34	14	69	32	22	446
1997	260	35	27	69	32	22	445
1998	238	34	46	69	32	22	441
Change in number	-58	-5	46	–	-33	-23	-73

There are currently over 5,000 non-elected local quangos (e.g. National Health Service trusts, grant-maintained schools, training and enterprise councils, further-education corporations). Compare this with the number of elected local authorities set out in Table 8.1. There are now some 23,000 elected councillors but almost three times this number of quangocrats – people sitting on the boards of non-elected local bodies.

The financial independence of elected local government is also rapidly being eroded. The single British local tax, the council tax, now accounts for under 20 per cent of local government's net expenditure in England and only 8 per cent in Wales. Local authorities thus control little more than a third of the 53 per cent of their local expenditure that they had as recently as 1989/90, and little more than a half of the 35 per cent they had in the early 1970s. This gives local authorities relatively little freedom to manoeuvre as increasing proportions of local spending are provided by central government. It is a desperate situation for local authorities, one characterised by a comment from the leader of Bury Metropolitan Council at the Labour Party local government conference in February 1998: 'If you really want standards, if you really want democracy, you have got to trust us with money. Without that, talk of democracy and structures is nothing but a sham.' A similar note was sounded by Sir Jeremy Beecham, chair of the Local Government Association at the launch of the consultation paper on democratic renewal in 1998: 'It is no good giving authorities a new look in terms of internal structures if they don't have the capacity to act decisively locally. That means greater financial autonomy.'

The relative lack of control over local finances enjoyed by local authorities is crucial not only from a democratic perspective but also from the standpoint of local policy making. Without a viable independent form of finance, local authorities are in danger of being 'captured' by a central government that provides an increasingly large share of the spending cake.

Elected local government, with its severe financial constraints, is today but one part of a complex mosaic of policy influence within a locality. Many of the tasks previously carried out by elected local authorities are now provided by non-elected agencies exclusively financed by central government. This has had important implications for the role of locally elected councillors: their operational role now tends to be less important than their representational role. Nevertheless, as we will see, it is a mistake to dismiss elected councillors as politically unimportant. Some, notably majority party leaders and committee chairs, remain extremely influential, albeit within a stringent financial framework set down by central government.

There have been serious questions raised in recent years about the representativeness of local councillors. A Local Government Management Board census in 1998 showed that male councillors outnumbered females by nearly three to one, most were aged over fifty-five and only 3 per cent were non-white. The census received returns from 98 per cent of all local

Table 8.2. *Councillor profiles, 1998*

	Finding
England	
Male (%)	72.1
Female (%)	27.8
Average age	55.4
Wales	
Male (%)	79.6
Female (%)	20.4
Average age	57.8
Work status (%)	
Retired	34.9
Employed full time	29.6
Employed part time	8.2
Self-employed	15.2
Not working[a]	11.9
Ethnicity (%)	
White	96.9
Indian	0.7
Black Caribbean	0.5
Pakistani	0.5
Other	1.4

[a]Includes unemployed, in full-time education and permanently sick/disabled.
Source: Local Government Management Board (1998).

authorities and almost 14,500 councillors – 67 per cent of the total. Table 8.2 provides an analysis of the findings.

The dominance of white, middle-aged men militates against local policy making which is sensitive to the needs of those who are currently marginalised, notably ethnic minorities and younger women. Indeed, in February 1998 the Labour Party launched its Project 99 initiative to make councillors more representative of their areas. As Hilary Armstrong observed, the age and ethnic weighting of councillors showed that local democracy was 'not as healthy as it should be'. Richard Penn, chief executive of Bradford Metropolitan Borough Council, emphasised that retention rates were a major factor as too many younger, female and ethnic minority councillors became disillusioned with their place as backbenchers and stood down after one term:

> Local government isn't a very friendly place for elected members in terms of practices and working hours.... Not everyone can be a decision maker, but

if they're drawn into engaging work instead of simply being lobby fodder they are likely to stay longer.

Local representatives, it seems, are becoming less and less representative of the communities they serve. The implications for local policy making cannot be ignored, hence the government's determination to enhance participatory forms of democracy such as citizens' juries, local opinion polls and local referendums.

Analysing policy influence

At the heart of the debate about policy influence inside local authorities is the relative importance of elected councillors and appointed officers. Three of the most influential analytical models are summarised in Box 8.1.

The formal model is grounded in the traditional legal approach to analysis. Policy influence is seen purely in terms of the formal structures of decision making – the council, committees and departments. Put simply, councillors are seen to make policy, while officers carry it out. In practice, however, a model that sees councillors making policy through the council and its committee system, while officers simply advise and implement, tells us more about what should happen than what actually happens. Nevertheless, this model should not be dismissed out of hand. During the Thatcher years assertive councillors of both the new urban left and radical right were dominant in a way which this formal model delineates.

The technocratic model sees paid officers as the dominant force in local policy making. Their power is said to be rooted in their control of specialist technical and professional knowledge not held by part-time, amateur, generalist councillors. This model, however, underestimates the knowledge, experience and skill of senior councillors. It is based on a stereotype of councillors as unintelligent and uninformed. Councillors can be active and they can be knowledgeable. In the early 1990s, for example, the ruling Conservative Party groups in the London boroughs of Westminster and Wandsworth and in the district councils of Wansdyke in Avon and Rochford

---

Box 8.1. *Officer–councillor relationships: three influential models*

1 *Formal* model – councillors make policy; officers simply advise councillors and implement policy.
2 *Technocratic* model – paid officers, because of their professional and technical knowledge, dominate the policy process.
3 *Corporate* model – senior councillors and senior officers jointly shape policy.

in Essex were particularly active over the introduction of competitive tendering – just as a decade earlier the 'municipal left' had introduced the subsidisation of public transport and council housing, as well as job-creation and anti-discrimination policies.

Nevertheless, the professional and technical knowledge possessed by officers is a very important resource and does enable them to act as powerful influences on policy, particularly in the absence of any positive lead from councillors. As professionals they are always there to fill any policy vacuum. It is up to councillors to set their own clear policy agendas and thereby ensure that there is no vacuum.

The corporate model (sometimes known as the joint elite model) has been developed in the light of perceived deficiencies in both the formal and technocratic models. It argues that policy making is dominated by a small group of senior councillors and officers. Blowers (1980, pp. 9–10) exemplifies this perspective:

> The power to make policy and take decisions is concentrated among a few leading officials and politicians. The interaction of these decision-makers, and the transmission of ideas and hopes and fears among them, reveals how power is exercised and to what purpose.

Numerous other studies have pointed to a similar 'joint elite' in places as diverse as Croydon, Lambeth and Newcastle upon Tyne. This model is very useful in distinguishing between senior councillors and officers and their more junior colleagues. This alliance of senior personnel is indeed very important in most authorities, but the model underplays the role of both junior councillors and junior officers, who can, on occasions, exercise influence. The corporate model also frequently presents leading councillors and officers as being a united and cohesive group, whereas in practice relationships are frequently characterised by tensions and strains.

Of the three models outlined above, the corporate model is widely recognised as the most useful but, as we have seen, like the other two, it has deficiencies. All three models shed some light on the distribution of policy influence inside local authorities. None is the last word on the subject.

The rest of this chapter looks at how the corporate model can be refined in order to provide a more realistic analysis. This is necessary because there is far more to an understanding of the distribution of power and influence than simply an analysis of the activities of the most senior personnel. In other words, the corporate model requires supplementing if a realistic picture of power relationships is to emerge. At the heart of the formal decision-making network is the committee system. This is discussed next, followed by an examination of other, non-elite influences upon policy making inside local authorities.

Box 8.2. *Some drawbacks of the committee system*

- Meetings are frequently deluged with detail; they should instead focus on deciding major or controversial issues.
- Insufficient attention is paid to following up previous decisions and monitoring performance.
- Committees take up the bulk of members' time, even though councillors believe that they should fulfil a wider representational role in addition to committee work.
- The value of time spent in formal committees is undermined in many cases by agreement on decisions in advance within a ruling party group.
- Committees can consume a large amount of management time, slow down decisions and duplicate each other's work.

Source: Audit Commission (1997, p. 3).

Broadening the debate

Committees are important arenas for decision making inside local authorities. They have many strengths: they open up decisions to public scrutiny and ensure that officers and contractors remain accountable for their performance. But, as Box 8.2 shows, there are also problems with the way the system currently operates.

One of the biggest problems is that of duplication. Even small decisions can take months to go through the network of committees and subcommittees, as Box 8.3 demonstrates.

Nevertheless, committees do provide back-bench councillors with a chance to influence policy, particularly when issues relate to their 'patch', that is, the ward or electoral division they represent. The corporate model ignores such back-bench intervention, which can occasionally be decisive. Without

Box 8.3. *Local authority committees – too cumbersome?*

In one council with decentralised offices, a relatively minor decision to change the structure – but not the overall cost – of the administrative staff was put to the neighbourhood services committee, cross-referred to the personnel committee and ultimately had to be ratified by the policy and resources committee. This process took some four months, with a total of thirty councillors spending time considering the matter – more than once in the case of those who were members of more than one of the committees concerned.

Source: Audit Commission (1997, p. 9).

wishing to exaggerate the influence of back-bench councillors, the committee, subcommittee and working party networks provide them with a means of influence which is on occasion utilised. Back-bench influence is occasional and specific but it does exist.

It is also important to recognise that the ruling party group as a whole, not simply its leading councillors, can have an important influence on policy making. Policy initiatives can and do emerge from the back-bench members of a party group; likewise, backbenchers can veto leadership proposals with which they disagree. Given the potential for factionalism within groups, a leadership can rarely take for granted the automatic support of all group members. In November 1995, for example, two majority group leaders – Stewart Foster in Leicester and Valerie Wise in Preston – were overthrown following votes of no confidence by their respective Labour groups.

A realistic model of policy influence also needs to incorporate inter-departmental tensions. Different departments (e.g. social services, treasurers', education, planning) represent different interests; at times of resource constraint, battles between them can be particularly intense. There are also professional rivalries – between, for example, the technical departments involved in land development: 'Planners, architects, housing managers, valuation officers and engineers all claim an involvement and there is a long history of rivalry between these professions' (Stoker, 1991, p. 102). Dominance of specific departments and professions will inevitably change over time; unacceptable policies will be delayed and favoured policies will be accelerated. Increased professionalisation within the local government service has meant that interdepartmental tensions are never far from the surface. They will spill over into the policy sphere with some regularity.

There is a further dimension – divisions *inside* individual departments. The size and diversity of many departments means that, in effect, the span of control a chief officer can exercise must be limited, thereby providing junior officers, often with greater technical knowledge by virtue of their more recent training, with scope for influence. For example, the planning and transportation department of Leicestershire County Council has the following eight major areas of responsibility: public transport services, traffic, road safety, highways, street lighting, environment, planning and waste regulation. The managers of such subunits can have a great deal of influence. To marginalise such officials is to undervalue their importance. They need to feature in any realistic model of policy influence inside local authorities.

There also needs to be a recognition of the dynamics created by a council being 'hung' or 'balanced' – those on which no single party has an overall majority of councillors. In 1979 one in seven councils was hung; by 1997/8 the figure was nearly one in three. This necessitates extensive interparty contact and negotiation. Bargaining becomes the order of the day because there is no elite of members from a single party who can be sure of delivering a policy programme. Leading councillors need to consult and secure the support of backbenchers before making alliances. Without such support collaborative arrangements cannot stick.

In hung councils senior officers have to assume different roles, working with and briefing spokespersons from several parties rather than just one. In 1998 in Leicestershire County Council, for example, Conservative, Labour and Liberal Democratic spokespersons were briefed before every committee meeting. In such circumstances officers can often perform a brokerage role, bringing the different parties together in order to negotiate a policy. On hung councils back-bench members can also find their position enhanced as in both committee and full council every vote can be precious.

Party politics

In the metropolitan areas of Britain, in most of the English counties and new unitary authorities and in the larger shire districts, there are fully developed party systems. Some 80 per cent of all councils fall into this category and because they include nearly all county and unitary councils they affect almost all British voters. Independent councils still survive but they are being inexorably squeezed, election after election.

Interestingly, despite its central importance, the party political dimension rarely features in diagrammatic representations of the organisation and working of councils. This is because it complicates an otherwise fairly straightforward picture of officers and departments servicing committees of councillors who make policy decisions which are then publicly approved in full council. In our earlier discussion we argued for a recognition of the importance of the whole party group (not only its leadership) in shaping policy. The majority group's manifesto becomes the council agenda. Councillors of the majority group will chair all committees and subcommittees. Each public committee meeting will usually be preceded by private pre-committee meetings of the different party groups, at which they determine their tactics: which issues they will focus on, who will speak to them, how they will vote. A hung council, on which there is no overall majority party, will (as we have seen) clearly operate differently in practice, but not in principle.

Whether or not one likes it, party politics at local level is not only here to stay, but has recently received a hefty boost with the spread of geographically larger unitary authorities. It provides the context within which decisions are made. The significance of party politics might not feature on formal policy-making charts inside local authorities, but its centrality is real enough. It must be recognised as such in any model of local policy making.

Fragmentation of decision making

While the centrality of the joint officer–councillor elite is not questioned, its exclusive dominance certainly is. This is because local authorities are political institutions – in both the narrowly partisan and broader senses of the word. They incorporate a whole range of additional actors and influences that can impinge on policy making, depending on an authority's traditions, culture, leadership, political balance and so on. In the real world the policy process is both complex and changeable.

That complexity has been exacerbated by the use of what we identified earlier as local governance and the consequent fragmentation of power and influence within local communities. Monolithic local authorities, controlling and managing the vast bulk of local policy making and public service delivery, are a thing of the past. As Hambleton reminds us (1997, p. 2): 'many of the public services which affect electors are now outside local democratic control. Health, training, urban regeneration and further education are among the services which are now the responsibility of appointed, rather than elected, bodies.' Consequently many major decisions about localities are made in private, by largely unknown board members. Hall and Weir (1996) identified some 5,166 quangos operating at local level. Box 8.4 lists the major players on the local pitch. Policy making within local

---

Box 8.4. *Players on the local pitch*

'There are all sorts of players on the local pitch jostling for positions where previously the council was the main game in town.' (Blair, 1998, p. 10)

Training and enterprise councils
Child protection committees
Health authorities
National Health Service trusts
Grant-maintained schools
Further education colleges
Police liaison committees
Police authorities
Fire authorities
Single regeneration budget partnerships
Probation committees
Drug action teams
Magistrates' courts committees
Development agencies
Joint planning committees
Joint consultative committees

Source: Blair (1998, p. 10).

communities increasingly incorporates these non-elected bodies. Models of local policy making must reflect this messy, non-elected universe. To focus solely on elected local government is to ignore an increasingly influential source of local policy.

In the same way, it is important to recognise that local authorities themselves have been increasingly constrained in their activities by central government during the period 1979–97. Financial pressure has been particularly severe. While there remains much innovation locally, it takes place in an increasingly constrained environment. The changing nature of central–local relations is an essential backdrop for any analysis of policy making inside local authorities. For enthusiasts of local autonomy the last twenty years have presented a depressing scenario of increasing central direction, which, they believe, threatens to undermine local democracy. There were signs in Labour's first fifteen months of office of a new era of cooperation beginning to emerge. In November 1997 a 'Concordat' setting out the principles of consultation was published. This delineated six major principles, including a promise to give local government greater authority and financial freedom. Hilary Armstrong sought to create a new, more meaningful, forum for central–local debate:

> Let us sweep away the formal, ritualistic gatherings of ministers and local government leaders which I think we all agree have become rather pointless affairs. We would like to replace these sessions with more coherent and constructive contacts on main service issues and finance.

Within the first fifteen months of the Blair government being in office, the Department of the Environment, Transport and the Regions launched discussions with the Local Government Association on more than twenty specific policy and service areas. There were also six consultation papers on local government reform:

1   local democracy and community leadership;
2   improving local services through best value;
3   business rates;
4   improving local financial accountability;
5   capital finance;
6   a new ethical framework.

The 1998 white paper further stimulated discussion. And to demonstrate its commitment to democratic local government, one of the government's first acts was to sign the European Charter of Local Self-Government. It subsequently ratified the Charter, which binds the UK government to safeguarding the basic rights of local authorities.

During the first fifteen months of the Labour government, therefore, local authorities were deluged with discussion documents, but the proclaimed spirit of partnership in central–local relations should not disguise the firmness of the government's demands for reform at local level. This was because the government saw local authorities as crucial agents for the implementation of its election pledges. Speaking of new policies on crime, jobs, health, education and transport, John Prescott argued: 'We can only deliver these pledges effectively with the cooperation and involvement of local government'. Hence the government's desire to see modernised, democratic and efficient local authorities.

Conclusion

Labour's 1997 manifesto promised that local decision making would be 'less constrained by central government' and once elected it emphasised the principle of meaningful dialogue with local authorities. As Hilary Armstrong promised local authorities:

> We are not just a new Government, we are a new type of Government. Our decisions will not be handed down from on high. We do not have a monopoly of wisdom and ideas. We want to hear your ideas and we want you to tell us what you think of ours.

At the same time, as we saw in the introduction, Tony Blair has made it clear that services will be transferred to voluntary bodies and business where individual local authorities are failing in terms of standards. In *Leading the Way* (1998, p. 22) he told local authorities, under the subheading 'If you change we'll reward':

> If you accept this challenge you can look forward to an enhanced role and new powers. If you are unwilling or unable to work to the modern agenda, then the government will have to look to other partners to take on your role.

In the new, fragmented world of local governance, effective policy making at local level appears to be the key to survival for elected local authorities. In the light of the 1998 white paper, directly elected mayors, executive cabinets and more streamlined local administrations are likely to emerge. More important, however, for the long-term health of local government is whether participation is widened and democratic renewal takes root.

Reading

Audit Commission (1997) *Representing the People: The Role of Councillors*, Audit Commission Publications.

Blair, T. (1998) *Leading the Way: A New Vision for Local Government*, Institute for Public Policy Research.

Blowers, A. (1980) *The Limits of Power*, Pergamon.

Department of the Environment, Transport and the Regions (1998) *Modernising Local Government: Local Democracy and Community Leadership*, HMSO.

Game, C. and Leach, S. (1996) 'Political parties and local democracy', in L. Pratchett and D. Wilson (eds), *Local Democracy and Local Government*, Macmillan, pp. 27–49.

Hall, W. and Weir, S. (1996) *The Untouchables*, Democratic Audit, Paper 8.

Hambleton, R. (ed.) (1997) *New Perspectives on Local Governance*, Joseph Rowntree Foundation.

Leach, S. and Stoker, G. (1997) 'Understanding the Local Government Review: a retrospective analysis', *Public Administration*, Vol. 75, pp. 1–20.

Lowndes, V. (1998) *The Future of Central/Local Government Relations: Rebuilding Trust?*, Local Government Management Board.

Stoker, G. (1991) *The Politics of Local Government* (2nd edn), Macmillan.

Stoker, G. and King, D. (eds) (1996) *Rethinking Local Democracy*, Macmillan.

Wilson D. (1996) 'The Local Government Commission: examining the consultative process', *Public Administration*, Vol. 74, pp. 199–219.

Wilson, D. and Game, C. (1998) *Local Government in the United Kingdom* (2nd edn), Macmillan.

9

The education issue: raising the standard or beating the retreat?

Lynton Robins

Britain's education system is in a state of near crisis. And, furthermore, there is nothing new in this, since the crisis goes back a long way into the history of state education. For example, the Schools Inquiry Royal Commission which reported in 1868 revealed that the standards found in British schools were far inferior to those found in European schools. Much the same story has been repeated time and time again by other royal commissions, government inquiries, Her Majesty's Inspectorate as well as by independent and academic surveys of one type or another. In this respect the wide-ranging authoritative report published in 1992 by the Organization for Economic Cooperation and Development contained no surprises. For there, at the bottom of the international league table on educational spending but at the top of the league table with highest pupil–teacher ratios, was Britain. Somewhat similar findings emerged from a 1997 international survey of standards in maths and science.

This chapter examines the politics of educational failure which have cast Britain in its by now familiar role of a poor performer in this policy area. It begins with a consideration of the different philosophies and practices which have competed for political support in the battle to raise standards, includes a discussion of a new consensus on education and concludes with an examination of some contradictions found in current policy.

The position of the educational left

The 1944 Education Act – the so-called 'Butler Act' – was a milestone in the history of British education which promised to make good the educational deficiencies revealed in wartime Britain. The Act was summed up in a slogan, 'education for all', and it was widely anticipated that the new system of secondary education being introduced would cater equally for the needs of all pupils and thereby bring about a general improvement in standards.

139

But today this Act is viewed to have been something of a failure insofar as it was never fully implemented, and those areas which were implemented had a negative impact on many children. Looking back at this important Act today, it is perhaps surprising that its author had little to say on either the purpose of education or the content of what should be taught, and that the Act was based on such basic and simplistic ideas about children's intelligence.

What were the principal faults of the Butler Act? Although the Act reorganised the administrative structure – reducing the number of local education authorities (LEAs) to 146, raising the school-leaving age to fifteen and establishing the first Minister for Education – its implementation reinforced the social and educational divisions which already existed in society. Educational thinking at the time tended to categorise children into three broad types, and the Norwood report of 1943 reflected this in recommending the establishment of three kinds of secondary schools:

1   secondary grammar schools for children 'who loved learning for its own sake';
2   secondary technical schools for children who 'delighted in applied science and applied art';
3   secondary modern schools for children who 'dealt more easily in concrete things than ideas'.

In the event, few secondary technical schools were ever built and so a bipartite system took shape during the postwar years in which an examination – the 'eleven plus' – decided which pupils would go on to grammar schools and which to secondary modern schools. Needless to say, secondary modern and grammar schools were not seen by parents, teachers, pupils or employers as being of equal status. Grammar schools had acquired a high prestige because of their strong links with higher education and the professions. But there were not enough grammar school places for all who wanted them, since only 20 per cent of eleven-year-olds could ever be successful in winning places. This meant that the education system had the undesirable effect of 'failing' 80 per cent of the nation's pupils who, at eleven, would be moving from their primary schools to secondary moderns.

It came to be of increasing concern that the divisions between grammar and secondary modern reinforced those damaging class divisions already found in society. Children from middle-class homes succeeded disproportionately in passing the eleven plus while children from working-class homes made up the vast majority of those who failed the eleven plus. Even those working-class pupils who did pass the eleven plus and were selected for grammar schools tended to do less well, once there, than their middle-class peers.

A loose grouping of liberal-minded Conservatives in central government, including Sir Edward Boyle as Education Minister, and some LEAs and others on the left campaigned for reforms which would remove the divisions of status, opportunity and social class caused by the operation of the eleven plus. The slogan of the 1944 Act, 'education for all', was reworded into 'comprehensive education for all'. With time, however, the case for comprehensive schooling became much more closely associated with the egalitarianism of the left and Labour than with the one-nation Toryism of Boyle and like-minded political colleagues.

It was argued that the establishment of a system of comprehensive education would result in a general raising of education standards. It was argued that the social selection effect of the eleven plus, with its early labelling of 'success' for the few and 'failure' for the many, resulted in the underachievement of the majority. Thus an educational reform which removed the cause of this social division would result in a general raising of standards. The establishment of comprehensive schools promised to do just this, since entry would be open to all social classes and not depend upon the outcome of selection. The end result was that no pupils would be labelled as educational failures and consequently be held back at the very outset of their secondary schooling.

Expectations about the impact of comprehensive schools were set high by their supporters. While the old system of grammar schools and secondary moderns represented a society divided by social class, the new comprehensive schools seemed to promise a classless society. This sort of thinking went further, with ideological comprehensivists arguing that an egalitarian education meant more than just abandoning the eleven plus. The practice of streaming pupils into different classes based on measures of 'ability' should be dropped also, since this led to divisions within schools which were just as undesirable as the old divisions between schools. Streamed classes, it was proposed, should be replaced by 'mixed ability teaching'. If schools did offer a view of future society, then many assumed that 'open schools' represented by comprehensives would produce the sort of 'open society' desired by many on the political left.

Education has always been used as a political tool, of course, even by those who profess the wish to keep politics out of education. During the 1960s there was a view on the left that not only institutional reforms but the organisation of the educational process itself – the curriculum – could be designed in ways which would bring about social and political goals. In other words, things such as 'classroom climate', the teaching methods employed, the arrangements of tables and chairs and even the design of the room itself could result in very different educational experiences, which, in turn, could shape distinct political orientations. It was argued, for example, that in the traditional classroom where the teacher is the only expert in the subject, the pupils end up depending on him or her. They play a largely silent and passive role in class, either writing notes or copying dictation. When pupils do speak or act, it is only in response to questions or requests initiated by the teacher. The position of the teacher, facing and in charge of the class, reinforces the impression of a division between one active person controlling the affairs of the, largely obedient, others. Power relations reflect those found in an elitist society.

On the other hand, a progressive teacher might organise the class to work together in groups on a project. This would mean that the teacher no longer claims to be an expert, since the projects usually cross a number of academic disciplines. The teacher, as 'manager of the learning process', learns alongside his or her pupils as an equal in the discovery of knowledge. Through cooperation with each other, members of the class discover knowledge for themselves and develop a wide range of educational skills. Much conversation and action are initiated by the pupils. Thus the class learns the value of cooperating rather than simply the rewards of individual effort, and the teacher is part of this interaction since he or she is not separated from the pupils by the status proffered by an academic discipline. Unlike the situation in the traditional class, here the entire ethos of the class is open, democratic and participatory.

How did the comprehensive experiment fare? There is a view that the growth of comprehensive schools together with the adoption of more progressive teaching methods failed both politically and educationally. First, there was never a glimmer of hope that 'open' comprehensive schools would contribute to the creation of an open society. Pupils left middle-class suburban and working-class inner-city comprehensives as divided in many ways as if they had taken the eleven plus, with the children from different backgrounds moving from school to their preordained roles in society. Secondly, neither the new comprehensives nor the new teaching methods had resulted in raising educational standards. The radical right drew attention to the defects of state schools in well publicised Black Papers, written by academics, which criticised progressive education methods.

The question of falling standards was central in a speech made by Labour Prime Minister James Callaghan in 1976. This speech, made at Ruskin College, Oxford, marked the opening of the great education debate in Britain, with the Prime Minister's doubts and concerns raising considerable anxiety in parents, teachers and employers. In this new, more fluid, situation '"Realistic" and morally conservative parents were allied with business interests against "irresponsible" teachers and educationists' (Johnson, 1991). A reconstruction of education, in which the radical right was to play a crucial role, was now under way.

The position of the educational right

During the 1970s the left had voiced much disappointment with the working of the education system, but looking back this played into the hands of an increasingly vocal right wing in education. The left, it was argued, had had its chance and blown it – now it was the turn of the radical right to tackle Britain's crisis in education. The radical right, influential in shaping Conservative economic thinking during the 1970s, was also determined to shape the Party's policy on education. Influential contributions to the great education debate came in the form of the Black Papers, and publications from the Hillgate Group, the Adam Smith Institute and the Institute for Economic Affairs.

These groups were not in full agreement about what was wrong with education nor over how it should be put right, but generally speaking they agreed that education had fallen under the control of 'producers' (teachers, unions, LEAs) and needed to be put under the control of 'consumers' (parents, pupils, employers). Thus the central thrust behind proposals from the radical right concerned ways of creating a market-led system in education. Consequently, a twin-track strategy developed which aimed to reduce the influence of vested interests while enhancing the role played by education's customers. The right supported policies which reduced the influence of the teaching profession, through measures such as the abolition of the Schools Council, as well as curbing local authority influence, by providing opportunities to opt out of LEA control and by total abolition, as in the case of the progressively minded Inner London Education Authority. At the same time, proposals to increase the role played by parents were crucial in right-wing policy making. It was argued that parents should be given as much choice as possible about the schools their children attended. And, furthermore, parents could make informed choices only if they had more information about the academic performance of individual schools than was currently available. Armed with information and the ability to choose, parents would send their children to 'good' schools, which would prosper. Poor schools would then be forced to improve so as to attract more pupils in the future or otherwise face the prospect of further decline. As Ranson (1990) states:

> For consumers to fulfil their allotted role as quality controllers in the market place they require some diversity of product, information about the scope of choice and the quality of performance, as well as the opportunity to choose. If schools were made to respond to the market 'there would be a built-in mechanism to raise standards and change forms and types of education in accordance with that market demand'.

He continued to elaborate the argument with a quotation from Sexton:

> 'In short, it supposes that the wisdom of parents separately and individually exercised but taken together becoming the collective wisdom is more likely to achieve higher standards more quickly and more acceptably to the public than the collective wisdom of the present bureaucrats, no matter how well meaning those bureaucrats may be.' (Quoted in Flude and Hammer, 1990)

One of the most popular proposals for increasing parental choice among the right was the introduction of education vouchers. A voucher-based scheme for the provision of pre-five nursery education was eventually implemented for a brief period running up to the 1997 general election. It was not judged to be a success, since primary schools dominated the voucher market, leading to the closure of many pre-schools (play groups), which resulted in less choice being available for parents.

Some educational thinkers on the radical right believed that education needed a reinjection of moral purpose and national pride. It was argued that during the 1960s the purpose of education had been subverted to the cause of social engineering from the true path of traditional education. Child-centred teaching methods, and new subjects on the timetable, especially those which embraced 'multiculturalism', should be dropped in favour of a traditional curriculum.

The key Conservative Acts

Many of the themes and ideas developed by the radical right can be detected in contemporary education policy. But it would be misleading to recognise the Education Acts of 1980, 1986 and 1988 as direct legislative expressions of 'new right' thinking.

The 1980 Education (No. 2) Act

This Act introduced the assisted places scheme, which was designed to allow a relatively small number of parents on modest incomes to send their children to private schools. This measure was consistent with a policy of increasing parental choice, although its critics saw it simply as a way of subsidising the private sector from the public purse. The Act also gave parents using state sector schools greater choice over which school their children would attend, by obliging LEAs to 'make arrangements for parents to prioritise the schools they wanted their children to attend and LEAs had a duty to comply with these preferences unless it would prejudice the provision of efficient education' (Savage and Robins, 1990).

The 1986 Education (No. 2) Act

The central purpose of this Act was to reduce the role of LEAs in the running of schools. It provided for more parent governors on school governing bodies which, with other changes, reduced the number of local authority governors to a minority position. The Act provided that each school governing body should consist of equal numbers of LEA nominees and parent governors, together with a few teacher governors and governors representing the community, the business community in particular. The Act extended the responsibilities of governors into areas of curriculum concern, and the 'theory was that if governing bodies could be made more important and made accountable to the parents this would enhance parent power' (Savage and Robins, 1990).

The 1988 Education Reform Act

This Act specified that a national curriculum be taught to pupils until they reached the age of sixteen. A core curriculum would include English, maths and science, together with seven foundation subjects – history, geography, technology, art, music, physical education and a foreign language. Religious education would also be taught as well as certain cross-curricular themes. The Act also introduced the national testing of pupils at four key stages of seven, eleven, fourteen and sixteen years old. The Act abolished the Inner London Education Authority and weakened the position of local authorities generally, by creating grant-maintained schools, directly financed by the Department of Education and Science. Parents of children at an eligible school could vote for it to opt out; having once opted out, a school could never 'opt back'. The Act also introduced local management of schools in order to improve the quality of management as well as making schools more responsive to 'customer' needs.

Choice and diversity

Under the premiership of John Major, Conservative education policy moved towards greater selectivity and tougher school inspections. In the worst cases, new 'hit squads' would take over failing schools. A 1992 white paper, *Choice and Diversity*, proposed a further weakening of local authority control by extending market principles: greater specialisation and subject diversity should be available, new arrangements would make opting out easier and a new funding agency for schools would assume what were once local authority responsibilities. In the run-up to the 1997 general election John Major declared that he would like to see 'a grammar school in every town', a policy stand which embarrassed Labour since much publicity surrounded Tony Blair's son attending a selective school in preference to his local one. As the election approached, the possibility of selection to primary schools was also on the Conservative agenda.

Labour in office

Labour's manifesto pledged 'zero tolerance of underperformance' in schools, which would be achieved through policies which accepted most of the

Conservatives' agenda. School tests would be retained and expanded with new baseline assessments, new school targets would be implemented and modified league tables would continue to be available to the public. Labour would retain the services of the controversial Chief Inspector of Schools, Chris Woodhead, who had aligned himself with the Conservatives' back-to-basics drive on traditional teaching methods. New Labour now accepted whole-class teaching, an hour a day in primary schools being devoted to basic literacy and numeracy, and fast-track streaming for the brightest pupils in secondary schools. Mixed-ability teaching methods, once popular with the progressive left, were now shunned by Labour. While Labour did not embrace Conservative ambitions on greater selectivity, the Party accepted that schools should offer greater specialisation. Of course, specialisation may involve an element of selection.

A Labour white paper, *Excellence in Schools*, continued to echo previous Conservative themes. In a move reminiscent of the Conservative idea of 'hit squads', Labour proposed that teams of elite teachers should be 'parachuted' in to run failing schools; Ofsted inspections would continue, although with longer periods for schools between inspections; and, finally, echoing Chris Woodhead's claim that 15,000 teachers were incompetent, Labour proposed establishing simpler procedures for dismissing poor teachers. Local authorities were not to regain the ground lost during the Thatcher–Major years. Opted out schools would continue as before but with grant-maintained status being replaced by an as yet undefined 'foundation' status.

It was only in the detail that the major parties differed. Labour was committed to a gradual phasing out of the assisted places scheme in order to fund smaller primary class sizes and to ending the nursery voucher scheme. The former involved a small minority of parents, and the latter a scheme which had been in place for only a matter of months. Labour's policy, like that of the Conservatives before it, was to continue the upward drive on standards without committing significant additional resources. As before, the pressure was on teachers to deliver the stricter education targets, with blame firmly attached to them should the policy fail.

Conclusion

What has been the impact of these dramatic changes on the education system? Rhodes has observed that the impact of policy can differ markedly from legislative intent and the sheer volume of legislation on education suggests that there will be examples of a gap between policy aspiration and operation. This concluding section examines areas in which policy has been counterproductive, risking a decline in standards.

Finance, good teachers and high standards

Devolving financial responsibility has resulted in some teachers being declared redundant. Since experienced teachers are the most expensive to employ, they are often the most vulnerable in terms of job security. Inexperienced teachers, even unqualified teachers, are cheaper and from a managerial point of view it makes sense to employ teachers at the lowest cost available. The importance of money to the running of any institution cannot be denied, but under financial delegation there are dangers that schools can become obsessed about fund-raising. Indeed, the 'good teacher' has been redefined by some cash-hungry heads as 'good fund-raisers' rather than individuals with classroom skills. Wallace (1990) explains how income generation takes over the life of a school:

> schools will put all income together, whether from the local authority, parents or local businesses, and regard them as one. It will be only on the private fund-raising side that increases can be 'earned', so that such activities will become more important. Fund-raising is likely to become a major activity. Some schools already raise more money privately than they receive from public funds for books, stationery and small equipment.

The policy of classroom testing, with results leading to the publication of school league tables, was challenged by all the major teaching unions. According to teachers, this policy undermined the quality of teaching since the new system operated in ways which were over-bureaucratic and over-complex, as well as producing results which were misleading. Indeed, a primary teacher with a class of thirty-five pupils was expected to make 8,000 assessment judgements in a year, a situation in which testing assumed as great an importance as teaching in terms of classroom priorities. After a threatened teachers' boycott of tests, the Conservatives then Labour accepted the need for more straightforward tests and less misleading league tables, which should be manageable without distorting normal schooling. However, recent research has revealed that publicly available results on the standard assessment tasks (SATs), intended to help inform parents' choice of primary schools, remain flawed, for summer-born children remain disadvantaged throughout the primary stage of schooling. What may appear as a better school to parents is one which simply has more autumn-born children on roll than its local rivals.

Secondary-school league tables can be equally misleading and actually work against the interests of less academically able pupils. Where schools are in stiff competition for pupils, some now prevent the less able from sitting public examinations so that their lower results will not dilute the school's league table average. Other schools have been tempted to 'dumb down' 'A'-level entries, even for the more able pupils, in the cause of improving their league table position, by redirecting students from 'hard' to 'soft' subjects. For example, in 1996–7 'A'-level entries to 'hard' economics declined by 15 per cent from the previous year, while entries to 'soft' business studies rose by a similar amount.

The denigration of teachers

It has been calculated that around an additional 100,000 teachers are needed in Britain's primary schools if pupils are to reach the same educational standard as pupils in Singapore or South Korea. The continual pressure on teachers to raise standards, to accept a greater administrative load and to be the focus for blame and criticism when policy fails has led to a collapse in teacher morale. As a profession, fewer want to join and more wish to leave. An advertising campaign attempted to reverse the 11 per cent drop in teacher training numbers in 1997, while restricted access to pensions had to be imposed to prevent a mass exodus of middle-aged teachers from schools.

The inevitable consequence of these employment patterns within the profession is either an increase in class sizes or the employment of retired, unqualified or semi-qualified staff to fill the vacancies. Neither measure holds much promise regarding raising standards.

The Ofsted inspection system is more combative than that of Her Majesty's Inspectorate of the past. But does a stricter system necessarily raise standards? Teachers are put under considerable stress, with Ofsted inspectors rating their abilities on a one-to-seven scale in ways which are unimaginable for doctors, lawyers or business people. Furthermore, Ofsted can actually damage the quality of education, as described in this account of the inspection process:

> A school may have up to a year's warning of an inspection.... During the preparatory period, schools tend to concentrate on perfecting their paperwork and management rather than their teaching methods. The pupils may be regarded almost as an irritant. There are stories of schools cancelling extra-curricular activities, including Christmas plays and concerts because an inspection was imminent. And once the inspection is over ... exhausted teachers think they can relax and a great many videos hit the classrooms. (Wilby and Griffith, 1997)

There can be no denying that policies developed during the Thatcher and Major administrations, continued in caricature by New Labour, have put education standards high on the political agenda. But without the commitment of significant additional resources for more attractive salaries and improved classroom facilities, such policies seem doomed to failure. The conditionally promised 5.1 per cent annual increase for education spending from 1999 to 2000 contained in Labour's comprehensive spending review seems insufficient to raise standards beyond a marginal improvement. First, any such increases will follow in the wake of a two-year freeze on spending at Conservative levels and, secondly, any substantial increases will depend upon the economy performing well. Furthermore, Labour's New Deal initiative to utilise the unemployed as classroom aides is little more than a reincarnation of earlier Conservative proposals to put a 'mums' army' into schools, a move designed to improve adult/pupil ratios at low cost. Without sufficient qualified, well rewarded and motivated teachers in adequately resourced schools, the pattern of poor educational standards compared with our trading rivals, noted in 1868, seems set for the foreseeable future.

Reading

Bash, L. and Coulby, D. (eds) (1989) *The Education Reform Act: Competition and Control*, Cassel.

Flude, M. and Hammer, M. (eds) (1990) *The Education Reform Act 1988: Its Origins and Implications*, Falmer Press.

Johnson, R. (1991) 'A new road to serfdom? A critical history of the 1988 Act', in Education Group II, *Education Limited: Schooling, Training and the New Right in England since 1979*, Unwin Hyman.

McVicar, M. (1990) 'Education policy: education as a business?', in S. P. Savage and L. Robins (eds), *Public Policy under Thatcher*, Macmillan.

Ranson, S. (1990) 'From 1944 to 1988: education, citizenship and democracy', in M. Flude and M. Hammer (eds), *The Education Reform Act 1988: Its Origins and Implications*, Falmer Press.

Savage, S. P. and Robins, L. (eds) (1990) *Public Policy under Thatcher*, Macmillan.

Wallace, R. (1990) 'The Act and local authorities', in M. Flude and M. Hammer (eds), *The Education Reform Act 1988: Its Origins and Implications*, Falmer Press.

Whitty, G. (1990) 'The new right and the national curriculum: state control or market forces?', in M. Flude and M. Hammer (eds), *The Education Reform Act 1988: Its Origins and Implications*, Falmer Press.

Wilby, P. and Griffith, L. (1997) 'On closer inspection', *New Statesman*, 31 January.

10

The politics of health

Bruce Wood

The nature of the health issue

Health is always high on the political agenda. Whether the issue of the day be 'mad cow disease', long waits for treatment, hospital closures, nurses' pay, the latest medical research findings, or faults in the screening of cervical smears, the Secretary of State for Health is rarely far from political controversy in a country where both the media and political responsibility for provision of health services are highly centralised.

Britons cherish their National Health Service (NHS). Pollsters have, ever since its establishment in 1948, found the NHS to be one of the country's two most popular institutions, usually second only to the royal family in the public's affections. Its core objectives – the provision to anyone, regardless of their social or economic status, of free health care on the basis of clinical need – are supported by all the main political parties. This bipartisanship meant that for the first forty years of the NHS the politics of health centred on what may be called micro issues (detailed and usually temporary, even if regular): disputes about abortion policy, water fluoridation, doctors' and nurses' pay, the standards of care in large long-stay mental hospitals, outbreaks of meningitis or food poisoning, and so on – and views about such issues crossed party lines most of the time. Hence at successive general elections health played a minor role in the campaign: it was in a sense a 'non-issue' because it did not appear to any party to be a vote winner.

From the early 1980s this began to change. The Thatcher governments of 1979–90 introduced a series of changes to the role, structure and management of the NHS, with their final 1989 radical reforms being implemented by the successor Major governments of 1990–7. The 1997 Blair government then introduced comprehensive proposals of its own. The politics of health became a macro (fundamental) issue of structure and purpose: the whole organisation and role of the NHS were, or appeared to be, up for analysis, review and reform.

150

Or not, as it transpired, because all governments of the period decided that it was politically expedient to work within the traditional core objectives of the NHS and to continue to fund the service from general taxation. This decision, a reflection of public esteem for the NHS (most notably recognised when Prime Minister Thatcher abandoned any thoughts of privatisation and declared the Service to be 'safe with us'), affected the politics of health. It meant that reform proposals focused on the organisational structure of the NHS rather than on its financial basis, and that political debate centred on managerial issues of efficiency, effectiveness and economy. The macro politics of health consequently have been defined by politicians narrowly, so as to exclude the two fundamental underlying issues of how much the state should spend on health care and how best to ration health services. As this chapter shows, these fundamental macro issues remain under the surface and have not gone away: managerial structural reforms have failed to resolve them.

The complex politics of health: everyone wants more

The above picture of health politics focuses on the major political parties and their leading spokespersons. It implies that the politics of health are best characterised as essentially open and public. But this is to oversimplify and to mislead: the politics of health, crises apart, are in reality both far more complex and a far more private process than that.

In Britain, as in all developed countries, health care is big. We spend as a nation almost as much on it as we do on food (between £15 and £20 a week). The NHS alone employs around one million people and to them must be added the tens of thousands who work in the pharmaceutical industry and for manufacturers and distributors of health equipment (from beds and bedpans to computers and body scanners) used in NHS offices, clinics and hospitals. Significant numbers of people also work in the small private health insurance and hospital and clinic sector. We use or consume a lot of health care, going to the general practitioner (GP) on average about five times a year and leaving with some nine prescriptions. We are hospitalised at great cost several times in our (average) lives. We are vaccinated as children and women have regular cervical smear and mammogram screenings.

This enormous range of activity inevitably spawns political and politico-administrative organisations. The NHS workforce is largely unionised, and more than forty separate trades unions are involved. Doctors (through the British Medical Association) and dentists (through the British Dental Association) have notoriously powerful national organisations and the medical specialties are largely self-regulated through a series of royal colleges (of physicians, of surgeons, of GPs, etc.). Then there are well over 200 patients' groups supporting those with specific diseases and illnesses (Alzheimer's Disease Society, National Asthma Campaign, etc.), 400 hospital leagues of friends, hundreds of local and national charities raising funds for equipment and research, and a network of official community health councils, all seeking to further the interests of patients and consumers. Suppliers of medical equipment and technology have their trade associations, of which the Association of British Pharmaceutical Industries is probably the best known and most influential as it campaigns for increased spending on prescription drugs on grounds of cost-effectiveness through preventing expensive hospitalisation.

The NHS itself has some 500 health authorities and NHS trusts (both with boards appointed by ministers) and thousands of GP and dental practices responsible locally for service provision. Its organisational hierarchy of management includes regional offices and the national NHS Executive, based in Leeds. National associations abound – of finance officers, of directors of public health and of authorities and trusts through the NHS Confederation. Politically, there are special-interest groups of MPs within each main party and on a cross-party basis: their scope ranges from the general to the highly specific (the All-Party Skin Committee monitors dermatitis and related diseases, for example). The Health Select Committee is the House of Commons' main investigatory body, monitoring the work of ministers and the NHS. Ministers are also advised by a range of official politico-administrative bodies, the most prominent of which include the Audit Commission and the Mental Health Act Commissioners. To sum up, the NHS exemplifies what may be termed 'government by agency', or 'quango-land', meaning government by a complex array of semi-autonomous appointed organisations.

Consider carefully the list of bodies in the two previous paragraphs. At first they appear to be very different, with some providing health care, some paying for it, some monitoring it and some setting quality standards. Some are political, some managerial; others are expert organisations and others again are consumer bodies. Potentially, there is plenty of scope for conflict between them: a patient group may want GPs to change their treatment patterns; hospital doctors may seek changes from the NHS trust which employs them; and so on. The politics of health centres around this potentially endemic conflict and the balance of power and influence is ever changing, particularly in the case of matters described earlier as micro issues.

Now consider an alternative analysis of these same bodies. In very different ways they all almost always want more. Patient groups seek better facilities and treatments; health sector unions higher pay; local health authorities larger budgets from the Secretary of State (who in turn presses the Chancellor of the Exchequer for a bigger allocation in the budget); and doctors press NHS trusts for state-of-the-art equipment, for example. The politics of health can now be portrayed as one of a battle for resources, with central government under constant siege from all sides. The late Enoch Powell, Minister of Health 1960–3, summed his experience up thus in his 1966 memoirs: 'one of the most striking features of the NHS is the continual deafening chorus of complaint which rises night and day from every part of it'. The macro issue of funding is at the heart of the politics of health and the intensity of pressure for resources suggests that many demands are unsuccessful. Hence the second and related macro question of rationing results.

Fifty years ago the founding fathers of the NHS did not foresee this. They believed that once the initial backlog of treatments was completed the health of the nation would be better and demands on the NHS would stabilise or even reduce. How very wrong they were! Their crystal balls were doubly defective. They failed to anticipate the emergence of 'new' illnesses, diseases, or treatable conditions (some genuinely new, others not previously diagnosed or not thought to be a matter for doctors). And they did not foresee the explosion of technology which has transformed health care, and which will continue to do so, not least through genetic research as well as new drug regimes. To illustrate, a handful of examples is listed in Table 10.1, with the invitation to extend both lists to several times this length.

Table 10.1. *'New' illnesses and treatments, 1948–98: some examples*

Illnesses	Treatments
Alzheimer's disease	Heart bypass operation
AIDS	Hip, knee, shoulder joint replacement
Asbestosis	Hormone replacement therapy
Drug addiction	Hospice care
Gulf War syndrome (under investigation)	*In-vitro* fertilisation
Legionnaire's disease	Organ transplant
Repetitive strain injury	Betaferon (new drug for multiple sclerosis)

Within only two years the assumptions of 1948 were found wanting. To its acute embarrassment, the 1945–50 Labour government found it necessary to curtail demand by breaching one of its founding principles and imposing prescription charges. The 'free' service was no more, and Nye Bevan (the minister responsible for creating the NHS in 1948), unable to accept this change of policy, resigned. Rationing had begun.

Government as a rationer of health-care services

Rationing had actually begun from the outset, and the 1950 prescription charges incident merely introduced an additional and a third method of containing or restricting the demand for NHS services. These three early devices, listed below, remain central to rationing fifty years later. The first two resulted from bruising and lengthy negotiations between Nye Bevan and the medical profession. In exchange for retaining their 'clinical freedom', the doctors had agreed to exercise this professional autonomy over clinical diagnosis and treatment within the constraints of fixed budgets for the NHS. That, and the inevitable consequence of waiting lists as demand and need outstripped the supply of resources, was acceptable to Bevan because there was no incompatibility with the egalitarian principle of treatment according to medical condition and need. Charges, however, were different: the Bevanites argued that even with means-testing there would be some inequity and the possibility that some patients would be deterred from seeking needed medical treatment.

Thus the three main rationing devices in the NHS were:

1   *Clinical freedom within political controls over budgets and staff numbers.* The total NHS budget was fixed centrally by government and allocated to local health authorities and other service providers. Numbers of hospital consultants and GPs were regulated nationally, on a locality basis, as well as through budgetary allocations.
2   *Waiting for treatment.* The numbers waiting for non-urgent hospital treatment reached half a million in the 1950s and have been above one million throughout the 1990s. The 'average' wait is currently about four months. There can also be waits for outpatient appointments with specialists, with GPs playing an important role by acting as 'gatekeepers' to specialist care.
3   *Charges for services.* Prescription and dental charges have been continuously in place since the 1950s. They were heavily increased by the Thatcher and Major governments, and in the 1980s new charges for eye and dental check-ups were introduced.

Political debate often revolves around semantics and the politics of rationing is an outstanding exemplar of this as successive governments have always sought to avoid using or even recognising the term. They prefer instead to employ phrases such as 'priority setting', 'cost-effectiveness' or 'the efficient and effective use of resources' as the Blair government put it in its 1997 policy statement *The New NHS: Modern, Dependable*. In a typical incident earlier in the 1990s the then Secretary of State for Health, Virginia Bottomley, once refused point-blank to speak at a major national conference simply because 'rationing' was in the overall conference title and she claimed not to recognise its existence. Yet the central precept of rationing, that the state cannot afford to provide a free, open-ended, demand-led health service, has never been in dispute. There has always had to be some form (or forms) of rationing.

This line of thinking is certainly not uniquely British. Across the whole of the developed world, the costs of health care have risen much faster than the general rate of inflation. Though Britain is unusual in having almost all of its health care provided directly by the state, in every other country the state is also a large-scale spender on health services and so cost-containment policies have been sought worldwide. Once these get beyond the inevitable initial drive to cut waste and administrative costs (always politically popular) they equally inevitably constitute rationing.

Structural reforms: ducking the real macro issues?

The attraction to all governments of focusing attention on organisational structures and management processes is clear. These symbolise red tape and this unpopular image makes them a popular target, suitable for reform through legislation. Reforms can then be used to claim that problems have been successfully tackled. Just as important, the debate can be limited so as to sidestep political minefields. In the case of the politics of health, this means avoiding the potentially insoluble issues of spending and rationing.

Hence the Thatcher and Major governments created new actors, new processes and new institutions in a series of reforms designed to revolutionise the NHS by strengthening its management and by operating it through a market-type system of buyers and sellers of health services. In the 1980s they introduced general managers (later styled chief executives) in each local health authority, based on the business model of operating large concerns, having first commissioned a 1983 report by Roy Griffiths, the managing director of Sainsbury's supermarkets. This was to replace a style of decision making known officially as 'consensus management', with unclear lines of responsibility, and it was widely perceived as a threat to the traditional professional autonomy of doctors in particular. The new general manager posts attracted many private sector applicants and later in the decade people from business backgrounds were increasingly appointed as non-executive and (very) part-time members of the boards of local health authorities. The historic public service ethos and culture of the NHS began to change under these two developments, neither of which required legislation because governments have discretionary powers to undertake many administrative moves.

Structural reform followed with the 1989 white paper *Working for Patients*, enacted into law in 1990. The key change was the separation of the purchasing of health care from its provision, both functions having previously been undertaken by district health authorities (DHAs). The DHAs were retained as purchasers while new NHS trusts became providers of hospital and community health services, with GPs continuing to provide primary health care. The aim was to introduce an 'internal market' whereby trusts competed with one another for contracts and DHAs searched for value for money in a way that they previously had not when, in effect, purchasing from themselves. Another institutional change created a further set of purchasers: groups of GPs could obtain 'GP fund-holder' status and a budget of their own to spend on trusts' services. By 1997 some 50 per cent of the 30,000 GPs had chosen to do so, adding to the appearance of lots of buyers and sellers operating a market system.

Naturally, given that spending and rationing were deliberately excluded from political discussion, this was all dressed up as the way to enhance efficiency and effectiveness. It reflected Conservative Party beliefs in the superiority of markets over self-regulated state provision. The rhetoric was of devolution of power to the new health authorities, GP fund-holders and trusts. At the same time, however, steps were taken to strengthen the central state. Parallel changes saw the extension of the Audit Commission's remit to the NHS (the Commission had been undertaking influential value-for-money studies in local government, based on the concept of the three 'E's – economy, efficiency and effectiveness – since the early 1980s) and the bolstering of the NHS Executive as the national body responsible to the Secretary of State for overall performance. A leading academic analyst, Professor Rudolf Klein, has described these changes as indicative of 'government anxious to centralise credit [but] to decentralise to disclaim blame' (1995, p. 127). Hierarchical control alongside budgetary control was designed to sidestep the macro political issues of spending and rationing, and additional spending on the NHS in the early years of the new market system helped too.

In a classic market-based system, customers (patients) can be expected to play an important role. The new NHS market did not give them individual purchasing power: this role was to be carried out for them by collective bodies – DHAs and GP fund-holders. Hence the frequently invoked term 'quasi-market' to describe it. However, patients' rights and expectations were deliberately raised through the publication of both the Patient's Charter and so-called league tables, annually, of hospitals' activities (officially entitled performance indicators). It was anticipated that this would result in improved service quality: one consequence of providing patients and potential patients with such information would be enhanced competition between providers. The Charter and league tables were also used by the central state as directives to local provider trusts: no patient to wait for an operation for more than two years; attention within five minutes of arrival at accident and emergency departments, and so on – with bad publicity resulting from failure.

Though avoided as much as possible during the reform process, the issue of rationing soon emerged, and in a more explicit way than under the old NHS system, whereby clinical decisions were left to doctors. Contracts between DHA purchasers and NHS trust providers had to specify the volume of care. By 1995 research studies were showing up instances of individual DHAs deciding no longer to purchase certain services such as tattoo removal or sterilisation reversal. The definition of exactly what constituted the basket of NHS 'health care' services seemed to vary from place to place, publicly and in ways that had not previously happened (though in practice there had always been varying service capabilities between areas, the official principle of a national service had been maintained by every government since 1948). A specific case – the refusal of a local health authority to pay for treatment for 'Child B' and the unsuccessful court action by the family – highlighted the apparent existence of rationing in the NHS but denials by ministers and health authority officials defused the issue.

Nevertheless, it is clear from the wider studies that a fourth form of rationing – reducing the range of NHS services – has been introduced to contain costs. The evidence is actually clearest in the case of earlier national policy decisions to close many thousands of long-stay geriatric and psychiatric beds in NHS hospitals. Those who would once have been hospital patients, receiving free care from the NHS, are now in nursing and residential homes. There they are classified as being in need of 'social' rather than 'health' care and, as a result, they are subject to a system of means testing which results in many having to contribute substantial sums towards their non-medical care.

By 1997 the new actors, processes and institutions stemming from the 1983–90 reforms were well established. Though there were mixed research findings about the effectiveness of the internal market, and though the Labour opposition had strongly opposed its creation, the incoming Blair government was in no position simply to turn back the clock. Under immediate pressure from many supporters who had anticipated at the very least an increase in expenditure on the NHS (even though overall public spending was to remain constrained) the Secretary of State initially behaved in the usual manner, discussed later. He claimed to be able to cut bureaucracy by £100 million a year, got the Chancellor to find extra cash (partly from a raid on the defence budget and partly through advancing sums planned for the following year's NHS budget), and thus bought himself time to review the situation.

Seven months after the Blair government took office, it published its proposals for another round of structural changes. The white paper *The New NHS: Modern, Dependable* (December 1997) contained both change and continuity. Thus GP fund-holding was to be abolished but primary care groups covering populations of around 100,000 would replace them in England (in accordance with wider devolution plans there were separate and slightly different proposals for England, Scotland and Wales). The 1990 purchaser–provider split was to be retained, though primary care groups (like GP fund-holders) fell into both categories by providing GP and community services but also purchasing specialist and hospital care. The internal market would be modified so that it no longer operated through complex annual contracts and expensive individualised billing procedures for cases which fell outside the main contracts (these arise because people fall ill, or are referred to specialist centres, away from their home area). Continuity of the policy of strengthening the central state and setting levels of service expectations was very apparent through proposals for a new NHS charter, a National Institute for Clinical Excellence, a Commission for Health Improvement and a bidding process to determine which localities are designated health action zones. The document was written around the concepts of quality and efficiency. It contained proposals on many micro issues (e.g. plans for a twenty-four-hour helpline; for speedier access to cancer specialists) and talked of structural change (with organisation charts to help the reader grasp the blueprint). But, as ever, the macro issues of spending and rationing were sidestepped. Even when, in the summer of 1998, the Secretary of State was able to announce a three-year plan to increase the NHS budget substantially (after the government's comprehensive spending review), he was careful to avoid suggesting that this would solve these issues.

Cost, quality, access

The process of rationing health care presents three simultaneous political issues – cost, quality and access – for governments to manage. Governments aim to contain spending levels while at the same time seeking to improve the quality of health care and maintaining and enhancing access to that care. But quality and access initiatives usually cost money because they involve both financial investment in new treatments and technologies and the creation of additional demands for care. Indeed, it was the link between access and costs which forced reform on to the public agenda in the 1980s and led the Thatcher government to devise the 1989–90 NHS structural reforms. Then public concerns, fuelled by the opposition and articulated by the media, focused on the apparent growth of hospital waiting lists and forced a government response to the political charge that it was under-spending on the NHS.

The twofold response of government typified the management of the politics of health and was to be repeated in 1997 by the new Blair government. First, from the mid-1980s, fairly small additional sums of cash were released each year. Styled 'waiting list initiatives', they were designed to defuse the immediate political crisis which hit the NHS every winter as seasonal demand increased. Secondly, by embarking on institutional and process reforms the government was able to deflect the underspending charge by suggesting that better management of resources could improve productivity. In the 1989–90 debates it claimed, for example, to have achieved a 30 per cent increase in hospital throughput in the 1980s. This was seen as evidence of the success of its earlier reforms to improve NHS efficiency such as the introduction of 'general management'. Noticeably, little or no mention was made of the impact on the statistics of new technologies such as laser surgery (which had enormously speeded up cataract treatment of the eyes, enabling patients to leave hospital often within hours of surgery). Nor was it clear how comparable the figures really were, as a system of counting by 'finished consultant episodes' (rather than by patient numbers) had been introduced: if two specialists saw a patient during a single hospital stay it counted as two cases.

The seemingly incompatible cost, quality and access issues have remained at the centre of the political agenda, albeit in the form of organisational reforms and waiting list problems, with the main parties arguing about the efficiency and effectiveness of first the 1989–90 introduction of an 'internal' market and, later, the likely impact on productivity of the Blair government's December 1997 blueprint for reforms to the NHS's structure. The micro issue of waiting times often still provides the focus for immediate debate, with party spokespersons swapping claims and counterclaims and a good deal of creativity in the construction and analysis of statistical data. The Major government, for example, sought to deflect attention away from the growth in numbers awaiting treatment by, in the Patient's Charter, setting a variety of target times – six months and one and two years – for the length of wait (as opposed to the length of the queue, which had comfortably topped a million and was approaching 1.25 million). This approach was copied by the Blair government. It proposed an appointment with a cancer specialist within two weeks of referral by a GP, quicker results from blood and other tests, and new telephone services both to offer instant advice from nurses direct to patients and to speed up the wait for a hospital outpatient appointment by cutting bureaucracy, while struggling to meet its manifesto commitment to reduce the length of NHS waiting lists (they continued to grow steadily in 1997–8). The Conservative and Labour reform proposals for the basic structure of the NHS may have differed somewhat, but their management of the politics of health shows remarkable intergovernmental similarity and continuity! In both cases, a consequence of micro policies to improve access and raise targets is that public demands and expectations are fuelled. This puts more pressure on governments, which, oddly, thus become victims of their own political rhetoric.

Political consensus, in principle, if not always about precise details, has also been apparent over another quality of care issue, the effectiveness of particular medical treatments. The 1989–90 reforms included the introduction of a system of medical audit in every health authority, with doctors reviewing the outcomes of care. Note that general managers were excluded from the medical audit process in order to avoid a political battle with the medical profession, which presses for the continued recognition of clinical autonomy. The 1997 plan sought to underpin local medical audit systems by establishing a new National Institute for Clinical Excellence to produce and disseminate clinical guidelines of best practice based on research evidence. Though outwardly about clinical quality, these and other quality moves (e.g. to reduce the incidence of cross-infections in hospitals) – further detailed in a July 1998 consultative paper, *A First Class Service: Quality in the New NHS* – are all closely related in practice to the cost-containment issue because politicians believe that there is scope to reduce the incidence of allegedly 'unnecessary treatment', and hence to cut spending on it. The 1997 white paper, for example, expected the new National Institute to 'give a strong lead on clinical and cost-effectiveness' – a phrase repeated in the July 1998 document: note its last two words.

In sickness and in health

The politics of health should include more than the treating and curing of illnesses, the focus so far. The NHS, however, has often been seen as a national 'sickness' service, used only by the ill. The prevention of illness and the provision of health education have tended to be low-priority issues throughout most of its history, though this has begun to change in the last decade. What is often styled 'public health' or health of the community (in contrast to the health of an individual) has re-emerged and its origins are traceable right back to the mid-nineteenth century, when the state's first forays into health care through the provision of clean water and of proper sewage systems got under way.

Public health successes in the twentieth century have included the virtual eradication through mass screening and vaccination programmes of a whole array of diseases, from tuberculosis and polio to smallpox, German measles and whooping cough. But new illnesses continued to be recognised, as Table 10.1 showed. That brief list included Legionnaire's disease, preventable through an effective public health approach, and AIDS, the target of an extensive, expensive and very frank health education campaign designed to change sexual habits to prevent or minimise its further spread.

Between 1990 and 1992 the Thatcher and Major governments initiated a range of public health initiatives. These initially included financial incentives (bonuses) for GPs achieving high vaccination and cervical cytology screening targets and running clinics aimed at illness prevention. This was followed by the publication of a package of some twenty-seven health targets in a bulky 1992 white paper *Health of the Nation*. Targets such as percentage reductions in smoking, in premature ('unnecessary') deaths, in suicide rates and in teenage pregnancies were set, with accompanying guidance on strategies for health authorities to achieve them. Though this emphasis on public health was not in itself politically controversial, there was criticism that the strategies, by focusing on each individual's responsibility, avoided acknowledging and tackling the relationships between poverty or low socio-economic status and health. The Blair government's own 1998 green paper on public health, *Our Healthier Nation*, sought to alter this through a so-called 'contract with the people'. Though strategies were outlined, there was little explicit information about extra resources or expenditure that might be needed to meet the four key targets outlined in it (heart disease and stroke; accidents; cancer; and mental health).

At first sight, illness prevention has the double attraction of both improving the quality of life and keeping NHS costs down by reducing treatments. Evidence of the latter is, however, at the very least unclear. Extra longevity of life adds to overall NHS spending by increasing the numbers of visits made to doctors and their resultant costs. And additional public health activity, whether it be via advertisements and educational materials, or clinics and screening tests, or preventive drugs (to lower blood pressure, cholesterol or stress for instance), requires funding, often with large sums of money involved.

Improving our health, then, is not a cheap alternative to treating sickness. Rather, it is yet another demand on scarce resources. Politically it is attractive to governments because it not only focuses attention on the popular question of how to live longer and be healthier, but it also enables ministers to take credit for improvements to health that may actually be due to technological advances at least as much as to political activities. Important as public health is, it is a micro politics-of-health issue. It has the capacity to deflect attention from the pressures on health-care funding and rationing even though, ironically, it can be portrayed as making both these key underlying macro issues more difficult to solve.

The issue of funding: is enough being spent?

Does government spend enough on health-care provision? The considerable use made by the NHS of the four main rationing devices identified earlier may immediately suggest not. But the need for and demand for health care are constantly shifting and seemingly ever increasing, making some degree of rationing take place in every country. 'Need' and 'demand' are elastic rather than absolute concepts, and there is no magic formula for the calculation of a single, 'correct', level of expenditure on health care.

Under successive postwar British governments, the long-term tendency has been for spending on health care to rise in response to the increases in both demand and need. The main parties dispute which of them has been the more generous spender, but the trend runs clearly across the

Table 10.2. *Spending on health care, 1990 and 1996*

Percentage of GDP			Per capita (US$)	
1990	1996		1990	1996
9.2	9.2	Canada	1,691	2,002
8.9	9.6	France	1,539	1,978
8.2	10.5	Germany	1,642	2,222
4.2	5.9	Greece	389	748
6.0	7.2[a]	Japan	1,082	1,581[a]
8.3	8.6	Netherlands	1,325	1,756
6.9	7.6[a]	Spain	813	1,131[a]
8.8	7.2[a]	Sweden	1,492	1,405[a]
6.0	**6.9**	**United Kingdom**	**957**	**1,304**
12.7	14.2	United States of America	2,689	3,708

Representative sample of the twenty-nine countries presented in the OECD data.
GDP: gross domestic product.
[a]Data for 1995.
Source: OECD, *Health Data, 1997.*

decades regardless of which party held power. So does the need to try to reconcile what appears to be a situation where spending and rationing both increase simultaneously. Are politicians allocating too little to the NHS? Or too much? Or is NHS spending about right?

One possible test is to compare cross-nationally. Here the 'evidence' in Table 10.2 is pretty clear: by the standards of other developed nations for which the Organization for Economic Cooperation and Development (OECD) publishes information, Britain is a below-average spender on health care. In 1996 seventeen of the twenty-nine OECD states spent more per head than Britain, with Switzerland spending almost twice as much and the USA nearly three times as much. Expressed in terms of national wealth, the proportion of gross domestic product devoted to health care is also low, with Britain's 1996 figure of 6.9 per cent placing it in twenty-first place in the league table.

Caution is, however, necessary when interpreting raw data such as these. First, the figures alone say nothing about how much health care is actually provided. Monies spent are an *input*; services provided are an *output*; and levels of health and longevity are an *outcome*. Britain might be a low spender because its NHS (which dominates all health spending, with only a very small private sector, unlike the case in many other countries) is very efficient, with high productivity and low administrative overheads; or because it pays its doctors, nurses and other staff lower wages than is the case elsewhere (certainly true in comparison with Germany, Canada and the

USA, for example); or even because the list of items included under 'health' varies from country to country (some may include spending on long-stay nursing and social care). Indeed, all three factors do apply and the OECD statistics are not technically 'robust': they do not fully compare like with like and they do not clearly relate inputs to outputs and outcomes (though attempts are being made to do so). Nevertheless, most health economists do judge Britain's spending in relation to health needs and problems to be below average. Even this conclusion is not decisive as all countries, including the big spenders, have been experiencing the macro spending and rationing problems of demand outstripping supply. Nor is it clear that high spending correlates with better health: data for life expectancy in OECD states show no significant relationship between health spend and age at death.

A second possible test is to focus on the rate of spending increase, to see whether governments have been as generous in their NHS funding allocations as they proclaim. Again, caution is necessary. All governments are inclined to express claims of 'growth' by comparing the rise in the NHS budget with the general level of inflation as measured by the retail price index. But health-care costs have clearly risen much more quickly than have the prices of the average household's purchases, for four main reasons.

First, staff pay has (like average British wages) gone up quicker as the general standard of living has improved. Secondly, drugs and health equipment have cost more as new products entered and continue to enter the market. Thirdly, demographic changes include longer lives, a rapid increase in the numbers of elderly citizens and consequent greater use of the NHS (some experts believe that this factor alone requires an increased spend of up to 1 per cent per year to meet it). Finally, public expectations have risen. British patients are said to be traditionally stoical and relatively undemanding in comparison with North Americans but they increasingly believe that medicine can do more for them and so demand action from their doctors. When these four and other more minor factors are examined, the NHS budget increases are usually all accounted for. Hence the political emphasis on efficiency and productivity, necessitated because spending allocations alone do not normally allow for any substantial growth in service provision beyond inescapable commitments. Finally, note that the figures in Table 10.2 show an increase in British health spending per capita of about 35 per cent between 1990 and 1996, a rate which is just about average for the sample shown.

Conclusions

The political spotlight moves from issue to issue. In the mid-1990s Health Secretaries of both main parties were, as usual, embroiled in a myriad of controversies. These ranged from the medical consequences of 'mad cow disease' (the emergence of a new and a possibly virulent strain of Creutzfeldt–Jakob disease) and isolated but fatal outbreaks of *E. coli* food poisoning to debates about the frequency of, and eligibility of elderly women for, mammogram screening and to the usual agenda of issues: waiting lists; hospital closures; failures of the policy of community care; fluoridation; and many more. Everyone continues to expect and want more, and governments continue to battle to satisfy those aspirations, or at least to contain or manage them politically.

These immediate political crises come and go, with many reappearing regularly. Most cannot be easily anticipated, but their limited longevity at any one time is normally predictable. At first sight surprisingly, they are not entirely unwelcome to politicians, because they tend to reflect symptoms rather than underlying causes. The plethora of such micro issues results in a politics of health in which the key underlying or macro issues of rationing and of spending receive little public debate, either in Westminster or in the media. Journalists prefer to focus on specific human stories rather than on general, relatively esoteric and seemingly academic statistical disputes. And politicians prefer to tackle the perceived problems of the NHS through organisational and structural change, thus focusing on processes rather than on the content of health care; on administrative rather than on clinical matters. The twin macro issues of rationing and spending ought, perhaps, to dominate the politics of health, but they do not. Nevertheless, an understanding of their permanent existence and influence, hidden just below the surface, is essential for the interpretation of those debates that do fill the health political agenda.

Reading

Allsop, J. (1995) *Health Policy and the NHS: Towards 2000* (2nd edn), Longman.
Appleby, J. (1992) *Financing Health Care in the 1990s*, Open University Press.
Baggott, R. (1998) *Health and Health Care in Britain* (2nd edn), Macmillan.
Ham, C. (1992) *Health Policy in Britain* (3rd edn), Macmillan.
Harrison, S., Hunter, D. J. and Pollitt, C. (1990) *The Dynamics of British Health Policy*, Unwin Hyman.
Hunter, D. J. (1997) *Desperately Seeking Solutions: Rationing Health Care*, Longman.
Klein, R. (1995) *The New Politics of the NHS* (3rd edn), Longman.
Mohan, J. (1995) *A National Health Service?*, Macmillan.
Ranade, W. (1997) *A Future for the NHS? Health Care for the Millennium* (2nd edn), Longman.
Walt, G. (1994) *Health Policy: An Introduction to Process and Power*, Zed Books.

11

Reforming welfare

Rob Baggott

Why reform welfare?

The British welfare state was designed to tackle five specific but interrelated social problems identified by William Beveridge in his 1942 report: want, disease, ignorance, idleness and squalor. More than fifty years on, it can be judged a successful project in that such problems are not as prevalent as they once were. Nevertheless, over the last two decades the modern-day equivalent of Beveridge's 'five giants' – poverty, illness, poor education and skill levels, unemployment and bad housing – have persisted and in some respects deteriorated. The welfare state has been criticised for failing to respond adequately to these problems and for being inflexible in the face of social and economic changes. It has also been attacked on other grounds: for undermining economic incentives, for placing too high a burden on taxpayers, and for being inefficient and wasteful. Together these arguments have provided a powerful impetus for welfare reform.

A number of social and economic trends have raised questions about the efficacy of the welfare state. For example, the proportion of the population of pensionable age rose from 12 to 18 per cent between 1941 and 1991 and is set to rise to around 20 per cent in the twenty-first century. Not only are there more elderly people, but their needs are more complex. Many now live in the community rather than in residential care and require a complex pattern of financial support and welfare services. Meanwhile, the family, often seen as the building block of society, has also changed dramatically. Divorce rates are high (40 per cent of current marriages will end in divorce if current trends continue) and the number of single-parent families has increased (a quarter of families with children are headed by a lone parent). Yet the welfare state was designed for the traditional family unit of a married couple and children. Although it is still the most common arrangement, even this has been altered by other factors, in particular the decline of the male breadwinner and the increase in women's participation in the workforce, neither of which was foreseen by the architects of the welfare state.

Furthermore, one of the key pillars of the postwar welfare state was the acceptance of the Keynesian approach to economic management, aimed at promoting full employment. By pursuing this approach, successive govern-ments effectively reduced the burden of the welfare state on the nation's finances. In addition, full employment contributed towards the cost of welfare as employees paid their taxes and national insurance contributions. In contrast, the growth of unemployment in the 1970s, followed by the abandonment of a full-employment policy by the Thatcher government, added to the demands on the welfare state. Unemployed people required income support; they needed to be rehoused if they defaulted on their mortgages. Unemployment was also associated with an increasing demand for health care, placing extra burdens on the National Health Service (NHS) (Smith, 1987).

Particular areas – the inner cities and large council estates of the old industrial conurbations – were seriously affected by long-term structural unemployment associated with the recession of the early 1980s. Their residents became trapped in a spiral of economic and social decline and benefited little from the boom which followed. As a result, those who remained in these communities had few employment opportunities.

By the mid-1990s one in five households headed by people of working age had no one in employment. For many, the welfare state ceased to act as a safety net and became an unavoidable way of life. Meanwhile, the number of people in poverty grew during the 1980s and 1990s (Joseph Rowntree Foundation, 1995; Hills, 1997). Between 1979 and 1993 the percentage of households living on half the national average income (after housing costs) rose from 9 to 25 per cent. At the same time British society became economically more unequal. Average income (taking into account housing costs) for the top tenth of the income distribution rose by 60 per cent between 1979 and 1993/4. Over the same period the average income of the bottom tenth actually fell by 17 per cent. Between 1979 and 1995 the top fifth of the income distribution increased its share of income from 36 per cent to 40 per cent of total household disposable income. The share of the poorest fifth fell over the same period from 9.4 per cent to 7.9 per cent.

Above the poverty line, job insecurity began to affect a much wider range of people, including the professional and managerial classes. The impact of the recession of the early 1990s was more widespread, affecting the middle classes and areas which had largely escaped the ravages of the earlier recession. Self-employment, part-time and casual work also became more common: the number of self-employed people rose from 1.9 million in 1979 to 3.4 million by the end of the 1980s. The prospect of a secure job for life seemed to become more elusive for many. Hutton (1995) characterised this as the 40:30:30 society – 40 per cent privileged, 30 per cent insecure and 30 per cent marginalised and disadvantaged. However, the welfare state failed to acknowledge this new reality and continued to treat unemployment as an unusual state of affairs for a few rather than a common experience for many people.

As employment prospects for the male breadwinner decreased, those for women improved. In 1971 only a third of the British workforce was female: now it is almost half. Many women benefited from increasing opportunities for part-time work; however, though this provided a useful addition to the income of the family it was insufficient to support it alone. Unfortunately, the welfare state was slow to catch up with this trend, with social security rules adversely affecting part-time workers. In many cases women were forced to give up part-time work because their partners became unemployed and could not claim benefits if they remained in employment. By the same token unemployed men and women were prevented from taking on part-time and low-paid work because of poverty and unemployment 'traps' created by the benefits system, discussed below.

As a result of these social and economic changes, the welfare state was increasingly viewed as inappropriate to modern needs. Moreover, new demands resulted in a rise in the proportion of national expenditure devoted to the welfare state. The potential cost of welfare is expected to grow even further, in view of the continuation of the social and economic trends discussed above. Nonetheless, the level of resources allocated to welfare should not be exaggerated (see Hills, 1997). Over the last twenty years, welfare spending in Britain has been relatively stable, at 21–26 per cent of national expenditure. Although there will be pressures for higher spending, their total effect on public finances has been estimated at less than 5 per cent of national expenditure over the next fifty years, no more than the increase in resources actually allocated between 1989 and 1992.

The Conservative governments of the 1980s and 1990s were particularly keen to reduce welfare costs, as a means of reducing public expenditure and tax rates. This was undertaken mainly by reducing entitlement to benefits (e.g. mortgage payments for social security claimants, invalidity benefits and raising the pensions age for women), reducing, freezing or not fully uprating benefit payments (e.g. child benefit and the state pension), abolishing benefits (e.g. unemployment benefit – replaced by the job seeker's allowance; emergency single payments for those in urgent need – replaced by a loans scheme), encouraging private funding and provision (e.g. private health insurance, mortgage protection insurance, private schools and residential care), imposing charges (e.g. for eye tests and dental checks and higher prescription charges) and by shifting the emphasis away from universal benefits claimed as of right (e.g. child benefit and the state pension) towards means-tested benefits such as family credit and income support.

But the welfare budget did not fall, partly because of the rising demands mentioned earlier and partly as a result of the Conservatives' policy of increasing the role of means-tested benefits. By the mid-1990s around a quarter of the population was dependent on means-tested benefits. This added to the costs of social welfare in several ways. First, it added to administrative costs: means-tested benefits cost more to administer than universal benefits. For example, the administrative costs of the means-tested social fund account for over a third of the cost of the scheme, while only 2.2 per cent of the cost of child benefit, which is not means tested, is spent on administration (Hills, 1997, p. 42). Second, the Conservatives' approach led to the creation of poverty traps and unemployment traps. These are disincentives produced by the withdrawal of means-tested benefits as people enter low-paid work, so that they in effect face punitively high marginal rates of tax and in some circumstances may be financially worse off in work than when unemployed. Means testing also created further disincentives in the form of savings traps. A savings trap occurs when people are worse off by having a small amount of savings (or an income generated by a savings or investment scheme) which prevents them from receiving means-tested benefits.

Though presiding over a large and increasing welfare budget, the Conservative governments of the 1980s and 1990s displayed an overt ideological dislike of the welfare state. First, they opposed the redistributive effect of the welfare state on the grounds that socio-economic inequalities were not only acceptable but necessary in order to create a thriving entrepreneurial culture. Second, the welfare state was viewed as an unresponsive public sector bureaucracy, a haven for restrictive labour practices, and therefore ripe for reform. Third, welfare was seen as a major cause of high levels of public spending and taxation. Finally, the postwar welfare state was blamed for undermining individual responsibility and morality by cushioning people from the consequences of their own actions (particularly with respect to marital breakdown and parenting) and by removing incentives to seek employment.

These arguments were increasingly influential, largely due to the acknowledgement of US critics of welfare, such as Charles Murray (1990, 1994). Murray argued that welfare dependency in Britain was likely to create a US-style underclass, with high crime rates, inadequate parenting and a refusal by the unemployed to take jobs. He was particularly concerned about the growth of lone parenting as a dangerous form of welfare dependency which could, if unchecked, destroy the social fabric. The currency of such arguments partly explains the 'demonisation' of single mothers during the 1990s.

These ideological predispositions, extremely influential in government during the Thatcher era and the Major years, continued to some extent under New Labour. For the Blair government espoused a communitarian approach to welfare, similar in some respects to the New Right perspective adopted by its Conservative predecessors. New Labour welfare is a marriage of individualism and collectivism, highlighting individual and community responsibilities as well as rights. It implies an attack on what Peter Lilley, the former Conservative Secretary of State for Social Security, called 'the something for nothing society' while at the same time seeking to improve the effectiveness and efficiency of collective welfare provision. Furthermore, the centre-left has recognised that the old welfare state must be overhauled for practical reasons. As the Commission for Social Justice argued, there is a need for an 'intelligent welfare state', which meets the needs of individuals and society more effectively (Institute for Public Policy Research, 1994). The centre-left sees a revitalised welfare state not only as contributing to a more civilised society but also as a means of promoting a more effective and competitive economy (Hutton, 1995; Field, 1995). Hence the continuation of the Tories' agenda to tackle the cost of welfare, fraud and dependency, along with the inflexibility, poor coordination and perceived lack of fairness associated with the welfare state. However, it would be wrong to see the intentions of the Blair government as purely and simply a continuation of the policies of Thatcher and Major. Indeed, it has declared an intention to be even more radical, the stated aim being to redesign the welfare state rather than merely tinkering with its worst features. However, as we shall see in below, political pressures seriously affected these plans.

The Blair government's reforms

After taking office, Blair appointed Frank Field, a long-time advocate of radical change, as Minister for Welfare Reform. This led to the publication in 1998 of a green paper, *A New Contract for Welfare*. However, tensions between Field and his superior at the Department of Social Security, Harriet Harman, and conflicts with the Treasury over the cost of reform undermined the initiative. It should be noted that the welfare review did not sit easily alongside the comprehensive spending review undertaken by the government on taking office. Both Harman and Field left the cabinet in the July 1998 reshuffle, amid considerable uncertainty about the future of welfare reform.

The Blair government has not as yet declared an intention to redistribute significant resources from the rich to the poor. Indeed, it has pledged not to increase basic or top income tax rates, key instruments of redistribution. Furthermore, its first two budgets left untouched some key middle-class benefits: contrary to some expectations, heavier taxation of company cars was not introduced, nor was child benefit for higher earners taxed, though both options remain a future possibility. Nevertheless, these budgets were mildly redistributive, according to the Institute for Fiscal Studies (*The*

Independent, 19 March 1998): the bottom half of earners gained between 0.5 and 3 per cent of their incomes; the top half lost 0.3 per cent of theirs. Moreover, the government's concern for the broader effects of inequality was reflected in the creation of the Social Exclusion Unit and by the identification of educational and health inequalities as key issues to be tackled. However, the extent to which these initiatives will attack the underlying causes of poverty and inequality remains to be seen.

Rather than a policy of redistributing incomes, the Labour government sought to target the specific causes of poverty, unemployment and welfare dependence. It set out the Welfare to Work programme, aimed at creating employment and training opportunities for young people, disabled persons, lone parents and long-term unemployed people. This programme aims to link the payment of benefits to employment and training, while offering opportunities through a series of 'New Deals' for each particular group. For example, building on the previous government's attempts to import US-style 'Workfare' projects, it intends to link benefits for people under twenty-five years of age directly to participation in training and job-creation schemes. Employers will receive grants and subsidies to encourage them to take on young people and train them properly. In addition, employment zones have been identified as a means of targeting areas of high unemployment.

Unemployment has been recognised as a key cause of poverty. However, poverty often results not from 'no pay' but from 'low pay'. The Blair government accepted recommendations from the Low Pay Commission for a minimum wage of £3.60 per hour, although it opted for a lower figure of £3.00 for younger workers. This was hardly a generous rate and reflected the government's concern to minimise the knock-on effect on pay differentials and wage claims, which could undermine its anti-inflationary policy. This decision also indicated a desire to maintain a good working relationship with employers, many of whom felt that a higher minimum wage will reduce their competitiveness.

A further area of reform concerns financial support for families and children. The much-maligned Child Support Agency, established by the Conservatives in 1993 as a means of obtaining resources from absent parents, was earmarked for reform in the green paper on welfare. In July 1998, proposals were put forward to simplify the assessment process that had caused so much anguish (pp. 59–60). In the 1998 budget, child benefit was increased, by 20 per cent over the rate of inflation for the first child, and poorer families with children were given additional social security benefits. In addition, a tax credit scheme was announced for low- and middle-income families, enabling them to claim up to 70 per cent of child-care costs. This dovetailed neatly with an earlier proposal, announced in November 1997, to provide funding for 30,000 'out of school' clubs for one million children. This scheme was intended to provide cheap child care outside school times, enabling women and single parents in particular to participate in the workforce to a greater extent. This built on initiatives introduced by the Major government to promote after-school clubs and remove taxation from workplace nurseries. The Major government had also introduced a voucher scheme to encourage an expansion of nursery education for four-year-olds, enabling some parents to enter the workforce a year earlier than otherwise would have been the case. The Blair government subsequently abolished the nursery voucher scheme and declared that funding would be available to enable all four-year-olds to have pre-school education.

Families on low earnings were seen as the beneficiaries of most of the proposals discussed above. They were also the main target of early efforts by the Blair government to integrate taxation and benefits. Over the years a number of radical schemes have been proposed to integrate the taxation and benefit systems in an effort to overcome poverty and unemployment traps and to provide greater incentives to seek work. However, only recently have such ideas been seriously acknowledged by policy makers. One radical idea which has attracted some support is the citizens' (or basic) income scheme. This involves the payment of a non-means-tested lump sum, to replace all benefits, including tax allowances, and set at a level to ensure a basic standard of living. Although the Blair government has no specific plans at present to introduce such a comprehensive scheme, it has announced steps to integrate taxation and benefits for certain claimants. In the 1998 budget, a working families' tax credit was announced for working parents on low incomes. This payment (scheduled to replace family credit from October 1999) is intended to boost the incomes of low-paid families and enable them to keep more of what they earn, thereby increasing work incentives. According to the government, families with a full-time worker will have an income of at least £180 per week following the introduction of the working families' tax credit.

Other radical ideas include possible changes to reinforce the contributory principle of social insurance. Such changes received support from Frank Field, the former Minister for Welfare Reform, who had long argued that individuals should be encouraged wherever possible to make additional provision for themselves (see Field, 1995). He suggested the development of additional schemes to supplement basic state provision, such as a graduated unemployment benefit scheme linking higher contributions to improved benefits, second pensions (see below) and schemes to cover long-term care. Although Field argued that the state should retain overall responsibility for ensuring that people are covered by welfare schemes – compelling them to do so if necessary – he acknowledged that non-governmental institutions such as friendly societies could play a key role in delivering particular services, alongside commercial insurance and state schemes. Despite his departure, such ideas are likely to influence policy developments in a number of areas over the next few years. The green paper on welfare reform stated that public and private sectors should work together to ensure that people are adequately insured against risks (p. 33). One area identified for the further development of such partnerships is pension reform. One in three pensioners are at or below the poverty line, though many fail to claim their entitlement to means-tested income support. There are a number of reasons why so many pensioners are dependent on such benefits. Since 1980 the basic state pension has not been uprated along with average earnings and those relying on this income have become relatively poorer as a result. Occupational schemes can supplement the state pension, but cover only half the population and tend to exclude part-time and short-term workers. Furthermore, the decline of a job for life and the rise of part-time and self-employment make occupational pensions a rather inflexible arrangement for the future. The state earnings-related pension scheme (SERPS) pays an earnings-related pension to those not in employer schemes, but this also excludes many women, part-time and low-paid workers and self-employed people. SERPS was reformed by the Conservatives in 1986 in ways which made it less attractive to contributors who, with government subsidies, were encouraged to take out private pensions. These subsidies were extremely expensive to the taxpayer – costing in the region of £9 billion. Moreover, many of those who opted out of SERPS and occupational schemes ended up financially worse off due to high charges and mis-selling of pension products by insurance companies.

Aside from raising the basic state pension dramatically to make up for the shortfall relative to average earnings, other options are to widen SERPS or to expand private provision within a comprehensive framework set out by the state. Present indications are that the government favours the latter option, though it has so far refused to abolish SERPS and may in fact extend this scheme to carers of sick and elderly people.

The main thrust of policy at present is to create 'stakeholder pensions', joint arrangements between the financial sector, employers, employees or self-employed people, approved by the state to provide additional private pensions for those people not covered by private or occupational schemes. At the time of writing the government is consulting on these options and there remain many unanswered questions, not least about the extent to which contributions will be subsidised by the state or cross-subsidised by those already contributing to pension schemes, and whether or not there will be an element of compulsion to get employers and individuals to contribute to pension schemes. The government is expected to set out its policy on pensions reform in greater detail towards the end of 1998. However, this was pre-empted to some extent by an announcement in July 1998 of a minimum guaranteed income for pensioners dependent on state support.

A related issue is the funding of long-term care for elderly people. In recent years the closure of NHS geriatric wards, coupled with the growing number of dependent elderly people, has led to a growth in residential care homes. Unlike the NHS, social care is not necessarily provided free at the point of delivery. Users of these services face a means test and if they have sufficient assets must pay for care. The Major government was particularly concerned about the likely impact of this trend on the middle classes, who faced being deprived of inheritances when elderly parents sold their homes to meet the costs of care. So it raised the level of assets a person could hold without having to pay charges and proposed that people could protect their assets further by taking out private insurance. Meanwhile, others joined the debate, the House of Commons Health Committee (1996) arguing that the costs of nursing care should be paid for by the NHS, while some preferred a state insurance scheme in which people in work would pay an additional national insurance premium to cover the costs of their future care (Joseph Rowntree Foundation, 1996; see also Institute for Public Policy Research, 1996). The Blair government initially distanced itself from these proposals, shelving the previous government's plans to encourage private insurance for long-term care while not explicitly backing an alternative funding scheme. However, in December 1997 it established a royal commission on the long-term care for the elderly, to examine further the various funding options, whose report is expected during 1999.

Social welfare services

During the 1980s and 1990s the following principles guided the reform of services in health care, education and housing:

- the extension of private funding and provision, curbing the rise of public expenditure;
- introducing management concepts, philosophies and practices imported from the private sector;
- monitoring and regulation of performance and quality of service;
- an emphasis on consumerism, flexibility and choice in service provision;
- the introduction of 'quasi-market' forces into the provision of public services.

These principles were pursued with varying intensity in different policy areas. For example, private provision was sought far more extensively in housing and social care than in health or education. The policies adopted also varied in detail; for example, in housing and education, public ballots were introduced to allow tenants and schools respectively to opt out of local authority control, whereas NHS hospitals were allowed to create self-governing trusts without such public approval.

The Conservative government often faced problems in implementing its policies and in some cases had to compromise and rethink its policy. For example, problems with the national curriculum and standard assessment tasks (SATs) in schools, highlighted by teachers, local authorities, parents and school governors, forced the government to amend the scheme (see Chapter 9). Likewise, the NHS internal market introduced by the Conservatives had to be modified because of a series of problems: the new system proved expensive to operate, producing a rise in administrative costs, duplication of services and fragmentation, all of which undermined the government's declared aim of improving the efficiency of the service.

The Blair government has accepted that many of the previous government's policies should not be reversed. For example, in relation to the NHS it retained the Private Finance Initiative – which involves the private sector in the financing and management of public services. It did not plan to reduce the role of the private sector in health care back to its pre-Thatcher level, though the 1997 budget did abolish tax relief on private health insurance for the elderly. Seemingly, the government had no intention to reverse the trend of rising charges for NHS services (prescription charges were raised in line with inflation in April 1998), nor did it immediately abolish charges introduced by the Conservatives, such as those for eye and dental checks, though eye test charges for the elderly were ended in 1998.

The Blair government stated its commitment to abolish the NHS internal market and GP fund-holding and has introduced new measures in an effort to improve access to services. For example, health authorities were told to plan improvements in the health of the local population, and in some areas health action zones were established to target particular needs. However, certain elements have been retained, such as the commissioning process whereby budgets are given to health authorities to pay for services provided by hospitals and community health-care trusts. The plan is to replace the internal market introduced by the Conservatives with a new scheme based on improved planning and cooperation between the different players: there is no intention at present to return to the previous system where these services were funded, managed and delivered by a single bureaucracy in each geographical area.

In education, too, many of the Conservatives' policies have been modified rather than abandoned. So far only the commitment to reduce class sizes for five- to seven-year-olds to thirty or less, the proposed abolition of the assisted places scheme (which enables children of less well off parents to attend independent schools) and some strengthening of the role of local education authorities (LEAs) in relation to school standards and governance contrast with the approach taken by the Major government (see Chapter 9).

The Blair government does not intend to bring grant-maintained schools back into local authority control, though LEAs will be represented on their governing bodies and must be consulted on admissions policies. The admissions policies of the remaining grammar schools will be decided by 'local parents' – though this constituency has yet to be clearly defined. The

LEAs will also be responsible for setting school budgets, but at the same time will be required to delegate more financial powers to the schools themselves. LEAs are to be given overall responsibility for education standards in their area and will be expected to intervene to improve the quality of education if necessary. Failure to do so could lead to the suspension of their powers. Failing schools face being taken over by new management teams and possible closure if they fail to improve. Education action zones are being established in areas where educational standards are particularly poor, involving among other things the recruitment of high-quality teachers and head teachers to underachieving schools, freedom to opt out of the national curriculum and a role in the financing and management of schools for private firms in partnership with LEAs and community groups.

The Labour government has also announced plans to introduce procedures to dismiss poor teachers. A General Teaching Council has been proposed as a means of improving standards and the status of the profession, though its role has not yet been fully detailed. It is expected that school inspections will be less frequent, but inspectors will have greater powers to inspect LEAs. In addition, testing is to be extended with the introduction of baseline tests for all pupils starting school. New national tests for nine-year-olds in English and maths are also being introduced. School performance tables have been retained, but in a modified form. For example, the secondary-school tables now show improvements in overall performance and may in the future include more information on pupils' progress, so that the 'value added' by the school is measured.

Labour's traditional hostility to independent schools is notably absent from the Blair government's proposals. Apart from the abolition of the assisted places scheme noted above, the government has gone out of its way to reassure the independent sector. In particular the charitable status of the independent schools seems to be secure for the foreseeable future. However, these schools are being urged to share their facilities with local schools and communities and to cooperate with them on academic matters. But this is only a voluntary scheme and there is no compulsion for the independent sector to make anything more than token gestures.

In the field of higher education, the government's policy has continued along much the same lines as that of its predecessor: a commitment to expand higher education, increasingly paid for by those who use it. The Major government established a committee on higher education chaired by Sir Ron Dearing, which reported shortly after Labour took office. Dearing's proposals included the abolition of free higher education for all, with students contributing a proportion of their tuition costs and the means testing of student loans as well as grants. Although accepting the main thrust of the report, namely that the costs of higher education should be shared among those who benefit, the government's policy differed from Dearing by proposing a means-tested fee structure (exempting students from lower-income families) and the replacement of maintenance grants with student loans.

Of all the areas of the welfare state, housing was perhaps the most deeply affected by the application of New Right principles during the 1980s and 1990s. The Conservatives' philosophy of a property-owning democracy promoted a rise in owner occupation from 52 per cent of homes in 1979 to 68 per cent in 1996, achieved largely through the sale of council houses. Local authorities were prevented from replacing this stock by financial constraints. Most new social housing – for those who could not afford to buy their own homes – was provided by voluntary housing associations. Meanwhile, the Conservatives sought to encourage local authorities to contract out the management of council estates. The private sector was stimulated largely through tax breaks for landlords, while on the issue of affordability, the Conservative government favoured 'market rents' subsidised by housing benefit rather than regulation of rents.

The Conservatives' policy on housing had many adverse social effects. Homelessness rose during the 1980s and 1990s (doubling in the 1980s alone). Owner occupation proved to be a disaster for many people as mortgage repossessions rocketed. The situation was compounded by the lack of good quality social housing. Rents rose sharply (by 30 per cent in real terms between 1989 and 1993 alone), mitigated to some extent by housing benefit. But because this benefit is means-tested, the problems of poverty and unemployment traps referred to earlier were further exacerbated. Consequently, the housing benefit bill rose rapidly, more than doubling in real terms between 1986 and 1996.

Despite the importance of good housing to health, wellbeing and community life, it has not been at the centre of welfare policy. The Blair government has agreed that councils may reinvest funds raised by council house sales in new housing, but the speed at which this occurs will be dictated by economic policy rather than by housing need. Action has been proposed to deal with some of the worst aspects of housing: a licensing system for landlords, improved rights for lease-holders, measures to avoid repossessions, new rules on house purchasing and expansion of the previous government's Rough Sleepers' Initiative. In July 1998, plans were announced to regenerate run-down estates and improve housing standards at local level. However, there is no plan to set housing standards nationally and to provide a plentiful supply of affordable and appropriate accommodation for those who need it.

In housing and other areas of welfare, the Blair government's policies have been shaped by its overall approach to economic management. Despite calls from within the Labour Party and from the public to increase welfare spending, the government's priority has been to establish a reputation for sound economic management. Before the 1997 election, and in financial statements after it took office, the pledge to maintain overall public expenditure totals set by the Conservatives was reiterated. Even so, some relaxation of the commitment to remain within existing departmental budgets did take place. In his first budget, the Chancellor of the Exchequer, Gordon Brown, used contingency funds to allocate extra funds to the NHS and education in the following financial year. A few months later additional funds were given to the NHS (from the trade and defence budgets) to deal with an impending financial crisis in the service. In the second budget, of March 1998, clearer signals were given that health and education would benefit from future expenditure plans in the forthcoming financial year (£500 million for the NHS; £250 million for the education budget). After the announcement of the outcome of the comprehensive spending review in July 1998, it became clear that some welfare services would receive additional funding. Health and education were to receive an additional £40 billion over the following three years, according to the Chancellor.

Despite this apparent generosity, control over public expenditure remained tight. Much of the new spending commitments will be absorbed by the cost of new welfare reforms. In addition, like its predecessor, the Blair government has sought to release resources through a reduction in management costs and by a more rigorous approach to fraud in the welfare state.

The future development of government policy

Having outlined the main arguments for reform and the current direction of welfare policy, we now turn to the wider political factors likely to shape future developments: competing ideological perspectives within the Labour Party and the government; the role of organised interests; public opinion and the media; and interdepartmental politics.

The Blair government's vision, as already noted, attempts to marry self-interested individualism with collective responsibility. It therefore espouses policies that are somewhat inconsistent with the kind of approach to welfare traditionally supported by the Labour Party, while at the same time developing Conservative policies introduced in the 1980s and 1990s. However, there are many within the Labour Party, not to mention the wider labour movement, who strongly question these changes (see Chapter 18). This is often portrayed as a battle between weak and weary 'Old Labour' and vibrant, victorious 'New Labour'. But the reality is more complex: for example, little is known about the extent to which the new intake of MPs will rebel against the policies of the leadership. The back-bench protests witnessed in the 1997/8 session of Parliament, on issues such as the planned cuts in social security payments to single parents, changes in disability benefits and on student fees and maintenance, may be an indicator of what lies ahead or could merely be 'teething problems' of a new government – it is simply too early to tell.

Organised interests close to the Labour Party are uneasy about the government's welfare policies. Trade unionists have urged a more flexible approach to public spending, while complaining about what they see as the damaging effects of policies inherited from the previous government. These sentiments are echoed by professional associations whose members are employed by the welfare state – such as teachers, doctors and social service staff. So far this criticism has been rather muted. Only groups representing claimants and the users of services have so far vociferously expressed serious concerns about the direction of policy.

Up to now, the Blair government has been given the benefit of the doubt. But this is unlikely to last, as the details of policy are increasingly fleshed out. There are some thorny decisions ahead, which are likely to produce considerable opposition from organised interests, including the regulation of professional and service standards (in education and health care, particularly). Much will depend on how the government approaches these issues. Will it seek a consensual approach, as it so often claimed it would, or will it use its huge majority in Parliament to push measures through?

Dealing harshly with special interests would not matter too much if the public were squarely behind government policy. But here, too, the Blair government must tread carefully. Even after almost two decades of overt government antipathy to the welfare state, the public are still clearly attached to it (Taylor-Gooby, 1996; Brook *et al.*, 1997). Public opinion polls consistently show that the growth of private health care and education has not undermined support for the welfare state. The vast majority of people prefer public spending on welfare services to tax cuts, particularly on health services and education. And there is little public support for a further extension of private welfare provision. However, there is considerable dissatisfaction expressed with particular services, providing some legitimacy for government action, notably on educational standards and NHS waiting lists.

On the other hand, there is considerable public opposition to radical reform proposals. For example, there is much support for increasing the basic state pension (Brook *et al.*, 1997), while second pensions are unlikely to be popular, particularly if there is an element of compulsion. Compulsion is not, however, necessarily unpopular, particularly if it is aimed at a specific group in the population identified as 'undeserving'. Compulsion of young people into work and measures aimed at getting single parents off benefit are likely to be seen as populist measures given the demonisation of these groups in recent years by some politicians and the media, and an attack on social security fraud guarantees popularity, given the tabloids' constant vigilance with regard to 'spongers and scroungers'.

The media play an ambivalent role in relation to the welfare state. On the one hand, they generally support the need for services such as state education and the NHS and reveal the plight of groups such as the elderly and disabled. At the same time, they mobilise criticism of other aspects of the welfare state, such as the benefit system. The danger for any government is that the reaction of the media is not always predictable. As the Conservatives found to their cost, the media can take up an opposing stance on an issue when it might be expected broadly to support the government's line. This happened notably on the issue of school SATs during the early 1990s, when there was strong media and public support for the demands for reform articulated by the teachers' unions and others.

Finally, obstacles to reform can arise within government itself. Government agencies have their own interests and policy preferences. They resent efforts to reallocate functions and reorder priorities. Hence on several issues the Blair government faces internal disputes between different government departments and agencies, which could jeopardise its plans. We have already witnessed serious disputes between the Treasury and the Department of Social Security. Efforts to develop social policies which involve the cooperation of agencies involved in health, education, employment, social security and social care are fraught with practical problems as each department digs in to defend its own turf. Moreover, pre-existing departmental conflicts can be exacerbated by personality clashes between ministers. As the conflict between Field and Harman illustrated, this can produce tensions within as well as between departments.

As previous governments have found, it is enormously difficult to reform the welfare state according to some master plan. Even where there is consensus for change, detailed proposals can produce a political backlash, leading to compromise or even to the abandonment of changes. Notably, the Blair government effectively reinstated cuts in single-parent benefit and diluted its plans to reform disability benefits after protests from pressure groups and MPs. It has since reiterated the long-term nature of its plans and made clear its intention to move forward on the basis of consultation and consent, in its 1998 green paper.

The government is right to pursue a modernisation of the welfare state, to ensure that it is affordable, efficient, proactive and appropriate to the needs of individuals. Yet the way in which it manages this process – with particular regard to ideological conflicts within the Labour Party, organised interests, public opinion and interdepartmental responsibilities – will be the crucial factor, not only in the success of the welfare reform programme but, more broadly, in determining its future political prospects.

Reading

Brook, L., Hall, J. and Preston, I. (1997) 'Public spending and taxation', in R. Jowell, J. Curtice, A. Park, L. Brook and K. Thomson (eds), *British Social Attitudes. The 13th Report*, Social and Community Planning Research.
Field, F. (1995) *Making Welfare Work*, Institute of Contemporary Studies.

Hills, J. (1997) *The Future of Welfare*, Joseph Rowntree Foundation.

House of Commons Health Committee (1996) *Long Term Care: Future Provision and Funding. HC 59, 3rd Report 1995/6*, HMSO.

Hutton, W. (1995) *The State We're In*, Verso.

Institute for Public Policy Research (1994) *Social Justice: The Report of the Commission for Social Justice*, IPPR.

Institute for Public Policy Research (1996) *Paying for Long Term Care*, IPPR.

Joseph Rowntree Foundation (1995) *Income and Wealth*, York Publishing Services.

Joseph Rowntree Foundation (1996) *Inquiry into Meeting the Costs of Continuing Care*, York Publishing Services.

Murray, C. (1990) *The Emerging British Underclass*, Institute for Economic Affairs.

Murray, C. (1994) *Underclass: The Crisis Deepens*, Institute for Economic Affairs.

Smith, R. (1997) *Unemployment and Health*, Oxford University Press.

Taylor-Gooby, P. (1996) 'Comfortable, marginal and excluded', in R. Jowell, J. Curtice, A. Park, L. Brook and D. Ahrendt (eds), *British Social Attitudes: The 12th Report*, Social and Community Planning Research.

12

Privatisation

Geoff Lee

This chapter considers the political and economic arguments surrounding privatisation. At the end there are appendices summarising the types of privatisation, the sums raised, and lists of past, present and future candidates for the transfer of services and organisations from the public to the private sector.

The arguments for nationalisation had consisted of an intermeshed set of factors: economic ones such as economies of scale, coordinated investment and the public control of monopoly power; political/economic impulses to preserve key industries such as Rolls Royce and British Leyland (BL); socio-political reasons such as the provision of uniform services and safeguarding regional economic development; and political determination to ensure the public ownership of key industries. A similar mixture is to be found in the rationale for privatisation. The chapter begins with a look at the political factors.

The political impetus for privatisation

Ideological underpinnings

It was a central tenet of Conservative political philosophy that the role of the state should be minimised, and the government which came into office in 1979 was clearly committed to rolling back the frontiers. In particular there was little liking for the nationalised industries: the eighteen largest employed 1.6 million workers, in protected or monopoly markets, with strongly unionised workforces and large debts. These 'dinosaurs' were said to increase the scale of public borrowing, increase taxation and cause unemployment. In the House of Lords, Lord Beswick noted the 'sick language' used by the Prime Minister and her colleagues in describing them as 'horrific, poisonous, debilitating, voracious and a haemorrhage' (*Hansard*, 4 February 1981).

Policy formulation

Yet while the political inclination may have been there, no radical programme for privatisation existed. In April 1977 John Biffen MP, later to become a cabinet minister, had called for the introduction of some private sector resources into nationalised industries but the Conservative policy study group had reported in 1978 that denationalisation 'must be pursued cautiously and flexibly, recognising that major changes may well be out of the question in some industries' (*Sunday Times*, 9 October 1983). The Conservatives were slow to reject completely the thirty-year Butskellite agreement on the boundaries of the public sector. For their 1979 manifesto they adhered to the so-called BP solution, of selling just under a half share in a few industries. Intellectual responsibility and guidance began to be added – from the Adam Smith Institute of Economic Affairs, the Centre for Policy Studies, and Professors Beesley and Littlechild.

When the government had to channel hundreds of millions of pounds into loss-making industries such as British Steel and British Shipbuilders, and as some of their manifesto sales were thwarted by economic and technical problems, it seemed even this small-scale process of privatisation would falter. An article entitled 'Whatever happened to the great sell-off?' in *The Observer* concluded of privatisation, 'The word hasn't yet made its way into any dictionary. Whether it will now do so is increasingly doubtful' (23 November 1990).

Policy commitment

A radical change in policy was signalled, however, by the Chancellor, Sir Geoffrey Howe, in 1981, with the declaration that the postal services, British Telecom (BT), the British National Oil Company and even gas and electricity were under consideration. Sir Keith Joseph, then Education Minister, has stated that in so attempting to deal with the problem and clear their desks, privatisation was a product of government, not opposition. It was very much in keeping with 'the resolute approach', but it was also carried by expediency – for example, passing Royal Ordinance to British Aerospace (BAe) enabled them to pass on the problems of restructuring and redundancies.

The 1983 manifesto promised to continue the process, and only as an afterthought were nationalised industries unsuitable for privatisation mentioned. Back in office, it was said that ministers were competing to bring industries to market as proof of their political virility. Having sold off assets worth £3.6 billion since 1979, the cabinet 'E' (economics) committee agreed to sell a further £10 billions' worth over five years – and it was clear that privatisation had become a central and distinguishing policy of the Thatcher government. John Moore, Financial Secretary in the Treasury and the minister responsible for privatisation, attacked the failure of the concept of public corporations and warned that 'no state monopoly was sacrosanct' (*Financial Times*, 2 November 1983). By 1983/4 the scale of the shift of the debate was astonishing – groups were then calling for the privatisation of the railways, coal, electricity, the universities, the BBC and more of the NHS. At the time, these claims were regarded as extreme, made for effect or as an indicator and reinforcer of direction. In response to the question 'what would be left at the end of the third Thatcher government?', Moore was said to have replied, 'the Treasury'. By then £25 billions' worth of assets had been sold.

Stockbrokers Grievson and Grant identified a package of £28.5 billion assets in 1984 and went on to suggest another available £55 billion which the government could sell.

The proof of ideological commitment is the willingness to privatise for nil gain; the introduction of private management into the two royal dockyards would have cost as much as it would save over three and a half years and selling Rolls Royce would involve writing off debts of £372 million, injecting another £100 million and yet still giving state support. The latter had the symbolic political attraction of reversing the Heath government's 1971 'lame duck' takeover.

Public opinion

Bolstering the government's case was a public opinion far from hostile to privatisation. A MORI poll in 1983 showed 39 per cent favouring privatisation against 21 per cent wanting more nationalisation (*Sunday Times*, 9 October 1983). Some £40 billion had been spent on nationalisation and write-offs since the war, but it was shown to be a vote loser. An ORC poll as early as 1978 had shown that 71 per cent of respondents (against 19 per cent) thought it to have failed and 78 per cent (against 13 per cent) believed Labour should abandon the policy (*The Times*, 10 July 1978). And in times of high unemployment, the unions' defence of jobs and index-linked pensions was muted.

A share-owning democracy

Just as the Conservatives sought to strengthen property-owning democracy (e.g. by council house sales), fostering a share-owning democracy was a political ambition. Share ownership in Britain trebled from 1979 to reach eight million shareholders in 1989 (six million of these holding privatised shares). By contrast, in the USA, 42.5 million citizens own shares, while most western countries are ahead of Britain.

The watershed came with the sale of BT, when a £7.6 million advertising campaign was launched by the government in the press and on the television to persuade people to buy shares and to participate in BT's future. The simplicity of the procedures was stressed, booklets on the City and shares and investments were provided, and incentives were offered in the form of £10 vouchers to offset rental payments and a one-for-ten loyalty bonus. Application forms could be taken to banks and post offices. In offering free shares and other incentives to BT employees, the government automatically had nearly a quarter of a million potential investors. The flotation of BT in November 1984 was hailed as a triumph for the government as two million people bought shares, many for the first time (small investors being favoured in the allocation of shares). Of BT's 233,000 employees, 96 per cent ignored union advice and applied for free shares. With so many investors, BT's annual general meeting is a twice-daily road show in five centres, preceded by 60,000 telephone calls and replies to 10,000 letters after a mailing of 1.5 million annual reports.

The sale of the British Gas Corporation (BGC) cost £20 million in advertising (twice that of BT) to reach small shareholders – the 'tell Sid' campaign was known to 90 per cent of the population and spawned jokes and cartoons galore.

The government could be content that there was a hard core who held on to ex-government stocks and were being advised to do so by investment analysts – for the 3.2 million investors in BGC in 1989, 800,000 held shares in other privatised concerns and 600,000 of the 1.13 million shareholders in the British Airports Authority (BAA) held equity in the others (International Communications and Data, for *The Independent*, 29 July 1989). By 1993, investors had lost the chance to sell for a quick profit but had been 'educated' to buy – less than 10 per cent of the second issue of BT shares were resold within a month.

Workers as shareholders

The idea of workers becoming shareholders in their own company is not new – Sir Alfred Mond, the founder of ICI, advocated this. Unlike cooperatives, worker share-holding leaves control undisturbed and has been advocated as the answer to socialism, in making workers 'capitalists'.

During the process of privatisation, worker share-holding had obvious attractions – it weakened opposition, particularly if free shares were offered, and was thought to impede renationalisation later. In the long term, it was identified as a motivator of staff and a means of increasing productivity – Keith Stuart, chief executive of Associated British Ports, was convinced that staff awareness had increased since workers had taken 8 per cent of the share-holding. Between 1980 and 1992 one million workers were transferred from the public to the private sector, over half had become shareholders and the proportion of state industry had fallen from 9 per cent of gross domestic product (GDP) in 1979 to 3 per cent in 1990. Besides weakening the trade unions, it was argued that worker share-holding, in producing lower wage claims, would assist the economy.

In November 1983 British Airways (BA), in preparation for its privatis-ation, offered its 36,000 workers low wage rises for two years in return for a profit-sharing bonus plan, with money held in trust for share purchase. The frequently cited example of worker share-holding success is the National Freight Corporation, where management took the initiative in 1981 and organised the biggest buyout in British industry. Seven years later, 82 per cent of the company was owned by employees, families and pensioners. When the company was floated on the Stock Exchange in February 1989 the average £600 investment at the time of privatisation was worth £60,000.

Workers in the six unions of the Yorkshire Rider bus company pushed for employee share ownership in 1988 and the electricity privatisation split the unions – while the National Union of Mineworkers (NUM) and the National Union of Railwaymen (NUR) opposed the sale, the eight unions most closely involved pressed for the best ownership deal for their members and consulted City experts. The management of the Vickers and Cammell Laird Belfast shipyards worked to persuade employees and residents to invest to the extent that 80 per cent of the workforce subscribed, with the share oversubscribed twice. To the anger of the NUM, both the Union of Democratic Mineworkers and the General and Municipal Boilermakers and Allied Trades Union (GMB) expressed interest in buying British Coal.

Profit-sharing schemes have been encouraged by the 1978 and 1980 Finance Acts, which conferred tax benefits on employees and companies. Nigel Lawson's 'popular capitalism' budget was, according to a poll, well received by 58 per cent of the nation – it offered tax incentives to buy shares and to belong to employee share schemes (7 per cent of workers now covered) and outlined a profit-sharing plan that would link 20 per cent of wages to profits. A survey of firms involved in share ownership reported that all of them had experienced an improvement in industrial relations (Burns, 1988).

This theme was taken up by Chancellor Gordon Brown when the Labour government took office in 1997. In pursuit of industrial democracy, he favoured voting rights being attached to share ownership. US studies had indicated that such participation in the long-term future of companies stimulated productivity, jobs and profits. In an effort to find promised 'commercial freedom' for the Post Office, without incurring the wrath of unions, the Labour government employed accountants KPMG and the Dresdner Kleinwort Benson investment bank to find an alternative to privatisation – in September 1998 this was thought to involve issuing a billion bonds to small investors. Lacking the volatility of shares, these were thought to offer a wider appeal to savers, not just share-owners.

Public borrowing

Between 1980 and 1992, privatisation revenue totalled £41 billion and the sale of council houses £5.5 billion. These sales of assets reduced the public sector borrowing requirement (PSBR – or the amount government has to borrow each year to balance income with expenditure). Additional expenditure is therefore possible by allowing a higher PSBR when these sales are added. In 1983/4, the total asset sales raised £3.1 billion, which lowered the PSBR by 30 per cent, from a target of £4.5 billion. For 1985/6, if the proposed sales were subtracted, the PSBR of £7 billion or 2 per cent of GDP would have to be doubled. Privatisation thus enabled the Tory government to cling to the monetarist claims of expenditure control and sound finance, while continuing to spend with a large deficit – keeping pressure off ministers. The Labour government quickly changed its mind about the merits of the Private Finance Initiative (PFI) – it was a way of delivering public services, using private money, while staying in the tight spending targets it had accepted. By September 1998 projects worth £10.5 billion had been agreed.

Civil service interference

Nationalised industries had to submit their investment and borrowing plans to the Treasury and report to their 'sponsoring ministry'. But beyond the formal controls there had been the 'lunchtime directives' to directors and other informal pressures – to set an example on pricing, wage settlements and to favour British manufacturers, for example with aircraft or computers. The chief executive of National Freight described privatisation as 'breaking out of the straightjacket' and the chair of Cable & Wireless (C&W) as an end to the 'psychology of restraint' – C&W had seen the 'dead hand' of the Treasury delay its plans and veto a vital project. The idea of being free to make commercial decisions and being rid of constant meetings with officials proved attractive to corporation boards and served the government's purpose of reducing the role and size of the 'bureaucracy'.

The commercial impetus for privatisation

Expansion

In freeing the corporations, the government believed they would be able to invest more, expand and meet international competition.

After takeovers of British airlines, BA took a minority stake of £390 million in US Air, to build a global airline. It moved this up a gear by forging a partnership with the larger American Airlines and changed its livery in 1997 to lose its 'Britishness'.

In 1981 BT lost customers as it raised prices to keep its £1 billion self-provided investment going. The Treasury had withdrawn the chance of raising a £360 million bond and BT had to be helped twice by raising its borrowing powers. Privatisation was intended to avoid this constraint and enable BT to compete with the privately owned communications company Mercury (and its backer C&W), Vodaphone cellular phones and, abroad, AT&T and the American 'baby Bells' (companies created by the partial break-up of AT&T's Bell company). Once privatised, BT began to expand overseas, particularly in North America – buying stakes in Tymnet, Dialcom and Syncordia, investing £1 billion in a global network and £3.24 billion in the American MCI company and then forming an alliance with AT&T. Similarly, BGC intended to re-enter oil exploration and production, won a contract, against international competition, in Kazakhstan and moved to invest £3 billion in South America. PowerGen made a £1 billion investment in Indonesia. By 1993 £10 billion had been invested abroad by privatised companies, with even the water companies winning overseas contracts (North West Water and Severn Trent to clean up Mexico City's systems).

Similarly, the government believed it had no place in the dynamic, competitive environment of oil exploration and production – so it hived off Britoil from the regulatory functions of the British National Oil Corporation. In August 1984 Jaguar Cars, hived off from BL, announced plans to expand production by 4,000 cars a year and employ 530 extra workers, to meet demand and German competition. Government supporters claimed that this was evidence that privatisation worked. Unfortunately, such claims have a short shelf-life, and Jaguar, taken over by Ford, was faring badly in the 1990s.

Nevertheless, this argument – for commercial freedom – persisted. In 1998 the chair of the Post Office, Neville Bain, was arguing for privatisation, warning that if it was milked for profits by the Treasury, its value of £3.25 billion would be halved in five years. There are now eight overseas companies in Britain handling mail. As ever, there was support from the Treasury – not simply because it saw the Post Office better able to take on foreign competition – but because of a sale's effect on public borrowing.

Efficiency

Nationalised industries' accounts have been poor measures of their performance, for in addition to problems of inflation and depreciation, governments have altered prices or levied profits. Supporters contended that the threat of privatisation so concentrates the mind that efficiency improves dramatically. British Steel's productivity rose 60 per cent over the ten years to privatisation in 1988 while its workforce was cut by 70 per cent; it moved from a loss of £1.7 billion in 1979 to a profit of £500 million. The same was true of British Coal, which in July 1992 reported a profit of £170 million, the highest in its forty-five-year existence. This performance was twice as good as that in 1991, despite restructuring and lower property rights, and was attributable to higher productivity and lower operating costs. Rover's newest plants approach Japanese standards, with the extra incentive that the Japanese car companies were manufacturing in Britain.

Government spokespersons commented favourably as BT restructured itself to be customer-facing, revolutionised its accountancy away from monopoly capitalisation and invested £17 billion, installing two digital exchanges a day and laying 1.2 million miles of high-quality fibre optic cable, matching Mercury's in the City. Mercury and then cable companies undercut BT by 12 per cent to 25 per cent for some calls and BT responded with discounts, redesigned bills and reliability on appointments. Nor did the regulator, Oftel, take a low profile, as predicted, as it stopped BT's links with IBM, obtained interconnection charges favourable to Mercury, after calling BT's bluff to go to the Monopolies and Mergers Commission (MMC). It ended the payphone monopoly in 1988, imposed new metering standards and reduced the tariff/pricing structure for customers from the retail price index (RPI) less 3 per cent to 4.5 per cent to 7.5 per cent in 1992, and insisted this price cut was passed on to domestic customers by a separation of accounting. The RPI – x formula was meant to determine price changes, where x was a factor reflecting expected efficiency gains. It forced BT to introduce dozens of price-cut schemes over the next decade.

In the summer of 1987 BT came under immense pressure following an engineers' strike in February and a National Consumer Council report naming it as the worst public service. By reallocation of resources and new standards, payphone availability rose from 75 per cent to 96 per cent as the number of them increased from 77,000 in 1984 to 104,000 in 1992, new business lines installed within six days of the request rose from 28 per cent to 60 per cent; faults cleared within two days rose from 74 per cent to 90 per cent. It accepted that compensation should be paid for delays in repairs and installation. This shock to the system ensured BT would continue its quest for quality.

With the exception of the water industry, which is allowed to raise prices up to 5 per cent above inflation, customers were deemed to have done well under the new regimes by the 1990s: electricity prices have matched inflation, gas prices have risen 20 per cent since 1986 while inflation was 40 per cent, and BT prices had fallen by 35 per cent in real terms by 1997.

By 2001 a third of prison inmates will be held in privately run prisons, at a saving to the taxpayer – from Securicor's £53 million at Parc gaol to £3 million at Group 4's Altcourse prison (Commons Public Accounts Committee, August 1998). This was at the cost of fewer staff, at lower rates, with poorer pensions. In a kind of 'customer satisfaction' (see below) the absence of the Prison Officers' Association meant that inmates enjoyed more liberal regimes in terms of time out of cells and purposeful work.

Customer satisfaction

By increasing efficiency and introducing new services, the customer benefits: from special offers from British Rail (BR); from BT's dash to modernise and its average 35 per cent price reduction on main services since 1984; from lower rates bills where refuse services have been put out to tender; from a choice of airline services on British routes with the start-up of companies such as British Midland; and, in towns like Hereford where competition on bus services was introduced, more frequent services and lower fares. The promotion of efficiency and removal of 'take it or leave it' attitudes became central to the advocacy of privatisation. There was even hope of more comfort on the buses as investment came through – £280 million in 1997 and an expected 20 per cent more new buses in 1998, in the wake of the Labour government's pro-public transport white paper.

The government could also claim to have taken steps to safeguard the public. In its Gas Bill it strengthened safety provisions – requiring a response to leaks within twelve hours (half the time required before); BGC was responsible for leaks on the customer side. For water privatisation, its second proposal in 1988 was stronger in that it created the National Rivers Authority to take over regulation, pollution control, fisheries and care of the environment. This separation of poacher and gamekeeper had been kept out of the 1987 version of the legislation by the opposition of the water authorities, which were in the main polluters with sewage. Expressing commitment to tough European Union (EU) standards and green policies, the government began to advocate the sell-off of water as an expensive but long overdue clean-up, requiring £3.5 billion for improving beaches, drinking water and sewage works. These improvements were woven together under John Major's Citizen's Charter of 1992/3.

The government learned from the BT and BGC experiences – not merely did it break up the electricity generating industry, but it included a money-back scheme for poor service from the start. Yet in 1989 the National Consumer Council stated that services had not improved, and wanted clear standards and mandatory automatic compensation.

Ideology and pragmatism

Dr Malcolm Pirie of the Adam Smith Institute neatly listed the ten benefits of privatisation:

- reduced government costs;
- companies can raise money on capital markets;
- government can concentrate on public goods such as defence and education, not trading;
- companies are more responsive to customers;

- they are better managed;
- better industrial relations;
- wider share ownership;
- higher capital spending;
- more competition and choice;
- lower prices.

However, the Conservative government almost just happened upon the policy of selling public assets. It certainly did not invent it: Chile sold assets in 1973; Edward Heath sold off Thomas Cook and Carlisle Pubs in 1970; and Labour sold 17 per cent of BP in 1977. Despite many obstacles, inconsistencies and embarrassments, it persisted and enlarged the process until privatisation not only came to be one of the government's main claims to success and its distinguishing feature but also a primary means of survival. For all the economic and managerial underpinning of privatisation worldwide, the issue of power cannot be ignored: Poland has had difficulties because it was reluctant to hand utilities back to communists; and in Britain the process reduces government and union control over the economy and favours Conservative interests at the expense of Labour's (Will Hutton, *The Guardian*, 11 May 1992). The Conservatives even began to advocate selling off EU civil service work.

Nevertheless, it seemed that privatisation's time had come on a worldwide scale. Germany began to speed up the sale of Lufthansa and Telekom, and sold shares in Volkswagen and Veba AG. Most risky of all, non-communist Russia moved to sell shares in 6,000 state companies for cash or vouchers in August 1992. Swedish, Turkish, Italian, Latin American and eastern European offerings accelerated the pace and only a shortage of capital held more back. The *Wall Street Journal*, after taking a swipe at France's economic nationalism, was satisfied that it was settled that the state had no role as a 'corporate shareholder' ('Ideology for sale', 13 August 1992). In 1997 worldwide privatisation receipts reached an all-time high of $100 billion.

By 1987 Treasury officials had advised twenty countries about privatis- ation and, appropriately, in 1989 embarked on a venture with the USA to sell the expertise to the developing world. In 1989 and 1990 £25 billions' worth of expertise was sold worldwide and in 1991 it was £40 billion; British firms were advising on half of all ventures. London was regarded as the centre of privatisation expertise – with think-tanks to advise and consultancies to implement strategy and regulation, Britain had the scale and variety of experience and thus acquired the techniques. This also suited the global aspirations of British companies and found new markets for merchant banks, which often worked for a success fee.

One assumption which has been accepted by parties of all kinds was that competition was more important than ownership. But a major study by the World Bank in June 1992 offered proof that 'privatisation' per se works. The Bank's methods were rigorous, separating the benefits and losses to all parties and assessing alternative courses of action for three privatisations in each of four countries. In eleven out of the twelve cases they calculated the net increase in wealth, which was highest for the privatisation of Chile Telecom, with a gain of 155 per cent on turnover. The Bank excluded gains not attributable to privatisation and explained the success – freedom to invest in four cases; setting higher prices was crucial to most. Consumers gained from four and lost from five; Labour cuts were significant (the Mexican government bankrupted Aeromexico and the new firm rehired only half the workforce); but workers benefited directly in three cases and none of the twelve cases studied had labour troubles. And the Bank showed that foreigners took large slices – in three cases more than indigenous buyers – but that often helped countries like Mexico to convince investors that they were serious (figures from *The Economist*, 13 June 1992).

General problems with privatisation

It was unlikely that the factors described above would weave together into a coherent strategy. The main inconsistency has proved to be between the ideological drive for liberalisation and competition, and the Treasury-led demand for maximum sales revenue.

Privatised monopolies

This inconsistency was exposed most clearly in the privatisation of BT and BGC, monopolies capable of generating annual profits in excess of £1 billion from the outset. Having decided against breaking up BT so the Treasury would gain most upon flotation and to create an international 'heavyweight', the government had to institute a regulatory agency, a quango, Oftel. Instead of new bureaucratic controls, of doubtful strength, many Conservatives demanded competition. That ministers were also trying to safeguard the fledgling Mercury at the expense of would-be leasers and resellers of BT lines in the lucrative business sector was only grudgingly accepted. Gradually, pressure to redress the situation increased – Mercury and BT lost their exclusive rights to computer communications over the network, and in 1991 their duopoly was broken by the licensing of competitors – Ionica, BR, the power companies, the Energis telecommunications company, and US carriers like Sprint were all keen to get into the most liberalised telecommunications market in the world. The Liberal Democrats were still basing their case on first principles – their 1992 election manifesto demanded the regional break-up of BT.

Confusion and break-up

When the BGC's oil assets were sold off as Enterprise Oil and only one-sixth of the shares were wanted by ordinary investors, the government was placed in the embarrassing position of blocking a bid from Rio Tinto Zinc (RTZ) for 40 per cent of them. While this was consistent with aims of promoting competition (RTZ has oil interests) and safeguarding small investors in an independent company, it alienated free market Conservatives and the City. Gas and electricity supply presented a similar dilemma – whether to break the production and distribution monopolies radically or simply sell the shares and apply regulation.

After the privatisation of BGC, industrial customers, who provided 30 per cent of BGC's income, found that they were being charged more than the domestic sector for their gas. They were angry at the differential pricing and won a verdict against the privatised giant from the MMC in 1988. The users were soon lobbying to break its monopoly. With the regulator, government and the Liberal Democrats in favour, and Labour against, this was a clear indication that the original sell-off had been defective. Having wasted £6.5 million of its shareholders' money on advertising, lobbying and public relations fighting the MMC, BGC began the process of dismantling itself. The severance of sales (Centrica) from transportation (TransCo) came into force in 1996, though the pilot deregulation in the West Country was rushed and chaotic, with computer breakdowns, hard selling, misrepresentation of competitors and disconnection threats. TransCo and the exploration and production arms became BG p.l.c. Though one and a half million consumers had switched suppliers (with two million waiting to do so) by April 1998, many were initially confused about different tariffs. However, they could save up to 20 per cent on bills and the two new companies focused on keeping customers and planned expansion. Instead of being trapped in BG (known as 'bloody goner') a year before, their share values rose by £6 billion. One is left with the question of why this was not planned properly from the outset, despite Treasury greed.

Market forces or the public interest?

Learning from such experiences, electricity was split up on both the generating and distribution side. On the former, it was soon evident that the split between National Power and PowerGen was no provider of true competition – the distribution companies were soon building gas-fired stations to escape the duopoly. Again free market principles were shelved, to safeguard nuclear power by trying to make the generators buy up to 20 per cent of power from non-fossil fuel, and then giving up on including Nuclear Electric in the privatisation.

Market forces meant that the industries did not to stay in their privatised pattern – the utilities were cash rich and had steady cash flows and were attractive to companies like Trafalgar House, which made the first move – for Northern Electric in 1994. Hanson followed by bidding for Eastern Electricity – this would result in tax advantages for Hanson, large payoffs for Eastern's directors and the price indicated that the company had been privatised for only a third of its real value. Such bids were also said to mean that the pricing regulation was seen as weak and that the companies were 'fat' in being able to mount campaigns against takeover, including extra share payouts. The government blocked the bids of Severn Trent and Wessex Water for South West Water on the grounds that mergers would prevent the regulator, Ofwat, making comparisons between the performance of separate companies. Yet they approved Scottish Power's bid for Manweb and only stopped the French group Lyonnaise from adding Northumbrian Water to its existing North East Water until it promised bigger price cuts. Nor were takeover bids confined to their own industries – North West Water bought Norweb, South Wales Electricity was bought by Welsh Water, Southern Water by Scottish Power, Centrica gas began to sell electricity and nuclear British Energy moved into gas generation.

The possibility arose that such mergers would create monopolies able to hold customers to ransom – a charge levelled from John Redwood on the Tory right as well as from Labour, which demanded that all takeovers be referred to the MMC. This was also true of companies beginning to integrate vertically – Eastern buying two power stations from PowerGen. The attempt of PowerGen and National Power to go 'downstream' by bidding for Midlands Electricity and Southern Electricity respectively (also nullifying the privatisation separation) was too much for senior Tories and was blocked by the government – though the MMC had seen no problem with the bids and Labour let PowerGen go ahead in 1998 and take over East Midlands Electricity.

The national interest or laissez-faire capitalism?

French companies had won water and rail franchises, but the main investors in privatised industries were the Americans. By May 1998 they had bought eight of the twelve regional electricity companies – C & SW of Texas bought Seeboard, CalEnergy bought Northern, Dominion Resources bought East Midlands, Southern of Atlanta bought South West Electricity, SCE Corp. bought National Power's pump storage business, Cinergy and GPU bought Midlands Electricity, Entergy bought London Electricity and Texas Utilities bought Energy Group (which includes the largest regional electricity company – Eastern Electricity). The first three of these buyers were under legal investigation in the USA – for anti-competitive activity, fraud and being a 'top polluter' respectively. In the USA, 5,000 experts and support staff safeguard the public interest (not a few hundred 'learners' as in Britain) and they let private enterprise nowhere near the water industry. The Labour government's windfall tax and tougher regulation in favour of the consumer, rather than competition, began to deter them – by September 1998 two had sold out and others were said to be divesting. But at the same time an American company moved in to take over Wessex Water. US hospital companies arrived in 1994 to buy into the NHS and other US companies moved in on the privatised railway companies. BR's freight operations had been split into three to encourage competition, but all of it was sold to Wisconsin Central Transportation Corporation, which already ran the Royal Mail and the royal train.

The process began to work the other way as the British companies sought sources away from the more tightly regulated domestic market, where there were calls for break-up or selling of power stations by the regulator: by October 1998 National Power had invested £1 billion in the USA, Scottish Power took over Cinergy and the National Grid targeted Pacificorp. PowerGen also tried large mergers and takeovers, amid rumours that predators were stalking it and National Power – a case of grow or be eaten.

Privatised predators

The Civil Aviation Authority's recommendation in 1984 that over thirty major routes be taken from BA and given to competitors produced uproar. BA hotly opposed the plan as producing no competition or benefit to the customer and retarding privatisation. In becoming efficient for flotation BA had become more of a threat to competitors. Privatised, it started to remove them, beginning with British Caledonian and DanAir. Its alliance with American Airlines would take in 60 per cent of traffic between Britain and North America and drew attacks from competitors and the EU. BA was later found to be using 'dirty tricks' to capture passengers from Virgin and was taken to court for using its power to create a cheaper domestic subsidiary (not having BA pay and conditions) to take on EasyJet and short-haul carriers.

The mergers described above and the emergence of companies like United Utilities, the expansion plans of PowerGen and other overseas takeovers and alliances all raised issues of control. After nine years, 60 per cent of the bus market was in the hands of the biggest seven companies, run by aggressive entrepreneurs; a quarter of all complaints to the Office of Fair Trading were about that industry and the MMC had carried out fourteen investigations – one in August 1995 strongly rebuked Stagecoach and Go-Ahead for acting 'against the public interest' in the north-east of England.

Value for money or just money?

When privatising Jaguar, the government was accused by the all-party Trade and Industry Committee of rendering BL and its privatisation less viable, and the government had to turn down a management–worker buyout of some of BR's hotels in order to try for a better price. A bitter dispute occurred over Britoil's capital structure, as the company tried to obtain government funds while the Treasury pressed for sale of assets to save money. The result was a Britoil perceived to be weak with insufficient reserves while the government was still accused of wasting money.

National policies or ad hocery?

Inevitably, others pressed the cause of privatisation to logical conclusions with demands for the break-up of monopolies, buyouts and decentralisation (CBI, October 1983) and widespread ownership of capital by giving shares away (the Stock Exchange chair).

At times the government was trapped between its own inclinations towards market forces and political expediency. After secretly negotiating with Ford to take over Austin Rover and having invited General Motors to discuss the trucks and Land Rover part of BL, it found itself assaulted by angry Tory MPs. Having followed orders to privatise BL, directors now began to bid for Land Rover and other offers, having been spurned, were then welcomed. All negotiations were eventually dropped.

Safety

In its determination to sell the electricity industry, the government had to deal with its awkward nuclear component. At first all of the latter was taken out of the sale and imposed as a levy on the rest. Then, to make money and despite safety fears, the newer nuclear plants were sold off (cheaply) as British Energy. The government had even considered a trade sale of nuclear power to a US company in 1996, without anything resembling an energy policy. The Labour government was left the task of merging British Nuclear Fuels Limited (BNFL), with its waste and reprocessing, and the old Magnox plants to decommission – at a cost of £4 billion to the taxpayer. BNFL still worked on plans for privatisation by passing on its liabilities to buyers or dumping them with the Treasury. In September 1998 the government moved on this largest remaining but most difficult sale by appointing advising accountants – but while the latter might like its yen-earning capacity from reprocessing nuclear waste, they cannot answer scientific problems about what to do with the stockpiles or the political pressures on Sellafield's safety record.

The first figures released by the Mines Inspectorate since privatisation showed that serious accidents in that industry had risen by 28 per cent. Nacods, the coal supervisors' union, claimed in August 1998 that owners had under-reported a 52 per cent rise in accidents – the sudden 400 per cent rise reported in one category showed the omission. After the second rail accident by an American-run freight company in 1996, there were claims that the run-down in investment and rushed sell-off was endangering lives. A similar claim was made against the privatised water companies in 1998 by fire chiefs – to meet their leakage targets, water pressure was being kept too low for the fire service's needs. In the same year they were blamed for adding to beach pollution for failing to invest in safe storm drains.

Special pleading

In deciding between state-owned Harland and Wolff and the newly privatised Swan Hunter shipyards for a £130 million order, the government was squeezed between Harland's cheaper bid under 'competitive tendering' (and appeasing Ulster Loyalists) and yet not wishing to see a new company go bankrupt in the north-east (where there were marginal seats) after it was virtually promised the order before flotation. Both yards were given work and survived.

Confusion

This surfaced in bizarre areas: there would be a £422 million subsidy for the Post Office; the privatised skill centres (set up with £11 million) went bankrupt in July 1993; and the government was accused of wasting £200 million as it sold National Transcommunications Limited (*Business Age*, February 1993). In trying to sell the Department of Trade and Industry's Insolvency Service the government spent £2.4 million on consultancy advice and then gave up the idea.

The wrong problem

Changes in ownership do not necessarily bring improved performance. Indeed, transferring ownership to pension funds and unit trusts, away from civil servants and politicians, may actually diminish accountability.

It has been argued that privatisation is desirable because all governments interfere with nationalised industries and only severance will provide a solution. This view discounts past proposed reforms such as that of the 1968 Select Committee on Nationalised Industries, which wanted a ministry for corporations, and the 1976 suggestion of policy councils by the consensus-seeking, tripartite National Economic Development Council. Today their recommendations sound as out of date as the structures themselves.

But some successes have been achieved in the public sector. BP thrived irrespective of majority or minority government share-holding, while C&W enjoyed steady success before and after privatisation. BL, as a private company, went bankrupt, while it improved dramatically in the public sector – against competition and under Sir Michael Edwardes (who could reassert tighter management and distance government influence) it showed signs of revival. British Steel's and British Coal's dramatic increase in productivity came in the public sector. The Post Office raised productivity 17 per cent in the five years from 1981 and was one of the most productive – in 1991 it doubled profits to £266 million in its sixteenth year without subsidies and the European Commission reported that 90 per cent of sixty-one million letters (thirty-eight million in 1981) were delivered within twenty-four hours in Britain, as well as Denmark, Ireland and the Netherlands, while in the other member states it was 30–40 per cent. The Centre for Policy Studies reported that the government was making a success of corporations by appointing uncompromising new chairs, such as Lord King (to BA) and Mr McGregor (to British Steel).

It could be argued that the only problems of the electricity industry were Treasury-induced price rises to grab revenue and 'fatten' them for privatisation, fulfilling the jibe of interference and prophecy of sell-off as a solution. Under no threat of takeover, BT and BGC's position led many to claim that competition and good management which responded to customer needs were more important than ownership.

The regulators

Nicholas Ridley, in an article eulogising privatisation, said that the creation of 'tough and clear regulatory regimes' protected customers from monopoly power and 'again we are leading the world'. This bears examination: in July 1992 the *Sunday Times* assembled a panel of six customer and utility experts to mark the regulators out of ten on accessibility, public profile, striking a balance between customers and industry, understanding the companies and efficiency in handling complaints. All four regulators were criticised for lack of toughness, fairness, lack of commitment to customers, acting in secrecy (and not publishing their salaries) – in contrast to the US system of regulation. Sir James McKinnon of Ofgas came top for his tough stand against BGC and forcing a 3 per cent price cut – in a sense he was BGC's competition. His eighteen months of rows led to BGC taking the issue to the MMC and gaining a review of the whole industry – including replacing the regulator by a panel.

British Telecom has had an unending acrimonious relationship with Oftel, its chair attacking the regulator for 'secret deliberations' with its competitors and calling for a watchdog to watch the watchdogs, or abolition. As in the gas industry, BT saw increasing interference by one non-accountable figure with policy making, but Carsberg, director of Oftel, scored low in the *Sunday Times* on 'fairness' and 'toughness'. In 1996 BT went so far as to take its regulator to the High Court for exceeding his powers by including a clause about anti-competitive behaviour in its licence – it lost. The electricity regulator scored low on every measure despite having the strongest powers and Ofwat was criticised for allowing water price rises and disconnections.

The progress of BGC seemed to show the flaw: in 1991 it increased prices by 35 per cent at twenty-four hours' notice and was threatened by legal action by Ofgas and power companies, and price cuts were forced; it clashed with the regulator the following year over its profits of £1.5 billion while one million people sought help to pay their bills; and in 1992 BGC was threatened with the courts and the MMC again and the government proposed to break the retail monopoly. Faced with this, BGC began a review to break itself up – into twelve districts, severing all links between exploration, production, pipelines (alone worth £6 billion) and global business.

By 1994 the regulatory regime was under severe criticism, seeming too much influenced by the industries, dependent on personalities, lacking expertise (argued by the Confederation of British Industry and experienced US regulators) and of being uncoordinated at a time when British and foreign energy and water companies began to merge or overlap in the services they provided. In that year Ofwat's new regime limited price rises to an average of 1 per cent above inflation over the next decade (1.5 per cent for the first five years, 0.5 per cent for the second five) – down from the original 5 per cent. Since privatisation, water bills had risen by an average of 74 per cent and would now rise up to 35 per cent over the next decade. Meanwhile, the water companies' share prices rose 99 per cent (against a FTSE average of 39 per cent) and their profits had nearly doubled to £2 billion in 1993.

In the City, where BZW had been urging the water companies to stand up to the regulator if a new regime was tough, their share prices rose and the regulator was condemned for betraying the consumers. Nor had he said anything about the £727 million wasted on 160 non-water projects. As their directors began to pay themselves large increases in salaries in the 1990s and drought and rationing (especially by Yorkshire Water) cast doubt on their competence, there was considerable anger.

In 1994 Stephen Littlechild imposed a one-off cut of 14 per cent on the regional electricity companies but then limited rises to 2 per cent above inflation – what he described as a 'crackdown' was regarded as a give-away and £1.1 billion was added to their market worth in forty-eight hours. They had outperformed any privatised utility (including water) on the stock market, their chiefs had trebled their salaries in four years and their prices had steadily outpaced gas prices to consumers since privatisation.

Oftel was beginning to wonder if it should loosen its regulatory regime and walk away from the pressures and complexities. With press coverage personalising the 'toughness' of regulators, it comes as no surprise that they responded to such criticism with harsher regimes in 1995/6: the RPI – x formula was making them guess at efficiency without adequate data (the Americans regulated profits rather than charges). They were forced to change decisions – Oftel changed its mind about its new regulatory framework, in reaction to complaints from BT's competitors in July 1991, and prevented the Treasury bringing in £11 billion by selling its remaining 48.6 per cent of BT shares, and Littlechild reopened his pricing review in 1995, after eight months, in the middle of the sale of 40 per cent of National Power and PowerGen, which led to accusations of sales under false pretences and incompetence.

In response, the Labour Party demanded 'windfall' taxes on large utilities and imposed one of £5 billion when it came to power in 1997. Others rejected the regulators' argument that they were responding to changing circumstances as the industries developed – wanting the MMC and customers to have more power and subjecting regulation agencies to review by parliamentary select committee, Audit Commission and the Office of Fair Trading. After reviewing the regulators' performance, the Labour government was committed to reorganising the system and putting the interests of consumers first, rather than fostering competition. When their green paper appeared in March 1998 it suggested merging the gas and electricity regulators, and promised guidance on how to pursue environmental and social objectives, including protecting those on low incomes. But the Treasury had stopped profit capping, retaining the RPI – x formula, with an 'error correction mechanism'. Critics could not see why the system should improve, with regulators depending on utilities for information, being fed overstated costs or understated revenue and productivity projections. Neither they nor the new 'independent' consumer committees were likely to get access to 'share sensitive/commercially confidential' information (unlike in the USA).

Left-wing critics and crusading or self-seeking privatisers had asked the same question – if it is such a good idea, why not privatise the management and leave the assets in state hands? This had been done in the NHS, so why was the case not made for leaving the assets of public utilities alone and letting private management compete for the job of running them efficiently, with the profits coming back to the Exchequer? Privatised companies may be free from the Treasury, but the British stock market, which demands quick profits and dividends, probably renders them even less efficient.

Political problems with privatisation

Management opposition

Three board members of BT and the British National Oil Corporation resigned over the privatisation issue. Nevertheless, management has largely concentrated on obtaining the best terms, resisting attempts to break up the corporations (BT, BL, BGC, BR, British Coal) or minimising regulation (the degree of control allowed BT for pricing). The most open opposition from within industry came from Sir Denis Rooke to the selling of BGC's showrooms, North Sea oil and the Wytch Farm oil field in Dorset; from Lord King and the BA board, who mounted a powerful campaign against ceding routes; and Sir Bob Reid ceased to be a favourite when he opposed BR's privatisation. Critics argued that these supposedly sympathetic chairs had not only delayed privatisation but impeded competition. The Institute of Directors also alluded darkly to key enemies in the civil service.

The BA sale had foundered several times over anti-trust lawsuits, jumbo jet defects, arguments over restructuring its balance sheet and downturn in business. In anger and frustration, Lord King organised a management buyout in March 1986, but this was blocked after a public row, amid speculation that there were plans to restructure BA into three or four airlines to promote competition and increase the sale price. Far from this happening, the powerful Lord King organised a takeover of British Caledonian and DanAir.

Opposition could come from more exalted quarters – it was said that the Queen had opposed the sell-off of the Royal Mail, although she had to consent to the 'de-crowning' of Parcel Force.

Union opposition

Unions have had good reason to oppose privatisation: over nine-tenths of workers in nationalised industries were union members, many in closed shops, while three-quarters of manual and one-third of white-collar workers in private manufacturing were unionised at the start of the 1980s. While some workers in successful enterprises, such as Amersham, have been unaffected, others in service industries have seen their pay, working conditions and security suffer. Initially, unions took strong anti-privatisation stances – in the 1982 annual conference of the Trades Union Congress (TUC), ten motions were submitted with demands for renationalisation without compensation, except in cases of hardship. In June 1994 Michael Heseltine told the unions that he no longer saw any need to talk to them about privatisation because he was 'liberating' their members from government. The following year the chief executive of North West Water advised the rail managers to 'eliminate or emasculate' the unions as opponents of change and privatisation. The successful bidder for the main east coast line thought the railways were run with a 'communist approach'. Action taken so far has included the following.

*   *Days of action*   These were taken by the gas and other unions (e.g. the National and Local Government Officers' Association; NALGO) against the sale of showrooms, and by 180,000 BT employees in six unions against privatisation in October 1982. In the case of BR, the National Union of Rail, Maritime and Transport Workers (RMT) organised day-long strikes in 1989 to try to protect job security. The same union

began a two-day action against the Labour government's plans to privatise the London Underground in June 1998.

- *Alliances* NALGO contributed £1 million to a fund and agreed to work with the National Union of Public Employees (NUPE) in the campaign against contracting out.
- *Campaigns* NUPE and Services to Community Action and Tenants organised local campaigns against contracting out services. The BT unions initiated a publicity and parliamentary campaign, the latter including a filibustering speech lasting eleven and three-quarter hours by MP John Golding, who was sponsored by the Post Office and Engineering Union (POEU). The unions then turned from generalised defences to critical analysis of efficiency, costs and consequences. The NUM promised legal, political and industrial campaigns, but this was subsumed by later mass demonstrations. The Prison Officers' Association expressed opposition by alerting the public to the mistakes of private contractors – they claimed success in the stopping of market testing in 1995, but the following year a further 2,500 support jobs were privatised.
- *Education of members* Members were advised against buying shares, for example by the Transport and General Workers' Union (TGWU) in National Freight Corporation and POEU and the National Communications Union in BT. The TGWU later tried to recruit and recover membership among the now often contracted out cleaning staff, but employer resistance and low pay were to impede its efforts.
- *Prolonged industrial action* There was bitter action against loss of jobs through contracting out at several hospitals and councils. In BT the POEU escalated its action in 1983, refusing to connect the rival Mercury's backers, and 2,500 engineers were suspended and £250,000 a week was paid out in strike pay.

Industrial action, however, was often met with the threat to privatise, as during the ambulance strike in November 1989.

Ironically, the privatised utilities tried to enlist union support in 1996 to oppose Labour's windfall tax, warning of the impact on jobs and investment.

Labour renationalisation

Labour's original policy was one of renationalisation without compensation but this was modified for the 1983 election manifesto. Given the sums of money involved, a future Labour government would have to resort to a combination of partial and selective reacquisition, cooperatives and employee involvement in decision making. In 1986 Labour explained that 'social ownership' would entail a public sector able to work outside cash limits, with corporations able to develop commercially beyond their standard roles. Shares in key privatised companies could be exchanged for the original sale price or kept as bonds with a rate of interest. As part of the policy review, the 1988 Labour conference was asked to reject 'Morrisonian' corporations and it accepted regulations in the interest of consumers and workers, rather than buying back. This employee share ownership plan was retained in the 1992 election manifesto, but Labour's priorities by then were to stop compulsory tendering in the NHS and to 'free' opted out schools from central funding by returning them to local authorities. Its renationalisation measures were limited to retaining control of the National Grid, to safeguard coal and stop the 'dash for gas' and they were reduced to urging the boycott of water privatisation. In 1997 Labour was clearer that its priorities, given the 'mess' and debt it was inheriting, would not include renationalisation. Its 1998 conference rejected a bid for partial renationalisation of the railways (deemed illegal) and accepted that the £20 million needed for the whole process was needed elsewhere. After removing Clause 4 (regarding ownership of the means of production) from its constitution, the Party, and especially the Chancellor, was willing to contemplate privatisations or joint ventures.

Public opinion

While there is no urge to renationalise, neither is privatisation seen as a priority. In 1983 it ranked seventeenth on managers' list of priorities (CBI/ BIM survey). A strong campaign was mounted against the BT sale, then a novelty, but it merely shifted those opposed from 37 per cent in December 1982 to 46 per cent in October 1983 (Gallup poll). Reported resistance to further privatisation seemed to increase as the sell-offs became more controversial: a BBC/Marplan poll of January 1988 found 57 per cent wanted postponement or abandonment and only 25 per cent wanted continuation. And at the end of the year, a MORI poll confirmed the results of three years earlier – a five-to-one majority against water being sold and a three-to-one majority against electricity privatisation (*Sunday Times*, 4 December 1988). The public still turned out to make a quick profit when privatisation went ahead. An NOP poll for *The Independent* asked about preferences of future ownership in October 1991, after twelve years of privatisation. The results are reported in Table 12.1.

A MORI poll in 1996 found that people felt public services should be under public control, by a margin of six to one, and that they were underinvested, by ten to one.

It could not be assumed that public opinion was informed, however; a Cabinet Office report in February 1993 showed that the majority wrongly thought that the National Westminster Bank, BA and ITN were publicly owned, and 20 per cent thought the Abbey National 'definitely' was. Nor

Table 12.1. *Public preferences (%) for ownership of companies*

Company	Government	Private sector
Water	62	29
British Rail	52	39
British Coal	52	35
Post Office	66	29
British Gas	55	37
Electricity	59	34

Source: NOP for *The Independent*.

would opinion be helped to clear-thinking when a bus company, almost given away in 1990, was deemed to be worth £5.1 million in 1993 and constituted a monopoly on a main route.

The unpredictability of public opinion continued to confound the expectations of privatised companies. Employers and employees were clear that consumers and shareholders had a better deal, often at their expense, but a survey in June 1992 found only half willing to say anything good about privatisation and two-thirds cited negative effects (28 per cent on price). No account was taken that water and electricity prices were increased to make profits for their pension funds as well as 'Sids', nor that BT's size and investment needs meant that it could be expected to earn '£100 profit per second' in 1997. While BT may have been slow to turn from money making to consumer awareness, it was attacked for poorer service and higher prices when the reverse was true.

The press focused on rises in directors' salaries up to private sector levels and drew selective comparisons, such as the high cost of local telephone calls in Britain, ignoring what were classed as trunk calls in the USA or the subsidies and protectionism in Europe. BR suffered the same loaded comparisons, despite lacking comparable state support to railways elsewhere, and was threatened with sell-off as a kind of disciplinary medicine. At the same time, privatised industries found their regulators were interfering more and more, effectively making policy in a way that civil servants never could (City and Corporate Counsel Survey, *The Times*, 29 September 1992).

But nothing could have prepared the government for the public reaction, directed at them through their backbenchers in October 1992, as they announced the closure of thirty-one pits, with the loss of 30,000 mining jobs. Coal managers were warning of potential trouble in mid-1991; the size of the shutdown was being openly calculated by the Rothchild's report of 1991, which went on to predict that only twelve deep pits could remain by 1995; it further stated that the government foresaw that four-fifths of the workforce would go in three years. The government declared it wanted a rapid sell-off and went ahead with its planned announcement before Parliament reconvened. They totally miscalculated the public sympathy for the mining families and the outcry and demonstrations that followed, by an electorate already fearful and depressed by the state of the economy.

What seemed logical decisions by privatised and soon to be privatised companies over redundancies mushroomed into a political crisis threatening the Major government. Amid large demonstrations in September 1992, the government was forced into a humiliating 'U' turn, promising a select committee into the whole energy policy while the pit closures were suspended. Later disclosures that the Prime Minister had agreed a Colombian coal import deal, that BP was fostering competition by importing Norwegian gas, and that British Coal had been investing for thirteen years in an Australian mining company which produced cheap coking coal all made an harmonious outcome impossible. In March 1993, the inquiry offered the pits only a chance of survival. As British Coal's losses rose, it moved to close more pits. It was accused of sabotage and, with little private interest in four collieries, managers pressed miners to go quickly to receive better terms. The government had been able to let 'market forces' work for them but nonetheless would rue their clumsy handling of the issue.

In 1997 the Labour government seemed no more inclined to intervene and was said to be preparing its damage-limitation strategy as the industry declined and another 5,000 jobs were lost. But in April 1998 the government did move to make the generators take twenty-two to twenty-five million tonnes of coal, securing two-thirds of the deep-mine pits and jobs.

Dubious motives – sweeteners, fat cats and sleaze

Initially it was said that the government was diverting attention from right-wing criticism and from aid to lame-duck industries such as BL or British Steel. The privatisation connections of Conservative MPs were condemned – twenty-one owned shares in cleaning, catering or laundry firms or were part-time directors or consultants and the Labour research staff traced the ninety-one Tory MPs with BT shares and identified multiple applications. In October 1987 former MP Keith Best was imprisoned for four months and fined £3,000 for making six applications. The City, too, was criticised as it had been paid over £2 billion by 1991 in fees, expenses, commissions and underwriting. The £250 million spent on the more difficult water and electricity privatisations dwarfed the £25 million 'Sid' campaign and made the government the third biggest advertiser in the country. The non-executive directors of TSB 'mutinied' over the £3.8 million to be paid to Lazards. The City received more than £128 million for the sale of BT and auditors subsequently found illegal multiple applications. Consultants had made £258 million by 1994. Rothschilds was given a bonus of £2 million on top of its £5.5 million fee for selling British Coal in 1995.

The government found that the rules were too indefinite to take action against profiteers buying shares. By the time of the BP sale in October 1987, with twenty-three outstanding prosecutions from the BA, BGC, BAe and TSB sales, the 'forensic' accountants were using a computerised tracking system. By August 1992 investigations continued into illegal share applications and 700 cases were brought before a special court. The Public Accounts Committee had criticised the lack of control in 1986 and a year later condemned the £281 million in perks (vouchers and loyalty bonuses) offered since 1981. It was noted that a £15 million speculative profit was made in the first day of trading of C&W shares and that TSB shareholders doubled their money on the first day. At the TUC conference in 1984, Rodney Bickerstaffe of NUPE concluded, 'wherever public need is met by private greed, corruption is not far behind.... For privatisation read profiteering, expense account lunches and sweatshop wages' (*The Guardian*, 7 September 1984). In fact there were complaints in the City that the government was using its influence to force down fees to an unrewarding level.

A study by the London Business School in November 1988 showed that salaries of chief executives rose by an average of 78 per cent in the year after privatisation and by 250 per cent in real terms since 1979. The Labour Party analysed the donations to the Tory election funds, including £50,000 from Rolls Royce in 1987, and noted that donors to the Tories in 1997 included those who had profited from rail privatisation or would do so from future ones.

One of the longest-running accusations was that Lord Young had mishandled the takeover of Rover by BAe, never valuing the land it was allowed to sell at a large profit. It was then revealed in 1990 that 'sweeteners' worth at least £44 million had been given. This led to intervention by the EU on grounds of non-competitive practice. Yet despite the £400 million that the Rover sale had cost taxpayers, by 1992 BAe was in such difficulties that the car company was destined for foreign ownership. Lord Young stayed in the firing-line in 1990 as he became chair of C&W within a year of awarding its UK subsidiary company, Mercury, a personal communications network contract. The issue widened as other ministers and civil servants moved to lucrative jobs and the word 'sleaze' entered the vocabulary (discussed in Chapter 15). Accusations were levelled too at the attempts of a Thatcherite favourite, Lord Hanson, to buy PowerGen and British Coal outright. Whitehall retaliated in time-honoured fashion by refusing to divulge which of the seventy-two new bus companies had made a 'killing'. In 1996 it was alleged that £6.9 billion of 'sweeteners' had been included to sell the controversial nuclear business, British Energy.

The government was able to get the second lowest ever underwriting (£33 million) for the water sell-off in 1989, because of 'competition' for the business, but spent £39 million advertising to attract 'Sids' to their allocated 30 per cent of shares. It was left to the National Audit Office in 1992 to reveal that discretionary 'completion bonuses' worth £2.2 billion had been paid to City companies, on top of the government's spend of £143.5 million on fees. The consultant gravy train did not stop with the sale – new regulators and their utilities paid them £100 million for advice. In 1995 the EU investigated the possible misuse of £400 million of its regional aid as 'sweeteners' for privatisations. Workers in the water industry regarded the write-off of £5 billion of debt as fixing a 'barrow boy price' for a vital public service.

Towards the end of the Major government the cloud of sleaze, which was to poison any chances of re-election, emanated strongly from the privatised industries. Cedric Brown of BGC received most opprobrium with his 75 per cent rise and £4 million pension at a time when the company was making 25,000 staff redundant over three years and reducing the pay of its retail staff. In addition to huge rises in salaries, a wave of windfalls followed from share options and shares, as executives left or companies were taken over. The chair of South West Water stood to make £1.3 million in this way, seventy-seven electricity executives held £70 million in share options, twelve other utility chiefs became millionaires and the Serious Fraud Office was called in when six PowerGen directors cashed in £3.5 million in share options before profits were predicted to fall. In the case of the railways (see below) the sums were even higher. Through 1995–6, 'fat cat' directors scrambled to cash in their profits as condemnation rose and lobbying around the 'dregs' of privatised assets – seemingly going to Tory allies before the curtain came down – was intense and unedifying. The earlier claim of the Conservative Party that this was 'our greatest success' was looking threadbare. The House of Commons Public Accounts Committee in March 1998 said that it thought the sale of Belfast Airport 'stinks from start to finish' – three civil servants had become multimillionaires by selling it on at a profit of £75.15 million, including a £5 million hotel, which they bought for £1. In the same month the Comptroller and Auditor General condemned the managers of the privatised water pension funds of crass incompetence, dereliction of duty and conflict of interest for losing £400 million. The *Daily Mirror* put it in its starkest terms by singling out two power and three water executives, who had received 69 per cent increases, as 'Fat Rats' (13 August 1998).

Share-holding

The idea of a wide share-holding seems not to have been realised, for after initial interest small investors tended to sell for a profit. Of 65,000 Amersham buyers, only 7,717 were left by October 1983. Of BAe's workforce, 10 per cent did not apply for their £50 of free shares. C&W shareholders reduced from 157,000 to 26,000 in a year, and BAe from 158,000 to 26,000 by the end of 1982. The number of BT shareholders fell from 2.3 million at the time of floatation to 1.58 million in March 1986, with the big institutions controlling 62.5 per cent of the non-government shares. By the end of 1988 BGC was losing 10,000 'Sids' a month as its share-holding fell from 4.5 million to 2.8 million, TSB lost 700,000 in six months and one-third of Rolls Royce shares changed hands in a ninety-minute scramble as profits were taken. Individual shareholders were left holding only 16 per cent of BA after the other two-thirds of the buyers took their 83 per cent profit. To avoid fixing prices too low, the government was increasingly turning to tender, on which City institutions bid low, meaning that the temptation of big gains for individuals was missing. By offering low prices on monopoly shares, it was argued that a false impression of risk capitalism had been given, and these large institutions were unwilling to take necessary risks or bring accountability to companies.

Despite the increase in absolute numbers, the proportion of the population holding shares has declined relative to 1978 – most of them are held by the older and more prosperous citizens. By 1992 it was clear that there was a difference between holding shares in service industries with quasi-monopoly power and trying the same in manufacturing: British Steel's shares halved from their 1992 peak of 409p and were on their way to one-third of their 1988 flotation. Doubts began to surface that some flotations had been underpriced and would fare less well in the long term: even BT was not performing as well as expected as a 'defensive stock' and the best hope for the rest seemed to be sound management in a growth industry (C&W) or a takeover – Jaguar's gains multiplied fivefold in five years due to Ford's takeover.

But while a year and a half of holding Eastern Electricity shares would have brought gains of 38 per cent and BT since 1984 had yielded 159 per cent, there were to be fewer 'Sids': the bonuses offered for loyalty with water shares could not remove the reality that Britain was more a nation of buyers and sellers (for a quick and substantial profit) rather than shareholders. The government itself seemed more interested in the flotations than the long term.

There was evidence, too, that companies regarded flotations as an expensive nuisance and welcomed the introduction of a system like Taurus, which required electronic codes and shorter periods to pay as likely deterrents. By August 1992 the proportion of the population with individual share-holdings had fallen for a third year to 20 per cent (having been 37.5 per cent in 1981 before privatisation) and in 1996, after massive flotations with free shares, private investors only held 20–25 per cent of shares on the stock market. In 1996 the Committee for Private Ownership reported that people did not understand the stock market and only 200,000 of the eight million buyers of privatised shares had invested in other shares. In the same year the chair of BGC said it cost them too much to have 1.8 million shareholders and the City ruled that companies which were floating could decide whether to sell to private investors or to institutions. In fact over half of British shares are held by financial institutions – 31 per cent by pension funds and 21 per cent by insurance companies. Overseas holdings are now 12 per cent, including 10 per cent of the shares of privatised companies.

Sociopolitical problems with privatisation

Decline in service

In October 1983 the chair of the publicly funded National Consumer Council warned of the dangers to consumers in privatisation – that less information would be available and that loss-making parts of the business – rural telephone boxes, bus services and railway lines – would wither. The Labour Party and the TUC thought their fears were justified when BT began to rebalance the tariffs to the advantage of long-distance and international callers and to charge for emergency repairs. Deregulation of bus services under the 1985 Transport Act left one-fifth of routes with no bidders. There was soon 35 per cent less rural mileage, compared with an 8.5 per cent cut in urban areas. Weekend, evening services and children's reduced fares all suffered and fourteen rival companies in Strathclyde helped bring traffic to a standstill in Glasgow in 1986. The National Consumer Council released a study in October 1990 showing that the number of bus journeys had dropped 16 per cent overall and 6 per cent in shire countries. After ten years the number of journeys outside London had fallen by 29 per cent, with journeys almost impossible to plan – the stipulated lack of cooperation meant that rival bus companies hid timetables from each other.

The National Consumer Council warned that gas prices would rise because the regulator, Ofgas, would be unable to prevent cross-subsidisation of industrial contract customers with profits from domestic householders. The BT-like price formula of RPI – x per cent, plus y per cent to reflect additional costs in buying North Sea gas, was not deemed to be strong enough.

Water privatisation raised social issues: metering (which the regulator refused to deliberate on) would be to the disadvantage of those in dirty jobs or large families. The British Medical Association wanted disconnections (over 10,000 in 1994–5) made illegal, including self-disconnections as pay-as-you-use meters were installed, masking the problems faced by poor families. (The Labour government stopped disconnections in April 1998.) By 1997 complaints about water bills reached an all-time high, with fifteen million out of twenty-one million querying them, according to the National Audit Office, and water pipe repairs dropped to an all-time low after privatisation – amid hose-pipe bans, a third of all supplies were wasted – 300 billion gallons a year. In September 1998 the Labour government acted to fulfil its manifesto pledges by moving against the unpopular industry, to cut bills by 10 per cent through the regulator and forcing them to cut pollution of rivers and beaches, on the advice of the Environment Agency and English Nature.

In a 1991 policy paper from the Department of Trade and Industry, gas fared worst among privatised utilities, with 102,000 complaints in a year. Complaints doubled between 1994 and 1995 to reach the highest level since 1987, and it received more in the first month of 1998 than it had during the last six months of 1997 put together. The Gas Consumers' Council reported in May 1998 that disconnections had trebled in the first quarter of 1998 compared with 1995 (i.e. since privatisation) – the MMC had earlier condemned the 'uncaring attitude'. Nor did the March 1998 green paper on utilities' regulation say anything about prepayment meters, which give the poorest consumers the means to cut off their water and gas supply and enable the utilities to claim they have not been responsible, and a government plan in May to cut fuel bills for poorer families was condemned as uncompetitive by the gas regulator.

By 1997 dissatisfaction with the privatised rail system was worse after two years than during BR's fifty-year reign (see below).

Councils and the public complained that privatised refuse services were inefficient and poor-performance penalties were imposed (*Sunday Times*, 3 July 1983). Similar complaints rose over NHS contracting. Rodney Bickerstaffe, for NUPE, said that the government had let in 'the Sewer Sharks' (7 September 1988). In August 1998 the charity Action for Victims of Medical Accidents reported that patients in private hospitals were more at risk, with one in five complaints now coming from that sector.

In the Prison Service it was recorded in 1994 that a quarter of escapes from escorts had been from those contracted to the private Group 4, that the staff at the private prison of Blakenhurst could not control inmates and it was the worst prison for assaults (seventy-three in three months) and that inmates were in charge at the new private Doncaster prison ('Doncatraz'), which had to be bailed out with public money because it was 'well below expectations'. Untrained staff were working on lower pay and poorer conditions, as budgets and numbers were cut (official research, based on a Coopers and Lybrand study). Though the private prisons may have more liberal regimes, that has been at the expense of safety – the Parc prison mentioned above had two suicides, two mini-riots, two officers taken hostage and a major failure in 'keyless technology' before it was even opened by Princess Anne in July 1998.

Prices

Besides the question of value for money for gas and telecommunications services, it became increasingly doubtful whether the consumer would benefit from later sales. Fears over water rate rises were confirmed by authorities, which raised prices up to 30 per cent in 1989, to ministers' fury. Water prices doubled in the ten years to 1998. The public (80 per cent against the sell-off) still turned out to oversubscribe to the sale by four times, in the expectation of a profit, but those profits for shareholders (of £9 billion in total, with a high of £850 million in 1998) were seen to be at the consumers' expense. The Consumers' Association dubbed utility privatisation a failure in a major review in 1995, with over-lax price controls and no real choice for customers. The electricity generators operated a pool system, which only they really understood, and there was no real fall in prices – even after the Labour government abolished this system and the regulator pressed for competition to bring a 10 per cent reduction in bills (September 1998), the advantage would still remain with the large, integrated companies. Ofgas had promised a price cut of 21 per cent in June 1997, a saving of £29 on the average bill, but a month later had to concede that this would not happen as the industry again favoured its largest customers.

After a two-year investigation by the Office of Fair Trading, ten bus companies were taken to court in April 1998 for price rigging.

Job losses

Privatisation was said to be costing jobs: 3,000 in the NHS, where contractors had been told they could abandon standard terms of employment and had cut full-time union members and used part-timers; 4,000 in BR's engineering division; and up to 9,000 bus jobs due to deregulation, abolition of metropolitan authorities and break-up of the National Bus Company into seventy units. Rover's takeover by BAe in 1988 led to two plant closures and 4,900 job losses. The sale of the Govan shipyard in April 1988 and encouragement of a millionaire bidder for Harland and Wolff gave rise to fears that the government was pulling out of, rather than privatising, British Shipbuilders. In December 1988 it closed North East Shipbuilders with 2,000 job losses.

The most serious job-loss programme was to be in the coal mining industry in 1992, with 30,000 mining and thousands of rail and community jobs to go in a matter of weeks. The gas, telecommunications, electricity and water industries together employed 900,000 in 1983 – after a decade of privatisation this was down to 400,000. This has not been offset by new jobs in competing companies. The retained workers are the cores of skilled employees, enjoying high wages, while the job losses have been among the lower-skilled 'peripheral' workers. The takeovers, mergers and foreign investments were all predicated on reducing costs, including jobs.

Legal–political problems with privatisation – ownership

The right of the government to sell public assets has been challenged, beyond the basic political objection to 'giving away' public investment.

The TSB's flotation in 1985 was postponed when Scottish depositors claimed it belonged to them and the claim was upheld in the Court of Sessions. After acrimony with the Bank, the Treasury pushed the Act through Parliament in 1985 saying that the TSB belonged to no one and established ownership with the successor companies. The law lords, however, in August 1986, published their decision that these had been state assets and the Treasury had given away £1 billion from the sale and £4,800 million in assets. The £5 million campaign to sell to one million shareholders had been started in July and the opposition called for the minister to be sacked for 'gross incompetence'. Controversy over ratepayer ownership of the water industry led to postponement of the proposals until after the 1987 general election.

Ownership policy encompassed the problem of privacy and national security: should private contractors be allowed to handle military data, including medical records, the Inland Revenue files or intelligence computers (all floated as proposals)? While internal markets and private contracting could be introduced into some public services, including the NHS, the Police Federation and chief constables refused to countenance privatisation eroding their role and the government retreated in 1995.

The government also had to accept defeat and delay at the hands of Law Lord Denning, who blocked the Dockyard Services Bill to privatise management in Rosyth and Devonport because a trade union consultation process had not been observed. The same argument was put before the courts in October 1992, that is, that the short time scale of days or weeks before coal mines were closed was illegal. Privatisation's reputation was not enhanced by Westminster's Council's sell-off of its cemeteries for £1. After court cases and rancour, the cemeteries were bought back in 1992 for 15p each, with a large maintenance contract for the existing owners.

Political–economic problems with privatisation – the national interest

It is contended that economies of scale dictate that some industries are organised on a national scale and that bringing competition into the telephone, gas or electricity systems simply produces waste through duplication.

Some industries were acquired for the public sector because of their strategic position, particularly the oil industry – beginning with BP before the First World War. Selling Britoil caused the loss of future profits and its cash flow into the Treasury. It had taken a 'golden share' in that company to prevent takeovers and monopoly, and the Treasury indicated it would block BP's £2.27 billion takeover in late 1987. But two months later it had changed its mind and the absorption went ahead. Yet the national interest did require the government to step in, through the MMC, and order the Kuwaitis to reduce their BP stake (acquired in the crashed privatisation – see below, under 'Timing') from 21.6 per cent to 9.9 per cent. Relations were strained until £2,000 million of shares were bought from Kuwait – by BP!

The imperative of control was claimed for BNFL and the Royal Ordnance factories. There was political uproar when it seemed that the state-funded microchip company Inmos would be sold to AT&T for a mere £50 million. Claims that the government had undervalued state assets to secure sales led to accusations that they were 'mortgaging the future' and 'selling the family silver' (Lord Stockton – former Conservative Prime Minister Harold Macmillan – in a speech to House of Lords in 1985). Margaret Thatcher had been unable or unwilling to privatise the Post Office (the Queen was said to be concerned). Michael Heseltine staked his reputation on selling off 51 per cent of Parcel Force and the Royal Mail, leaving the Post Office Counters in public ownership, but opposition from the Treasury, Ulster Unionists, fourteen Tory backbenchers and a petition of two million signatures forced a complete climb-down in November 1994 – leaving the Labour government to decide how to let the Post Office compete in a rapidly changing technological environment.

Some 18.6 per cent of the BT shares went to foreigners and over £100 million was taken in immediate profit by them. And in 1989 the government made an agreement with the European Commission to raise the ceiling on the foreign holdings of Rolls Royce and BAe – whether European 'foreigners' or not, these defence industries were defined as too sensitive for such treatment.

Another furore met the secret talks to break up and sell BL to US companies, because £2.4 billion had been put into recapitalising BL since 1975 and attempted explanations that BL could no longer survive were rebutted by the charge that BL exports were worth £1 billion per annum. Complaints of anti-Americanism were swept aside as critics spurned 'dogma and defeatism' (Ted Heath). The sale of Rover and Royal Ordnance to BAe ended with calls for a judicial inquiry into its mismanagement. Losses at Rover of £2.7 billion were written off in 1988, on top of £500 million the year before. As BAe took over and shut two plants, shareholders were offered only one-quarter of what they wanted. It then transpired that BAe could make over £1 billion on the land sales of Rover and Royal Ordnance (the two had cost £340 million). The opposition and the Public Accounts Committee criticised this collusion in asset stripping. By 1997 BMW took over Rover, Britain's last 'home' major car manufacturer, with little complaint, except from their erstwhile partner Honda, but then began to seek public money as the price of retaining jobs and the Longbridge plant in October

1998. Even Rolls Royce cars fell into German (VW's) hands in 1998. There had been a shift in mind set.

The government was said to be neglecting the national interest by allowing gas and oil companies to deplete reserves without effective control. This resurfaced in the 1992 general election when the Tories clarified that they would not retain a department of energy, but let market forces drive, without a policy. This raised awkward questions: was it in the national interest to close pits at the expense of increasing coal imports and thereby worsen an already gloomy balance of payments? Why did the Germans subsidise their coal, if not to avoid dependence abroad? Why had the previous privatisation of electricity left distribution companies seeking bargaining power against two supposed competitors – National Power and PowerGen – by building cheaper gas-fired stations in the 'dash for gas'? Why could the monopoly BGC sell to the highest bidders, neglect previous gas reserve depletion policies and, in the process, almost as a consequence, destroy one-third of the coal industry and 100,000 direct and indirect jobs? Even Margaret Thatcher intervened to try to save the national coal industry. And was it not embarrassing that while British Coal was unsubsidised, the nuclear industry received a subsidy that would have enabled coal to be given to the electricity industry free? That old Magnox nuclear stations could not be sold or safely shut down seemed less of an explanation than another layer of government bungling through conflicting objectives. Backed by warnings from the cross-party Department of Trade and Industry Select Committee in April 1998 that the country should not become over-reliant on gas, the government ignored legal threats from gas generators and scruples about aiding the privatised RJB coal industry. Especially telling was the case that Britain's reserves would run out in twenty years, by which time 70 per cent of electricity would be dependent upon gas – and therefore upon imports from Russia or Algeria. The argument that gas was cheaper could be queried if the cost of building new stations was included, and the environmental argument could be addressed by requiring cleaner coal-generated emissions.

The BAA came under criticism in 1989 as it raised charges, invested abroad in Indianapolis and blocked a fifth Heathrow runway, while at loggerheads with the Civil Aviation Authority. This highly profitable company was accused of looking after its shareholders first.

A special share was inserted in regional electricity and water privatisations to stop merger or takeover, but these were only for a limited period. While some were retained as being of strategic interest (e.g. TransCo's gas pipeline) other 'golden shares' began to be removed – BT's at its own request in 1997. Even BAe and Rolls Royce asked for the 29.5 per cent ceiling on foreign ownership to be scrapped. US companies began to move into the new privatised arena and by 1997 they had seven of the twelve regional electricity companies, were bidding for more and talking of merging their operations. A 'shadowy' Saudi group, based in Athens, became the largest shareholder in the National Grid.

Financial problems with privatisation

The mechanics of selling state assets often proved to be difficult and politically embarrassing.

Capital structures and controls

It often takes public industries time and money to bring their accounts into line with those of private companies. BT's treatment of fixed assets led to qualifications on its accounts, a long argument took place over Britoil's capital structure, BR's franchises could offer only notional guesses as to profits and restructuring cost £649 million.

One particular problem is the cost of honouring pension arrangements. Of the £52 million raised by selling National Freight, £49 million was used to pay off the pension scheme deficit, and to do the same for the Royal Ordnance factories entailed the government paying out £100 million more than the sale raised. To cope with the problem, BA closed its scheme to pay off the £1.25 million deficit (but the cost of running the scheme will enact a charge on profits). While BAe did not present such problems and was attractive to the market, the huge writing-off of debts in the case of industries such as BA and the Associated British Ports opened the government to attack. In 1994 Nuclear Electric was found to have milked its pension fund of £70 million to fund redundancies and in 1996 the National Grid was ordered to pay back £55 million to its pension fund. Legal advisers to BR's £8.5 billion pension fund told the trustees that the deal they had done with the government in 1993 was inadequate in terms of future protection and, if proof of the danger were needed, the National Audit Office in 1996 told the government to pay back £200 million which it had 'raided' from National Bus when it privatised it ten years before.

The government was in the difficult position of honouring commitments (down to concessionary travel for BR hotel staff), exercising control in the public interest (e.g. through Oftel) and still trying to convince the market to buy – in BA's case this led to a government promise not to exercise its influence as a shareholder.

The government has had to write off vast sums of public investment/ debt, for example £43 billion with Rover, £5 billion with British Steel and £5 billion with the water authorities. Some £250 billion had to go into restructuring Parcel Force and the power generators stalled their sale with a debt of £800 million. For British Coal £1 billion in capital allowances were made available, British Energy had its debt cut by the same amount and for Railtrack the subsidy was as high as £2 billion; the government tried withholding disclosure of its expenditure on rail sell-off fees (but it was revealed to be £450 million).

Timing

The government found it very difficult to get the timing of sales right. The Amersham issue was twenty-four times oversubscribed, 75 per cent of Britoil was left with the underwriters, Associated British Ports, BA and Jaguar were thirty-five, thirty-five and four times oversubscribed respectively, and five-sixths of Enterprise Oil was unwanted. The all-party Public Accounts Committee twice looked at and criticised the government's record, recommending phased sales.

Analysis of the sale of the National Freight Corporation, BP, Amersham, ABP, BAe, C&W and Britoil showed that by June 1984 the share prices had risen to the extent that £799 million had been lost – to speculative gains in a rising market. BAe shares had risen 143 per cent. Critics pointed out that this was an opportunity cost worth sixteen NHS hospitals. The *Daily Mirror* dubbed it 'jumble-sale politics' (28 June 1984).

Problems in this respect worsened as the market, which doubled in Thatcher's first five years, went down – wrecking the enterprise flotation. The ultimate disruption came in October 1987, when the stock market crashed in the middle of the huge £7.2 billion BP sale and the Bank of England had to offer a buyback facility. The biggest miscalculation was the sale of British Energy in 1996, when the shares dropped 10 per cent on the first day, incurring losses for 600,000 small investors.

After the sale of BT, the Labour opposition claimed that the fivefold oversubscription and the 45p (or 90 per cent) premium when the market opened meant that the government had wasted £1.3 billion in addition to spending £320 million on the sale and was guilty of 'criminal incompetence' (House of Commons, 4 December 1984). The shares for the electricity distribution companies were oversubscribed by 10.7 per cent, leading to the predictable government claims of a 'great success' and Labour accusations of an 'under-priced ... swindle'.

The most controversial handling of shares was that of the twelve electricity distribution companies. There were claims of underpricing – shares shot up later, which favoured outsiders rather than local customers; of allocating tiny amounts; and of delaying share despatch so small investors could not take an early profit. Investors in Railtrack could secure a 25 per cent return in the year before the 1997 election. In March 1998 the Tories and their stockbrokers (with a £1.8 million 'success fee') were condemned by the National Audit Office for selling off AEA Technology for £228 million, when its price then shot up to £575 million.

Occasionally, however, the government got it just right. Labour attacked the sale of British Steel as underpriced but the financial pundits predicted a bigger flop than BP. In fact it was 3.3 times oversubscribed – proving a market for water and electricity – yet it opened at a 2p premium and there were no quick gains. Nevertheless, the Commons Public Accounts Committee accused the government of underestimating the profit forecasts of British Steel by over £100 million before privatisation.

The average return on all privatisations was 598.5 per cent compared with an average of 353.9 per cent for the FTSE index of shares. A £1,000 investment in shares in each of the twenty biggest sell-offs would have been worth £140,000 in 1996 (Datastream and Guinness Flight figures in the *Sunday Times*, 26 May 1996).

Investment

Floating huge concerns like BT and BGC created fears that a 'crowding out' of other investment – in gilts, industry and building societies – would take place. Experts warned that higher interest rates and an appreciation of sterling would follow, putting pressure on companies' profit gains. When five big building societies floated themselves in 1995–6, giving away thousands of free shares, there was a boom in consumer spending, leading to several rises in interest rates. The building of Eurotunnel had been fraught with near disasters, and this was hailed by some as the proof that private sector finance just could not meet large national needs. This seemed reconfirmed when, in January 1998, John Prescott refused London and Continental Railways an extra £1.2 billion (on top of the existing subsidy of £1.8 billion) to build the Channel Tunnel link. Unwilling to lose the project, in June he agreed to underwrite £3.7 billion of a £5.4 billion complex refinancing deal with Railtrack. This was part of the PFI funding, which the Treasury claimed had saved taxpayers £500 million. Yet there was no proof that the private sector could produce services more efficiently and to quality standards, and the state was signing for guaranteed returns lasting over twenty years – would the buildings/services last that long? Nor was this extra spending but a displacement.

The railways – a privatisation too far?

British Rail seemed at first sight to be a prime candidate for return to the private sector. The 1989 series of one-day strikes led to government threats to sell it off and BR topped the league of public dissatisfaction: in 1992 complaints had increased by one-fifth during the year despite John Major's campaign for better service. But in 1990 the government had been told that BR's finances were so shaky that privatisation should be postponed for ten years. The following year a 'dowry' of investment money was suggested, but the £144 million deficit in 1992 put the change in doubt because privatisation itself was likely to double the subsidy to £1 billion a year or to raise commuter fares by 65 per cent. This was largely because BR's subsidy was the lowest in Europe (0.7 per cent of GDP there, against 0.14 per cent of GDP in Britain). It also highlighted the absence of a transport policy, with car use (including for two and a half million company-car owners) apparently free.

The uncomfortable parallels with British Coal continued, with a report suggesting that 15,000 jobs would go with a sell-off. The government was unable to agree a policy before the 1987 election, as three departments disagreed with each other – Malcolm Rifkind at Transport wanting a big sale, the Prime Minister wanting regional companies, and the Treasury favouring splitting BR.

After the 1991–2 recession and £17 billion in tax increases, the Major government needed the revenues from privatisation before facing the electorate and it was also suggested that this would demonstrate their right-wing credentials to Euro-sceptics. The accounts of the twenty-five potential separate rail operators and three rolling-stock companies were too theoretical to meet the demands of a City sell-off and the public might well regard such sales as too much of a risk. Nor was there time to complete this quickly enough to transfer enough to the private sector to be able to subsidise the sale of Railtrack – the owner of the infrastructure (especially with Labour likely to stop the process if it had not gone too far). As a result the sell-off was undertaken in great haste, with many questions unanswered and with parliamentary debate guillotined (Japan had taken six and a half years to privatise its railway) and low morale and uncertainty in the industry. The 'trade sales' to existing companies produced an appalling deal for taxpayers, who lost £1.1 billion according to the Audit Commission. The public subsidy to twenty-five of the operators was £1.81 billion by 1996/7 and the three rolling stock companies (sold for £1.7 billion) were resold – one via a Japanese bank – for £2.7 billion, making personal profits of £15 million, £16 million and £33 million for their 'fat cat' chief executives. The sale of the Great Western franchise in March 1998 would make another set of former BR managers multimillionaires, sharing £10 million, though the public were still providing a £184 million subsidy. The House of Commons Public Affairs Select Committee condemned the failure to insert claw-back clauses and stop such easy profits in August 1998.

British Rail cost £649 million to restructure (50 per cent higher than estimated) and was primed with £745 million in 1995. Railtrack was sold off for £1.8 billion. Its valuable property assets were not fully accounted for and it is now worth £5 billion. The rail sell-off cost the taxpayers £1.4 billion – with £680 million going on fees and direct payments – by far the most expensive and rushed privatisation.

In return, the service has been underwhelming. The Health and Safety Executive warned in March 1998 that parts of the network were unsafe and it could start prosecutions – far from responding positively, Railtrack announced an £80 million saving on its repairs bill and was found to be using incompetent contractors. Responding to the Executive's reports and claims that two-thirds of rail managers did not trust Railtrack on safety, the Commons Transport Committee began its own investigation in May 1998 and that same month the Health and Safety Commission demanded that £250 million be spent on safety. In August 1998 Railtrack admitted its own safety procedures were inadequate, following the derailment of a goods train in Wiltshire. Leaving stations unmanned and dispensing with guards (to raise profits) was also seen as endangering vulnerable passengers.

The Central Rail Users' Consultative Committee reported 'a truly dreadful performance', with total complaints up by 82 per cent during the first year since privatisation, with highest dissatisfaction about punctuality – up 145 per cent and accuracy of information at stations – up 152 per cent. In September 1997 they were fined £500,000 for their 'chaotic' inquiry service, and yet a year later there had been a 246 per cent rise in complaints about the accuracy of information. Figures released by Opraf, the franchising agency, in August 1998 showed a continuing deteriorating performance on punctuality, reliability and customer satisfaction: 257,000 trains were delayed and 47,000 were cancelled during 1997–8; punctuality worsened on forty-six of the sixty-four routes and reliability decreased on thirty-three routes; twenty-five routes failed to meet their Citizen's Charter targets for the period ending June 1998. Some other companies claimed their franchises were not long enough for the investment and tried to get more journeys out of older, failing engines, but Connex had to admit that its new trains broke down every 3,000 miles while the old slam-door ones went for 40,000 miles. An investigation by the *Sunday Times* (20 September 1998) showed that steam trains in India, Pakistan, China and Ghana were more reliable and punctual (in May 1998 it had similarly proved trains were faster in the last century). Yet South West Trains, which was threatened with a £1 million fine and the loss of its franchise in 1997 for sacking so many of its staff and failing to reach nine of its twelve satisfaction benchmarks, still made a profit of £800,000 (together with the Island line) for its owner Stagecoach in 1997. Even Virgin's brand image began to be tarnished by the inclusion of its West Coast line among underperformers – it was bottom of the punctuality league, with 71.3 per cent of trains on time (but it too made a profit of £13.5 million in 1997–8). Given the 1995 price cap on certain fares, some operators were raising the price of cheap 'saver' fares by as much as 20 per cent (more than double the rate of inflation) and the levels of compensation for failed service are low and difficult to acquire. Meanwhile, despite the new complications of multi-ticketing, more penalty fares were being imposed on supposed 'cheats'. The group Save Our Railways was in no doubt that BR used to do better than this 'dismal failure'. Many experts thought poor service on unprofitable lines was a prelude to closures.

In response John Prescott, Deputy Prime Minister, effectively sacked the rail regulators in September 1998, threatened rail operators with larger fines, that they would lose their franchises if they did not improve, and announced a bill to set up a stronger Strategic Rail Authority.

The wider context

After initial enthusiasm, it was realised that privatisation was no panacea for eastern Europe, where Hungary, Poland and the Czech Republic thought it would take twenty-eight years to privatise half their companies, as two-thirds were near bankruptcy. In Slovakia, Bulgaria, Albania and Romania there were charges of bungling, corruption and political chicanery. The process was stopped in the Ukraine.

Whether one supports privatisation in Britain or not, it cannot be denied that the light of open scrutiny and debate entered the murky corners of nuclear decommissioning, water pollution, discriminatory prices and the direction or absence of key policies.

Appendix 1. Types of privatisation

- Denationalisation – this term was employed before 'privatisation' came into fashion. While some industries, such as BR and BL, could be returned whence they came, most privatised companies were never in the private sector.
- The sale of 100 per cent of the shares of a newly created (but still publicly owned) company, either on the stock market, for example with Amersham International, Enterprise Oil and BGC, or to management and workforce, for example with the National Freight Corporation, Leyland Bus and Unipart. This was an ever-changing pattern – the management which bought out the National Express Bus Company in 1988 was replaced by a buy-in of new managers and investors.
- The issue of 51 per cent, that is a majority, of shares in a newly created public company, for example with BAe, Britoil, BT and the water and electricity industries.
- The issue of 49 per cent, that is a minority, of a public company's share, for example with Associated British Ports.
- Placement of shares with investors – for example 24 per cent of British Sugar, and Rover with BAe, most of British Coal with JMB Mining – by waiting for a suitable bidder and arranging transfer.

- Hiving off and outright sale of profitable concerns, such as Sealink, Travellers' Fare and hotels from BR, Jaguar from BL/Rover and shipyards from British Ship Builders.
- The sale of shares and the removal of custodianship/aid, for example through the former National Enterprise Board (as was done with Ferranti and ICL).
- Joint ventures with the private sector, as was done with Hoverlloyd and BR Hovercrafts, Allied Steel and Wire (British Steel and GKN).
- Permitting competition in place of former monopoly, for example with Mercury in telecommunications (25 per cent government owned), private generation and sale of electricity, and private coach companies.
- Permitting and stimulating private contractors to tender for public services. Southend and Wandsworth Councils led the way on refuse collection. By September 1984 all but thirty-five of the 223 district health authorities had complied with the circulars requiring them to put catering, cleaning and laundry out to tender. Sometimes called 'intrapreneurship' it encourages competition for public service jobs, including from incumbents.
- Introducing finance into large projects, such as road building (Civil Engineering Economic Development Council) and the December 1987 Eurotunnel share issue.
- Opting out: allowing schools and hospitals to cease to take their funding and oversight from local or regional authorities. Their basic budgets are provided by a central government department and they have more discretion over how to manage their affairs. The Conservative plan in 1992 was to enable all schools to opt out, even at a cost of £600 million and despite research showing no major improvement in standards. By then there were 156 hospital trusts, put together at a cost of £40 million, and NHS patients were paying £1 billion in charges.

Some of the categories above were interlinked: often the sale of a majority of shares was the first stage in selling off the whole; private sector takeovers occurred as worker–management buyouts failed (e.g. with BR hotels) and the government directed who could not own industries (RTZ's share of Enterprise Oil, and that Thorn-EMI and not AT&T should buy Inmos). Despite official disclaimers, the Conservative Medical Society published a pamphlet, *All Private Patients Now*, in 1991 and a *Sunday Times* poll showed that 62 per cent thought the NHS would be privatised after the 1992 election. Charitable status and tax relief on health insurance meant that £120 million a year was being given to private health care in the 1990s, at a time when the NHS was desperate for funds.

Social service departments were to make more use of voluntary agencies and charities and the Department of Health and Social Security sold twenty centres for homeless people. In July 1986 the Department of the Environment revived its plans to compel tendering for refuse collection, school meals, vehicle fleet maintenance and street cleaning. New town asset sales had brought £700 million by 1987 with £1 billion's worth of assets more to sell, and councils were even thinking of selling 480 playing fields to raise money (the first attempt, by Oldham, was rejected in court in 1992).

Meanwhile, central government continued to hive off or contract out – Treasury computer operations and army pay, dental and medical services (the last group being part of a reorganisation to free 4,000 soldiers from front-line duty). The Cabinet Office report of July 1988 revealed that 100 agencies were to be hived off – 75 per cent within a decade. The newly elected Conservative government of 1992 promised a 'rolling revolution' in line with their 1991 paper *Competing for Quality* and the Citizen's Charter – targets included planning, publications, naval surface surveillance, managing hostels and, radically, advice to ministers – their increasing use of external management consultants had opened new vistas. In 1993 the government began 'market testing' the privatisation of NHS consultants, Companies House, the Police National Computer, the Public Records Office and the census, for a £1.5 billion 'saving'.

Appendix 2. Privatisation income: Treasury summary

	£billions
1979–80	0.4
1980–1	0.2
1981–2	0.5
1982–3	0.5
1983–4	1.1
1984–5	2.0
1985–6	2.7
1986–7	4.5
1987–8	5.1
1988–9	7.1
1989–90	4.2
1990–1	5.3
1991–2	7.9
1992–3	8.1
1993–4	5.4
1994–5	5.5
1995–6	1.0
1996–7	1.0
Total	62.5

Appendix 3. Main sales of nationalised industries and other assets to date

Note: not all sale figures are available.

	£million
1979/80	
BP (5 per cent)	276
ICL (25 per cent)	37
Suez Finance Co.	57
1980/1	
Ferranti (50 per cent)	55
Fairey (100 per cent)	22
British Aerospace (51 per cent)	195
Automation and Technical services etc.	91
Prestcold (100 per cent)	9
Motorway service stations (to THF)	28
1981/2	
British Sugar (24 per cent)	44
Cable & Wireless (50 per cent)	182
Amersham International (100 per cent)	64
National Freight Corporation (100 per cent)	5
1982/3	
Britoil (51 per cent)	225
Associated British Ports (49 per cent)	46
British Transport Hotels (100 per cent)	40
International Aeradio	60
1983/4	
Britoil	293
BP (7 per cent)	565
Cable & Wireless (25 per cent)	260
1984/5	
JH Sankey	12
Scott Lithgow	12
Lye Tinplate	16
Enterprise Oil (100 per cent)	392
Wynch Farm Oil (50 per cent)	215
Associated British Ports (48.5 per cent)	51
Inmos	95
Jaguar Cars	295
Sealink	66
British Telecom (51 per cent)	3,700
1985/6	
Britoil (48.8 per cent)	450
Royal Ordnance factory, Leeds	11
Hall Russel Shipyard	
Cable & Wireless (22.7 per cent)	558
Trustees Savings Bank	1,000
Warship Building Yards (Vickers, Yarrow, Swan Hunter, Vosper)	140
British Aerospace (48.4 per cent)	400

1986/7

National Bus Company	250
BA Helicopters	13.5
Unipart	52
Leyland Bus	4
Royal Ordnance	190
Leyland Trucks (40 per cent holding new venture with DAF)	
DAB	7
Istel	26
British Gas	7,720
British Airways	900
British Technology Group (ex NEB)	

1987/8

Rolls Royce	1,080
British Airports Authority	1,275
BP (31.7 per cent)	7,240
Dockyard management	
Ship repair yards	20

1988/9

Travellers' Fare (from BR to management)	20.6
Govan Shipyard (to Norwegians)	
Rover Group (to BAe)	150
Professional and executive recruitment (first civil service activity to be privatised)	
British Steel	2,500
Girobank (from Post Office)	300

1989/90

Twelve electricity distribution companies	5,200
Electricity generating companies	5,400
Short Bros	30
Property Services Agency	10
Water companies	5,300

1990/1

Speke and Luton airports	
Port of Bristol	36
Ninety state-owned ports	
New toll roads and second Severn Bridge	270
British Telecom	1,800
Ninety-nine hospitals 'opt-out' from local authorities	

1992/3

National Express	90
Naval Dockyards	
British Rail freight and parcels divisions	–
British Rail's 2,500 stations	1,000
Post Office: Parcel Force, Royal Mail	
BT (22.5 per cent)	3,200
National Power (40 per cent)	1,200
PowerGen (40 per cent)	800

Main sales of nationalised industries
and other assets to date 1992/3 continued

	£million
1992/3 continued	
Scottish Electricity	835
Marketable debts, e.g. BT	4,000
One hundred canal and riverside properties	1.5
Northern Ireland Electricity	1,000
Northern Ireland Water	
Docklands Light Railway	
Medway Trust Port	15
(sold eighteen months later for £104 million)	
Remaining thirty-eight bus companies' property	11
Property Services Agency (£3 billion budget and 23,000 staff)	10
(resold for eight times the price in 1996)	
Twenty-four local airports	600
British Technology Group (defeated in Lords, 1991)	
Floated on stock market 1994 for £100 million	28
1993/4	
British Coal (to RJB Mining)	815
Electricity debt	850
Forestry Commission (despite Prime Minister's pledge).	
The process was stopped under Labour in 1998 – £95 million	
to buy it out over three years	2,200
1994/5	
Remaining public shareholdings in BT, BA, BP, BAA, electricity, etc.	1,300
Privatised industry debts	1,600
Third instalment on BT	1,600
Insolvency Service (aborted)	2.4
Two prisons market tested for privatisation	
One-thousandth school opted out	
PowerGen and National Power (40 per cent)	4,300
1995/6	
Ten London bus companies	
BR workshops	25
British Rail Red Star parcels (to its managers)	£1
National Grid	5,000
1996/7	
Three rail rolling stock companies	1,742
Twenty-five rail franchises	
Railtrack	1,800
British Energy	1,400
HMSO	70
Atomic Energy Authority	224
Dole offices	800
Treasury building	200
Ministry of Defence married quarters	1,500
Residual privatised industry shares	257
Benefits Agency Medical Service	300

1997/8
Commonwealth Development Corporation   500
Mini-cab firm wins £1 million a year London ambulance contract
Social security property and computer systems
Energis (25 per cent) from National Grid   1,000

Approximate total   £63 billion
(£80–£90 billion at today's prices)

Appendix 4. Privatisations under way or mentioned

Some £200 billion of assets owned by government departments – land, houses, estates – were ordered by the Treasury, under Gordon Brown, to be sold to finance other needs. In June 1998 he announced a package of 'partnerships' to raise £12 billion over three years – these included:

* BNFL – accountants appointed in September 1998 to advise on its sale;
* National Air Traffic Services (£1.5 billion) by 2000 (but withdrawn in October 1998 on safety grounds);
* local authority assets worth £2.75 billion;
* Royal Mint;
* Commonwealth Development Corporation;
* Belfast port;
* motorway service stations;
* Ministry of Defence land;
* student loans.

Also mentioned or under way are the following:

* Royal Opera House (supported by the Commons Culture Select Committee in June 1998);
* London Underground (private and public funding) by April 2000, to attract £10 million of private money – £7 billion is needed to modernise the network and £3 billion to maintain the existing system. The first part would be BAA's building of the tube to its new Terminal 5;
* Meteorological Office;
* Channel 4;
* Tote;
* Companies House;
* civil service management;
* toll roads (Birmingham Northern Relief Road proposed to be first);
* police patrols (July 1998 proposal by government and chief constables).

Reading

Adam Smith Institute (1992) *Eastern Promise*, Adam Smith Institute.

Adam Smith Institute, *Omega Project Reports*, Adam Smith Institute.

Bishop, M., Kay, J. and Mayer, C. (1994) *Privatization and Economic Performance*, Oxford University Press.

Burns, P. (1988) *Industrial Relations Review*, November.

Centre for Business Strategy (1988) *Does Privatisation Work?*, London Business School.

CIS (1982) *Private Line*, CIS.

Hall, R. (1986) 'Privatisation and British politics 1979–86', *Teaching Politics*, September, pp. 460–76.

Newman, K. (1986) *The Selling Of British Telecom*, Holt, Rinehart and Winston.

O'Connell Davidson, J. (1993) *Privatization and Employment Relations: The Case of the Water Industry*, Mansell.

Price Waterhouse (1992) *Privatisation: Learning From the UK Experience*, Price Waterhouse.

13

Crime and punishment

Bill Jones

Every one is concerned about their physical wellbeing and the safety of their property; the question of law and order is therefore both perennial and worldwide. This chapter considers the current state of law and order in Britain, examining: its place in political ideas; the extent of crime; causes of crime; and responses to crime.

Law and order and political ideas

Attitudes to the subject tend to revolve around assessments of that nebulous concept, human nature. Some thinkers have been pessimistic. Thomas Hobbes, for example, adduced that without the shielding machinery of the state – an order-inducing 'Leviathan' – life would be 'solitary, poor, nasty, brutish and short'. Machiavelli was more to the point, 'it may be said of men in general that they are ungrateful, voluble dissemblers, anxious to avoid danger and covetous of gain'. He believed chaos could be precluded only through the establishment of an all-powerful state. Other thinkers were more optimistic. Rousseau believed 'man is naturally good and only by institutions is he made bad'. Marx agreed, asserting that 'environment determines consciousness' and that it was the harsh competitive world of capitalism which corrupted humankind's innocent natural cooperativeness and fellowship. It followed that lawlessness could be solved only by a radical reordering of society, which would then refashion the nature of people themselves.

Traditionally, Conservatives have tended to occupy the pessimistic end of the spectrum. Their 1979 manifesto described 'respect for the rule of laws' as the 'basis of free and civilised society'. They tend:

- to see the problem of crime from the point of view of its victims rather than its perpetrators;

- to support the deterrent policy of tougher sentences;
- to believe individuals have free will and should be made accountable for their actions – it matters not what one's position in society may be, everyone faces the choice between right and wrong, keeping the law or breaking it, and anyone who breaks it should be in no doubt as to the penalties they face.

Labour and Liberal Democrats have tended to be closer to the other, optimistic end, arguing that:

- crime has social causes (e.g. poverty, unemployment) which are curable through social policy;
- tougher penalties and police powers can impinge on civil liberties, robbing the criminal of the rights to which anyone in a civilised society is entitled.

As the 1970s drew to a close, Margaret Thatcher was unrelentingly tough on crime: 'The demand in this country is for two things: less tax and more law and order' (*Daily Telegraph*, 29 March 1979). Her manifesto claimed Labour had 'undermined' law and order and 87 per cent of Tory candidates mentioned the subject in election addresses. It had the desired result: an ITN survey on election night revealed 23 per cent of respondents claimed to have switched their support to the Conservatives primarily over this issue. A MORI poll in 1985 revealed that 45 per cent of those questioned judged the Tories best equipped to deal with the growth of crime compared with only 19 per cent for Labour and 9 per cent for the Alliance.

This situation persisted for about a decade until, significantly, Tony Blair, as shadow Home Secretary in 1992, began his long march to the leadership by transforming Labour's profile on crime from allegedly soft to a much harder stance. According to Blair's biographer he has always held the views of 'being tough on crime; tough the causes of crime' which he established so effectively during this time (Rentoul, 1996, p. 271). He quickly moved his party closer to the Conservatives and his successor as shadow, Jack Straw, continued the process, annoying many of his own party's supporters by attacking beggars in the street and 'squeegee merchants' who annoyed motorists by importunately demanding their custom. Suddenly it was Labour Home Affairs spokesmen, as well as Conservative ministers, winning applause at conference with right-wing-sounding speeches on law and order. Labour's record in government has tended to reflect continuity with the policies of the previous government in this area. It is ironic that Tories accused Labour of ushering in a crime wave and then presided for eighteen years over an increase of serious crimes of over 100 per cent.

Is there a crime wave?

Before examining this question the two major sources of statistics should be identified. First, there are the 'people figures', those crimes reported to police by victims. Second, there are the 'victim figures', those collected every few years as a result of Home Office British Crime Surveys (BCSs) of crimes the public have had committed against them. According to the latter, crimes have not increased as sharply as the police recorded figures (see Figure 13.1). Indeed, during the 1970s one BCS concluded the actual rise in theft and burglary was only 1 per cent a year instead of the 4 per cent recorded figure. In other words, it was the proportion of crimes reported which leapt forward. Most experts attribute the difference to the prevalence of property insurance requiring a police reference number before claims can be made. Other experts challenge the 'crime wave' thesis, arguing the following.

- Much crime is relatively trivial, recorded or not. The 1984 BCS showed that over 60 per cent of vandalism, motor vehicle thefts and burglaries from the person were not reported to the police because no damage was involved and no property taken. In 1984, two-thirds of all home burglaries involved thefts of property worth less than £100.
- E. G. Dunning's study (1987) of violent disturbances revealed that while reported violent disturbances in Britain had increased since the

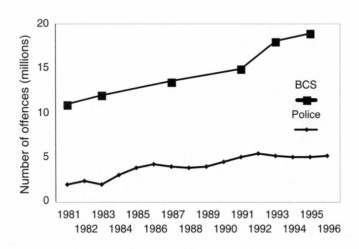

Figure 13.1. *Number of offences (millions) recorded by the BCS and by the police (twelve months to June). (Source: Home Office.)*

war years, the rate for 1975 was less than one-third that of 1900, despite a 46 per cent population increase during that period.

- The growth of laws and regulations plus the abundance of material goods in a consumer society mean there are now more crimes to commit.
- More efficient police recording procedures – supported by a 10 per cent increase in police numbers since 1979 – help to explain why police record more crime.
- The chances of being the victim of crime are still very low; just over a decade ago a statistically average person aged sixteen could expect:
  (a) a robbery once every five centuries;
  (b) an assault resulting in injury every century;
  (c) a burglary in the house once every forty years.

As the BCS notes, 'small upward changes in either reporting [method] can all too readily create a "crime wave"'. The small reduction in crime between 1991 and 1995 was seized on by Michael Howard as evidence of his success, but *The Guardian* (23 April 1997) quoted the BCS's finding that 'the reason for the fall is that police recording practices changed: a significantly smaller proportion of crimes reported to the police, found their way into reported police statistics in 1995 than in 1991'.

So is it possible to conclude there has been no crime wave, merely statistical anomalies? Not really. Crime has indeed soared by any standards and the inner-city riots in the early 1980s, the miners' strike clashes of 1984–5 and the poll tax riot in 1990, plus the demonstrations against road building, animal exports and hunting, have reinforced public awareness of living in less law-abiding times. This impression is clearly distorted; according to the 1997 BCS, three-quarters of the public believe crime to be on the increase, while the reality is that it has fallen in recent years. The 1997 figures revealed a drop of nearly 9 per cent during 1997 – the largest drop in postwar history and the first time the overall figure has fallen below five million since 1989. In 1993 there were 5.5 million recorded crimes and only 4.6 million in 1997, with big decreases in robbery, burglary and breaking into vehicles. The 1998 figures were even more encouraging (see Table 13.1), with a 12 per cent fall in car crime and a 13 per cent fall in robbery. These figures were unusually matched by the 1998 BCS figures, which recorded decreases in burglary and big declines in thefts of vehicles and thefts from vehicles. But there is still cause for concern, with crime totals still 50 per cent higher than in 1980, violent assaults up by 5 per cent, sexual offences up by 6 per cent, and rapes up by 11 per cent.

Statistical averages mask the fact that for some groups of people the risks are much higher than for others. For example, in 1998 wealthy suburban dwellers faced a 3.7 per cent risk of burglary, while inner-city households

Table 13.1. *Percentage changes in notifiable offences (twelve months ending March 1998 compared with previous twelve months)*

	Percentage change
All offences	-8
Theft from vehicle	-12
Theft of vehicle	-15
Theft from shop	-3
Theft from person	-4
Theft of pedal cycle	-5
Other theft/handling	-4
Burglary in dwelling	-15
Burglary, other	-12
Criminal damage	-9
Arson	+2
Fraud and forgery	+1
Violence against the person	+5
Sexual offences	+7
Robbery	-13
Other offences	+8

Source: Home Office.

faced a 19.3 per cent risk; owner-occupiers in rural areas faced a 3.3 per cent risk; low-income inner-city residents a 10.0 per cent risk. Similarly, women over sixty-five faced a 1 per cent risk of suffering violence to the person, while young men aged sixteen to twenty-four years faced a 21 per cent risk.

Moreover, statistical averages mask the fact that for certain people, that is young working-class males, especially blacks, living in the inner cities, the risks are much higher. For example, studies suggest you are twice as likely to be burgled if you are an unskilled worker than if you are a professional. Thirty-five per cent of burglaries occur in the inner-city area according to the 1984 BCS and while 12 per cent of householders on poor council estates had been burgled in the previous year, only 3 per cent suffered similarly in the middle-class suburbs. Those most at risk from crime are those least able to afford it: working-class people themselves. And the figure that a house is broken into every thirty seconds in Britain and the fact that 40 per cent of British men have a criminal record by the time they reach forty offer no grounds for complacency.

A report covered in *The Guardian* (12 October 1998) disposed of a satisfaction British people have comforted themselves with for some time – that at least our crime levels are not as bad as those in the United States. The report, conducted by the US Justice Department, revealed that in 1995, the chances of being robbed were 7.6 per 1,000 people in England and Wales, compared with 5.3 per 1,000 in the USA. Even worse, burglary rates in England and Wales were reported to be twice as high as in America. However, criminologists point out that comparisons are difficult and that crime in US inner cities is much higher than that on this side of the Atlantic.

Fear of crime is arguably as much of a problem as crime itself, blighting people's lives and exacerbating the situation by emptying the streets of people whose presence might otherwise deter law breakers. BCS evidence reveals 60 per cent of elderly women living in inner-city areas felt 'very unsafe' when walking alone in their locality after dark. And 24 per cent of all women aged between sixteen and twenty-four never go out on their own at any time of the day for fear of attack. Forty-one per cent of all women aged thirty and under confess to being 'very worried' about the risk of rape. The irony of these statistics is that the feared risks are out of proportion to real risks: women over sixty, for example, are the least likely to be victims of an assault while of those most likely, men aged sixteen to thirty, only 1 per cent felt 'very unsafe'. Those aged under twenty-nine are thirteen times more likely to be mugged than pensioners.

The government inquiry into fear of crime, chaired by Michael Grade, felt strongly that media presentation of crime contributed towards unrealistic fears. Its first report recommended, perhaps feebly, that the publication of crime statistics should be reduced from four times a year to two, to 'reduce the opportunity for sensational and terrifying headlines which contribute nothing to the public's knowledge and understanding of the facts about crime' (letter to *The Guardian*, 15 November 1993). Even a brief examination of one week of the tabloid press's coverage reveals that Grade's hopes have scarcely been fulfilled, despite the acceptance of his recommendation on crime figures. Moreover, the 1996 BCS revealed one-third of the large sample interviewed believed violent crime and rape to constitute one-third of all crimes instead of an actual figure of 6 per cent.

The causes of crime

Gap between rich and poor

A young offender from Liverpool in a London Weekend Television *Weekend World* programme in December 1987 put this thesis starkly: 'Some people have got jobs, they can go out and buy the things they want. But we're on the dole, we haven't got the money so we go out robbing to get the money.' Inevitably, poor people will be tempted to steal when there is so much abundance surrounding them, especially when so many social values and publicity seem to enthrone material goods and make them synonymous with success, pride and desirability.

The Conservative governments of 1979–97 used to downplay the connection, claiming it was an insult to the law-abiding poor and pointing out that during the 1930s recession, when unemployment was at record levels, crime was much lower than today. However, the researches of Simon Field in the Home Office revealed a close positive correlation between poverty and crime and eventually ministerial statements began to acknowledge the link too.

Prosperity encourages certain crimes

Paradoxically, prosperity may have a causal connection with some crimes. In October 1997 Chris Nuttall, Director of Research at the Home Office, argued that the recently announced increase in violent crime was connected to a buoyant economy, which released more income for expenditure on alcohol: 'It appears that alcohol is more related to levels of violent crime than drug consumption.' He said the figures reinforced 'the link between the economy and crime with buoyant times producing a rise in violence and sex offences and recessions producing a boom in property crime.'

More potential crimes

Once domestic arguments were dismissed by police but new legislation has brought them into the official figures. A growth of regulation and rules affecting an increasingly complex pattern of living also contributes to a higher recorded crime rate.

Underclass

The US sociologist Charles Murray argues a new 'underclass' has arisen in the USA and Britain – a large minority supported by benefits and crime. Children are socialised into a world where there are few male parents to provide role models and few jobs to occupy them productively when they reach maturity. Instead, they admire those who flout the rules, stealing, dealing in violence, drugs and so forth. It is difficult for children in such circumstances to resist the lure of easy money and the excitement which stealing cars and other forms of crime provide.

Values have declined

Many older people claim increases in crime are a product of declining values, a loss of respect for religion, authority, family and the law. Often research into social attitudes, however, reveals that such fears characterise all generations; so parents in the 1940s feared 'Americanised youth'; in the 1950s, the teddy boys; in the 1960s, mods and rockers; in the 1970s, punks and so on. There was no golden age.

Media

The conviction persists in the minds of many that the media are breeding a race of citizens who are either indifferent to violent crime or are practitioners of it. Advocates of this view cite the fact that if television is so effective at selling products on the market, a diet of a murder every few seconds on the same medium and in films (e.g. *Child's Play III*, said to be a factor in the Jamie Bulger murder, *Natural Born Killers* and *Reservoir Dogs*) must have some hidden but catastrophic effect upon the human consciousness. Research into the subject has been inconclusive as cause and effect between stimuli and human behaviour are so difficult to identify.

A report from the University of Birmingham which came out in early January 1998 was no exception. It concluded most teenagers were unlikely to be affected by violent films but that for those in 'vulnerable situations', films which glamorised violence might encourage them to commit such crimes (*The Guardian*, 8 January 1998). Some opponents of censorship, like Michael Winner, the film director, found it difficult to accept the conclusions of the report: 'If films and videos create violence, then how do we explain the Victorian era when it was much more dangerous to walk the streets?' A further study based on the island of St Helena, reported in *The Times* (12 January 1998), revealed that children in this closed environment watched the same programmes as their British equivalents but did not develop the same profile of anti-social behaviour.

Hereditary factors

Much recent work undertaken into genetics has suggested that many behavioural characteristics are the result of inheritance. This is still very speculative but it could be that criminal tendencies are inborn and the growing art of gene therapy might even be able to identify the rogue genes and replace them before or after birth.

Responses to crime

Policing

Conservatives have long believed a strengthened police force is an essential response to the increase in crime. Accordingly, between 1979 and 1992, they raised spending on the police by 87 per cent, increased numbers in England and Wales by 16,000, and police pay rose by 30 per cent. The 1984 Criminal Evidence Act extended police powers regarding stop and search, searching premises and holding suspects without trial for up to ninety-six hours instead of the previous twenty-four. However, the police were not happy with the Independent Police Authority for investigating complaints in the place of the police-run system it replaced. Critics argued the following points.

- Police support for the harsh public-order requirements of Thatcherism was bought by pay increases.
- Police activity is not that cost-effective in that:
  (a) only a fraction of their time is spent fighting crime, with some two-thirds spent on paperwork and other duties;
  (b) a report in *The Economist* (2 June 1993) suggested that police in London had 'given up', frequently letting criminals go with cautions as processing cases was too time-consuming.
- The 'clear-up' rate of reported crimes has been falling for a number of years. Figures depend on the type of offence but the overall percentage fell from 40 per cent in the late 1970s to 25 per cent in the early 1990s.
- Despite earlier denials, some police forces proved to be riddled with corruption, including elements of the Metropolitan Police and the notorious West Midlands Regional Crime Squad.
- A report by the Policy Studies Institute revealed widespread racist and sexist attitudes, together with drunkenness on duty.
- A series of high-profile convictions were reversed upon appeal including the Birmingham Six, the Guilford Four and the Maguire Five, not to mention the Bridgewater Three.
- The progressive increase of powers by the nine Criminal Justice Acts 1979–97 – from 1851 to 1979 there were only five – has eroded civil liberties dangerously. Moreover, the establishment of the National Reporting Centre seemed to some to presage a 'national militia'.

Zero-tolerance policing

This approach was based upon the policy of New York's Mayor Rudy Guliani. During his first four years in office he reduced the crime rate in one of the world's crime capitals by 40 per cent: murders down by 61 per cent; armed robberies by 47 per cent; rapes by 13 per cent. But the thrust of his policy was on street-level crime – fare dodging, intimidatory begging, vandalism, graffiti – the things which give out signals an area is uncared for, neglected, not closely policed. With his Chief of Police William Bratton, he put officers on the beat again, back into the local communities. And guarding against and pursuing the minor seemed to deter the major crimes. Both Labour and Conservatives jumped on the bandwagon. Zero-tolerance policing of the notorious Kings Cross district vastly improved the quality of life for residents; employing similar tactics, Chief Constable Ray Mallon in Hartlepool cut crime by 27 per cent over 1994–6. However, *The Economist* (15 March 1997) reported mixed reactions among the police themselves.

The Police Federation says it requires hugely increased resources and more officers; Bratton had 7,000 new recruits to deliver the policy while the New York Police Department already had twice the strength in terms of police per head as Britain. Others predict only a temporary respite once petty crimes come under control and ineffectiveness once less densely populated areas are covered by the scheme. Worse still, the approach could worsen race relations as a hands-on approach antagonises ethnic minorities. Charles Pollard, Chief Constable of the Thames Valley Force, is doubtful of the uncompromising zero-tolerance method, believing the community approach to be better: coordinating social workers, voluntary workers and council officials. Such an approach in Marlow, Buckinghamshire, reduced crime by a third in six months at a cost of a mere £917 just by leafleting residents and talking to publicans and trades people.

In June 1993 the Sheehy report on policing was presented, criticising: 'top heavy' rank structure; 'ineffective' management structures; and promotion based on service rather than merit. The report suggested scrapping three senior ranks and much else dear to the heart of the police establishment. The Police Federation attacked it hysterically and, after huffing and puffing, Home Secretary Howard backed down on some major issues. For Labour, Jack Straw avoided conflict with the police and assumed a generally supportive stance.

Sentencing

The appropriate sentence to hand out to criminals is a matter of intense debate. For example, *The Guardian* (10 March 1998) highlighted the fact that a man who had bludgeoned his wife to death was given six years while a number of women who had killed abusive husbands were given life. Sentences vary considerably in different parts of the country.

Right-wing Conservatives believe in retribution and deterrence: heavy sentences are the antidote to crime. Thatcher told a conference of US lawyers in 1985 that 'the very real anxiety of ordinary people is that too many sentences do not fit the crime'. Sentencing policy appeared to reflect this feeling; penalties were increased for sex and violent crimes throughout the 1980s.

Judges ultimately decide on sentences and the 1996 BCS discovered they are not held in high public esteem: 64 per cent of the 16,348 respondents thought they were to a greater or lesser extent 'out of touch'. Publicity is given to judges who seem to live in a world apart from ordinary people. Mr Justice Harman, for example, in February 1998 asked in court 'Who is Gazza?'; he was also ignorant of the game he played. This state of affairs has existed for years as judges are drawn from the very small world of barristers, most of whom have received an elite education. In 1987, 70 per cent of senior judges had been to public school and 80 per cent to Oxbridge; by 1997 the figures were 82 and 88 per cent, respectively.

On the other hand, the public seems to be similarly ignorant of sentences actually handed out. Three-quarters believe judges to be too lenient while underestimating the severity of sentences handed down. Half the sample thought that only half of those convicted of rape were sent to prison while the real figure was 97 per cent. Similar mistakes were made in respect of muggings and house burglaries. Interestingly, when respondents were given fuller facts of a case, they tended to agree with the judge's sentence.

Conservative Party conferences regularly call for stiffer sentences and their Home Secretaries, aware of the complex reality, tend to become trapped by the rhetoric they employ to satisfy their own supporters. Responsible ministers like Whitelaw and Hurd resisted the temptation but others, like Michael Howard, tended not to.

Capital punishment

Surveys regularly show three-quarters of the population favour a return of this penalty for murder. From 1979 onwards scores of eager new Tory MPs crowded into Parliament after each election having made capital punishment part of their election addresses. When it has come to the vote, however, many changed their minds, as Table 13.2 illustrates.

The answer seems to be that even the most enthusiastic 'hangers' think again when confronted with the case adduced against their own retributive and deterrent arguments: it would be a retrograde step for a civilised society; Britain in any case has a low level of homicides – 681 in 1996 (10 per cent fewer than the previous year) compared with 23,000 in the USA; there is no evidence to suggest murders have increased appreciably since the death penalty was abolished; it would put pressure on judges and juries; it would mean that those wrongly convicted would die unjustly; and

Table 13.2. *Numbers of MPs voting for capital punishment, 1979, 1983 and 1988*

	19 July 1979	13 July 1983	7 June 1988
Conservatives elected in:			
1987			42
1983		64	55
1979	57	43	38
before 1979	174	141	71
Other parties	12	15	12
Total	243	263	218

Source: *The Economist* (11 June 1988).

it would give political terrorists a ready-made martyr's crown. During a debate on the issue in June 1988 Home Secretary Douglas Hurd pointed out that:

> Fierce honorable argument immediately after the event is one thing. It is quite another to institute slow, cold processes of justice, with months filled with arguments of lawyers and the hearing of appeals, at the end of which the Home Secretary may decide, long after the event, that the offender should cease to exist. An execution in this way can surely give only fleeting satisfaction, if any, to the public or those who knew the victim.

The House agreed: by a free vote it voted 341 to 218 against the reintroduction of the death penalty. In February 1994 the margin was even greater.

A survey reported in *The Guardian* (12 October 1998) revealed that 66 per cent of the population believed capital punishment should be re-introduced. Interestingly, the results were socially skewed so that 70 per cent of the lowest-earning groups favoured its return compared with only 47 per cent of students. There was no difference, however, between the attitudes of men and women.

Prisons

Prison as a response to crime attracts much criticism:

- To deprive people of their liberty is a severe sanction, which should be used only rarely, for example 'only where there is extreme danger to the community' (Lea and Young, 1984, p. 267).
- The aim of prison should be to rehabilitate and not to 'bang away' criminals out of sight and out of mind. Even hardened criminals can, with care and sensitivity, be rehabilitated and saved for society.
- Less than 10 per cent of those in prison are murderers, rapists and armed robbers, while one-half are there for persistent non-serious offences for which alternative sentences could be found.

Conservatives and prison

Custodial sentencing comprises a central part of the debate about sentencing. The Tories began in 1979 calling for 'short sharp shock' treatment for young offenders and longer prison sentences for adult criminals. Four new institutions were opened for young offenders but it soon was shown that the reoffending rate was unaffected and young offenders returned to the streets stronger, fitter, wiser and meaner. The policy was abandoned. After the 1982 Criminal Justice Act and with the help of Hurd, the prison population fell, with the number of juveniles halving over 1984–9. Hurd and his junior minister John Patten judged prison 'an expensive way of making bad people worse'. After 1988 numbers continued to fall for six years. But then Michael Howard took over and decided to play to the right-wing gallery with his statement that 'prison works'. He changed the laws which kept many minor offenders out of gaol, helping to push up numbers by 50 per cent by the time of the election, when he was seeking to introduce mandatory sentences for serious offenders, much to the indignation of judges and just about everyone associated with penal policy.

Labour and prisons

Jack Straw, Howard's Labour successor, is keen to divert offenders away from prison but, in the opinion of *The Guardian*'s Polly Toynbee, he needed, like Hurd and in his malign way even Howard, to lead his sentencing shift more aggressively. She recorded how prison numbers were still leaping ahead under the inertia of the previous regime. With numbers at 64,000 (up from 42,000 in 1978) Richard Tilt, Director of the Prison Service, foresaw the 70,000 mark being breached by 1999, which would require twenty-four new prisons, costing £2 billion. Each prisoner costs £600 a week. 'The basic fact remains we are underfunded to provide full constructive programmes for prisoners.' Too many merely sit in their cells and a half are likely to reoffend. 'Some of the people coming into prison could be dealt with as effectively in the community and at a very much lower cost. I am worried at the size of the prison population and the rate at which it is expanding'

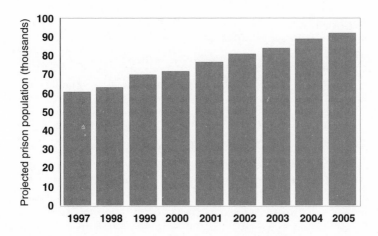

Figure 13.2. *Projected prison population, England and Wales (1,000s). (Source: Home Office.)*

(see Figure 13.2) (*The Guardian*, 29 January 1998). In April 1998 the prison population stood at 66,800, a rise of 11,000 in less than a year, and was rising at over 1,000 a month. The prison population by 2005 could be as high as 92,000 if present trends continue.

Non-custodial alternatives

Government has been interested in a number of such alternatives.

Victim restitution schemes have been very successfully experimented with in the USA – where offenders are confronted by their victims and asked to make amends. On 11 February 1998, the BBC screened a documentary based on such a scheme run by the Thames Valley Police. It showed meetings involving victims, offenders and family members; despite the pain involved for all parties, the policy seemed to be effective in releasing anger, inducing contrition and reinforcing law-abiding attitudes (see also below under 'Crime prevention').

Community service orders, whereby offenders work off their debt to society through undertaking worthwhile tasks, have been in existence for some time. Few were used in the early 1980s but they achieved more popularity and usage later on in the decade and a higher profile in 1993 when fiery French soccer star Eric Cantona was given such a sentence after kicking a fan who abused him verbally; he filled it by coaching inner-city young children at soccer.

Other alternatives to prison, like cautions, probation and supervision orders, are also urged by those who think prisons counterproductive. 'Tagging', whereby convicts are not imprisoned on condition they wear a small electronic transmitter and report regularly to the authorities, has also won approval and may be used more widely.

The problem with all alternatives to prison is that public attitudes tend to be negative: they are seen as 'soft' options, when a tough no-nonsense approach is needed. On this, as on so many aspects of sentencing, the public is woefully ignorant and a major programme of public education is necessary.

Juvenile crime

The year 1993 saw an eruption of youth crime. Two prominent cases concerned a man kicked to death who intervened to stop vandals in Cardiff and, worst of all, two ten-year-olds convicted for the murder of two-year-old Jamie Bulger on Merseyside. Home Secretary Kenneth Clarke spoke of 'the need to identify and control the really persistent nasty little juvenile offenders'. Half of all young men and a third of young women admit to having committed a crime and one-quarter of offenders are under eighteen. The Audit Commission produced an estimate in 1996 that young offenders commit seven million crimes each year, costing victims and the state £4 billion. The police solve as few as 5 per cent of these and only 1.3 per cent end up being charged.

The Conservatives' military-style detention centres for young offenders reflected society's concern that most crimes are committed by men aged sixteen to thirty. The experiment, however, was a failure, with a recidivism (return to crime) rate of 80 per cent within two years of release. Youngsters are not rehabilitated by such sentences or shown the error of their ways; they are merely, through meeting other offenders, socialised into crime more effectively and return to the streets wiser and more determined not to get caught. This last is something which declining clear-up rates (see above) show is not an unrealistic aspiration.

The reoffending rate after first prosecution is about 40 per cent and it rises sharply after that. It costs more to keep young offenders in a detention centre than to send them to Eton and because the proportion of fifteen- to nineteen-year-olds in the population as a whole is set to rise over the next ten years and offenders now take longer to detach themselves from a life of crime, the problem will get worse.

In 1991 the imprisonment of fourteen-year-olds was abolished in favour of community sentences, but the outcry over the Bulger case presaged a tougher approach. By July 1997 there were seventy-one girl juveniles (under seventeen years) held in adult institutions and 1,294 boys. Sir David Ramsbotham, the Chief Inspector of Prisons, challenged these practices, which violate the United Nations Convention on the Rights of the Child, to which Britain is a signatory. While the Convention is not embodied in British law, the 1989 Children's Act obliges local authorities to intervene to protect children from 'significant harm'. Sir David found conditions so bad in the Glen Parva centre in Leicestershire he discontinued his inspection and at Chelmsford prison he found a 'nineteenth century attitude to the treatment of young offenders'.

Despite his unwholesome attempts before the 1997 election to upstage Michael Howard in terms of being tough on youth crime (e.g. calling for curfews and for parents to be made legally responsible for their children's actions) Jack Straw has been more constructive in office and has won support from the usually liberal prison governors. According to Polly Toynbee:

> They believe he genuinely wants to divert sentencing away from prison, catching and treating young offenders early. They like his plans for young offender teams [police, social workers, schools and courts] to make community sentences work, so courts trust and use them.... Straw talks their language.
> (*The Guardian*, 18 February 1998)

Crime prevention

Many criminologists argue it would be cheaper to spend money preventing crime rather than on the vast superstructure of apprehension and punishment. A number of possibilities exist.

- A greater sense of community awareness and responsibility should be inculcated, as in China and Cuba, with their street committees.
- France has set up a powerful crime-prevention council with branches in all major towns. These target educational and training programmes for young people; France is the only EU country regularly reporting substantial falls in the rate of crime.
- Property can be made more secure via better car theft protection measures and the requirement of photographs on credit cards, which caused this type of fraud to plummet in Sweden when it was introduced.
- Neighbourhood watch schemes should be extended, whereby neighbours undertake to watch out for each other's property. Some 40,000 schemes existed by the early 1990s, though some reports suggest they push crime out of the suburbs and back onto the street.
- The Holme Wod estate in Bradford established a special force to target known offenders and the burglary and joy-riding rate fell by 61 per cent.
- Victim contact seems promising. This idea, already touched on, originated in the tribal way Maoris approach crime in New Zealand, through a conference with the victim, the offender and his/her extended family. Charles Pollard of the Thames Valley Force reported on its results in October 1997. He claimed the reoffending rate among youngsters facing cautions had fallen from 30 per cent to 4 per cent. *The Guardian* (18 October 1997) quoted a victim, Julia, who confessed to nerves before meeting the fifteen-year-old boy, Darren, who took her car. The reality was not daunting and she felt, after explaining how she felt and communicating with him, she could put it all behind her. For his part Darren said, 'When I committed the crime I didn't think of the consequences.... I am now convinced I will stay on the straight and narrow. I know exactly what she went through and if I had ended up in court I would never have been told.' His father added, 'Since the conference he has certainly quietened down.'
- Some local communities, despairing of effective police action, have either hired outside patrols or set up their own. Some of these initiatives have been very effective but others have demonstrated a worrying tendency for vigilantes to pursue suspected offenders and mete out harsh to savage arbitrary justice. Police forces tend to be wary, especially as former convicts have been discovered offering their services commercially in such schemes.

• In the USA, property crime has fallen sharply and, apart from the demographic explanation of fewer young men in the population, some experts attribute the effect to the Head Start programme begun in the 1960s, when Lyndon Johnson was President. For the past thirty years, some 700,000 children from the highest crime areas have been given two years of nursery education. It was modelled on a Michigan experiment, which revealed that the children involved in such schemes, now in their thirties, tended to thrive, with lower crime rates, higher college qualifications, better jobs and more home ownership. Accordingly, the British Home Office plans in 1999 to spend an extra £200 million on intensive nursery education in high crime areas.

Reducing Offending: the Home Office report of July 1998

This report drew on forty years of criminological research and set as its target 'to ensure the long term trend of a 5 per cent annual increase in crime in this country is reversed', according to Chris Nuttall, Head of Research for the Home Office. The report sought to explode myths surrounding the debate about crime, concentrating on what seems not to work as well as what does and might do so more effectively.

What does not work includes: merely increasing police numbers; random patrols (useful only in reducing fear of crime); charging more suspects (counterproductive for young offenders); community policing (useful only in improving the public image of the police); responding quickly to emergency calls (dubious overall effect); zero tolerance (short-term benefits only in limited areas – can be counterproductive in the longer term).

What does seem to be effective includes: targeting repeat offenders to secure good evidence; directing patrols to 'hot spot' areas; targeting repeat victims; and identifying patterns of crime and seeking to establish underlying causes.

However, the headlines from the report concerned its debunking of the notion that 'prison works'. It suggests the prison population would need to rise by 25 per cent to achieve a 1 per cent reduction in crime. As *The Guardian* editorial of 10 April pointed out, 'the system only deals with one out of every 50 recorded crimes'. A much more coordinated approach across a broad front is required. The editorial concluded ministers should try harder to educate the public in the lessons of the report, pointing out that people are not as punitive as tabloid editors would have us believe. The paper also warned against complacency over the fall in recorded crime: 'This year's 4.6 million is likely to be as good as it gets'.

In his keynote speech to the Labour Party conference at Blackpool in 1998, Tony Blair highlighted a recommendation from the *Reducing Offending* report when he announced the extension of zero-tolerance approaches to twenty-five crime 'hot spots' throughout the country. Once the target area has been chosen, New York police computer software would analyse crime patterns (e.g. street robberies or domestic burglaries) before police and other agencies moved in to tackle the problems.

Reading

Benyon, J. and Bourn, C. (1986) *The Police: Powers, Procedures and Properties*, Pergamon.
Dunning, E. G. (1987) In G. Gaskell and R. Benewick (eds), *The Crowd in Modern Britain*, Sage.
Lea, J. and Young, J. (1984) *What Is To Be Done About Law and Order?*, Penguin.
Reiner, R. (1993) *The Politics of the Police*, Wheatsheaf.
Rentoul, R. (1996) *Tony Blair*, Warner.

14

Environmental policy: too little too late?

Geoff Lee

This chapter examines the impact of environmental issues on British politics and the linked European and international dimensions. As well as reviewing the problems, public opinion and the response of pressure groups and political parties, the implications of the 1997 general election are covered.

Professor O'Riordan, of the University of East Anglia, traces three threads in the evolution of environmental consciousness: the first was 150 years ago, in the romantic age, when Wordsworth, Chekhov, Emerson and Thoreau believed the elements of nature had a life of their own; 1900–20 saw the emergence of the environmental technocrats, who wished to sustain, irrigate and manipulate; the third phase started in the 1960s, when the media began to relate to environmental issues, whether it was the *Torrey Canyon* oil tanker polluting the Cornish coast, or the Flower Power movement in America associating anti-Vietnam War protest with the use of the defoliant agent orange. Publications and protest against civil nuclear power stopped the programme in the USA.

During the last period, regulations and pressure groups started. An important book published in Britain was *Only One Earth* by Ward and Dubos, in 1972. The proceeds of this went towards the United Nations (UN) Conference on the Human Environment. Also in 1972, the Club of Rome commissioned a study from the Massachusetts Institute of Technology; the resulting report, *Limits to Growth*, showed that the world could not sustain its levels of economic and population growth.

The global dimension

The First United Nations Conference on the Human Environment

The 1972 Stockholm conference put environmental issues on the agenda and the World Commission on Environment and Development was established in 1983. This produced a report which said the depletion of resources could not continue. The UN proposed a new summit. In the twenty years after Stockholm, two billion people had been born, fifty million children had died because of polluted water, 500 million acres of trees had been felled and 500 million tonnes of topsoil lost. It was estimated that £165 billion would be needed to clean up – three times the wealthy countries' aid budgets.

The Rio de Janeiro 'Earth Summit', 1992

After three years of negotiations and twenty-four million pages of reports, 30,000 people descended on Rio in 1992, followed by 131 world leaders.

A key issue, not dealt with in European environmental politics, was population – the quarter of a million people born each day. The Vatican acted with the help of Argentina and the Philippines to have the word 'contraception' removed from a treaty and was attacked by the British.

The summit agreed upon: a treaty to slow global warming; a treaty to protect wildlife; moves to stop the spread of deserts; measures to stop the pollution of the seas; Agenda 21 – an 800-page action plan; a declaration of principles to have a Sustainable Growth Commission and an Earth Council and a statement of principles on forests.

Winners. These were the industrialised countries. The USA refused to sign the biodiversity treaty, seeing a danger to patents and wetland exploitation. Britain helped weaken the global warming treaty to enable the USA to sign – the document lacked targets for improvement. Agenda 21, on toxic waste and many other subjects, was not legally binding. The General Agreement on Tariffs and Trade (GATT) was kept off the agenda. The World Bank and the UN Sustainable Development Commission emerged with control over programmes.

Losers. These included the debtor countries, which pay £50 billion interest per annum. The G77 developing countries, led by Malaysia and India, made sure forests lost out, with no treaty resulting. The UN bodies most generous to poor countries lost – Japan had overtaken the USA as lead donor, partly because it saw financial gains to be made from environmental technology. The world's forty-three poorest nations and indigenous people gained nothing in this supposed 'North–South' dialogue. Britain's manoeuvring there led the hundreds of pressure groups in Rio to vote them the third most negative country, after the USA and Saudi Arabia.

Eastern Europe

One reason for Europe's reluctance to increase help at the world level was the realisation of the extent of the disaster in eastern Europe. Poland had been used as a toxic dumping ground, pollution and unsafe nuclear stations were sited throughout eastern Europe, and in the former USSR 290 areas were dangerous to health, together constituting 16 per cent of the land, an area as big as western Europe. In October 1992 it was reported that one-sixth of Russia was unfit for habitation. It was also reported that the Soviet navy had dumped thirteen nuclear reactors and 17,000 barrels of toxic waste in the Arctic.

The Berlin Climate Conference, 1995

The conference of 166 countries was set up at Rio to reduce emissions of carbon dioxide. At this stage the industrialised countries were trying to hold to 1990 levels by the year 2000. The main opposition came from members of the Organisation of Petroleum-Exporting Countries, which feared for their exports. The European Union (EU) pushed for progress, knowing that in its absence, targets beyond 2000, on the agenda at Kyoto (see below), would be very tough to agree.

The Kyoto Summit, 1997

Some 10,000 delegates from 164 countries met to negotiate a new protocol to the Climate Change Convention, setting targets and timetables to reduce greenhouse gases during the first twenty years of the twenty-first century. Delegates had their own warming problems – thirty were admitted to hospital during the first week, suffering from dehydration or exhaustion. Not all were there to help – the Global Climate Coalition of oil, gas, automobile and heavy-industry companies was proud to be 'defending American jobs' by wrecking any deal on targets. Australia was criticised for seeking an 18 per cent increase in emissions. Warnings were made about threats to share prices of polluting firms and the Australian tourist industry.

Britain, with its own target of reducing emissions of carbon dioxide by 20 per cent from 1990 levels by 2010, worked hard for an agreement, trying to persuade the Americans at the highest levels. The EU was seeking a 15 per cent cut by itself, Japan and the USA. These two countries objected that the EU countries could do deals among themselves, allowing Germany and Britain to make larger, easier cuts, and other countries to do less, such as Portugal and Greece.

The deadline for concluding the summit kept being extended and the G77 block of developing countries (including India and China) kept waiting. What emerged angered them – reductions of 6 per cent by Japan, 7 per cent by the USA and 8 per cent by the EU, and with loopholes such as trading in emissions, so the USA could buy notional reductions from a run-down Russia and cut by only 3.5 per cent. A deal was done with China that the USA could keep its demand over trading in reductions of levels if the developing countries did not have to reduce emissions. Trading was allowed up to November 1998, without which the USA would not ratify the agreement. Many thought the price of achieving the first legally binding treaty – a 5.2 per cent cut by thirty-eight countries over fifteen years – had been too high.

The American administration and the British, led by Deputy Prime Minister John Prescott, who was acknowledged to have done most to save a deal, hailed the outcome as 'historic'. The EU Environment Minister thought it 'not good enough for the future' and Greenpeace said it was 'a tragedy and a farce'.

But down in the marketplace, BP's share price had gone up as it invested in renewable solar energy (Exxon had been voted the second-worst wrecker in Kyoto); the City of London was keen to start domestic trading in emission permits (already common in the USA, where greens could buy and then destroy them); and the USA automobile 'dinosaurs' started to announce low-polluting, fuel-efficient cars for 1998 – so as not to lose business to the Japanese.

Leeds Castle Summit, April 1998

As well as dealing with ongoing pollution issues, the environment ministers of the seven leading countries and Russia addressed the issue of green crime. Smuggling banned chemicals (chlorofluorocarbons – CFCs), waste and wildlife was thought to rival only drugs, being worth £24 billion. Much was coming, via organised crime, from Russia. The illegal wildlife trade was worth £5 billion and illegal timber worth £15 billion.

Building on an idea by Mikhail Gorbachev in 1993, and in the wake of massive forest fires, the idea of having UN 'green helmets' to deal with such emergencies had surfaced again in March 1998.

Public opinion

Concern about the environment has been increasing steadily, according to surveys commissioned by the Department of the Environment. Table 14.1 shows the percentage of respondents in such surveys mentioning an issue as one of the most important the government should be dealing with.

As well as these surveys, MORI annually checks eleven factors indicating public concern, including donations to environmental groups, use of lead-free petrol, purchasing 'green' products, or belonging to a pressure group – saying yes to five of these classes someone as a 'green activist'. In 1991 31 per cent in Britain were so classified, twice as many as in 1989. An opinion poll in June 1992 by *The Guardian* and ITN indicated that 70 per cent would be willing to pay higher taxes for improving the environment, and the 1993 survey by the Department of the Environment showed that in response to the proposition 'The polluter pays even if goods and services

Table 14.1. *Percentage of respondents mentioning an issue as one of the most important the government should be dealing with*

Issues	1986	1989	1993
Unemployment	75	26	46
Health/social services	22	32	29
Environment/pollution	8	30	22
Crime/law and order	17	17	21
Education	14	13	17
Economy in general	4	10	15
Pensions/social security/child benefits	15	18	12
Housing/mortgages	8	15	9
Rising prices/inflation	4	17	6
Public transport	1	3	5
Income tax/VAT	–	–	3
Europe	–	–	3
Defence/nuclear weapons	–	–	3
Council tax	–	8	1

Source: NOP surveys of random samples of 3,200 adults in England and Wales, commissioned by the Department of the Environment.

cost more', agreement had risen from 27 per cent in 1986, to 31 per cent in 1989, to 62 per cent in 1993. But such pledges have been made before, notably about being willing to pay more council tax for local services, and they have not been translated into votes. Interestingly, 89 per cent thought environmental protection was government's responsibility, compared with 78 per cent for business and only 72 per cent for farmers.

In the USA, so-called yuppies had given way to 'gruppies', many of whom were 'greenoids' obsessed with the environment. In May 1995 some five million people turned out in 300 towns and cities to celebrate the twenty-fifth anniversary of Earth Day.

Legitimacy and media coverage

Britain followed in May 1995 with One-World Week. The Prince of Wales appeared in a BBC programme, *The Earth in Balance*. He had earlier chided the EU deadlines on eliminating greenhouse gases for being ten years too late. The Duke of Edinburgh highlighted his concern in the Dimbleby Lecture, and the Queen used her Commonwealth message to talk of global warming. The Archbishop of Canterbury had spoken of his fears at the Festival of Faith and the Environment in September 1989.

Through these statements and other television programmes, from the well established *Survival* to *Panorama* on 'The big heat of global warming' to Radio 4's *Costing the Earth*, media coverage informed, alarmed and rendered protest legitimate. The Sunday press carried features: *The Observer* and Friends of the Earth (FOE) enjoined us to 'Save our countryside', the *Sunday Times* pursued the 'Water rat' polluters and, in its 'Campaign to clean up Britain', declared that Camden was 'dirtier than Khartoum' (1 October 1989). The most successful was *The Observer*'s 'Toxic tips' campaign, complete with skull and crossbones – pre-publicity about lists of all tips, including the fifty-nine most dangerous, caused strong reactions, a sell-out of the supplement and 10,000 inquiries for more detail. Similar features appeared on filthy beaches, cases of 'planet abuse', acid rain in Poland, 'Planet in peril' and 'Green motoring'. On the other hand, the launch of an environmentally conscious newspaper, *The Planet*, on 16 June 1996 lasted only as long as that first copy.

These influences began to translate into action by middle-class citizens, who blocked the building of another supermarket in Bristol, the M3 motorway extension and lorries trying to export veal and other live animals. As well as taking non-violent direct action, much to their own surprise, they began to put their money where their beliefs were – ethical and green investment grew faster than the rest of the market (twenty funds with £300 million by 1992). In 1998 FOE launched its own personal equity plan!

Consumerism

In 1989 it was said that the public would pay more for green products. The *Green Consumer Guide* helped them choose and polls showed that such products had doubled their sales. Companies began to label their products as environmentally friendly. Car companies, washing-powder producers, Michael Heseltine and the consultants PA chided that British firms were not jumping on the green bandwagon, and in 1991 a register was published showing the progress of 100 British companies.

The labels did not always count for much: both the British Institute of Management and the Consumers' Association showed that many claims were bogus. Companies which played green at home but operated differently abroad, including BP and ICI, were taken to task. By April 1990 it was confirmed that consumers had lost belief in green claims (National Consumer Council). By 1993 supermarkets were withdrawing 'green' detergents and other products, less than 1 per cent of food was organic and four out of ten people thought the labelling was a device to raise prices and did not care if toiletries had been tested on animals. The National Consumers' Council concluded that the claims 'were often woolly, meaningless, unverifiable, open to multiple interpretations, confusing or of no real benefit ... many people give up trying to buy green altogether' (*Sunday Independent*, 21 May 1996). In October 1998 the *Sunday Times* revealed that the Soil Association had allowed the addition of sodium nitrate to so-called 'organic' foods by supermarkets to extend shelf-life. Oxford University's Environmental Change Unit verified the findings of the Consumers' Association in September 1998 that up to 40 per cent of fridges were wrongly overstating their eco-efficiency.

The other negative side to consumerism is that supermarkets demand perfection, specifying width, shape and colour and requiring large, cosmetically perfect fruit and vegetables. Over 2,000 tonnes of apples were 'officially' destroyed in 1996. As Rob Harrison of the Ethical Consumers Association pointed out, 'a bent carrot is just as good as a straight one' (*The Observer*, 16 August 1998).

Members of Parliament

If the public was expecting to be guided by its elected representatives, investigators showed that they would be disappointed. *The Observer* highlighted how MPs had voted on environmental issues (29 March 1992). In addition, seventy-five MPs were asked five basic environmental questions – only twelve answered correctly, and of thirty who declared themselves especially interested, only three got the right answers (Rosemary Collins and Terrance Brownhill for the *Sunday Times*, 16 July 1989).

Pressure groups

By 1980, 1.8 million people had joined environmental pressure groups, and in 1989 four million, while the groups' income had risen from £38 million to £237 million.

The spectrum of beliefs and tactics is wide – from those enjoying royal patronage to groups flirting with terrorism.

Established groups

At the respectable end of the spectrum one finds the Royal Society for the Protection of Birds, with 850,000 members and a growing income of £28 million in 1992, despite recession. The Society declined to join the acid rain debate.

The Woodland Trust has now bought 500 properties, including 1 per cent of Britain's surviving ancient woodland. Only 10 per cent of Britain is woodland compared with 25 per cent in Europe and the Trust has been planting 118,000 broadleaf trees a year, rather than with conifers, which are planted in commercial forestry for a faster return on investment.

The National Trust, with 1.5 million members, has broadened its activities but remains a solid insider pressure group, using its access to policy makers to influence decisions.

The World Wide Fund for Nature, with 120,000 members in Britain, has become more involved with other environmental groups. Its colour supplement with *The Observer* concentrated on saving rain forests, which could contain cures for diseases such as cancer.

The Council for the Preservation of Rural England also exercised its influence within Conservative circles, while becoming a major objector at the inquiry on the Sizewell nuclear power station.

The Joint Nature Committee for Great Britain was formed when the Nature Conservancy Council was split into three. Despite its 'respectable' position, the government was embarrassed when its chair resigned after three months, to stop their meddling.

The Countryside Commission met with the Rural Development Commission and the English Tourist Board in April 1990 to find a balance between tourism and protection of sites.

Transport 2000, founded in 1973, campaigns to cut road traffic and improve public transport and cycling. Its annual budget of £250,000 is funded by the rail industry (GEC and ABB), local authorities and trusts. It campaigns for taxes on company cars and joins road-building protests.

The Consumers' Association was formed in 1957, has 800,000 members and a staff of 500. It tests consumer goods and publishes *Which?*.

The Sustainable Agriculture, Food and Environment Alliance came together in 1991 to campaign for changes in farming, including the use of fewer pesticides. Its 'Food Miles' on long-distance transport produced meetings with the leading supermarkets.

Compassion in World Farming was born in 1967 to end factory farming and the live export trade. Its 40,000 members' demonstrations, boycotts and media campaigns stopped the veal-crate system in the Britain.

Friends of the Earth began activity in May 1971 when 1,500 non-returnable bottles were left at Schweppes' offices with the slogan 'Don't Schhh ... on Britain'. FOE grew to over 200 local groups, 230,000 members and an income of £5.3 million in 1994/5. It has adopted different tactics, including working with *The Observer* to publicise its research, as described as above. It tracks the record of water companies, helped phase out the use of CFCs in aerosols by threatening boycotts, and played a leading role in obtaining an Endangered Species Act. FOE is adept at using the law to defend the environment; it sent a copy of the toxic tips data to the EU Environmental Commissioner, and looked to the same authority when it believed power privatisation did not cater for anti-pollution equipment rules. FOE is usually called upon to comment on issues and respond to government statements as the main source of opposition, which it does with precision and often derision. It now has an Internet site where people can record pollution from any factory and has worked on 'solutions' such as the 700,000 jobs policy adopted by Labour. On its twenty-fifth anniversary in 1996 it was deemed by many to have lost its way and to be in need of a new mission. But its work goes on – in September 1998 it produced a league table of power companies and their commitment to renewable and environmentally friendly policies, so that consumers could choose a supplier on other than 'cheapest price' grounds under the new competition.

A potential pitfall for respectable groups is that they become 'neutered' by being drawn in as advisers to the government. In 1974 FOE representatives entered into discussions to make bottles returnable – after six years of talking they walked out, by which time companies had introduced cheaper bottle banks. Three former directors of FOE work on Britain's aid policy, act as an adviser to the Environment Secretary, and advise Prince Charles, respectively.

Similarly, environmental groups attacked the Groundwork trusts set up in 1981 to clean up city fringe areas – the trusts were denied promised funds and were excluding more independent groups. And the sixty-five Farming and Wildlife Advisory Groups were said to have been dupes, used by farmers to prevent legal controls.

One failure was the attempt to build a green consumer group, Ark, with the backing of pop stars. Jonathan Porritt, director of FOE, disliked its glitz and arrogance, while another activist thought that the 'last thing we need now is another nice, middle class cop-out campaign group'.

Interest groups

The Trades Union Congress (TUC) joined in drawing up environmental policies in 1989 and it had particular interest in providing legal protection for workers who refused to handle toxic waste. This had occurred in Liverpool among dockers and in Leeds to railway men. It wanted imprisonment for company directors who broke the rules and was reassured that research (such as that of Professor Pearce of Cambridge University) showed that jobs would be created in fighting pollution.

The Confederation of British Industry (CBI) called for taxation to encourage smaller company cars, for investment in railways and roads, but preferred heavier lorries because they are more efficient. The British Institute of Geographers wanted stronger restrictions on road transport. The TUC and CBI have in common a deep suspicion of green taxes, especially in the private sector and energy-intensive industries.

The consultancy KPMG (1997) in its *Survey of Environmental Reporting* found that nearly 80 per cent of UK companies 'now address' the

environment in their annual reports and they had experienced major
business benefits:

- a stronger internal commitment to improved environmental performance;
- the ability to demonstrate progress in environmental management to
  stakeholders;
- the identification of areas where management systems needed to be
  strengthened;
- better public relations and increased employee awareness of the environmental policies and goals of the company;
- 'two companies in our survey, BAA and National Power, also found that
  environmental reporting had contributed to new areas of business
  opportunities.'

The UN research on worldwide green reporting in December 1997
showed that companies were increasingly releasing sensitive information
and a quarter of the sample of 100 reports had been externally verified
(only four had in 1994). The Body Shop ranked first and British Airways
fifth, but British companies still lagged behind leading countries. The
shareholder activist group Pirc demanded standardisation in reporting in
March 1998 because of the 'ad hoc and variable' approach to reporting.
Michael Meacher, Environment Minister, threatened to name and shame
companies that did not publish an environmental report in April 1998,
saying that if Marks and Spencer could, so could House of Fraser.

Nevertheless, it was becoming clear that 'green' investment made sound
business sense: £2 billion was so invested in Britain, more than twice as
much as the rest of Europe (though still behind the USA, where 10 per
cent of investors have an ethical portfolio). At the UN meeting of 200
financiers in September 1998 Meacher was able to show these stocks had
outperformed other stocks. Shares on the FTSE index and done twice as
well during the fall in that summer and had actually risen in Asia during
the collapse there.

Smaller businesses (99 per cent of the environmental business sector)
tended to lose out to big company lobbying of government. Unlike Japan,
which gives tax incentives for energy-saving equipment, and the USA,
which gives tax credits for solar, geothermal or anti-pollution measures, the
British Treasury has never been of a like mind. Similarly, the deregulators
at the Department of Trade and Industry (DTI) opposed intervention to help
environmental initiatives, despite lobbying from businesses which were
losing out to Germany, Japan and the USA. Tough regulation there had
led industries to invest – as a result Germany has a 29 per cent share of
this $400 billion a year market, the USA 22 per cent and Britain only 6
per cent. The Environmental Industries Commission, which lobbies for 175
companies in this sector, could not overcome Tory antipathy. The Labour

Trade Secretary Margaret Beckett was more open to public–private joint ventures to help these small businesses grow.

Radical groups

These are groups differentiated from those above by their willingness to break the law. The Green Party was content to let members take individual decisions not to pay electricity bills because of nuclear generation, but did not advocate it as policy. One pressure group that had to wrestle with that dilemma, the Campaign for Nuclear Disarmament (CND), turned green in 1989 as the Cold War ended, to deal with the problem of nuclear waste. CND had lost its main fund-raiser, the Glastonbury Festival, to Greenpeace.

Greenpeace overshadowed FOE during the 1980s as it gained 150,000 members in three years, to reach 400,000, and worldwide it went on to reach 4.8 million members in 1990. Many of its confrontational tactics were inspiring and successful; these included collecting radioactive waste from pipelines off the Cumbrian Coast, positioning themselves between whales and harpoon guns and in dinghies beside ships throwing drums of toxic waste overboard (this was subsequently banned in Britain), spraying baby seals with dye to deter trappers, occupying an army firing range in Cyprus, and camping in Antarctica until its exploitation was banned.

Greenpeace acted as a centralised organisation and carefully channelled its education and publicity through separate trusts with charity status. Priding itself at being at the sharp end, it attracted enemies as well as followers – the employers' vetting agency, the Economic League, had Greenpeace members on its list, and its sailing into French Pacific nuclear test zones led to French secret agents blowing up its ship, *Rainbow Warrior*, killing one member in 1986 (as a result membership doubled in eighteen months). The French boarded and confiscated its boats during the renewed protest of 1995.

Using its advertising agency, Yellowhammer, it produced a professional and powerful poster and film of a model dressed in furs walking down a catwalk and trailing blood and splashing the audience. Feminists and furriers showered this first-ever X-rated commercial with abuse, and the advertising world showered it with awards. In 1991 Yellowhammer produced a grisly film of dolphins being killed, as part of the case to preserve Antarctica. It produced an alarmist advert in 1995, 'You're not half the man your father was', showing genitalia shrunk by polychlorinated biphenyl pollutants in the sea; the evidence was not there to support it – but it made its impact, heightened by the controversy. Greenpeace was also prepared to use the law, bringing the first private prosecution against a chemical company for illegal discharges into the Irish Sea. It enraged ministers with 'green' policies to sell by getting its reports out first – giving reasons why Britain was still the 'dirty man of Europe'.

Hit by recession and a drop in US contributions for opposing the Gulf War, Greenpeace International cut its budget by $9 million in 1992, sold the largest of its seven ships and sacked 25 per cent of its 500 campaigners. More radical groups added that Greenpeace had gone soft and bureaucratised. In 1997 it was even producing a cable television show and launched a credit card. On its twenty-fifth anniversary in November 1996 it was attacked by its founder members for its fat salaries and lack of inspiration, leading to a drop in membership of three million. In moving to find 'solutions' – less noble and chic than defending the planet – it was being drawn into dialogue with industry and the need to meet customers' wants – would they want electric cars or worse air conditioning?

It still achieved its most newsworthy success in 1995, however, when it boarded the Shell oil platform Brent Spar, which was to be dumped in the North Atlantic. The organisation of a major boycott of petrol stations in forty countries forced the company to back down and reconsider dismantling. The fact that Greenpeace's claims about the amount of waste oil on board were inaccurate did not detract from the impact – public opinion had beaten the company's high-level lobbying. Its final victory came in January 1998 when Shell announced they would dismantle the platform and parts would be reused to build a new quay.

In 1997 they occupied Rockall for forty-eight days and a BP rig off the Shetland Islands for a week, until they were arrested and their assets frozen in court. The last attempt to stop them like this – by British Nuclear Fuels Limited (BNFL) in 1983 – failed when supporters paid their fine.

Earth First was founded in the USA in 1980 and employed sabotage – of developers' machinery and spiking metal rods into trees to stop felling. Others were gaoled for trying to blow up power lines. As warned in their journal, *Live Wild or Die*, eco-terrorists resorted to arson in Colorado in October 1998 to damage the ski industry. To labels of eco-terrorism were added eco-fascism when a founder opposed both aid programmes and seeking a cure for AIDS to keep the population down. The century-old Sierra Club, the largest US environmental group with half a million members, was pro-population control and wanted to ban immigration. A meeting of Britain's Earth First in Wales in 1996 drew 3,000 members.

The Earth Liberation Front in Britain has 1,000 members, working in cells; they have been arrested for blocking the M3 and occupying docks importing timber. They crossed the line into criminal damage by raiding a Fisons compound and the threat of using explosives has been made.

The kidnapping of an Exxon chief was ascribed as to a radical group calling itself Rainbow Warriors. In 1994 a British magazine called *Terrarist* described how to make bombs and grenades and buried mines for use against construction workers, security men and police; another group, Justice?, produced a hit-list of construction companies in 1995. Prepared to use crossbows, mantraps and booby-traps, these 150 hard-core activists were often expelled from protest sites.

In Britain a new form of direct action emerged in 1994 with eco-warriors, who built tree houses and elaborate tunnel systems to stop the clearing of sites for development. One of the PANSEs (political activists not seeking employment) – Swampy – became a celebrity. Protests by these new, often middle-class protesters, included the M11 link road, M3 extension and Newbury bypass – the government had been warned two years earlier of such direct action. The first anniversary of the work at Newbury in January 1997 was marked by violence, damaged and burned machines and arrests. The cost of clearing the A30 road-widening scheme site in 1997 was £200 a minute. By the time the Manchester Airport extension site was occupied, the tunnels had steel doors, concrete obstacles, ventilation and food stores; the costs of clearance were enormous. Direct-action groups were increasingly coordinating their efforts, using the Internet and e-mail. In September 1998 trainee eco-warriors from Sweden, Poland, France and Germany came to a training camp at Greenwood in Staffordshire to learn the arts of tunnelling, tree-house dwelling and other tactics.

Deep ecologists derive their faith from Professor Naess, who lives on a Norwegian mountain. Their principles include respect for all creatures and their diversity, a reduction in human population, change away from present policies, and precedence given to the quality of life.

The familiar splintering at the fringe occurs as eco-anarchists, such as Bookchin, condemn the biocentrists, who want to demote humankind – middle-class people equating us with snails.

Given these differences, it comes as a surprise that over 150 green groups did agree on measures to deal with environmental problems in May 1990, and declared themselves ready to hold a shadow summit to the G7 meeting of the rich countries' leaders.

Between these groups and the 'establishment/exploiters' was very little in the way of mediation, except for the attempts made by the Environmental Council, a charity with financial backing from 500 companies and hundreds of public and voluntary organisations. The opposition to development did sometimes bring pressure groups, local residents and councillors together, such as the demand in September 1998 for a 'blue belt' for the River Thames to control 'trendy and fashionable' commercial development.

Genetically modified food

In 1998 an issue did emerge which united pressure groups – genetically modified (GM) food. The Monsanto Corporation led the way with 100 million acres under cultivation on four continents and launched a £1 million campaign in Britain to convince people of the benefits of such crops. Direct action came with the destruction of crops on twenty-five of its 325 sites; in August twelve protesters in Devon were arrested for destroying a maize crop to stop pollination; other groups are GenetiX Snowball, Lincolnshire Loppers, Captain Chromosome and Genetic Super-heroes – a mixture of groups with a background in roads and nuclear protest (including Earth First) but with many new middle-class protesters. In June they established an umbrella organisation, Genetic Engineering Network, a website and the *Genetix Update* newsletter, sent out by e-mail and fax – for which there has been heavy demand. Direct action and arrests have also occurred in France and Ireland, and though the Swiss approved the crops after heavy lobbying, there was disquiet on the Continent and Greenpeace claimed to have mobilised a quarter of a million German consumers.

Greenpeace, FOE, the Green Party and the Soil Association wanted to ban the introduction altogether, but establishment groups like the Consumer Association, the Women's Institute, Townwomen's Guild and Royal Society for the Protection of Birds and English Nature wanted a moratorium of between two and five years. Even Oxfam and Christian Aid doubted the claims that greater crop yields from the longer-lasting, pesticide-free crops would cure world hunger. Prince Charles spoke out against the ethics of playing God and the dangers if something went wrong (new toxins or a consequence like bovine spongiform encephalopathy – BSE, or 'mad cow disease') and in July when the head of the Environment Agency, Lord de Ramsey, was found quietly growing Monsanto's GM sugar beet on his estates, there were calls for him to dig up or resign. The government departments involved were split, with the DTI and the Ministry for Agriculture and Food for the experiments, and the Departments of Health and Environment less keen. Organic farming makes up 0.36 per cent of the whole – far less than our neighbours – and the Treasury was criticised again for doing nothing to foster its growth.

It was rare to find such united opposition – in several polls up to six out of ten were against any GM foods. In contrast to EU law and government policy 85 per cent of people wanted GM food separated at source and 95 per cent wanted it clearly labelled in shops (ICM/*Guardian* poll, 4 June 1998). There was anger about the lack of consultation or debate, with international or European law supervening, and about the growing power of Monsanto – worth £22 billion, a sixfold increase in five years, patenting its way along the food chain. Monsanto always lobbied hard when faced with opposition – an edition of the *Ecologist*, which attacked the company, was pulped by their printers in September 1998 without consultation – seemingly the first time they had been scared of libel action in twenty-nine years. It was claimed that President Clinton had 'leaned' on Tony Blair to allow the GM crops to continue. Following health doubts connected to experiments on rats, Britain announced it would set up a watchdog on GM foods to look at ethics and health issues, in September 1998.

British party politics

The Conservative Party

In office, 1979–92, a major change came with Margaret Thatcher's 'conversion' following her reading of a paper on global warming and a major speech in September 1988 to the Royal Society. She followed this with an address to the UN General Assembly in November 1989, when she called for protocols on ozone depletion, climate change and the preservation of plant species. She wanted half of Britain's waste recycled by the end of the century and urged international cooperation based on free trade. The Prime Minister was clearly out to claim a leading role, as a scientist as well as a world leader, and in 1989 invited representatives of 120 countries to London to discuss depletion of the ozone layer. The Tories could claim environmental credentials – they campaigned against whaling, favoured lead-free petrol and began to clamp down on Sellafield emissions and subsidies for intensive farming.

It was reported later that, after the Greens' success in the 1989 European elections, the Prime Minister had 'secretly instructed three ministers – Chris Patten, Lynda Chalker and David Trippier – to get green issues off the agenda by the next general election; they did it with a judicious blend of fair words, personal decency, and small (but well-hyped) policy changes' (Geoffrey Lean in The Independent, 23 May 1995).

Thatcher's claims came under scrutiny: Britain's earlier blocking of CFC bans, its worsening rivers, toxic waste imports and the lack of action on acid rain. Like most pressure groups in this period, the environmental ones were excluded from policy making and were not invited to her seminars, still less the cabinet committee she chaired on green issues. Doubts were expressed about her belief that privatisation of electricity would assist cleansing and after a year the environmentalists contrasted progress on one and a half issues against failure on twenty-seven – from sea dumping, toxic waste imports (up 50 per cent) and aid to developing countries.

The seemingly easy 'free market' solution that the polluter should pay, embraced by Environment Secretary Chris Patten, began to come unstuck, condemned as 'socialism by the back door', and the ministers responsible for privatising water and electricity realised the financial and political costs of passing on the price of a clean-up to the consumer. Initiatives on insulation and energy efficiency were scrapped. The Prime Minister's UK 2000 project, launched with film of her picking up litter and intended to stimulate green thinking, ended after a year (in the words of one of its founders 'as a total cock-up'). An attempt to have Whitehall use recycled paper was dropped because it would triple prices, and when the white paper Our Common Inheritance appeared, it was condemned as platitudes based on encouragement, with the ideas of Professor Pearce about taxing polluting goods dropped.

The 120-clause Environmental Protection Bill gave new powers to councils to control pollution in their areas. After a year the pressure groups could point to an absence of resources, targets and results. After a blunder by John Gummer, the Agriculture Secretary, which implied that he would inherit pollution powers, John Major announced in 1991 that a new green 'police' would exist when regulation was consolidated. But the threat had gone from the green impetus of 1989, when Michael Heseltine condemned the government's lack of urgency. In the 1992 election, Heseltine, now Environment Secretary, was claiming a world lead on the subject, with the 1990 Act and the addition of £36 million to recycling and protection forming 'a green revolution in government'.

But shortly after, the Transport Secretary was saying new roads were good for the environment, Baroness Chalker expressed her anger at the decline in the aid budget to 0.27 per cent of gross national product, the Treasury cut out key specific jobs on conservation, and the Green Bill, with its new agency, was dropped from the Queen's speech at the opening of Parliament.

In economic and political trouble in the autumn of 1992, the Conservative government began to backtrack on promises made at the Rio summit – on its aid budget, on 'green farming', on the work of the Renewable Energy Advisory Group and on energy conservation; in October the government was being threatened by the European Court again over pollution. Their white paper that month looked to 'market forces' to work for the environment, and John Major's pledge to keep the Forestry Commission in the public sector was explained away as an incorrect, 'hurried' election draft. While John Gummer at the Department of the Environment was increasingly enthusiastic and Kenneth Clarke introduced a genuinely green tax, on landfill, the Treasury and DTI and big business lobbyists were stronger in their non-interventionism.

The Labour Party

There has been a thin green line through socialism – traced from the Peasants' Revolt, the Diggers and Levellers, Robert Owen and William Blake. Current supporters include Tony Benn, who goes back to Marx and the fundamentals of ownership, and Ken Livingstone, who links environmentalism to issues such as feminism – the former Greater London Council under his leadership passed many environmental measures and lorries can still be seen in London carrying their noise-restriction badge.

The Party went into the 1983 general election with mere references to 'balanced' approaches to energy, but before the 1987 election it had changed its platform significantly. The Socialist Environment and Resources Association and FOE worked on Labour's policy committees and produced a Charter for the Environment in 1985. The defeat of Militant gave this theme more chance; the Marxists regarded the issue as a diversion from the class struggle. A key victory for the greens was over the 1986 conference decision to move out of nuclear power by closing some stations and not building new ones – this was in the wake of Chernobyl and intense lobbying by greens.

The Labour Party has had a problem of having to listen to differing voices from the unions – the Transport Workers and National Union of Seamen were out to protect their members, the mineworkers were against nuclear power for self-interest as well as principle, while the electricians were for it. A specific problem was that Sellafield was in the constituency of Jack Cunningham, Labour's environment spokesman, which resulted in the odd policy of being willing to complete the THORP nuclear reprocessing plant but not to use it. Despite all indications that the environment would feature in the 1987 general election, it was given little space in the manifesto and did not feature in the campaign.

More urgency was generated by the Green Party's success in the European elections, not least because analysis indicated their support came from Tories and centre parties. (Tories were careful to restrain attacks on the greens in case these were mistaken as anti-environmentalism.) In 1989 Labour concluded that the Conservative government's attitude was one that was improving their position in the polls and attacked Thatcher as the 'Green Goddess', unable to improve the environment because of Tory adherence to free-market 'dogma'. They claimed the government had failed on a range of policies – cleaning beaches, cutting research spending, and was abusing a £1.2 million research fund to trial water meters.

The government was accused of fiddling its estimates of carbon dioxide emissions by 7 per cent to make the real reductions from 30 per cent to 20 per cent easier to reach.

In 1990 the Party began to put its green agenda together under Bryan Gould, while Neil Kinnock talked to FOE and Greenpeace. They began to leak intentions to have a environmental strong executive body modelled on US lines and having green courts for polluters. They were willing to use tax incentives but shied away from a carbon tax because of the miners' interests. *An Earthly Chance* was published in October 1990: it promised that Labour would re-examine the road programme, tax company cars more heavily, protect Antarctica and reduce carbon dioxide emission to 1990 levels by 2000 (five years earlier than the Conservatives). Greenpeace criticised it for breaking its promise to cancel THORP. The Tory response was that these were 'back of the envelope calculations' (Chris Patten, 8 June 1990).

After the 1992 election defeat and change of leadership, the Party began a consultation exercise entitled 'Why the environment matters', under a commission which would report to the 1994 annual conference. In this phase there was an emphasis on protecting the poor against the imposition of carbon taxes and water metering. In the revised policies in the next manifesto and general election the Party had moved to broader considerations and (cautious) compulsory policies.

The Liberal and Social Democratic Parties

Traditionally, the Liberal Party was seen as the mainstream party most closely allied to environmental issues. Much to the green Liberals' consternation, it was the new Social Democratic Party (SDP) that set the pace in 1985 with its *Conservation and Change* policy document. The main green movement was more impressed by the proposal for a cabinet minister to deal with environmental concerns than with the concept of 'green growth', which is regarded as a confidence trick. The Liberals responded with their own research under Simon Hughes (who considered standing as a Liberal and Green candidate). On their 1979 platform, Porritt and Winner (1988) commented 'there are only so many patch-up symptom-solving environmental reforms one can legislate into being before having to look at inherent causes in the industrial system' and on the issue of nuclear power 'the bland hand' of the 'alliance apparatchicks' made sure that any radical policies were smothered in the 1987 election. In the Liberal/SDP merger of 1988 the Greens not only condemned the fudging of the leaders but castigated the Liberal Ecology Group, the Young Liberals, and the SDP Greens for failing to fight for their beliefs.

Like the Labour Party, the Liberal Democrats (wrongly) saw the environment as a significant issue in the 1992 election and sought to recapture this ground, declaring in 1989 that the Greens were fifteen years behind them and, like the Labour Party, writing them off as politically impotent. In 1990 they began to advocate an integration of economic and environmental policies, envisaging an 87 per cent rise in petrol prices by 2005 and a 30 per cent reduction in carbon dioxide emissions by that date. Having put themselves forward as the mainstream party most concerned with green issues, they took insurance by linking its benefits to National Health Service costs, as pollution would cease to affect fourteen million people, and offering tax reductions to those who responded by conserving energy. They thought that the Green Party would 'self-destruct when their two wings of totalitarianism and liberalism tear themselves apart', and, turning to the Tories, Malcolm Bruce said 'the only thing that's green about them are their wellies' (*The Guardian*, 15 September 1989).

The Green Party

The Guardian (23 September 1989) traced the Party's ancestry to:

> 17th century Digger utopianism ... 1960's alternative life-style politics ... the modern Incarnation of the 19th century anti industrial tradition of New

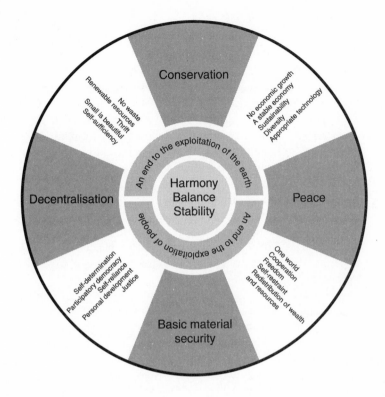

Figure 14.1. *Diagram adapted from an early Ecology Party leaflet, showing basic green policies*

Harmony, Charterville, the garden city movement and the green belt campaign ... increasingly the mouthpiece of English pacifism ... middle-class non-conformism. It is the party of both earnest vegetarian rationalism and mumbo-jumbo astrological nonsense.

The Party began life in 1972 as 'People', and had coral and turquoise colours. These were sufficiently ineffective that the Ecology Party emerged in 1975 under green colours. After a heated debate, the Party aligned with European counterparts by calling itself the Green Party in 1985. Figure 14.1, from an early Ecology Party leaflet, shows how little the basic philosophy and politics have changed. As with other small parties with strong principles, the Greens were prone to splits – an attempt in 1986 to adopt a more centralised constitution led to a splinter 'Mainstream' organisation going into the wilderness. In the early 1980s the major parties were paying no heed to environmental issues and in the 1983 general election their 670 votes per constituency was 10 per cent down on 1979. In 1987 the 134 candidates obtained 1.4 per cent of the vote and their membership was still at the 1979 level of 5,600.

In the following local elections, however, they won 4 per cent and then 8 per cent in the county council elections. The £250,000 required to fight all the European elections in 1989 was a gamble many did not wish to take. In the event, they achieved a major breakthrough, taking 15 per cent of the votes – 2.3 million – the highest ever achieved by any green party. The other thirty European green parties gave the British party attendance and voting rights at their meetings.

Clearly, there is a distinction to be made between support for the Party's policies and its votes. Polls revealed that only 12 per cent of voters were aware that it wished to leave the European Community and was opposed to economic growth. But 72 per cent believed they advocated cleaner air and 61 per cent that they wanted cleaner water (Harris poll in *The Observer*, 17 September 1989).

Analyses showed that Green voters were middle class and from the right and centre, making a close parallel to the Liberal/SDP Alliance protest voters outside general elections. A 1984 poll had shown that the earliest members had not belonged to a previous party, again a parallel with the political 'virgins' of the SDP.

Within the Party there was a difference between the 'dark green' fundamentalist members, who believed in major changes to the economy, and the 'light greens', who believed that the world's problems could be managed. Tim O'Riordan classified the former as eco-centrists, in contrast to the latter, who were techno-centrists. These differences between holistic fundamentalists, dubbed by Jonathan Porritt as 'Utopian impossibilists', and realists were to come to the fore after their success in 1989. This split also happened in the German Green Party and led to defeat in the federal elections in 1991.

At their 1989 conference the Greens confronted the challenge and put forward a nine-member national executive, a regional council and a clear leadership structure – in the past they had eschewed this in favour of a collective leadership. This move 'Towards a green 2000' was led by Jonathan Porritt, who told them to 'grow up' at the Wolverhampton conference. Here the chair resigned on stage when opposed and fringe groups such as Green Anarchists, Teapot 2000, red Greens, animal rights activists, Christian greens, and leaders of the travellers' convoy all stood in the way of a move into mainstream politics. Like CND, the Greens had to contend with left-wing infiltration – Sara Parkin opened the conference warning against 'parasites', tried to form a pact with Labour and the SDP and urged a policy of proportional representation. This failed, as some speakers continued to demand the overthrow of capitalism and others saw the streamlining of the Party as an 'act of terror', though all the 'red' amendments were rejected. And their eight-year policy of population reduction to thirty to forty million for Britain was made less specific as they moved towards Porritt's platform of green consumerism, sustainability, ecological security and internationalism.

Nevertheless, David Icke, who was to resign in 1991, stated that 'For us, values come before policies and our values are not negotiable' (*Sunday Times*, 17 September 1989) and they remained split over keeping their membership subscription at £15 rather than reducing it to attract new members.

The doubling of membership to 15,599 by 1989 and polls that suggested that 45 per cent were willing to vote Green one day ensured that the main parties turned to attack them: Paddy Ashdown dubbed them new 'Calvinists' who saw humankind as 'just another pollutant', and Conservatives saw 'bigoted Marxists, ecofeminists, and vapid romanticists' (Nicholas Ridley, July 1989), 'nimby [not in my back yard] hypocrisy ... in the pursuit of publicity' (Simon Jenkins, 13 August 1989).

By 1990 the Greens were playing down their no-growth policy and credit restrictions. They raised £150,000, fought the local elections with 1,500 candidates and gained control of Stroud Parish Council. In 1991 they rejected pacts with other parties and were set to contest marginal seats. But they remained committed to policies against cars, fertilisers and NATO, which were to surface in their manifesto and put them outside the mainstream. In opposing centralised finance and an uncontrolled market economy, they joined the unlikely bedfellows of the far-left and far-right national parties.

After the 1992 general election, in which they polled only 1.9 per cent of the vote, and the resignation of leaders, the Greens went in steep decline: from a membership of 18,500 in 1990, it was down to 7,500 in 1992. The reasons given were lack of leadership (by 75 per cent), a poor campaign, with funds of only £50,000 (£300,000 was needed), and the loss of every deposit. Faced with factions like the Vegan Quakers, Pagan Greens, New Agers and 'batty old Ladies along for the Elderberry Wine' it is not surprising that Parkin and Porritt moved back into the pressure groups – where membership was still five million. And, despite the election, a cross-party survey of 123 MPs showed a growing awareness – 85 per cent wanted pollution from power stations to be reduced, 74 per cent wanted a rapid reduction in carbon dioxide emissions, and 70 per cent wanted mandatory collection and recycling of ozone-damaging chemicals.

In November 1993 the Greens relaunched their journal and movement – the cover of the former was a copy of the Beatles' Sargeant Pepper album cover, with the four central figures being Porritt, Parkin, Anita Roddick of the Body Shop and botanist David Bellamy. Inside, Porritt provided an analysis of the bursting of the green bubble due to recession and suggested

that the political route for the Greens was 'impossible' – people should vote
for the greenest electable candidate. Local actions were more important
than harping on about the Amazon's problems, and he was optimistic given
the changing attitudes of many businesses towards the environment.

In 1996 the Green Party debated whether to stand at all in the coming
general election and instead gather support for European elections and the
long term. But they retained official policy – to field at least fifty candidates
in order to get a television broadcast, retain their credibility at other levels
of government and put across their message.

In stark contrast, the German Greens stood a chance of taking office
in a coalition with the Social Democrats by 1998.

The 1997 general election manifestos

The Conservative manifesto

In 1992 the Conservatives had set out in their manifesto over 64,000 words
in packed columns of statements interspersed with bullet-point policy
proposals in blue boxes, with no photographs. It seemed they were determined
to eliminate accusations of being 'tired' after thirteen years. In 1997, in
total contrast, the document had coloured photographs, montages and
graphics. 'Rural communities' and 'Environment' formed two of the sections
of 'The best place in the world to live'. As their achievements, the Tories
claimed:

- The area of green belt had doubled since 1979.
- Water and air quality in Britain had improved significantly.
- Britain was said to be one of only a few nations on course to meet
  the commitment to return emissions of all greenhouse gases to 1990
  levels by 2000. 'We are leading the world in reducing the level of the
  "greenhouse gases" that cause global warming and pressing for policies
  that will enable the world to sustain development without long-term
  damage to the environment'.

Small bar charts were used to show the use of lead-free petrol rising
from 1 per cent in 1987 to 69 per cent in 1997, and British beaches
complying with EU standards rising from 66 per cent in 1989 to 90 per
cent in 1996. They were now confident enough to set these out in a
separate 'Green manifesto'.

Future policy proposals were:

- to continue to protect the green belt from development, making sure
  that derelict and under-used urban land was developed in preference
  to green-field sites;

- to set tough but affordable targets, with published environmental strategies to improve air quality and banish city smog – with tighter standards on vehicle emissions and pollution crackdowns around the country;
- to aim for sustained improvements in water quality, at a pace which industry and consumers could afford;
- to develop labelling of products that would give consumers information to show the environmental impact of how they were made;
- to continue to use the tax system and other incentives to encourage the use of vehicles and fuel which did not pollute the environment;
- to continue to explore policies based on the principle that the polluter pays – those who contaminated the land, polluted the environment or produce harmful waste would be made responsible for their actions and pay for the consequences.

In 1992 the subject made up 2.4 per cent of the total document, and concerned four of the 426 policies. In 1997 the Party claimed more, though hedged some of its 'beginnings' and 'intentions' with qualifications, and the subject still only made up 1.1 per cent of the whole.

The Labour manifesto

The environment was no longer merely covered in a 'Families' section, as in 1992, but spread across five of the ten policy areas. The opening 'Contract with the people' stated, 'We will put concern for the environment at the heart of policy-making, so that it is not an add-on extra, but informs the whole of government, from housing and energy policy through to global warming and international agreements'.

Labour promised to promote new green technologies and businesses – energy conservation, efficient energy use and renewable solar and wind power (with no economic case being made for nuclear power). One of the four options for 250,000 people aged under twenty-five who had been unemployed for over six months would be a job with an environmental task force, linked to a citizens' service programme. There was also a promise to 'help you get more out of life' – taking no risk with the future, unable to escape unhealthy water, polluted air and adverse climate changes. All departments of state would promote environmental policies and Parliament would have an environmental audit committee.

Thus, across the manifesto it was claimed that there was an environmental drive combined with economic and social progress. This was especially true of transport policy, where Labour intended to work with the automotive industry to produce 'smarter' cars with lower emissions, and conduct a strategic review of the roads programme.

Under 'Clean up politics' they set out the achievement of:

Labour councils ... at the forefront of environmental initiatives under Local Agenda 21, the international framework for local action arising from the 1992 Earth Summit. A Labour government will encourage all local authorities to adopt plans to protect and enhance their local environment.

Under 'Give Britain leadership in Europe', a 'new environmental internationalism' was required to deal with threats to the global climate, including ozone depletion. It promised to strengthen Britain's cooperation in the EU and to 'lead the fight through our target of a 20 per cent reduction in carbon dioxide by 2010'. The policy would be pursued through trade negotiations and they would work for a new protocol in Japan in 1997.

This was all in line with Labour policies in 1992 (3 per cent of the content of the 1997 manifesto concerned environmentalism, compared with 3.5 per cent in the previous one), but institutional promises had changed – while the Tories' handling of the crisis over BSE (bovine spongiform encephalopathy) was condemned in the manifesto, there was no longer a promise of an independent Food Standards Agency to monitor quality.

The Liberal Democrat manifesto

Just as the Labour Party had stressed that environmental protection should not be an 'add-on', the Liberal Democrats said it must be 'built into every economic decision and every area of government policy', with an opening commitment 'To save energy, cut traffic congestion, stop the unnecessary destruction of the countryside and stem the tide of pollution'. The Labour Party had changed the emphasis from 1992 and pointed to the economic, export opportunities of 'green industries' and the Liberal Democrats began by saying that there would be no extra taxation, but different taxation – of pollution. Previously they had opened with protection of the countryside. But the basic policies were the same and the coverage comparable – 11.7 per cent in 1997 to 13.5 per cent in 1992.

The promises covered the following points.

1   A greener economy:
    - to set 'tough' new targets for the reduction of traffic pollution and waste, including a 30 per cent reduction in carbon dioxide emissions from the 1990 level by 2012 (but in the manifesto five years before the target had been tougher – 30 per cent by 2005);
    - to cut VAT and taxes on jobs, and make up the difference by taxing pollution instead;
    - to adopt a green action programme, with new 'indicators of quality of life, progress and wealth';
    - to protect the local environment, especially to reduce road congestion;

- to improve the way environmental policy was made – putting environment and energy policy in a separate department and to give the Environment Agency more powers.
2   Transporting people, tackling pollution:
- to invest in public transport, with road pricing to finance new, cleaner public transport;
- to treble the freight and double the number of passengers carried on Britain's railways by 2010;
- to encourage people to drive more fuel-efficient cars by cutting car tax from £145 to £10 for cars under 1600 cc, and raising the duty on fuel;
- to reduce the need to travel, through the planning system and information technology.
3   Warmer homes, saving energy:
- to stop wasting half Britain's energy requirement, by increasing fuel bills, and thereby tackling global warming;
- to launch a national homes insulation programme, starting with the two million lowest-income households – saving them £85 a year;
- to introduce a carbon tax (gradually) and reduce VAT and national insurance – 'a tax on jobs';
- to improve energy efficiency standards on materials and so on, cutting VAT to 8 per cent on them;
- to promote renewable sources of energy and combined heat and power schemes, ending nuclear power research and subsidies.
4   Protecting Britain's heritage:
- to clean up Britain's rivers and beaches, ensuring that water companies paid for a major part of the investment, and ending polluting discharges in ten years;
- to tackle marine oil pollution, with tougher rules on safety and high-risk areas;
- to reform land use planning, protecting wild life, coasts and areas of beauty or scientific interest;
- to green the countryside, by contracting with farmers to use more environmentally friendly methods.
5   Thinking globally, acting locally:
- to introduce schemes or to back EU standards for reuse, recycling or repair;
- to promote EU labelling of ecologically friendly products.
6   Promoting animal welfare:
- to improve conditions of rearing and transporting animals, to ban animal testing for some products and to review the law on experiments, enforced by an animal protection commission;
- to give a free vote on hunting, to ban snares and to try to halt the trade in endangered species.

In a separate section on 'Rural communities', the Liberal Democrats continued their demand for reform of the Common Agricultural Policy (CAP), for the protection of green-field sites from urbanisation and for the promotion of safe food through a food commission accountable to Parliament.

And in the final section, 'Britain in the world', they wished to press for legally binding targets on the emission of greenhouse gases and other pollutants, and for the creation of the 'environmental equivalent of the Geneva Convention' to outlaw 'gross acts of environmental destruction' in wars.

The nationalists' manifestos

Plaid Cymru spent 12.3 per cent of its bilingual manifesto on environmental issues (compared with 7.5 per cent in 1992). It was a continuation of the values and policies expressed before. The focus was on sustainability, protection of wild species, local recycling, insulation and low-energy lighting. Closing nuclear power stations was, like the Labour Party's rationale, seen as a chance to develop a new technology needed by the world. They took particular satisfaction in external support for wind power, which they had advocated 'in the teeth of fierce opposition', and wanted other alternative energy sources developed.

The Scottish National Party dropped its 1992 detailed 'medium-term recovery strategy' and offered only a standard manifesto again, with the same priorities and headings. 'Helping all of Scotland' made up one of the ten sections (5.8 per cent). Land, 'healing' agriculture, forests, crofting and fishing came first, before moving on to repeat its vague references to recycling and retaining the Environmental Protection Agency. Similarly, the reprocessing of nuclear waste was ruled out, with a new section on an 'opportunity for Dounreay', in that its decommissioning and a new renewable energy centre could be seen as reassuring to those working there.

The Green Party manifesto

This was printed on recycled paper and was shorter than any of the preceding ones. As in 1992, it set out a choice between themselves and 'conventional grey parties'. It stressed their honesty and realism – that reducing pollution would not be the main concern of those struggling to survive. Their four main themes were: greening the economy; rebuilding communities – dealing with crime, education, transport and so on; policies for health – homelessness, the National Health Service, pollution and food; and Britain's place in the world – the EU, defence, exploitation and trade. It is very clear that this was a mainstream manifesto covering the same issues as the other parties. At the 1992 election they had led with three areas – immediate action to aid the earth's life-support systems; action to build local communities and economies; and action to create new and more productive forms of work. Then, more than twice as much space was given to setting out and describing the problems than to the promises or policies.

In 1997 it was proposed that green taxes would be imposed to reduce resource use and limit pollution, but they said this would be balanced by reductions in job-penalising taxes like national insurance and income tax and by a restructuring of VAT, to bring back some zero ratings. Their approach was far less aggressive and punitive than before. They reaffirmed their previous guarantee of an automatic weekly income for everyone, with a basic income scheme to replace benefits and allowances. Measures of gross national product would be displaced by economic 'sustainability indicators'. On the key issue of global warming, the Greens offered a target like the other parties – 20 per cent from 1990 levels by 2005 – but spoke of basing them 'on the best available scientific evidence ... replace those currently set for political expediency'. Their only other target was to raise recycling of household waste over five years from 25 per cent to 60 per cent.

Taxing the value of land was now 'in stages'; there was no reference to 'returning the profit to the community, localising banks and even currencies'.

Cycle lanes, stopping the building of motorways and trunk roads and reintegrating the rail network were no longer linked to 'workers' participation in companies' decision making and the fostering of cooperatives'. Cutting road traffic by 10 per cent from 1990 levels by 2010 again sits inside the debate parameters of other groups.

Undesirable arms trade would be banned and some of the debt of developing countries would be cancelled.

Nuclear power would be phased out, but the five-year target was dropped, as was the controversial dropping of mortgage tax relief over ten years – the oft-mooted pending use of money from the sale of council houses to build houses was substituted.

The idea of handing out energy-efficient light bulbs free of charge seems to have faded since 1992.

Rural communities would be assisted by assaults on the CAP but the Greens now found merit in EU targets on water and soil quality.

Withdrawal from NATO no longer featured, though export of arms and nuclear disarmament did. A more international perspective appeared in the aim to give 0.7 per cent of gross national product to aid within five years.

Like CFCs, ozone-depleting gases would be banned, but a national environmental protection commission to coordinate all control did not feature.

The National Health Service was deemed to be in need of more funding rather than the previous 'community health focus, high technology medicine being "rigorously assessed" and a more holistic approach taken'.

While a bill of rights, proportional representation and dropping quangos and having citizens' initiatives were in line with their populist past, they almost seen tame compared to some 1992 proposals which the Greens offered as targets to their opponents – devolving revenue-raising and other powers to district level, a ministry for women's affairs, improved prisoners' rights and conditions improved and 'racist' immigration controls removed.

The 1992 mixture of a dramatic decentralisation of economic power, controls and initiatives, and the reversal of nearly every policy and assumption of the previous decade, was a startling contrast. In 1992 the other parties could attack its premises and implications with ease. This time it was the convergence of the Green manifesto that was remarkable. On its back cover they offered a tick-box form of their policies to contrast them with those of the 'grey' parties, but in truth the chasm was not there.

The 1997 general election campaign

In the 1992 general election campaign the environment and its related issues, transport and energy, received 1 per cent each of the radio time and nothing in the tabloids. Most stories originated from within the media and from press conferences – manifestos ranked behind meetings as insignificant stimuli. Similarly, in 1997 the coverage focused on the opinion poll gap that the Tories could not close, sleaze and personalities. It was only after the election that the 'green' elements of the Labour platform began to emerge, amid warnings from pressure groups that it had better not be rhetoric this time.

The Labour government

As well as taking a lead at Kyoto on global warming, the Labour government started to move on domestic green issues. Among its windfall taxes it wanted £5 billion from the oil companies, given that the latter's investment in the North Sea was over and they had escaped petroleum revenue tax since 1983 and benefited from lower corporation tax. It intended to raise the Tory landfill tax rate but looked for more far-reaching solutions. The UK produces 120 million tonnes of domestic and industrial rubbish annually, buries 85 per cent of it (59 and 20 per cent in France and Denmark respectively) and having set a target in 1990 of recycling 25 per cent by 2000, in 1997 the rate was 7.5 per cent. In June 1998 the government proposed to extend recycling, preferably from doorsteps, but the threat was there of extra council tax for conspicuous consumers. This was merely one of a series of policy problems and vacuums left by the Conservative government. There was a legacy of environmental problems.

The countryside

Labour saw green taxes as a growing source of revenue. In February 1998 it proposed one on green-belt development, scrapping its target of 4.4 million new homes by 2016 and looking to use inner-city and derelict land. Following the Countryside March by 300,000 through London in March 1998, the government sought to re-establish its credentials and said that only 40 per cent of new homes would be built on greenfield sites, with 60 per cent (10 per cent more than before) going to brownfield sites. The government also sought to alleviate the effect of green taxes on the countryside by offering 'tranquil zones' where pedestrians would have right of way; cheaper costs for country motorists; and village closures to be limited.

Vandals and landowners who damaged the countryside, especially Sites of Special Scientific Interest, would have to repair damage and the fine rose from £2,500 to £5,000 – welcome but hardly radical!

The government also prepared to take on the farming lobby to stop the uprooting of 7,500 miles of hedgerow a year, with new laws and fines – the earlier 1997 Tory measures had loopholes relating to species and economic loss that meant only a fifth of hedgerows were covered. They stopped the privatisation of the Forestry Commission (with half publicly owned woodlands gone) in July 1998 by setting aside £95 million effectively to buy it out over three years. But Britain was fourth from bottom on forestry management in Europe, largely due to having the worst score for pollution (and only had 2.5 per cent of remaining forest under protection) (WWF, May 1998).

Traffic congestion

John Prescott, Deputy Prime Minister and head of the Department of the Environment and Transport, also declared an end to the 'predict and provide' policy to one of listening to local views. But this was never an easy issue. New Labour voters wanted new houses in the south, where there was less brownfield town land and yet they did not want to lose the countryside! His own department and experts began to predict that five million homes would be needed by 2016 and that would mean two million on greenfield sites. Prescott rejected Hertfordshire's plans but pushed ahead with the biggest incursion into the green belt since the war, near Stevenage, and won a High Court ruling in August 1998 to impose another 12,800 houses on West Sussex. MPs and pressure groups attacked the confusion and lack of clear policy.

John Prescott began the debate on traffic congestion, attacking the 'two-car culture' and announcing an orbital rail link for London in August 1997. In July 1998 the government published a white paper which was the first integrated transport policy for twenty years. It began by rejecting the freedom of car ownership and choice of the Tories – we now travel twenty-five miles per person per day, as opposed to eight miles in the 1950s; by 2016 urban motorway journey times will have risen 69 per cent and on rural motorways by a fifth (at peak hours by 88 per cent); gridlocks would be the norm; the cost to business, health and the climate would be considerable. Between 1974 and 1996 the cost of rail and bus fares have risen by 50 and 75 per cent, while the real cost of motoring has fallen by 3 per cent. Measures therefore proposed were a careful bringing together of separate initiatives with a balance of 'carrots' and 'sticks':

- to stop the school run (20 per cent of peak-time traffic) safe routes to school would be found, with more power given to wardens, pedestrianisation and street widening, more routes, crossings and less waiting at traffic lights – the paper speaks of pedestrians being treated like trespassers in their own towns;
- providing better public transport as an incentive to park outside cities, copying many of the new integrated transport schemes under way in Edinburgh;
- if that does not work, enabling councils to levy congestion charges – for entering cities at peak times (£2 in the Scottish capital and £4 suggested for London);
- non-residential parking charges, including against delivery (white van) drivers and speed limits of twenty miles per hour;
- taxing six million company parking spaces (thought to lead to 60 per cent of peak-time traffic) and airport spaces (up to £500)
- a tax on out-of-town shopping centres, unless they can show steps to ease congestion, such as subsidising a bus service, home deliveries, or staff transport (the supermarkets had successfully lobbied against an automatic tax);
- electronic tolls on motorways and trunk roads, starting with the M8 to generate £100 million a year to upgrade the Glasgow–Edinburgh rail and road links;
- banning cars from 'greenways' where superbuses would run;
- a Commission for Integrated Transport would advise ministers on developments and implementation across sectors;
- a Strategic Rail Authority to demand quality and investment targets from operators – Prescott effectively sacked the previous regulators by not renewing their contracts and he threatened to cancel franchises.

Polls tend to indicate that the public would be prepared to switch to public transport. To the proposal 'Government should give a higher priority to environmental policy even if it means penalising car drivers' – 66 per cent agreed and 27 per cent disagreed, with only a 1 per cent adverse drop since 1997 (*Guardian*/ICM poll, 9 September 1998). If motorists failed to respond to 'carrots', charges would rise sharply and councils penalised if they did not produce adequate five-year plans with targets, to improve air quality, traffic reduction, public transport and road safety after consulting business and residents. They would be encouraged to form partnerships with bus services. These government-approved plans would be introduced on a non-statutory basis in 1999, covering 2000/1 to 2004/5. Prescott's target was said to be zero growth – with an expected rise of ten million cars in the next twenty years, that means a reduction of a third of journeys made. It means getting one in ten motorists to give up using their cars and the rest to use public transport more. Motorists are offered:

- a national system of better information for journey planning, with through ticketing and interchanges;
- new roads or road/motorway-widening where appropriate (including the M25 near Heathrow) – thirty-seven of the previous government's 140 road schemes were giver the go-ahead in August 1998;
- better-maintained roads, with regulation of roadworks and disruption;
- a Motorists' Charter, with provisions against rogue wheel-clampers and dubious second-hand car sales people.

The CBI, RAC, Transport 2000 and FOE all welcomed the white paper. Prescott had to wait for his legislation in a crowded timetable and there were reports that Tony Blair was wary of alienating middle-class car drivers with taxes (at least before the 2002 general election). But he expressed his support and knew that his commitment to reduce emissions of carbon dioxide by 20 per cent by 2010 requires a major contribution from cars (a third of the cut). Those taxes would also raise £1 billion by 2005. It was axiomatic that fuel duty would rise, with larger cars paying more.

The Committee on Medical Effects of Air Pollutants, a government advisory body, reported in January 1998 that just the immediate effect of pollution (mainly traffic fumes) was to hasten the death of between 12,000 and 24,000 vulnerable people a year and cause 24,000 hospital admissions. With a fifth of vehicles exceeding emission targets, the government offered free testing in eight cities. The March 1998 budget cut the vehicle excise licence for smaller cars and gave £50 million for rural bus services. In April the Department of the Environment funded an EU scheme to promote electric and fuel cell vehicles in all 1,400 European cities with populations over 100,000 – Oxford joined. Meanwhile Leeds introduced a lane for vehicles only carrying more than one person.

Pollution

Prescott, who in 1983 had swum in the Thames as a protest against nuclear dumping, planned to use Britain's presidency of the EU in 1998 and the Year of the Oceans to press for a treaty on seven dumping threats and over-fishing. In June he took the lead on greenhouse gases by Britain offering to make a 12.5 per cent cut as part of the agreed EU targets on the Kyoto 8 per cent reduction and on reducing acid rain and improving air quality by limiting sulphur dioxide, nitrogen oxides, lead and the sulphur content of heavy fuel. The Environment Secretary agreed to the cessation of all dumping in the North Sea in twenty-five years and the Energy Minister John Battle brought forward by two years measures to regulate the offshore oil industry. The Department of the Environment began the first fully integrated study into global warming on 5 June 1998 – World Environment Day, looking for the plusses, negatives and trade-offs. But the government did not escape censure – that it was still prepared to dump some oil-rigs at sea at the end of their lives (though in Portugal in July 1998 Prescott agreed to remove all twenty-seven British steel rigs over 10,000 tonnes). When it published its first pollution report in May 1998 it was criticised for not using actual figures – 'the only thing the Treasury understands' (though an independent economist put the cost of pollution at £22 billion a year).

Water

After privatisation, water company profits rose from £1.3 billion in 1990 to £2.1 billion in 1997, but it was pointed out that serious pollution had declined by three-quarters over that period, 89 per cent of bathing areas met required standards compared with 66 per cent in 1988 and drinking water met 99.7 per cent of safety standards. That did not stop the Water Inspectorate reporting in June 1998 that one in four people refused to drink tap water and more than half were not fully satisfied with its quality. Nor were those at the dirty end – groups like Surfers Against Sewage – impressed. Moreover, consumers have paid for 83 per cent of improvements, rather than investment by borrowing. The regulator, Ofwat, sought to pressure John Prescott to place the burden of the required £46 million improvement needed on to consumers again. The government demanded price cuts as well but, as ever, there would not be enough to satisfy public and pressure groups.

Emissions from energy production

This dilemma was also true of the energy sector, where the government inherited a comparable mess of privatisation legacy, urgent issues and political no-win decisions. As noted in Chapter 12, the Labour government moved to stop the dash for gas and save 9,000 jobs in fifteen privatised pits by guaranteeing set purchases by the generators (October 1998) though this reversed their previous policy and raised the issue of the polluting effects of coal burning, not least from our European neighbours who inherited the acid rain. They had to accept that nuclear power had a role in the policy mix – a case put strongly by the Trade and Industry Select Committee in June 1998, which also pointed out the investment made and the lower emissions from newer stations. They still had no answer about what to do with the waste and, as an unwelcome warning, the government had to fine its atomic weapons plant £22,000 in August 1998 when two workers were contaminated with plutonium. They also accepted nuclear waste from Georgia, to help prevent proliferation and nuclear terrorism – assailed by Greenpeace and FOE in a knee-jerk response – they wanted it pushing on to Russia. More embarrassing was that the safe facility chosen to reprocess this waste, Dounreay, was closed two months later in June 1998 as being completely unsafe. It was claimed by managers that its closure, with a £400 million clean-up bill, was needed to save the nuclear industry. The THORP reprocessing plant was closed in May 1998 because of leaks (thought to require £1 billion to mend) and in July Michael Meacher said they were prepared to close Sellafield because it could not achieve zero discharges. John Prescott had to fight his fourteen colleagues in Portugal in July 1998 who wanted it closed: under the deal he struck, eight of Britain's old stations will close within ten years and Magnox reprocessing at Sellafield will stop by 2020. After all-night negotiations he agreed to the French ban on discharges of radionuclides (unstable atoms). Equally tough on the French industry, BNFL said it would have to spend millions of pounds to meet these abatement levels. Greenpeace described the agreement as 'historic' and an end to reprocessing.

Stephen Littlechild, electricity regulator, claimed renewable energy was too expensive in September 1998, but the following month the government pressed on with its policy to provide 10 per cent of Britain's energy from renewable sources by 2010. It had been reassured that the cost of wind and landfill gas schemes had fallen 23 per cent. Predictably in this sector some greens (Council for the Protection of Wales) had decided that the 200-foot wind turbines were intrusive. The government was not prepared to go as far as the EU, however, which in March 1998 proposed to invest £110 billion over ten years on renewable power like wind, sun and water. It would not raise his own target to 12 per cent and thought the UK contribution to the fund would be £1–£3 billion.

BSE (mad cow disease)

Labour's motives were questioned for opening an inquiry in March 1998 into the BSE problem, especially by the National Farmers' Union. In fact it revealed again the culture of secrecy, with officials fearing a panic if they said anything; there was ministerial buck-passing; scientists admitting they were blundering around in the dark and decisions were taken to protect the industry rather than the consumer, twenty-seven of whom had died. At one time the Tories considered killing the entire beef herd; in any case, eight million will be killed by the year 2000 and the bill by then will be £4 billion. In January 1998 the government introduced a new standards agency that would put the consumer first; besides monitoring the safety of food, it would lead or share policy on GM foods, additives, chemicals, labelling, animal feed; it could commission research and coordinate law enforcement. Meacher had moved to ban dangerous pesticides, some akin to nerve gas, in July 1998. An agency was timely: in a *Guardian*/ICM poll on 9 September 1998, to the proposition 'Food is becoming safer to eat', 32 per cent agreed and 52 per cent disagreed (7 per cent worse than 1997).

Conclusion

We are left with the question – why has an increasingly aware and concerned electorate not translated its desire for a better quality of life and a safe environment into clear political action?

The first response must be the truism that people vote according to their economic wellbeing and prospects – now dubbed the 'feel good factor'; their next major concern was the National Health Service.

A second explanation is that many of the environmental concerns are long term and though voters do want a safe planet for their children, the issues are both complex and remote. As long as politicians and experts seem to be offering explanations, especially to the immediate problems of pollution that affect them, they are content to be reassured. Consumers ceased buying as much bottled water and began buying beef again as the scares passed.

A third but less significant factor is that voters who are familiar with alternatives and the implications of green policies do not like all they see. Higher prices, taxes on car use and major economic changes are not immediately attractive, even if adopted by a major party. In the case of third parties, the 'wasted vote' syndrome comes into play.

Jonathon Porritt's statement that the 'bubble has burst' may have been true of Britain's Green Party politics after 1993. Yet lead-free petrol, recycling, public awareness and company action were valuable gains, and the processes of scientific revelation, public education and political incorporation of environmental issues continue.

Tom Burke sounded a warning:

> The brutal truth about the politics of the environment is that all the successes of the past quarter century have been no more than tactical victories in the long retreat for the environment in the face of inexorable pressure from a rising population with rising income that it spends unwisely. The agenda of

the easy politics is very familiar: air and water quality; waste from contaminated land; endangered species; chemicals and radioactivity.... The hard politics of the future will be very different ... food security, fish stocks, water availability, forests, climate change, transport policy. (*The Independent*, 6 May 1996)

This was echoed by the World Wide Fund for Nature in October 1998 when it produced a Living Planet Index – showing that humans had destroyed a third of the natural world of animals and plants in the last twenty-five years. The problems described here will require radical concerted action that has not fully developed yet, but the magnitude and vital nature of these environmental issues keep forcing themselves on the future British and international agendas.

Appendix: a chronology of environmentalism

1971	Friends of the Earth formed
1972	Stockholm Conference on the Environment
1973/4	Toxic waste fed for nine months to cattle in Michigan
1974	Flixborough chemical plant in Humberside exploded, killing twenty-eight people and damaging seventy-two houses
1976	Seveso – a toxic cloud was released in northern Italy; this was revealed only after ten days; 40 per cent of births were subsequently with defects
1977	Reprocessing of nuclear waste at Sellafield agreed
1978	*Amoco Cadiz* oil tanker pollutes 130 miles of coastline
1978	Love Canal – toxic waste forces the evacuation of a US town
1979	Three Mile Island nuclear accident – effects are still unknown
1982	Worldwide agreement to ban commercial whaling
1983	Britain begins to move to lead-free petrol
1984	Bhopal – toxic gases kill and injure thousands in India
1986	Chernobyl nuclear reactor in the Ukraine explodes, causing cancers and mass evacuation
1986	French sink Greenpeace ship *Rainbow Warrior*
1988	Seals die in North Sea from pollution
1988	Agreement to phase out CFCs at Montreal
1989	*Exxon Valdez* oil spill off Alaska of eleven million gallons costs £1.8 million to clean up
1991	Five-year moratorium on mining in Antarctica
1991	Ozone depletion found over the Antarctic
1991	Aral Sea shrinks as water is diverted
1991	Kuwait oil fields burn after the Gulf War
1991	Chelyabinsk – the site of the USSR's nuclear programme – is revealed to be the most dangerous eighty square miles on earth (a hundred times worse than Chernobyl)
1992	UN Earth Summit in Brazil
1994	The Black Sea is an acknowledged cesspit for sixteen countries and 160 million people. Its fish catch of 100,000 tons is an eighth of that in the 1980s
1994	Ferry companies agree not to transport live animals
1994/5	Serious traffic pollution in London linked to rise in asthma

1995	First ozone hole found over the Arctic
1995	Greenpeace force Shell to stop dumping of Brent Spar oil platform at sea
1995	Anti-car pollution protesters stop London rush-hour traffic
1996	Nuclear bomb accidents in 1957–8 revealed to have contaminated Berkshire. The Ministry of Defence admitted to forty years of radiation tests on humans
1996	The Russian branch of Greenpeace march on Lake Kaskovo, the most chemically polluted lake on earth – the life expectancy of locals is only forty-two years
1996	The Dead Sea has lost twelve of its forty-five miles in forty years and has dropped sixteen metres because of mineral extraction
1996	'Mad cow' disease (BSE) linked to Creutzfeld–Jakob disease in humans – EU bans beef exports
1996	Pesticide dangers linked to Gulf War syndrome, having been ignored since 1951
1996	The *Sea Empress* spills 72,000 tonnes of oil off Milford Haven, killing thousands of seabirds and contaminating thirty-eight sites of special scientific interest on 125 miles of coastline – costing the government £100 million
1997	New York summit – Tony Blair raises issues of clean water and criticises US stance on global warming at the UN
1997	Indonesian forest fires cause smog and devastation in South East Asia
1997	Kyoto Summit on Global Warming sets soft targets
1998	The government bans the first genetically modified crops – a blow to the £250 million biotechnology industry
1998	The government changes its policy on building new houses on green-belt land
1998	Transport white paper

Reading

Barr, J. (ed.) (1971) *The Environmental Handbook*, Friends of the Earth.

Carson, R. (1962) *Silent Spring*, Penguin.

Club of Rome (1962) *The Limits to Growth*, Earth Island.

'Greening in organisations', *Journal of Organizational Change Management*, Vol. 1 (4).

KPMG (1997) *Survey of Environmental Reporting*, KPMG, London EC4Y 8BB.

North, R. D. (1995) *Life on a Modern Planet: A Manifesto for Progress*, Manchester University Press.

Porritt, J. and Winner, D. (1988) *The Coming of the Greens*, Fontana.

Schumacher, F. (1974) *Small is Beautiful*, Abacus.

15

Sleaze: standards in public life

Geoff Lee

On 18 January 1995, the first day of the Nolan Inquiry into Standards in Public Life, Professor Ivor Crewe drew the distinction between the public's past healthy cynicism about politicians' motives (also true in other major democracies like the USA and India) and the effect that 'sleaze' had produced – that two-thirds (64 per cent, according to a 1994 Gallup poll – see Chapter 2) now believed 'most MPs make a lot of money by using public office improperly'.

It should be remembered that while the matters detailed below were central to the debate, all kinds of other 'sleaze' were contributing to the picture – trials of footballers and demands for a public inquiry into the affairs of football clubs; the revelations of discriminatory sales of council houses by Westminster council ('homes for votes') and surcharges of £37 million; the rows over the fortunes being 'earned' by privatised utility directors (seen against the backcloth of all directors' pay soaring by 500 per cent or nine times the rate of inflation over the previous decade); and the directors of the collapsed Barings Bank seeking £100 million in bonuses when affected pension funds and charities faced losses (condemned in the media as 'outrageous greed'). In December 1997 up to thirty officers in the Flying Squad were being investigated in the biggest police corruption scandal for twenty-five years; in January 1998 250 members of Scotland Yard were being investigated for corruption by a 'ghost squad' from other services; and in September 1998 police in seven forces were being investigated for drugs, bribery and robberies. Nor was sleaze confined to Britain – there were scandals in Hong Kong, Japan, Singapore (Leeson's involvement in the collapse of Barings) and the 'black economy' in Greece, Spain and Italy was said to be short-charging the European Union (EU) by £10 billion in April 1998.

Political sleaze also affected attitudes to a privacy law, currently under study by Lord Mackay: many were sympathetic to the idea of curbing the worst excesses of the tabloid press, especially those affecting ordinary citizens or members of the royal family. But when John Major was considering the idea, he had had to keep away from any accusation of protecting MPs from embarrassment.

October 1994 – the beginning of a crisis

The Major government was dealing with a *Sunday Times* story that Mark Thatcher had benefited from his mother's name to become a multimillionaire in a £20 million arms deal, that Lord Archer had been dealing in Anglia Television shares while his wife was on its board during a takeover, and that MPs were willing to ask parliamentary questions for cash. *The Guardian* published documents from lobbyist Ian Greer to Mohamed Al-Fayed about the questions to be asked by Neil Hamilton, a junior minister, on his behalf. Tim Smith, another minister, was also named as a 'key player'. Labour members of the House of Commons Committee on Standards and Privileges walked out in protest at the secrecy imposed on their inquiries into 'cash for questions', while holding back from resigning for fear of letting the government abort the inquiry – raising questions about whether the Commons would have the competence and the will to regulate itself. At the same time it was revealed that the Railtrack bosses who had failed to end the sixteen-week strike would receive £2,000 bonuses and zone directors 40 per cent rises for hurrying privatisation along.

Meanwhile Jonathan Aitken was juggling letters to the Cabinet Secretary and the press from the Ritz Hotel manager to show that his wife and not a wealthy Saudi businessman had paid his bill.

David Hunt had been given the job of heading off further damage by increasing the accountability of quangos, amid accusations of 'favours' there. The government's strategy was to try to ride out this storm and to counter the rise in popularity of Tony Blair by offering insubstantial legislation. It failed lamentably. All the elements of what became known as 'sleaze' were in place. They ran for over three years and propelled the Conservative government to a crushing electoral defeat.

The House of Fraser affair

The takeover of the House of Fraser, including Harrods, stems from the mid-1980s. Lonrho's bid had been prohibited by the government and yet the alternative and successful bidder, the Al-Fayed brothers, were condemned by inspectors from the Department of Trade and Industry (DTI) in 1990 for lies and deceits but were not disqualified as directors. Criticism of the Al-Fayed brothers seemed strongest from Mr Wardle, the junior immigration minister, who was responsible for the applications for British citizenship of the brothers. In October 1994 all were trying to distance themselves from the affair. Home Secretary Michael Howard was denying involvement with the applications and imposing an injunction on the *Financial Times* from publishing a damaging article; the Prime Minister was being pressurised to repudiate accusations that Mr Howard, when a minister at the DTI in 1987, had been improperly influenced by a Lonrho 'family connection'; Mr Hamilton was writing to *The Guardian* denying any involvement when a minister and explaining his free stay at the Al-Fayed's Ritz Hotel in Paris, while threatening the newspaper that he would sue just as he had the BBC some years ago (for £500,000). In taking sides between Tiny Rowlands of Lonrho and the Al-Fayeds, there were doubts about the mixture of genuine business, personal dislikes, racial undertones and financial payoffs.

Cash for questions

Parliamentary questions do not come cheap – researching and answering the 50,000 written questions a year cost taxpayers £97 per question. Nor are they all genuine constituency issues, but instead the increase in the number of questions asked each year reflects the growth of the £30 million a year lobbying business, which has seen the number of firms quintuple since the 1950s.

The origin of this cash-for-questions scandal came from a leading businessman who told the *Sunday Times* that he had paid MPs to ask parliamentary questions on his behalf. The newspaper said it could not divulge this without revealing its source, and instead approached ten Labour and ten Conservative MPs to do 'consultancy work' by tabling written questions. Conservative MPs Graham Riddick and David Tredinnick agreed to do so for £1,000 cheques and they were suspended as parliamentary private secretaries when the story was published in July 1994, and were later suspended from the Commons, one for ten and the other for twenty days (thereby losing a few thousand pounds in salary). Tory claims of entrapment and there being no other evidence of such activity were to be blown aside by Mohamed Al-Fayed's sense of injustice and outrage.

Hamilton asserted that he had asked two parliamentary questions on the House of Fraser affair since 1987, but *The Guardian* traced and published four more since that date and asserted that Greer and Hamilton had worked together for Al-Fayed until April 1989. Hamilton emphatically denied receiving any payments from Al-Fayed and had registered his previous interests on becoming a minister. When *The Guardian* persisted in its allegations, he sued for defamation.

In contrast, Tim Smith confirmed receiving money from Al-Fayed between 1987 and 1989, and not declaring this information in the Register of Members' Interests until late in this period, and he resigned from the government.

On 1 October 1996 Hamilton dropped his libel case against *The Guardian*, which had as its main headline that day 'A liar and a cheat', and he was forced to resign on 26 October 1996 when other allegations were made. More information followed and moved the scandal closer to John Major when David Willetts (a key aide) and other whips were shown to have advised him on how to block an inquiry into Hamilton. Willetts was forced to resign his Cabinet Office job in December 1996 after the Commons Committee on Standards and Privileges Committee accused him of 'dis-sembling'. *The Guardian* continued to pursue John Major about his knowledge of sleaze in this area as Tim Smith began to reveal more evidence to the Commissioner for Parliamentary Standards, Sir Gordon Downey, a former Comptroller and Auditor General, in March 1997.

The problem was known to extend to the House of Lords. In February 1995 the respected Lord Lester told an internal inquiry that he knew of four colleagues receiving substantial sums for putting questions to ministers.

Arms sales – the Scott inquiry

The collapse of the Matrix-Churchill trial in November 1992 showed the government was willing to see the prosecution of three businessmen in the arms-to-Iraq affair, even though they were aware of their activities. Ministers Heseltine, Rifkind, Garel-Jones and Ken Clarke all signed public interest immunity certificates designed to stop vital information reaching the defence and it was alleged that Jonathan Aitken had been preparing to do so, despite a clear breach of self-interest. The subsequent outcry and the Scott inquiry showed that Parliament was being consistently misled on arms sales. In June 1995 Scott let it be known that he rejected the claim by William Waldegrave, Alan Clark and Lord Trefgarne that their agreement to relax restrictions in December 1988 was not a change of policy.

In 1995 *The Independent* alleged that Aitken was present, as a director of BMARC, when the company agreed to arms shipments to Iran via Singapore, in breach of government and United Nations embargoes. Minutes, withheld from the Scott inquiry, showed he had attended five key meetings between 1988 and 1990, not the three he claimed. Michael Heseltine, Trade and Industry Secretary, admitted to the House in June 1995 that there had been widespread failure in his department to scrutinise export licences – 74 per cent were incorrectly filled in.

The Scott report

Ian Lang and the government had eight weeks to prepare their response to the Scott report to the House of Commons on 16 February 1996, with a team combing the report for good news; 'big guns' like Lord Howe and

Douglas Hurd were brought out to cast doubt on the validity of the inquiry's procedures, and the timing being carefully stage-managed. Lang declared that there had been no conspiracy to imprison businessmen, that there was no change in the guidelines for exporting arms, that legal advice given at the time was correct and that, while mistakes may have been made, ministers and officials had acted in good faith. The opposition had only three and a half hours to study the 1,800-page/five-volume report in a closed room. Nevertheless Robin Cook and even some Tory backbenchers could easily punch holes in the government's selective account – he said that Parliament had been repeatedly misled, that they knew about the 'supergun' a year before it was seized by Customs, that they were prepared to blame civil servants and that they had instructed them not to issue any material that criticised ministers. The two ministers under most pressure were William Waldegrave for having misled the House and Sir Nicholas Lyall for ignoring Michael Heseltine's reservations about the use of public interest immunity certificates, as it raised important legal and constitutional issues. By 18 February the *Sunday Times* was showing in an NOP poll that two out of three voters wanted the two to resign.

Whitehall's attempt to deflect or bury the Scott report with a flood of documents had not worked – he singled out individuals who had offered 'unsound' and 'flawed' advice. The theme that comes through strongly from the report is the culture of secrecy and cover-up – 'gagging orders', disclosure of information, evading export controls and a lack of ministerial account-ability and coordination of intelligence – none of which drew clear government proposals for reform. The damage limitation and 'spin' did not last as the report was studied and though there may have been no 'killing phrases', there was a cumulative picture of secretive conspiracy at Parliament's expense. By 19 February Lang was admitting that fear of criticism over the change in arms policy, including in the USA, had led to the failure to inform Parliament. John Major was criticised for not giving full information, under 'Questions of Procedure for Ministers', but then an official raised the possibility that he had known about the change of guidelines six years previously. It was no longer certain that government could win the vote on the Scott report in the Commons. Three Tories had defected in the last five months and it was only by promising a Tory 'waverer' that 'gagging' laws would be modified that the government won the vote, 320 to 319, on 27 February 1996.

The Jonathan Aitken affair

Kept out of office by Margaret Thatcher since 1974, Aitken had used the time to build a fortune through a financial services company, partly funded by the Saudis. John Major brought him into office in 1992.

In May 1994 the Cabinet Secretary responded to *The Guardian*'s first information that the minister for procurement at the Ministry of Defence had stayed at the Al-Fayed-owned Ritz Hotel in Paris at the same time as Saudi and Syrian financiers and former business colleagues. These were said to be coincidental meetings with some of his daughter's godparents.

When it was alleged that the bill of £1,000 had been paid by Mr Ayas, which would have been a breach of 'Questions of Procedure for Ministers', explanations and correspondence flowed to the effect that his wife had really paid it, and it was a clerical error. As *The Guardian* continued to press on the details and publish letters, it claimed the Ritz bill was issued after it started to investigate. While angry Tory MPs rallied to Aitken in October 1994 and criticised the Prime Minister for not defending Hamilton as well, there was deep unease.

Granada Television's *World in Action* then reported that he had received £1 million from the Saudis to buy a health farm and had tried to arrange for women to entertain a member of the Saudi royal family. In April 1995 he sued *The Guardian* and threatened *World in Action*. As stories circulated about his directorships and the Scott inquiry findings of arms supplies, he resigned from the cabinet in July 1995.

After losing his seat in the 1997 general election, the libel case against *The Guardian* and Granada Television went ahead in June of that year (the offer to Aitken to drop the case and let each side pay its costs was turned down). He was questioned about links with the Saudis and with dealing with secret arms commissions and was shown to have lied to the Cabinet Secretary and to Parliament. His lies over the Ritz Hotel bill gradually came apart, even though he had tried to verify the story by using his wife (who left him) and his daughter (whom the police decided not to prosecute). On 21 June 1997 he withdrew his case and *The Guardian* ran the headline 'He lied and lied and lied' – and said he had been 'the amoral architect of his own downfall'. His marriage had broken down and the former Chief Secretary to the Treasury was left disgraced, with a legal bill of £1.8 million. In September 1998 legal proceedings began against him for perjury, conspiracy and perverting the course of justice. Aitken had been described as a gambler – his fall was spectacular. A story with a clear moral theme? Well, in fact, Aitken was hired as a 'consultant' by GEC-Marconi, Britain's main electronics defence business, in March 1998, to win Middle East arms contracts.

Outside interests

As the spotlight moved around Westminster, several Members were illuminated not fully dressed. Tory MP Michael Colvin had told *The Independent* in 1990 that introducing clients to policy makers 'would be very unwise of MPs.... I think that's prostituting their profession'. In 1994 it was revealed that he had failed to disclose a consultancy with a South African public relations firm which had earned him £10,000 in 1991 and he was listed as an adviser to the Federation of Retail Licensed Trade, Northern Ireland, Caledonia Investments, Meridian Broadcasting, Thames Heliport, and CUL Aerospace, and had two company directorships and extensive farming interests.

Meanwhile Dr Charles Goodson-Wickes, MP for Wimbledon, had six company directorships, and consultancies to public relations, pharmaceuticals and construction concerns. A major *Observer* investigation in 1995 found that at least £3 million was earned from 275 directorships by 100 MPs – the majority being Tory. Pride of place went to David Mellor, who, following his resignation after revelations of an affair and a holiday paid for by a member of the Palestine Liberation Organisation, was feted as a millionaire, earning £300,000 a year as a politician, broadcaster and holder of ten consultancies worth £100,000 (his former cabinet salary was £67,000).

Consultancies are favoured because they do not carry the legal obligations of directorships. The 168 MPs holding 356 consultancies were earning £3 million from them. Especially favoured were those which involved lucrative Middle East connections, where 'introductions' were valuable. In January 1995 it was revealed that ministers and MPs were employing eighteen known lobbyists as researchers (access to the register of researchers is restricted).

The Independent wondered whether these would fit Margaret Thatcher's definition of 'real jobs' and poured scorn on the usual rationale: that these kept MPs in touch with the 'real world' and enabled them to do their jobs better. If so, why need they be paid? Such involvement could take place anyway (especially as most MPs are not overburdened with ministerial work). The rationale that MPs needed to supplement their meagre pay no longer held any weight after their unpopular rises. Labour MPs managed on the pay, with less personal wealth, and union sponsorship made little difference.

One argument was that accepting gifts, fees and so on did not imply any obligation. The Tories, however, had warned the electorate against believing there was a 'free lunch' in the world. The *Independent on Sunday* (23 October 1994) said the Tories now 'expected us to believe in 5 free dinners and 3 free breakfasts at one of Europe's most expensive hotels ... the overwhelming message of this ... is that money talks.... The Conservatives offer no wider values or aspirations.... The Right looks to individuals to restrain their own greed. It has not worked.'

The following month it was revealed that Sir Paul Beresford, junior housing minister (on a salary of £45,000), had been allowed to continue his work as a dentist for nearly half the week, raising further doubts about the judgement of the Cabinet Secretary and John Major. By mid-1995, as Nolan reported (see below), a poll commissioned by the University of Essex showed that only 28 per cent thought it acceptable for MPs to do any outside work and only 3 per cent would allow them to receive fees from companies.

The position in the House of Lords was felt to be worse – there was no register of interests and there were many examples of lords declaring an interest in representing a client as a consultant and then going on to put their case in a debate. As many as 100 of the 1,200 peers were being paid (up to £15,000 a year). Lord McIntosh, Deputy Labour Leader in the Lords, dismissed the fact that they were unpaid and could not manage on their allowances as no reason for avoiding closer scrutiny. In July 1995 it was proposed that lords could not speak in debates in which they had an interest. When Nolan reported, the Lords agreed to establish a register of interests.

Perquisites

John Major made public the rules for ministerial conduct in 1992 – that 'they must not accept gifts, hospitality, or services from anyone which would, or might appear to, place him or her under an obligation'. This seemed not to have occurred to Environment Minister John Gummer when he failed to declare that a food company had paid £2,600 to help him restore a pond on his land. The Treasury paid Norman Lamont's £4,700 legal fees to evict a sex therapist from his private property.

Many MPs were discovered to be beneficiaries of upgrades from economy to first-class air travel, for themselves and their families, and in 1994 ministers' wives had enjoyed travel worth £35,000. The airlines regarded this as 'legitimate lobbying'. The same could not be said of Inland Revenue inspectors, investigating wealthy businessmen, who were being given thousands of pounds' worth of foreign trips, villas, casino visits and gifts (*Sunday Times*, 30 October 1994).

In February 1996 Neil Hamilton's name appeared again, in connection with free hotel stays paid for by US Tobacco and later that year having received furniture and paintings from lobbyist Ian Greer.

National Health Service (NHS) auditors discovered a £500,000 relocation perks scandal and banned a chief executive from serving again.

Conflicts of interest

A commonly recurring source of unease and anger was the employment, by privatised industries or City finance companies, of ministers who had been involved in the sell-off process – Norman Tebbit by BT, Lord Young by Cable & Wireless, Lord Walker by British Gas and Sir Norman Fowler by the National Freight Corporation. Less obvious cases came to light – that Douglas McGregor had worked for Hill Samuel before 1979 and was in their pension scheme, that the company then advised the government on rail privatisation and McGregor had rejoined the company, 'not knowing if any pension payments had been made' and not declaring these matters in the Register of Members' Interests. In February it was alleged that Associated British Ports received preferential treatment in developing Cardiff docklands because Lord Crickhowell, on its board, was Welsh Secretary from 1979 to 1987. In the same month it was reported that Lord Wakeham, who joined the board of N. M. Rothschild amid controversy about its role of advising the government about electricity privatisation, had awarded them a large contract when they were not the highest bidder.

A 1975 memorandum by Sir John Hunt, Cabinet Secretary, had said any curbs on ministers' employment after leaving office would be 'impracticable' and would be complicated by changes of government, though civil servants had to obtain permission before taking another job within two years of leaving.

In January 1994 Alan Duncan MP resigned as a parliamentary private secretary for having used 'right to buy' rules over council housing to make money in property deals with a neighbour.

Northern Ireland Minister Michael Mates resigned in June 1993 following revelations that he had lobbied on behalf of Azil Nadir, the fugitive and bankrupt Polly Peck businessman, had solicited the loan of a car and had given him a watch with the inscription 'Don't let the buggers get you down' on it.

Ten ex-ministers held consultancies with firms that had received £20 million from the overseas aid budget in one year and £8 million was awarded to companies contributing to the Tory Party. This was uncovered by a Labour MP's questions, as a follow-up to the Pergau Dam row, when British aid seemed to be linked to arms sales to Malaysia.

Sir Jerry Wiggin was forced to apologise for putting an amendment to a bill in a standing committee in the name of a colleague, without the latter's consent. The amendment would serve the cause of outside interests he represented and would stand more chance under his colleague's name because he was a member of that committee. Members of both main parties were angry that it was not referred to the Privileges Committee by the Speaker – many regarded this as more serious than cash for questions and thought he was 'getting away with murder'.

Patronage

In the 1980s there were 10,000 jobs available on quangos every year. The Labour Research Department found that nearly £2 million had been given to the Conservative Party or its affiliates by companies whose directors sat on NHS trusts. Tories, including peers and former MPs, were six times more likely to be appointed to trusts than Labour supporters.

A former Tory party fund-raiser and Monaco-based businessman, Mr Rowe-Beddoe, was being paid more than £70,000 a year to run the two most important quangos in Wales, while continuing his full-time job as chair of a Monte Carlo company. By the end of 1994 there were twenty-four wives and husbands of Tory MPs or peers with paid jobs on quangos and thirty-three former Tory candidates who had failed to be elected in the 1992 general election. A BBC investigation showed that directors of companies which donated money to the Conservative Party were three times more likely to hold quango posts than those of companies which did not – Marks and Spencer shared twelve jobs among nineteen directors, while Debenhams and John Lewis (non-contributors) had none. Senior members of the big five trade unions had a one in thirty-five chance. Richard Branson was later to claim that he had not won the licence to run the national lottery because he refused to donate money to the Conservative Party (*The Independent*, 4 September 1998). Labour MP Alan Milburn's research showed that three in five top civil servants obtain quango jobs and he commented 'Whitehall is infested with a "jobs for the boys" culture. Unlike the rest of the population Sir Humphrys are finding nice little earners when they retire' (*The Observer*, 14 May 1995).

The government responded to allegations by conducting an eight-month inquiry – in February 1995 they proposed: open advertising of posts; easier nomination; consultation with the chief whip; an end to multiple appointments; codes of conduct; information on membership via the Internet; and rules for ministers when a relative was involved. Many thought this was not enough and at the same time no alterations were made to total discretion on receiving gifts and there were no changes on ministers and civil servants taking outside jobs. The number of the latter leaving to join consultancies had quadrupled in five years – in 1988 it was one in eight and in 1993 it was one in two. As Nolan moved in to stop payments for sitting on such boards, *The Guardian* identified the main 'quangocrat' as Sir Brian Shaw, who received £4,000 per day from the Port of London Authority.

'Fat cats'

The high salaries, pay awards and the share benefits of business leaders, especially those in privatised industries, began to surface in the press and fuel political debate in the early 1990s. This was led by the report that British Gas was lowering the earnings of some workers while in November

1994 awarding a rise of 75 per cent to Cedric Brown, its chief executive, to make his salary £475,000 a year. The Prime Minister refused to defend this. At the annual general meeting on 1 June 1995 some 4,000 shareholders refused to reappoint the board – while proxy votes from City institutions overturned this, it was an unprecedented protest.

The Labour Party calculated that fifty directors of privatised industries were £1 million better off through salaries, share options and pension rights, while they had shed 150,000 jobs. All twelve chairs of English regional electricity companies made £1 million, six made at least £2 million, and the part-time (three days a week) chair of Eastern Electricity had had a rise of £33,000 to reach £250,000 a year by 1995. In total the utility chiefs had over £100 million of uncashed share options (seventy-seven electricity executives alone had £70 million). At the same time the £300,000-a-year chief executive of PowerGen had topped up his income by taking on three 'little' outside jobs worth £36,000 a year.

The Labour Party then turned its attention to the twenty-five directors of the privatised water companies, who were sharing £25 million in pay, share options and pensions by 1995 – nine out of ten having more than doubled their salaries since privatisation. The chair of North West Water earned 571 per cent more than his predecessor. The 'fattist cat' was said to be Sandy Anderson, who made £40 million in seven months from a railway buyout.

The salaries of 237 NHS trust directors (£141 million) would pay for 11,000 nurses (Labour research, in *The Guardian*, 2 January 1995). In May 1995 directors of the National Grid were already under attack for dealing in share options before flotation – it was then revealed that they were using the tax loophole of transferring their options to their wives, making profits of hundreds of thousands of pounds. *The Observer* conducted extensive research into utility chiefs and found they were awarding themselves £350,000 on average – to the anger of the government and Tories who regarded them as 'jumped-up civil servants' who had been handed this £40 million chance on a plate. Amid the almost daily disclosures of rewards John Major conceded in March 1995 that legislation might be needed.

The Greenbury Committee, led by the Confederation of British Industry (CBI), was encouraged to look at directors' pay for the government, but the cause of self-regulation was not helped by Sir Richard Greenbury himself receiving a pay rise of 17 per cent and share options worth £91,000 while the Committee was at work. His Committee recommended that gains from share options be taxed as income. When the Chancellor immediately introduced the tax on all such gains, including the lower paid, Greenbury repudiated the move, angrily rebutted claims that his report had no teeth and, given the intrusions into his private life, he wanted nothing more to do with the matter.

Princess Anne told the Chambers of Commerce that they must correct the image of greed and serving their own short-term interests – in a politically sensitive area a member of the royal family would only comment in the light of strong public opinion.

The issue would not go away easily with a change of government. In July 1998 it was revealed that directors had awarded themselves 18 per cent increases, ignoring calls for restraint. The TUC President, John Edmonds, called them 'greedy bastards' at its conference in September 1998.

The Committee for Standards in Public Life

The 1987 New Parliament Register set out nine categories of interest, including remunerated directorships; remunerated employment; remunerated professions; interests where the client's interest requires MPs' services because of their membership; financial sponsorships; payments and benefits received from foreigners. In fact MPs took a very wide interpretation about what was declarable – a gift to Norman Lamont of £18,000 to settle legal bills was not registered because it was anonymous. The Select Committee on Members' Interests accepted this, but said that in future anonymous gifts should be declared. In a major report in 1992 the Committee tried to tighten the rules by declaring that MPs did not have a high degree of discretion to decide on relevance.

There were increasing demands that an independent and public inquiry be held to reassure the public about MPs' interests. This was backed by the Labour and Liberal Democrat leadership, by former Conservative Chair Norman Fowler and by an increasing number of MPs with legitimate directorships who looked askance at those offering services as lobbyists and consultants.

By October 1994 John Major was said to be bringing forward a code of conduct for ministers, lobbyists and MPs' outside interests. But Jeremy Hanley, Fowler's successor as Party chair, was still maintaining that MPs' behaviour was 'ultimately for MPs themselves because they had the experience of the workings of Westminster'. It did not seem to have registered that the government was being tarnished as the first for seventy years to be systematically abusing power and that some MPs feared that the price to be paid would be giving up all outside interests.

When the full Register of Members' Interests was passed to the press by MPs, the issue was raised of who scrutinises the leading scrutineers – Sir Geoffrey Johnson-Smith, Tory chair of the Committee on Members' Interests, held four non-executive directorships and three consultancies, while others had shareholdings and had received gifts of overseas visits. It was also 'puzzling' why fifty MPs of different parties needed to make 'fact-finding' trips to Cyprus during the warmest months.

The Nolan inquiry

The Committee for Standards in Public Life was announced by the Prime Minister on the same day that Neil Hamilton was told to resign. Its remit was large – it covered all public servants, all councils and quangos, lobbyists, but not party funding, though pressure to look at the latter began before the inquiry and its chair, Lord Nolan, seemed willing to investigate this subject. Nolan also expressed a preference for open hearings. Yet John Major was indignant that many opposition MPs were not satisfied and sought to become 'witchfinders-general'. Rather, they saw an all-party solution being applied to a one-party issue – that 'such pollution is the result of one government being in power too long. Hubris and opportunism combine to degrade old standards' (Hugo Young in *The Guardian*, 27 October 1994).

The Nolan report, 12 May 1995

The Nolan committee laid down seven 'principles of public life' to guard against 'the slackness in the observation and enforcement of high standards':

1 *Selflessness* Holders of public office should take decisions solely in terms of the public interest. They should not do so in order to gain financial or other material benefits for themselves, their family or their friends.
2 *Integrity* Holders of public office should not place themselves under any financial or other obligation to outside individuals or organisations that might influence them in the performance of their official duties.
3 *Objectivity* In carrying out public business, including making public appointments, awarding contracts, or recommending individuals for rewards and benefits, holders of public office should make choices on merit.
4 *Accountability* Holders of public office are accountable for their decisions and actions to the public and must submit themselves to whatever scrutiny is appropriate to their office.
5 *Openness* Holders of public office should be as open as possible about all the decisions and actions that they take. They should give reasons for their decisions and restrict information only when the wider public interest clearly demands.
6 *Honesty* Holders of public office have a duty to declare any private interests relating to their public duties and to take steps to resolve any conflicts arising in a way that protects the public interest.
7 *Leadership* Holders of public office should promote and support these principles by leadership and example.

The report also suggested the following:

- There should be a ban on paid work for lobbyists.
- A ban on consultancies would receive widespread support, including from many MPs. It recognised that this could not be achieved quickly, as 30 per cent of MPs had entered into legal arrangements to undertake consultancy work. But it should be addressed urgently.
- The Register's rules on declaring interests should be set out in more detail and a code of conduct for MPs drawn up. It should be open to scrutiny and the financial value of the Members' interests should now be declared.
- The report contained unanimous support for an independent Parliamentary Commissioner for Standards, who would maintain the Register of Members' Interests and give advice. Disciplining MPs would still be the responsibility of the Privileges Committee.
- Former cabinet members would be subject to the same rules as top civil servants – forced to wait for three months before taking a job and vetted for two years.
- When appointing to quangos or NHS trusts there should be an independent element. The existing Public Appointments Unit should be taken out of the Cabinet Office and put under a newly created Public Appointments Commissioner.

Each took what they wanted from the report: government supporters that it was stated that the situation was not as bad as portrayed; MPs that they could continue with their consultancies (left a grey area), though 69 per cent resisted any independent involvement in complaints against them; the opposition regarded it as a condemnation of falling standards and wanted to press on to look at the House of Lords, where there was no register and where lobbyists were taking advantage of looser conventions, and into political funding.

Opposition to the report

Sir Geoffrey Johnson-Smith, chair of the Commons Select Committee on Interests for fifteen years, spoke for many backbenchers in resisting disclosure of income, and was supported by Sir Edward Heath and Theresa Gorman. Perhaps that is not surprising – *The Observer* had reported after three months' research that:

> having fees paid to a company that provides the MP's services – instead of the money being received directly as income – enables the MPs to considerably reduce their tax bill. Small companies, which most 'service' companies are, only pay tax at 25 per cent whereas the same income if paid to the MP directly would probably face tax at 40 per cent. MPs who use such companies include Sir Edward Heath ... Theresa Gorman ... Charles Goodson-Wickes. (15 October 1995)

When asked by Tony Blair whether he accepted disclosure, John Major had to dodge the question, given the hostility towards Nolan and his own handling of the situation. Major insisted that a select committee was needed to study and implement Nolan, and accused Labour of treating it as a political football. If Labour boycotted the select committee, the Tories would act alone. This all slowed the original plan, and the omens did not look good – MPs had had a chance to deal with this matter in 1969 under the Strauss inquiry and the Register was accepted fully only after twenty years. Tory backbencher Alan Duncan harangued Nolan in the street: 'You are about to obliterate the professional classes' representation in the House of Commons. It is a very dangerous game.'

Richard Needham, former trade minister, undermined the case of self-regulation when he admitted joining GEC three months after leaving office, partly to beat Nolan's stricter rules.

John Redwood, having resigned from the government in July 1995, to oppose John Major, attacked Nolan's interference in parliamentary self-regulation.

Implementation

The government accepted almost all forty-five of Nolan's recommendations. On 7 July 1995 the Commons voted for the following:

- to disclose MPs' earnings from consultancies (in bands);
- to ban paid advocacy, including questions and amendments;
- to restrict them speaking in debates in favour of paid interests;
- to appoint a new Commissioner for Standards;
- to register all contracts with the new Commissioner;
- to approve in principle a code of conduct.

The government's attempt to avoid full disclosure of earnings was defeated. Those voting for secrecy held twice as many consultancies, and eleven of the twenty-three Tories who voted for disclosure were in marginal seats.

It did not take long for the new Parliamentary Commissioner for Standards, Sir Gordon Downey, to obtain his first case – in November 1995 former minister Patrick Nicholls was accused of offering his services for water company shares.

In March 1996 Tory MPs were threatening to wreck the new code by splitting their contracts, arguing that much of their outside work did not depend on their role as an MP. Downey warned that mass evasion would bring the House into disrepute.

Sexual misdeeds

This aspect of our politics is put into sharp context by happened to US President Clinton in the autumn of 1998, following the publication of the

Starr investigations. But at the time domestic sexual misdeeds on the part of politicians fed the tabloids and the mood of disillusionment with politicians.

The Conservatives have been more tolerant of these indiscretions. David Mellor looked certain to survive as a minister despite the revelation of an extramarital affair, until a paid holiday came to light. But by adopting a platform of 'Back to Basics' and 'Family Values' they raised the stakes. Tim Yeo's love child cost him his job when his local party refused to support him.

In March 1992 Alan Amos resigned after allegations of indecent activity with another man on Hampstead Heath. In January 1994 David Ashby admitted sharing a bed with another man while on holiday in France. Lord Caithness resigned as Transport Minister after his wife committed suicide, her parents blaming his friendship with another woman. Gary Waller MP admitted fathering an illegitimate child whose mother was then secretary to the chair of the 1922 Committee. In February 1994 Stephen Milligan MP was found dead, dressed in women's clothing, having asphyxiated himself during auto-erotic sex. Hartley Booth admitted a relationship with his former research assistant and resigned as a Foreign Office parliamentary private secretary. In May 1994 Michael Brown resigned as a government whip following newspaper stories of a friendship with a civil servant in the Ministry of Defence who was involved in gay sex.

In April 1995 Richard Spring, an aide in the Northern Ireland Office, resigned after the News of the World reported a *ménage à trois*, and Rod Richards, junior Welsh Office minister, became the tenth minister to resign over an affair in June 1996. By this time there had been seventeen resignations from John Major's administration connected to sleaze.

While there was less public antagonism towards sexual revelations, they could still harm the Tory Party. Their position in Scotland was weak enough without losing Sir Michael Hirst, chair of the Scots Tories, during the 1997 election campaign – resigning over allegations of a homosexual affair.

Weak and corrupt government

John Major had set up the Scott inquiry in the wake of the collapse of the Matrix-Churchill trial, thus buying time. But the latitude given to Scott and the departures from legal procedure dragged the proceedings on for three years amid leaks.

Having dithered over dismissing ministers found guilty of sexual aberrations, in the era of 'Family Values', MPs could not understand why Major stood by Hamilton for so long. Neil Hamilton has always claimed his innocence and he refused to resign in 1984, with the agreement of the Prime Minister, who had perhaps seen too many ministers go already. But with columnists in ten newspapers backing The Guardian in demanding that

Hamilton make his case from the back benches, many thought the judgement of the Prime Minister and the political nouse of Cabinet Secretary, Sir Robin Butler, were in doubt. Further evidence forced Major to demand his resignation and set up the Nolan inquiry.

Sir Robin Butler presented a six-page report to the Prime Minister in October 1994 which said 'there were other allegations passed on to you or by your informant. I have looked into all these, so far as I am able, and the Chief Whip and I have put the allegations in detail to the ministers concerned'. They accepted their denials of some of these 'odd' allegations. The use of an 'informant' had meant that the Cabinet Secretary had not been able to approach Mohamed Al-Fayed, and this left questions over this 'intermediary'. Did this one-off (Nolan) inquiry not subvert the five-year investigation into House of Fraser by the DTI? Why was the investigation moving so slowly? Was Tim Smith in office after confessing?

A MORI poll in May 1995 showed that 78 per cent of people believed alleged misconduct against ministers should be handled by an independent commission or the police (11 per cent were willing to leave it to the Prime Minister, and 12 per cent to Parliament). By the summer of 1995 Tory backbenchers were blaming Major for setting up the Scott and Nolan inquiries, leading them into a trap, and there was press speculation about the merits of replacing him with Heseltine rather than have a damaging election challenge.

Dirty tricks information

Using the 1984 Data Protection Act declarations, *The Observer* found that Conservative Central Office was ready to gather and pass on personal defamatory information about political opponents, including lifestyles, sex lives, habits and credit-worthiness. It also stated that the Cabinet Office had used private detectives to gather information on members of cabinet committees.

Martin Bell was to be surprised by the tactics used against him by a desperate Tory Party in Tatton in the 1997 general election.

Labour's problems

The Conservatives did their best to accuse Labour leaders of not declaring trips or hotel stays – for example John Prescott at Gleneagles in May 1994, but this did little to stop the sleaze finger being pointed at them. Nonetheless, Labour was not without problems of its own.

In 1995 it became known that criminal elements had infiltrated Labour councils in Liverpool, Greater Manchester, and North Shields. Labour politicians in Birmingham were accused of trying to 'buy' safe House of Commons seats. The Party in Scotland began its own inquiry into Paisley South, Paisley North, Renfrew and Inverclyde in April 1995. But the Labour Party moved quickly when evidence of wrongdoing was found in councils and the Tory condemnations never seemed to work long enough. When Monklands Council in Edinburgh was found to have ruled through nepotism and Catholic sectarianism in June 1995, all seventy councillors were immediately suspended.

Local councillors had been given the freedom to decide what to pay themselves. Some councils, such as Birmingham, Newcastle, the London boroughs and Sheffield, realised they had been offered 'a poisoned chalice' and did not act. Some did and this was seized on by ministers – Michael Heseltine saying Nottinghamshire councillors were putting their 'snouts in the trough'.

When Jeremy Hanley tried to exploit the situation in the local elections of May 1995 by dubbing Labour councils as 'corrupt', it backfired on him and led to speculation on his suitability for the job of Party chair. Not all council scandals were Labour's problems – in addition to the surcharges at Westminster, Surrey County Council and the borough of Brent were accused of fraud and sleaze respectively.

Political funding

Contributions to the Tories from big business fell from 54 per cent in 1990 to 27 per cent in 1994, leaving it with a £15 million overdraft and more dependent on rich anonymous individuals. A dissident Charter group inside the Party was demanding reform.

In 1992 it was revealed that the Conservatives had received £440,000 from Asil Nadir, £1 million from Octav Botnar, the former boss of Nissan UK who was wanted by the Inland Revenue, and £500,000 from Tony Budge, the brother of privatised coalmine-owner Richard Budge, who was facing trial for the disappearance of millions of pounds. In 1994 Nazmu Virani, who was gaoled for fraud over the collapse of BCCI, said he gave thousands of pounds over many years.

In 1996 the Prime Minister was said to be 'hired out' at the Premier Club (of which he was patron), where a donation of £500,000 to the Conservative Party would bring business people to the dinner table of the most powerful politicians. In the latter half of 1996 it was claimed and detailed that Tory Party donors were lining up for bargains in last-ditch privatisations, such as Her Majesty's Stationery Office.

The Al-Fayed affair led to the revelation that he had made a political donation of £250,000 plus gifts, hotel rooms, hospitality and offered help with Arab states. In return he clearly expected no investigation into the

House of Fraser/Harrods takeover in 1985, and after a 1987 report commented unfavourably upon his conduct, he expected that to be repudiated. After the collapse of the Hamilton libel case it was shown that lobbyist Ian Greer channelled money (between £500 and £5,000) into the 1987 election campaigns of twenty-one MPs, including Norman Tebbit and Michael Portillo. Greer was forced to resign from his company in October 1996 – he stated that he had raised over £750,000 for the Tories over ten years.

A group of Muslim mosques were said to have transferred as much as £5 million to Tory Central Office (*Sunday Times*, 27 April 1997). It was claimed that a businessman who helped the Serbian Tigers – ruthless paramilitaries in Bosnia – had given the Tories thousands of pounds.

Tony Blair announced on taking office in 1997 that Lord Nolan would investigate party funding – resisted by Major for two years. Nolan, however, declined because he wanted to review his reforms so far and check if his recommendations on quangos, trusts, housing associations and grant-maintained schools had been implemented. It was to fall to his successor, Sir Patrick Neill, to undertake this work, but only after he had been accused of being duped into letting Labour off the hook by advising them to return Bernie Ecclestone's £1 million donation (during the Formula One cigarette advertising row in November 1997 – see below and see also Chapters 1 and 16). They tried to make a similar sleaze connection between the funding of Lord Sainsbury and policy on big business. The Tories could still be counterattacked at this point as they were unwilling to disclose individuals' private donations.

A compromise was reached in December 1997, when William Hague agreed with the Committee on Standards in Public Life to disclose the amounts received over the last five years but the anonymity of donors would be preserved. The names of donors of over £5,000 would be given only from July 1997. Labour still claimed that their declared £28 million spent on the 1997 campaign did not include written-off debt – the 'real' £47 million included foreign donors and 'black holes'.

The 1997 general election

The manifestos

The Scottish National Party, Plaid Cymru and the Green Party stuck to their traditional issues and priorities – only Plaid Cymru noted that 'Sleaze and corruption thrive in an atmosphere of political patronage'.

'Reforming politics' was the sixth of eight sections in the Liberal Democrat manifesto; condemning quangos, secrecy and party funding (as usual), they singled out the need for 'tougher rules' in the Commons 'for their conduct, behaviour and outside sources of income'.

'The constitution' was the last section of the Conservative manifesto; they took credit for a new civil service code and for setting up and implementing the Nolan committee and its recommendations, and claimed they had made government more accessible. Most of this section concerned the Union and Northern Ireland.

The Labour document was more specific in its penultimate section 'Clean up politics' – this referred to Tories 'afflicted by sleaze and profit from foreign donations from secret supporters'. They promised to implement Nolan's recommendations fully, while the committee would investigate how party funding could be reformed – until then the sources of all donations would be declared over a certain sum.

As usual, the two main parties led with their prime areas – the economy, education, jobs and the NHS.

The campaign

John Major tried hard to draw a line under the sleaze allegations to prove that the issue had been dealt with, and wanted to move the agenda to his economic 'successes' and a counterattack on Labour's policies. He failed. The sleaze just kept on coming:

- Michael Heseltine and John Major had to counter accusations that they had attempted to undermine the neutrality of the civil service by asking them to do political work (November 1996).
- Jerry Hayes MP was accused of having an affair with a young man, three days after Major had spoken again on family values (January 1997).
- Twenty-three quango officials left with a £1 million payoff (February 1997).
- A claim of hypocrisy was made when it was revealed that £500,000 had been paid in 'golden handshakes' to seventy-one ministers who had resigned from the Major government – including those for sleaze or sexual impropriety.
- The Education Minister Eric Forth was accused of being involved in tobacco lobbying (March 1997).
- Sir Marcus Fox, chair of the 1922 Committee, faced investigation for not registering directorships in three US companies.
- Gordon Downey now had another investigation into Neil Hamilton, following Greer's revelations on gifts and expenses (March 1997). On 21 March 1997 Downey's third report cleared fifteen MPs but left eight without a verdict. Six of this group were contesting the election.
- John Major warned that if any newly elected MP was found guilty, he would favour expulsion. Unfortunately, in March 1997, local constituency associations were free to ignore such 'hints' and Tatton kept

Neil Hamilton and Beckenham voted to keep Piers Merchant (accused of an affair with Ms Cox, a teenage club hostess). Tim Smith resigned and further pressure was put on Merchant as he was secretly photographed with Ms Cox.

- As a result of the Tatton decision, an anti-sleaze candidate, broadcaster Martin Bell, stood against Hamilton, as the other opposition parties withdrew. This drew even more media attention.
- By proroguing Parliament seventeen days earlier than he needed to, Major faced accusations that he was trying to bury Downey's reports.
- Tory Party chair, Brian Mawhinney, was named in a scandal involving a political lobbyist and was said to be soliciting honours for clients who donated to the Conservatives (April 1997).
- A Tory agent had plotted to finance a Green Party candidate to take votes from Labour in a marginal seat.

After two weeks of the election campaign, the Tories had been unable to get sleaze off the agenda and saw their attack on union power peter out. There were calls from Labour, Liberal Democrats and some Tory backbenchers for the recall of Parliament to clear up Downey's findings. The Tories had gone down in the polls to 28 per cent while Labour had gone up from 50 per cent to 55 per cent.

Labour built on the issue by offering more safeguards, making Downey more independent and full time and to give him more staff – this was billed as making him a 'sleaze buster' and 'sleaze hunter', possibly at the head of a new National Audit Office.

In the aftermath of the Tory defeat, the final parts were played out. In October, Hamilton, who had lost his seat to Bell, was condemned by Downey for breaking Commons rules and misleading Michael Heseltine, but Downey was not able to deliver a clear verdict on the charge of taking money directly – leading to calls for strengthening of the process. (Hamilton could have a last hollow laugh in January 1998 when Bell was found to have bungled his election expenses and had to pay back an undeclared legal bill of £9,400.) Al-Fayed was now claiming to have paid another top Tory £30,000. Tim Smith was condemned for taking money. Piers Merchant stood down in October, after winning his seat but admitting to deceit about his affair.

The Labour government

'New Labour' had to contend with the same pressure against sleaze, in the changed climate. Even Lord Steel, former Liberal leader, had to be defended from the charge of profiting from his defence of hunting.

Jack Straw saw MPs being subject to criminal law and if guilty of taking cash for questions they would face seven years in gaol for bribery. Some

Labour ministers were now refusing to see their Tory shadows if they knew they were acting for external interests, even if they were acting within the rules. Tony Blair concurred with Nolan's ideas about a 'misuse of office' criminal offence by any official or elected representative.

The government had problems of its own, however:

- It suspended Mohammed Sarwar, the new MP for Glasgow Govan – accused of bribery. He was charged with electoral fraud and perverting the cause of justice in December.
- It suspended Tommy Graham, accused of smearing MP Gordon McMaster, who committed suicide. He became the first MP to be expelled by the party for eight years in September 1998.
- A Labour MP, Bob Wareing, was suspended for seven days and forced to make a humiliating apology for falsifying a declaration to cover up a private company he set up.
- Lord Simon, who had given up his £750,000 BP salary to join the government, had to sell his £2.25 million in shares and give away profits to charity, amid claims of 'conflict of interest'.
- It still had a local government legacy of sleaze to deal with – in Doncaster, the west of Scotland, Humberside, Nottinghamshire – up to thirty councils – often involving police investigations. Individuals or whole parties were suspended.
- Robin Cook, the Foreign Secretary, announced the end of his marriage and an affair with a researcher, whom he then married.
- Two ministers had to admit to not declaring a free hotel stay in Geneva when in opposition and on what they thought was a United Nations visit.

The Labour leadership could cope with the above, as part of the old system. Tony Blair could point to Labour's readiness to root out wrongdoing and promise reforms, such as the reform of local government with binding codes of conduct (April 1998), an end to one-party town-hall regimes and a standards commission for the new Scottish Parliament. In June 1998 he also attacked MEPs' allowances, which could add £100,000 a year to their salaries.

Labour did though have to contend with issues where their political handling was unsure and mistakes were made.

The Robinson tax row and after

The Observer's 1995 research had covered Geoffrey Robinson's income from his company Transtec: 'He argued that there is too much secrecy about outside earnings. "What we earn while we are MPs should be fully disclosed". Mr Robinson had worked hard for his money. Other MP collectors of non-executive directorships, less so.' In contrast *The Observer*'s leading editorial on 7 December 1997 was 'Robinson shames our democracy'. Robinson was the Postmaster-General and a member of the Treasury team responsible for taxation. At the end of November it was revealed that he was a beneficiary of a £12.5 million offshore trust based in Guernsey. But in his capacity as a Treasury minister he had just set a maximum saving limit of £50,000 on which tax relief would be allowable in the new independent savings accounts. Robinson insisted that he had done nothing illegal and was supported by Blair in the Commons and other ministers – determined not to be 'bounced' by media coverage as John Major had been. But Chancellor Gordon Brown had always attacked such tax-avoidance schemes, Labour had promised a 'crackdown' in its manifesto, and Labour backbenchers, unhappy about benefit cuts, did not like such practices. The affair then took a depressingly familiar route – there were more investigations of the links between Robinson's companies and associates, threats to sue from Robinson, and claims that he had made a £200,000 profit after becoming a minister, and that he was linked to offshore trust in Bermuda. Downey promised to investigate his declaration of interests, and on 21 December 1997 *The Observer* accused him of breaking the law in not revealing all his share dealing. An NOP poll in the *Sunday Times* on that date showed 58 per cent thinking he was wrong and 25 per cent that it was his own affair, and it was claimed to show that people had less faith in the Blair government as a result. The Commons Standards and Privileges Committee found that he should have registered some directorships, in July 1998, but broadly cleared him of serious wrongdoing and he stayed on.

Cash for access – 'cronyism'

Motor racing chief Bernie Ecclestone made a £1 million donation to Labour before the general election and offered a smaller second sum after it. This led to trouble when the government reversed its pledge on banning cigarette advertising from sport, in allowing Formula One racing exemption, because of the impact it could have on British jobs. To counter the accusations of lobbying, Tony Blair had to appear on television and apologise for the handling of the affair and reassure people there was no breach of trust. Sir Patrick Neill had been consulted about the donation and because of the impression of a connection, he advised that it be given back. Labour proposed to give it to a cancer charity to restore some faith, but not easily – the Party had a problem, being £4.5 million in debt.

As a result, Sir Patrick Neill's Committee on Standards in Public Life began to investigate party donations. His recommendations were a surprise to Labour in that they included non-financial sponsorships and donations

in kind – including union premises, equipment and staff. Other recommendations, in October 1998, include the founding of an electoral commission
to monitor donations 'for influence'; powers to investigate and prosecute
party leaders; disclosure of the identity of major funders; making statutory
the voluntary agreement to disclose donors of over £5,000; the banning
of foreign donations.

Alistair Campbell, Tony Blair's press secretary, came under attack over
Rupert Murdoch's reported use of the Labour leader to sound out the Italian
Prime Minister about BSkyB expansion there. It was alleged that business
people had been encouraged to contribute advice and £11 million before
the election.

The government has had to worry about other donors, some of whom
have taken unpaid jobs on quangos, and many of their City backers did
them no favours by taking large wage rises while the Chancellor called for
wage restraint. By now the Tories could criticise from the moral high
ground, denouncing ministers who cut their tax bills by arranging business
taxes with their local authorities, and Frank Dobson, Health Secretary,
found himself under fire for bias in placing Labour councillors and supporters
on the boards of the NHS trusts (he denied replacing 'Tory deadheads with
Labour deadheads'). Deputy Prime Minister John Prescott was cleared by
Downey of breaking parliamentary rules on declaring a donation but he
said the matter should be referred to Lord Neill's committee. The new
Labour MP for Newark, Fiona Jones, was prosecuted over making a false
declaration of election expenses.

In fact the top 350 companies have cut by half the amount they have
given political parties over the last six years; the Tories are the main beneficiaries
with £1.3 million in 1997, while Labour quadrupled the amount they
received in 1994, but still had only £116,000 (Pirc Research, *The Observer*,
1 February 1998). Now Labour seemed to be favouring their financial backers
on task forces and in policy areas – Tesco, Caparo and Northern Foods.

Nevertheless, the ethical credentials of some sponsors of their conference
in September 1998 drew criticism from Amnesty and Friends of the Earth,
while Sainsbury's withdrew their support. Labour raised more than £1
million in sponsorship and offering £200 per head to shake Tony Blair's
hand at the gala dinner – a double standard of their headquarters drumming
up support, while ministers were being told to keep a distance. An *Observer/
ICM* poll at the time (27 September 1998) showed voters dissatisfied that
Labour listened too much to 'bosses' and not to 'working people'.

Lobbying – secrets for cash

In May 1998 *The Observer* reported that Number 10 policy adviser Roger
Liddle and lobbyist Derek Draper bragged that they could gain access to

anyone in power. The newspaper claimed it had affidavits and refused to be put off by government 'spin'. It was said that Draper received faxes almost every day from Peter Mandleson's office. Its editorial of 5 July 1998, entitled 'Disfiguring our democracy', castigated Labour lobbyists and demanded a Freedom of Information Act. There were alleged leaks of budget secrets by Gordon Brown's adviser, Ed Balls. While there was no suggestion that Labour politicians were profiting, as under the Tories, they were urged to rid themselves of hangers-on – a theme adopted by Tony Blair, who threatened ministers and civil servants with the sack if they leaked information (July 1998). Liddle continued to deny offering to help an American energy firm and remained but Draper was suspended by his firm, as William Hague accused Blair of 'protecting ... money-grubbing cronies'.

Sierra Leone

With echoes of the arms-for-Iraq affair came 'arms for a coup' – provided by Sandline, a military consultancy. The issue in May 1998 was whether the Foreign Secretary, Robin Cook, any of his ministers or Foreign Office officials had known and approved of the toppling of the unpopular regime. Amid confusion and retractions about whom had been told what, Cook managed to fend off the Tory assault on him.

The spoils of victory

- Ministers were criticised for taking partners on foreign trips – John Major even stepped in to say he had never allowed that.
- Labour spent £7.4 million on hospitality, with many celebrities in five months – £2 million more than was saved by the cut in single-parent benefit. The publication of lists of pop stars, actors and business donors, whose actual contributions were not disclosed, did not quell the unease. Some of the latter had become peers or acquired govern-ment jobs.
- Lord Irvine, the Lord Chancellor, spent £650,000 refurbishing his residence, with £59,000 spent on wallpaper.
- The *Sunday Times* reported that Margaret Beckett's official flat had cost £65,000 to refit and should have been included with the rest of her income.
- Cabinet 'enforcer' Jack Cunningham spent £15,000 on chairs and a table made of rare mahogany in August 1998.
- Their political advisers – 'spin doctors' – cost £2.6 million a year.
- The Tories could now play the comparisons game – that Labour's £11 million spending spree could have paid for 573 teachers, 819 nurses

or 2,700 hip replacements. They also wanted to know the cost of Cherie Blair's new kitchen!

- In September 1998 Chris Mullin was warning that the distaste for sleaze that had brought Labour to power could turn against them and turn them out.

It has become clear that the system has changed – Downney investigated the cases of thirty-five MPs and Nolan's work is deemed a success. It is likely that the next stage of scrutiny of interests by MPs needs to be changed, given that MPs cannot cope with the quasi-judicial workload and are prone to political positions or pressure. But the climate has also changed – some of the secrecy has been pushed aside and there is less public tolerance of 'sleaze'. Even Martin Bell, the 'clean' citizens' MP, had to start into the detail of why legal fees were not in his election expenses.

Reading

Leigh, D. and Vulliamy, E. (1997) *Sleaze – the Corruption of Parliament*, Fourth Estate.

16

Party finance

Graham P. Thomas

The issue of party finance has become one of the most acute controversies in British politics. The secretiveness which surrounds the sources of finance of the major political parties has been adversely commented on by a variety of critics, while accusations of sleaze and corruption have been made about the financial affairs of both major parties (see Chapter 15). Even the Liberal Democrats, who derive little benefit from institutional sources of finance, have been accused of undue secrecy.

Since 1945 the pattern of party fund-raising has remained largely unchanged, although there have been developments in the methods used. Both main parties now use computerised, direct-mail appeals to members and supporters, although a comparatively small proportion of finance is thus raised. Neither Labour nor the Conservative Party has a sufficiently large membership to be self-financing. The Liberal Democrats do largely finance themselves, but have to exercise great self-restraint in controlling spending.

The Labour Party's sources of finance

Labour in the past depended heavily on the affiliated trade unions, which provided some 80–90 per cent of the income of Head Office and over half of the total national income of the Party, which included constituency and regional fund-raising activities. At the national level, affiliation fees and donations (especially at general elections) were vital to the Party's viability, while the sponsoring of candidates provided vital finance to a considerable number of constituency Labour parties (CLPs). Links between the sponsoring union and its MPs varied, but in general unions did not place direct pressure on them to follow the union as opposed to the Party line. On those occasions when there was a clash between the attitude of the sponsoring union and the parliamentary party, most MPs supported the Party rather than the union. Whether a Labour MP rebelled against the parliamentary leadership was related much more to membership of bodies such as the Tribune Group than to whether or not the Member was sponsored.

Although the power of the trade union block vote at conference has been a significant factor in Labour Party history, it has traditionally been used in support of the parliamentary leadership, except on issues such as the imposition of a prices and incomes policy or attempts by Labour governments to restrict union autonomy. Labour governments tended to ignore conference decisions they found unacceptable. Although in the period 1980–3 the annual conference took several decisions which were opposed by the leadership (or at least reluctantly accepted) the union vote has traditionally been divided between the left and the right. Thus criticism that the unions dominate the Labour Party is misleading, as unions rarely act in unison. Since 1983 the bulk of the union vote has been behind the leadership in seeking to modernise the Party and to rid it of far-left elements.

In recent years the Labour Party has introduced further organisational changes aimed at reducing the significance of the union block vote in the Party's affairs. There are several reasons for this move. One is to limit the political damage done to the Party by Conservative attacks on the influence wielded by what are referred to as the Party's union 'paymasters'. Another factor is the hope that trade union affiliated members will join as individuals, thus boosting the Party's finances.

Although a few unions maintain a direct link with their sponsored MPs, union sponsorship of Labour MPs was virtually ended in 1995, to be replaced by 'constituency plan agreements' between unions and selected CLPs. This involved some union money going to support constituency activities in return for union representation on the CLP's general management committee. The change was stimulated by the desire to separate individual Labour MPs from directly received union funds and thus to reduce the ability of the Conservatives to accuse Labour of being under the thumb of the unions. It was also a factor of the need, in the wake of the appointment of the Nolan committee, to reduce the chance of the Party and individual MPs being accused of sleaze. By the early months of the 1997 Parliament, around 100 constituency plan agreements were in place, concentrated in marginal rather than safe seats with the intention of building up Labour strength in these crucial constituencies.

Over the twenty-five years before sponsorship was ended, the relationship had in any case ceased to be one between the union and an individual and had become one between the union and the CLP. This meant that the payment was to the *party* rather than to an *individual*, unlike when MPs act as consultants. Relationships between unions and their sponsored MPs were not close, partly because of the need to avoid giving political opponents ammunition and partly because of House of Commons rules forbidding outside bodies giving instructions to Members. Sponsorship by the Co-operative

Party also came to an end. Twenty-six Labour candidates, all of whom were elected, ran under the Labour and Co-operative banner in the 1997 election, but with the Co-operative Party as a sister party rather than a sponsoring organisation.

The reliance of Labour on trade union donations is still marked and there remains some uncertainty about the role of unions in funding the Party. In 1994 just over half of its income came from unions, a gradually declining proportion, and polls of Labour supporters displayed unease about the importance of the unions in funding. However, Labour could not afford to lose this steady support, despite its success in diversifying its fund-raising efforts.

The Party has also sought to increase its contributions from individuals. In recent years, a national membership scheme has been introduced, enabling the Party to make direct-mail appeals to members, who are increasingly middle class and comparatively affluent. This method was pioneered by the Social Democratic Party (SDP), which modelled itself on US political parties. Labour's electoral recovery after 1992 was accompanied by a much stronger financial position than it had enjoyed in the past. This means that while the unions continue to play an important role, Labour has diversified its sources of funds and managed in most years to generate a surplus. In turn, Labour was able to fight the 1997 election from a much more secure financial base than in past contests.

A major new development has been the willingness of individuals and businesses to support Labour. In the past, corporate donations were few in number and small in amount, while individual donations were dwarfed by those received by the Conservatives. More recently both trends have changed. The Animal Political Lobby gave the Party £1 million, continuing a long history of Labour links with animal welfare organisations. The late Matthew Harding, vice-chair of Chelsea Football Club, gave the Party £1 million. Other people from the business community made large donations, some arguing that the Tories were no longer the party of business. Figures from the media such as Melvyn Bragg and Greg Dyke also contributed. Particularly significant was the name of David Sainsbury, who had previously been a major giver to the SDP. Some corporations also made large donations; some of them had previously supported the Conservatives. A few companies switched directly to Labour, while others kept a foot in both camps by giving to both parties. Tate and Lyle, a long-time donor to the Tories, reduced its contribution to that party and gave to Labour for the first time. The Labour Party Business Plan was largely financed by individual donations from members or supporters or by dinners to attract money from individuals rather than from institutions. Money also came to Labour via the Industrial Research Trust, which it claimed funded research projects by the leadership. The Trust is reported to have received several large donations from companies and individuals, raising ethical issues similar to those which so adversely affected the Tory Party. In the run-up to the 1997 general election, the Conservatives attacked Labour over the manner in which the Party was financed by the unions and by union donations to help fund the leader's and deputy leader's offices. 'Blind trusts' were set up, which meant that the leader and deputy leader did not know the sources of the funds and so, it was claimed, could not be influenced by the donors. Attempts by several Tory MPs to persuade the Speaker to intervene failed. The Parliamentary Commissioner for Standards also cleared Labour of any impropriety, having approved the arrangement before it began.

Labour and the Ecclestone affair

Labour has traditionally argued that large corporate donations pose a threat to democracy, which increased the Party's embarrassment when the donation from Bernie Ecclestone was made public.

In the manifesto for the 1997 general election, the Labour Party stated that smoking is the greatest single cause of preventable illness and premature death in Britain and promised to ban tobacco advertising. In June 1997 the Health Secretary Frank Dobson repeated the promise but added that there was no intention to hurt sport, which would need help to find other sponsors. However, in early November the government announced that it proposed to exempt Formula One motor racing from the expected European-wide ban which was expected in December. The decision soon escalated into a major political row in which the Labour Party and the government were accused of sleaze and Tony Blair's probity itself was called into question.

It soon became apparent that after the election Tony Blair had met Bernie Ecclestone, the boss of Formula One, and Max Mosley, another major figure from the world of motor sport, known to be a long-time supporter of Labour. They had warned that the ban would lead to the loss of 50,000 full-time and 150,000 part-time jobs and the loss of export earnings, figures widely thought to be an exaggeration.

Initially the political storm centred on Tessa Jowell, the Minister for Public Health, who made the announcement. She was forced to deny a conflict of interests after it became apparent that her husband had been a non-executive director with a Formula One company, an issue the opposition took up with vigour, pleased with the opportunity to accuse Labour of a mixture of hypocrisy and incompetence. Downing Street denied that there had been any impropriety, saying that all the rules had been followed and that the Cabinet Secretary and Lord Nolan, chair of the Committee on Standards in Public Life, had been informed of the position and had raised no objection.

The government's embarrassment grew as the press reported that Ecclestone, previously a generous contributor to the Conservatives, had made a donation to the Labour Party before the general election. Although the Party vigorously denied any link between Ecclestone's donation and the decision to exempt Formula One, the row continued, dragging Tony Blair into the firing line. The advice was sought of Sir Patrick Neill, who had replaced Lord Nolan; he said that the donation should be returned on the grounds that those in public life should be judged not just by the reality but by the appearance. Labour then promised to repay the loan, adding that it would be difficult to raise the money at short notice.

For some days the Labour Party refused to divulge the amount of the donation but eventually had to agree that it amounted to £1 million, a sum far higher than had previously been thought. The manner in which this information had to be dragged out of a reluctant Prime Minister was reminiscent of similar episodes under the Conservatives and did much to damage the reputation of Blair and of the Party he leads.

The government then announced that it would legislate to make compulsory the disclosure of donors who gave in excess of £5,000 and to ban foreign donations. It was also decided to refer the matter of party funding to the Neill committee, which would be asked to consider the option of state funding of political parties. Blair repeatedly said that he wanted to create a 'level playing field' and to avoid the troubles which clouded President Clinton's second term, during which he was repeatedly accused of improprieties in raising campaign funds.

The row might have seemed a gift to the Conservatives. However, in the Commons their reaction was somewhat muted. Although some Conservative MPs accused the government of giving in to the Formula One lobby because of Ecclestone's donation, William Hague, aware of his Party's vulnerability on this issue, concentrated on the issue of incompetence and the breaking of manifesto commitments. Blair replied by attacking the Conservatives for never returning a donation, however tainted its origin, a reference to the Asil Nadir episode (see below). The most wounding interjection came from Martin Bell, the independent MP who had unseated Neil Hamilton on an anti-sleaze platform, who asked the Prime Minister, 'Have we slain one dragon only to have another take its place with a red rose in its mouth?'

Interviewed on BBC1's *On the Record* (16 November 1997), Tony Blair took the unprecedented step of publicly apologising for the handling of the Ecclestone affair but defending the policy decision to exempt Formula One racing. In a highly personal defence of his action, in which he claimed to be 'a pretty straight sort of a guy', he accepted that there had been the appearance of a conflict of interests and agreed to publish the note which had been taken by his civil servants at the meeting. He also challenged the other parties to reveal details of donations and repeated his intention not to put Labour at a disadvantage compared with the Tories, as had been the case up to that point.

The affair rumbled on for some time and then faded from the headlines. The consensus among both politicians and commentators seemed to be that

although nothing corrupt had taken place the affair was mishandled by
the Party and government, something all the more surprising for a party
which prided itself on its news management as well as on its superior moral
probity. Blair's reputation suffered a blow, although how damaging politically
this was is difficult to say.

The Conservative Party's sources of finance

The three main sources of Conservative Party funds are constituency
associations, corporate donations and individual donations. As published
accounts do not give much detail and do not distinguish between corporate
and individual donations, information is hard to find. Company donations
have usually provided around 60 per cent of the Party's central income
and approximately 30 per cent overall. Conservative constituency associations
raise significant sums through social events, local appeals and so on. In
addition, the Conservative Party benefits from individual donations, some
large, both to the Party centrally and to local associations; around one-
fifth of the income of Conservative Central Office is thus provided. In recent
years the source of these donations, details of which are a carefully guarded
secret, has caused considerable unease both to outside observers but also
within the Party. The Charter Movement, a group within the Party calling
for greater democracy and openness in its affairs, has voiced criticisms of
this secrecy. One of the most vociferous critics has been Eric Chalker.

The role of corporate finance and the secrecy surrounding Conservative
Party finances cause much concern. Although the 1967 Companies Act
(subsequently amended) requires that firms publish details of donations of
more than £200 for a political purpose, the definition of a 'political
purpose' is not comprehensive enough to prevent 'conduit' organisations
such as the now-disbanded British United Industrialists collecting money
for transmission to the Conservative Party, which allows the Party to claim
that it receives only part of its income from corporate donors, and allows
companies to avoid the embarrassment of showing political donations in
their accounts.

There were other suggestions that the Party receives money in ways
designed to avoid public scrutiny, possibly in contravention of the law. In
1989 there were allegations in the press about so-called 'river' companies
(named after British rivers) formed specifically to channel money to the
Conservative Party. The arrangement allowed it to receive company donations
without having to pay tax on certain kinds of donations. The secrecy of
Tory fund-raising has led to accusations of covert understandings between
the Party and business, to the detriment of the public interest. Attempts
to change the law to allow shareholders to block political donations from
their companies were resisted by the Conservative government, which

overturned a Lords' amendment to the 1989 Companies Bill. Foreign companies are not bound by the Companies Act and do not need to declare political donations.

The proportion of companies donating to the Conservative Party is quite small, although some are clearly large givers. Finance and property companies, food, drink and tobacco firms and construction companies are especially prominent. In recent years the Party has become reliant on fewer companies, which therefore pay an increasing share of the sums donated. Information derived from company accounts shows that of the top 4,000 companies in terms of turnover, 242 (6 per cent) made political donations between May 1991 and May 1992; around 95 per cent were to the Conservative Party. In that year the largest donation was £167,000. The average amount was around £5,000. Individual donations do not need to be declared by the giver and there is no legal obligation on a party to declare either corporate or individual donations.

Over the years, there have been many accusations about the purchase of both political influence and abuses of the honours system. All governments have to some extent been attacked for misuse of the system; accusations that honours were given for services to the governing party have been commonplace. However, there were especially fierce criticisms of the connections between the Tory Party and business between 1979 and 1997; the link between honours and company donations has often been pointed out. Margaret Thatcher was accused of having given peerages and knight-hoods in return for substantial donations. It was suggested that industrialists were ten times more likely to be awarded peerages or knighthoods if their firm gave money to the Conservative Party. However, it is difficult to establish a causal link and defenders of the system point out that these were successful people who had been given an honour in recognition for their work for the British economy. Conservatives counterattacked by pointing out that left-wing critics forget the honours given in the past to trade union leaders whose unions had made very significant contributions to the Labour Party.

During John Major's time as Prime Minister there were accusations that the Conservative Party was receiving money from foreign business people, including the Greek shipowner John Latsis, who donated at least £2 million, and various Hong Kong figures. John Major hosted a party for Asian business people in Number 10 Downing Street and was reputed to have assured them that no changes would be made to British tax laws for people who operated businesses in Britain but were technically resident abroad. The allegations were that the Conservatives were maintaining these tax rules in order to ensure donations from wealthy individuals.

Then came the Asil Nadir case. Nadir was making donations to the Party, allegedly in the hope of a knighthood, while facing charges of theft and false accounting; these gifts were not revealed in company accounts. Some

£440,000 was received by the Party, which denied that it had any responsibility to ensure that the Companies Act was being observed. It was later revealed that he had attempted to persuade the then Treasurer of the Party to try to get the charges dropped. The Conservative Party accepted that the money would be returned should it be found to have been stolen from shareholders (at the time of writing this had not been done).

Several conclusions can be drawn. Conservative politicians, while denying that the Party accepted money from foreign governments, stressed that foreign citizens have every right to make donations if they have a commercial interest in Britain.

> This is a contentious position. Many of those who make donations from abroad do not possess the vote in this country, yet they are permitted to make donations which indirectly may affect the outcome of elections here. By suggesting that such donations are legitimate on the grounds of financial interests, the implication is that economic interests bestow similar rights to those of citizenship. (Fisher, 1994, p. 68)

The practice of receiving foreign donations is forbidden in Canada and pressure has grown for a similar ban in Britain.

Another point concerns the number of claims about dubious practices in the Conservative Party, raising serious issues concerning public confidence in the political process. Secrecy fuels suspicion, of both the donor and the recipient, and leads to the conclusion that there is something to hide, even when this is not the case. This is particularly significant in the case of individual donors, where there is no obligation of openness. Although John Major and other Conservative politicians argued that a donor's privacy should be respected and that disclosure might discourage giving to political parties, pressure has grown for donations over £5,000 to be made public.

In the period following the 1992 election the unpopularity of the Conservative Party was reflected in its financial problems. The deficit reached £19.2 million in 1992/3, although it gradually fell during that Parliament. Much of this deficit was due to overspending. The Conservative Party's financial difficulties were increased by the loss of or reduction in the size of corporate donations. Donations have varied according to the electoral cycle, producing problems, as parties need a regular flow of money. To some extent the decision by companies such as British Airways or SmithKline Beecham to end or reduce donations was based on falling profits. It was also due to shareholder unrest, and increasingly companies are consulting their shareholders before making donations, or to the wish of international companies to end donations to one party only. This indicates that such donations are less likely to be resumed in the future. An additional reason was the growing feeling that Labour would form the next government; the desire to be on the winning side (or at least not to alienate the next government) influenced many corporate and individual decisions.

The Tories did have some success in raising new sources of income, although these turned out to be highly controversial. Donations from foreigners continued to pour into the Tory Party. Much money was raised from various Hong Kong residents and some critics said that the motive for the giving was to ensure favourable tax concessions or to guarantee the right of entry into Britain after the hand-over to China. It was also alleged that money had been given by individuals linked to the war in the former Yugoslavia; although this was denied, the Party is reported to have ordered an internal investigation.

Two 'clubs', the Premier and the Millennium, were set up; members received a number of benefits. Membership of the Premier Club involved the opportunity to meet ministers, while a more expensive scheme allowed members to attend dinners with the then Prime Minister. The Millennium Club conferred opportunities to meet and network with senior ministers in a variety of social settings; it was reported that members were advised that payments need not be disclosed as political donations in company accounts but could be classified as 'entertainment'. The targets were individuals and private companies which had done well out of the Conservative government, rather than large corporations.

This raises ethical and political questions about using access to ministers as a way of raising party funds. It also means that access (and presumably influence) is available to some and denied to others, the criterion being the ability to pay, not the justice or the importance of the cause, an issue also raised by the Ecclestone affair.

Constituency associations made interest-free loans, a practice which raises few if any issues of democratic concern. Private sources also made such loans, including one sum of £4 million, which may subsequently have been turned into a gift. This, if correct, would have been the largest single gift ever recorded, dwarfing other donations and even most payments to Labour from the unions. There was constant speculation about the links between donations and honours or membership of quangos. Membership of boards of quangos was often associated with donations to the Party. All these raise concerns about the link between donations and commercial benefits for the donors.

In the run-up to the 1997 general election, there was a marked increase in corporate donations to the Tory Party, more than wiping out the Party's deficit.

The centre parties' sources of finance

Little information is available about Liberal Party funding until the 1970s, when its national income was about one-tenth that of Conservative Central Office, although it was at less of a disadvantage locally. However, lack of money was a major factor in the reduction in the number of Liberal Party candidates in the postwar period, and it was not until the 1970s that the Party managed to contest the bulk of seats. The emergence of the SDP and the formation of the Alliance improved the financial position of the centre parties. Using new forms of fund-raising, in 1981 the combined funds of the two parties reached nearly a quarter of that of the Conservatives and in the 1983 general election it was nearly half that spent by the Tories nationally. However, the reliance of the SDP on a few large contributors, especially the Sainsbury family, meant that when that support was reduced the financial position was uncertain and this was a factor in the collapse of the Party.

In the two years up to and including the 1997 general election, the Liberal Democrats spent £3.3 million, the vast majority of which was raised from Party members. The Party's income is largely raised by Party head-quarters through direct-mail appeals to members and supporters, and donations, mainly from individuals. Corporate donations amount to less that £50,000 a year and a small amount is raised from companies which take stalls at the Liberal Democrats' biannual conferences. In addition, the national party receives a proportion of membership subscriptions. Liberal Democrat members join a 'state' party in England, Wales or Scotland and 40 per cent of the income (some £475,000 per annum) goes to Cowley Street, the Party headquarters; the other 60 per cent goes to local or regional parties.

The 1997 Liberal Democrat manifesto said the Party would clean up politics by reforming the way parties are funded and limiting the amount they can spend on national election campaigns, with no increase in real terms on existing amounts. Each party would have to publish its accounts and list all large donors (individuals, trusts and private companies), although no precise figure was stated. The Liberal Democrats advocate state aid for political parties, related to votes gained at the previous election and the seats to be fought at the next, but only half of the total should be funded by the state. All state funding would be made conditional on parties publishing full accounts, which should specify the source of all large donations. All this would be supervised by an electoral commission. This issue will be considered later.

Party finance – the controversy

The precise significance of the way political parties are funded is hard to assess because of the difficulty in obtaining full and reliable information, about either the extent or the sources of funds. Whether legal regulation of party funding should be introduced has been raised on several occasions. The 1974 Labour government set up a committee under Lord Houghton to consider the question of state aid to political parties. Its report, which advocated subsidies based either on the number of votes a party gained at a general election or on its representation in the Commons, was issued in 1976 but was not acted upon before Labour fell from office. Criticisms from a variety of sources about the role played by business and the unions in the financing of political parties led the Hansard Society for Parliamentary Government to establish a committee of investigation. Its report, *Paying for Politics*, said:

> Many people are concerned that, because of their small membership, the two major parties have become over-reliant upon institutional sources of finance – companies and trade unions. This is seen as an unhealthy development in a democracy where there are a large number of other interests which seek representation. (Hansard Society, 1991, p. 10)

The report recommended state aid for 'duly qualified' political parties on the basis of a matching contribution to that raised by the party itself; for every £2 raised by the party in individual donations, £2 would be given from public funds. There would be a limit to the total sum available and a formula would determine the meaning of 'duly qualified' and how much each party would receive. The committee hoped that the proposals would lead the parties to broaden their appeal, to seek new members and to encourage them to seek a large number of individual donors rather than to rely on a small number of large donations. No action has so far been taken on this report.

The Commons Home Affairs Select Committee examined the question of party funding and its report was released in March 1994. Its terms of reference were:

> [to] examine the case for and against state funding of political parties, excluding their work inside Parliament; the methods by which the parties are at present financed; the adequacy of those funds for the tasks which the parties perform; and the desirability or otherwise of controls over the sources of finance or other statutory requirements being placed upon donors or recipients. (House of Commons Home Affairs Select Committee, 1994, p. v)

The report was signed by the six Conservative members of the Committee; the five Labour members issued a minority version. The majority report largely expressed satisfaction with the current position, whereas the minority report was highly critical and called for a major overhaul of the law on state funding. In their evidence on whether there was a case for state funding the parties were divided: Labour, the Liberal Democrats, the Green Party and the Northern Ireland Social Democratic and Labour Party were in favour, the Conservatives, the Ulster Unionists, the Scottish National Party and Plaid Cymru against. These illustrate one of the central problems surrounding party funding. It is an intensely party political issue and yet any eventual reform must achieve a cross-party consensus, otherwise when the governing party changes new measures are likely to be brought in to alter the balance of political advantage. Any reform must also satisfy public opinion, which will need reassurance that the changes will be more than a cosy compromise between politicians.

The significance of party funding

The effects of their respective patterns of fund-raising on the parties are hotly contested. The Labour Party regularly attacks the Conservatives for being beholden to big business, while the Conservatives accuse Labour of being in the pockets of union bosses. However, some commentators believe that both accusations are oversimplified: a natural identity of interests and sympathies – not money – is the basis of the link between each of the main parties and its institutional sponsors. According to this view, the close connections between Labour and the unions would remain even if the unions ceased to be the Party's main source of revenue, while the Conservatives would continue to be pro-business even if corporate donations declined.

Party finance is important in several respects:

- Money spent on election campaigns may enable parties to influence voters.
- Contributions may affect policy making in directions favoured by those who provide the money.
- The internal structure of power within the party may be affected.
- The cost of politics and of campaigning may affect the pattern of political recruitment, perhaps by deterring those without adequate means from standing for Parliament.

Although the raising and spending of money by the local party associations remains important, spending centrally is now greater and much more important, given the growing cost of electioneering. The impact of such spending on the outcome of elections is hard to assess. The availability of free party political broadcasts limits the impact of press advertising and gives some advantage to the less well off parties, especially given that the parties cannot advertise or buy time on radio and television. Limited public funding is already available. All parliamentary candidates receive free use of halls for election meetings and free postage for one election address to each voter. In 1987 it was estimated that this subsidy amounted to £13.2 million for the Conservative, Labour and Alliance parties combined. In addition, subsidies are paid to the opposition parties in Parliament for research and secretarial costs, based on the support which the parties gained at the last general election. Called 'Short' money, after Edward Short, the Leader of the House who helped to introduce it, in 1996/7 it provided £1.53 million to the Labour Party, £316,000 to the Liberal Democrats and smaller sums to the other opposition parties. 'Short' money is to be spent only on the parties' parliamentary work, which is rather illogical as it merely releases party money to be spent outside. The leaders of the main parties, especially the Prime Minister and cabinet, are given protection by the security forces and the annual conferences of the main parties get police protection. Such sums are small compared with those given in comparable western democracies and are directed mainly at electoral activity rather than the day-to-day running of complex and expensive organisations. Despite this help to the opposition parties, there is a general academic consensus that the greater financial resources of the Conservative Party were a significant factor in its domination of the British political system in the twentieth century.

Both parties in government have changed the law to try to protect their sources of funds and handicap the opposition. In 1946 the Trade Union Act replaced 'contracting in' with 'contracting out'; this increased the number of trade unionists paying the political levy from 2.9 million in 1945 to 5.6 million in 1947. The 1967 Companies Act obliged companies to disclose political contributions exceeding £50, later raised to £200. The Trade Union Act 1984 required unions to ballot their members on the existence of a political fund every ten years; the hope was that this would reduce the flow of union funds to the Labour Party. All those unions which have held ballots have voted to retain the political fund. Unions have been successful in maintaining the flow of funds to the Labour Party, despite the fall in union membership and in the number contributing to the political levy.

The 1997 election campaign was expensive. Both major parties raised and spent very large sums of money, greater than in any postwar election. The effort required put both party organisations under great strain. It is difficult to be precise about the sums involved, partly because of the secrecy which attends such matters and partly because of the subsidies provided by the state in the form of free broadcasts, hire of halls and so on. In the twelve months up to polling day, Labour claimed to have spent over £13 million from central party funds and the Conservatives £20 million, compared with the Liberal Democrats' £700,000. These amounts included the spending on leaders' tours, help to constituencies, advertising, private polling and research and the salaries of staff recruited for the campaign. Labour seem to have outspent the Conservatives on polling, making considerable use of focus groups to test policy suggestions and to try to ascertain how 'New Labour' was going down with the electorate.

As has increasingly been the case in the postwar period, the biggest expenditure was on advertising, for the two big parties largely on posters.

The Conservatives were given help by press advertisements placed by Entrepreneurs for a Booming Britain and by the maverick businessman Paul Sykes, although his Euro-scepticism may have rebounded on the Party. The trade union Unison also spent large sums on press advertising, warning workers of the dangers (as the union saw it) of a fifth Conservative term. The main parties cut back considerably on press advertising and were massively outspent by the Referendum Party, which paid out over £6.7 million to various newspapers. The Liberal Democrats were short of cash and spent little on press advertising.

The reform of party finance

Voluntary donations to political parties grew in the period following the 1883 Corrupt and Illegal Practices Act, when business people saw them as a way of seeking honours. Both the Conservative and Liberal parties used the sale of honours as a way of raising funds. Especially in the case of the Conservative Party, this had an effect on its organisation, in that central Party finances had to be kept secret. No formal Party accounts were kept and contributions were held by the main fund-raisers, with the process involving a very small number of people. Little has changed over the years. Fund-raising is kept strictly confidential and the preserve of a small and select group.

Modern institutional fund-raising began with the advent of the Labour Party, which received support from the unions. This led the Conservatives to seek support from business to supplement that received from wealthy individuals. In the postwar period, institutional corporate funding became the predominant form of fund-raising by the Conservatives. However, in recent years there have been a number of developments. The most important have been the re-emergence and growth of large personal contributions and the use of commercial methods of fund-raising. Both major parties have used dinners and other social events to raise large sums of money and it is clear that donors expect and receive some tangible benefits. Besides enjoying a meal, donors can meet senior party figures and at least get the chance to put across their views and seek to advance their commercial interests. However, such access is not in itself a guarantee of influence or special treatment. The party may not take any notice of the special pleading, faced as it is with a multitude of cross-pressures and with electoral opinion. On the other hand, those who do receive this form of access are likely to have an advantage over those who do not. Although in a perfect world parties should be funded entirely by individual subscriptions or voluntary donations by individual supporters, this does not occur anywhere and in every democracy some form of state aid is required, perhaps supplemented by donations from companies or unions.

Three patterns

As Bogdanor (1997, pp. 149–50) points out, there are broadly three alternative patterns of party financing.

1 *State aid to parties* This is the system in many European countries. In Austria, Denmark, Finland, France, Greece, Norway, Portugal and Sweden parties which gain seats in the assembly get aid in proportion to the number of votes or seats won. There is usually a threshold below which parties do not receive support. An important factor seems to be the degree of consensus in the country concerned, which means that taxpayers do not resent or fear their money going to political parties.

2 *Tax relief for donations* The arrangement in the USA and Canada is that state aid follows from the decisions of individual citizens, whose donations to candidates and parties qualify for tax relief or tax credits. In return, there are legal requirements concerning democratic accountability and openness.

The system in Germany is a mixture of these two. There is state aid for parties and for election expenses and to all parties which win seats in the Bundestag to establish research institutes. Parties cannot get more from the state than they can raise from their own supporters. Individual donations up to a certain sum are tax deductible. Trade unions cannot make political donations, although companies can.

3 *The British system* No cash state aid is provided for parties outside Parliament. The main parties rely to a large extent on institutional donors. This is an unusual pattern; Britain is the only country of the European Union (EU) not to give aid to parties outside the legislature. Union support for the Labour Party has been gradually falling as a percentage of the whole amount as the Party has been increasing its revenue from individual donors and members. The trade unions' position has also been weakened, as Labour has transformed itself from a party based on delegate democracy to one based on direct democracy. The bulk of Conservative funding comes from donations from individuals and companies, the remainder being given by constituencies or raised from the sale of publications. Company contributions have fallen as a percentage of the total, which means that personal donations now make up the great majority of Tory Party funds. Thus in no other country do institutional donors play such a central role.

However, despite the enthusiasm of Bogdanor and others for state funding of political parties, there are drawbacks. *The Economist* (15 November 1997) reported that in 1992 the German constitutional court declared that state funding should be reduced on the grounds that the political parties were becoming over-dependent on the public purse. Nor does the problem of sleaze disappear when parties are funded by the state. There have been scandals in France, Spain, Germany and Japan, and in Italy public funding was ended as it was felt that it actually increased corruption rather than the reverse.

In the USA changes in the methods by which funds are raised have contributed to the weakening of the influence of political parties and the rise of candidate-centred campaigns at all levels of the US political system. One effect of this has been the soaring cost of electioneering. Because of concern at the influence of corporations and unions, laws were passed restricting direct contributions by these bodies. This led to the growth of political action committees, which channel money to candidates. Since the mid-1970s they have channelled over $159 million to candidates as well as spending large sums to defeat other candidates or to advocate or attack particular policies or causes. Because they raise large sums by direct appeals to members or sympathisers, political action committees have contributed to the rise of single-interest politics, helping even more to weaken traditional party structures and contributing to the fragmentation of the US political system.

The case against state funding

Those who oppose state funding do so on several grounds:

- Direct state aid would endanger the principle that parties (and other organisations with political aims) exist in a 'voluntary' capacity. There is a danger that governments would attempt to control the process to their own advantage, leading to constant tinkering with the legal position.
- There is a danger that state funding would end the need for parties to seek members in order to raise funds, thus making them remote from their supporters and further alienating the public from the political process. Fund-raising acts as a cohesive force in party political activity. There is no guarantee that public funding would improve the performance of parties.
- It can be argued that donations by companies and unions are legitimate expressions of political action, so long as the process is fairly regulated by law and is open to public scrutiny. Existing party alignments represent real divisions within society and, rather than distorting the political system, donations by the unions to Labour and business to the Conservatives indicate that legitimate interests are being represented.
- There is great difficulty in deciding who would benefit from state subsidies; issues of who would decide which parties would receive funds, whether independents and 'fringe' candidates would be eligible and whether individual citizens would be forced to contribute to parties not of their choice and to which they may have rooted or even moral

objections need to be addressed. Minor (perhaps 'extreme') parties may be given an artificial stimulus by the injection of state funds.

- Public subsidies could either strengthen central party organisations at the expense of the grass roots, leading to an over-powerful centre, or could have the reverse effect, as in the USA, making the national parties largely redundant. This has opened the way to the phenomenon of candidate-centred campaigns, in which the emphasis is on individual candidates being responsible for their own fund-raising and election campaigns. This has had major consequences for party cohesion and discipline and for the ability of parties to aggregate and articulate interests across the political spectrum.
- The public may become cynical at the sight of politicians voting for public money to be channelled to their parties and perhaps to be denied to others.

The case for state funding

Commentators such as Justin Fisher take issue with those who oppose state funding. Because of the importance of parties in the democratic system, the state should help to sustain them. It is questionable whether the parties *would* become even more detached from their members. In the postwar period both major parties have lost members and have found it harder to raise money from that source, although more recently Labour has somewhat reversed the tide. Also, there is no necessity that state funding should be on the basis of electoral support. It could be allocated on other bases, such as 'matching' other types of fund-raising, as in the USA, or on the basis of party membership. This would give parties the incentive not just to recruit members but to keep them. In this way, state funding could *increase* the level of political participation rather than reduce it, as critics suggest.

The first argument above against state aid was that parties are voluntary associations and so it would be undemocratic to require citizens to contribute to their upkeep. Bogdanor (1997) believes this is a flawed argument, because it assumes that *private* finance is necessarily *voluntary* finance. Companies contribute to political parties without seeking the approval of their shareholders, while unions rely on the inertia of their members regarding the political levy. Also, the state already aids political parties, so the argument is over the extent and scope of state aid, not whether or not it should exist.

There are several arguments in favour of some form of state aid.

- It would limit the unfair financial advantage enjoyed by the Conservatives and reduce the dependence of the two main parties on institutional support. This would prevent privileges being given to certain interests, while others are unfairly disadvantaged.

- State aid would improve the financial position of the central party organisations and allow the parties to concentrate on policy making (thus encouraging more coherent and practical policies), recruiting members and so on, rather than having to emphasise fund-raising.
- It would fund the research and policy-making activities of the parties. Opposition parties lack sufficient funds to conduct well thought out policy options and have to rely on small teams of party workers, advisers and special-interest groups affected by government legislation. State aid to British parties would enable them to establish genuine research organisations, as has been the case in a number of European countries.
- It would prevent parties such as the Liberal Democrats and other smaller parties being disadvantaged because they cannot command institutional finance.
- It would avoid the situation whereby some trade unionists and some company shareholders contribute to causes of which they do not approve. However, Labour supporters point out that trade unionists can 'contract out' of the political levy; shareholders have no such right.
- It could be a device to increase participation. Far from freeing parties from the need to raise their own funds, it could be made conditional on increased party activity, such as membership. In the USA and Canada, state aid is 'triggered' by individual decisions about donations.
- Such a scheme would require much greater clarity in the definition of a political party and some degree of public accountability in how they are run. At present, parties do not exist as legal entities and they have no legal personality. The law treats parties as though they were private clubs. Labour and the Liberal Democrats are in law unincorporated associations, the components of the party being separate entities although legally bound together by contract. The Conservative Party exists as three separate elements: the parliamentary party, Central Office and the National Union. They are not linked together contractually. This ramshackle system is to be changed by the reforms to party organisation announced by Hague in late 1997.
- Supporters of state subsidies point to the experience of other countries, especially in Europe, which have introduced similar changes.

Were the legal status of parties to be clarified, it would be possible to modernise the law on election expenditure. Although the spending of individual candidates is controlled, there is no limit on the national spending of the parties. This introduces much unfairness into politics, especially as much spending is not confined to the election campaign itself. In Canada there is a ceiling on party expenditure, based on the number of constituencies being contested by the party and the number of electors in those constituencies. All expenditure must be authorised by a named official within the party. This prevents or minimises extravagance and fraud.

One problem is that it is easy to evade such restrictions by channelling money to related but theoretically non-party organisations. Also, independent bodies could of their own choice (or perhaps through secret links to the parties) spend money promoting that party or this, or that policy or this. Such expenditure would have to be brought within the law. In Canada no independent expenditure which might affect the outcome of an election is allowed. Although in the USA the Supreme Court held that expenditure limits violates the First Amendment guaranteeing freedom of speech, it also said that those who accept public subsidies do have to abide by expenditure and contribution limits.

State funding could be used to help secure a fairer and more rational pattern of institutional finance. This would be especially true if its introduction heralded further reform. Company donations could be subject to controls similar to those imposed on trade unions. Companies could be required to establish a political fund following approval by shareholders, which would have to be renewed every ten years. Individual shareholders could opt in provided union members were also required to contract in rather than out.

Suggested reforms

Several reforms have been proposed:

- The state should subsidise party organisations and candidates.
- Public grants should match small individual donations; for every pound raised by a political party the state would provide an equal amount.
- Election spending by the parties should be limited.
- Parties should have to publish their accounts.
- Donations from unions and companies should be banned.
- Contributions by companies should have the same legal restrictions as those imposed on the unions.

The question of disclosure

There are two principal concerns about voluntary donations:

1 whether they should be publicly disclosed;
2 whether they are desirable for the health of democracy.

The main argument against forcing the parties to disclose the source of their funds is that individuals have a right to privacy and that no one else has a legitimate interest in disclosure. However, some argue that in the case of large donations this right is outweighed by the public interest in knowing whether such donations bring access or influence. It may be wrong to prevent people or institutions giving money to the party of their choice, but the voters need to be able to make a judgement as to the motives of the donor. Attempts to equate giving to political parties with donations to charities, which no one thinks should be subject to public scrutiny, are misleading. The stakes are much higher. It is in the interests of representative democracy that the public has a right to know who is financing parties that compete for power and control over their lives. Besides the argument that disclosure helps maintain public confidence in the democratic process, openness is an aid to fighting corruption.

Another issue is whether there should be a threshold above which donations should be made public. A problem is that the size of the donation may be related to the size of the party: a donation of £1,000 may be crucial to a small party and so capable of exerting influence; a donation of that size would not have much impact on a large party. It would also be administratively difficult for parties to have to identify and publicise the names of a mass of small donors. One additional point is whether it is healthy for a party to obtain the bulk of its money from one source or for a few large donors to dominate the process. This may mean that limits should be placed on the size of donations. Large donations may unfairly advantage one party, parties may become over-dependent on one source, withdrawal of which may handicap that party, or the threat of withdrawal may be a source of undue pressure. By limiting the size of donations the parties will be forced to seek finance from their grass-root supporters and so widen political participation.

Evidence from abroad, especially the USA, suggests that parties and their donors do not find it difficult to evade regulations. However, provided the law is clearly drafted and rigorously administered, it should be possible to overcome this problem, especially if the parties kept in mind the electoral consequences of sleaze, both personal and party.

The Neill committee

In October 1997 Sir Patrick Neill QC (later Lord Neill of Bladen), the newly appointed chair of the Committee on Standards in Public Life, promised an inquiry into party funding. Although no terms of reference had been announced, Neill said that the question of limiting national spending would be addressed. Other probable changes would include the banning of foreign and secret donations. The Prime Minister said that all aspects of the funding of parties would be examined to ensure openness and transparency.

The report was published on 13 October 1998. It proposed the biggest reform of party funding in British history, which would be backed by punitive sanctions and heavy fines. In his letter to Tony Blair, Lord Neill said:

> Many members of the public believe that the policies of the major parties have been influenced by large donors, while ignorance about the sources of funding has fostered suspicion. We are, therefore, convinced that a fundamentally new framework is needed to provide public confidence for the future, to meet the needs of modern politics and to bring the United Kingdom into line with the best practice in other mature democracies. (*The Guardian*, 14 October 1998)

Neill referred to spending by the parties as a 'political arms race' which needed to be curbed.

The main recommendations were:

- foreign donations to be banned;
- blind trusts to be abolished;
- all national donations of £5,000 and local donations of £1,000 to be made public;
- anonymous donations of £50 or more banned;
- £20 million cap on party campaign budgets at general elections;
- tax relief for parties on donations up to £500;
- tripling of state funding to help opposition parties in Parliament and a new £2 million fund for policy research;
- shareholders to approve company donations and sponsorship;
- new laws for referendums including equal state funding for 'yes' and 'no' campaigns;
- the establishment of an Electoral Commission, with powers to police the system, ensure openness and enforce the spending cap.

The report received a warm welcome from the Home Secretary Jack Straw, making it likely that the bulk of the recommendations will become law by the next general election. The government immediately announced that it was acting on the recommendations regarding the Scottish and Welsh elections. A £1.5 million ceiling was put on spending by each party for the Scottish Parliament and £600,000 for the Welsh Assembly.

All the parties welcomed the report, including the Conservatives, who had fought hard to be allowed to keep their financial affairs secret. The Tories attacked the government for delaying legislation so they could 'cherry-pick' the recommendations and called for legislation to be introduced in the next Queen's speech. The government retaliated by promising that new controls on party funding and spending would be in place by the next general election, and attacked the Tories' refusal to agree to the implementation of the recommendations in advance of legislation. The Labour Party urged that the Conservatives and Liberal Democrats voluntarily agree to disclose donations and ban foreign funding in advance of legislation.

Disclosure of donations over £5,000

This would introduce greater transparency to party funding and end claims that money can buy influence and would make it less likely that there would be accusations that donations are used to gain access to ministers, to influence policy or to obtain consideration for an honour or appointment to some public body such as a quango.

In evidence, all the big parties said they agreed with the need to publish the names of donors of £5,000 or above, although the Conservatives did not want to disclose the exact amount. Lord Neill said he did not accept this point. Public disquiet would not be ended by partial disclosure. There is a vast difference between a donation of £5,000 and one of £1 million, and the implications of the two donations differ fundamentally. The public interest outweighed the individual's right to privacy and the risk that donations might dry up is one which would have to be taken. If the parties suffered a shortage of funds, consideration would have to be given to a measure of state funding.

The names of donors who gave money to local parties would have to be given, to prevent the appearance of improper influence being sought over local decisions such as planning applications or the granting of contracts.

The report proposed that there should be a £1 million cap on any donation at general elections, something which will affect wealthy individuals and organisations such as trade unions, although this will not apply to referendum campaigns. Companies offering donations or sponsorship will have to obtain permission from their shareholders once every four years, putting them in a similar position to trade unions.

Blind trusts

The Committee called for a complete ban on the sort of blind trust which was used to fund Blair's office between his election as Labour leader and the victory in 1997 and which raised several million pounds. The report said:

> The committee rejects the very concept of such blind trusts as being inconsistent with the principle of openness and accountability. Moreover, there must be considerable doubt whether they ensure anonymity. While we do not impugn the integrity of those who administer such funds, the cynical will always be ready to conclude that a donor can easily let it be known to the beneficiary that he or she had made a substantial contribution to the relevant blind trust.

Foreign donations

All foreign donations should be banned, although an exception might be made in Northern Ireland to allow supporters of the Social Democratic and

Labour Party and Sinn Fein living in the Irish Republic to contribute. The report said that every large party, including the Tories (who raised millions in Hong Kong before the last election), agreed with this recommendation. The report stated that:

> At a time when the whole question of the funding of political parties is being re-examined, it is right to take this opportunity to lay down the principle that those who live, work and carry on businesses in the UK should be the persons exclusively entitled to support financially the operation of the political process here.

Parties would still be able to raise money abroad from British citizens.

Tax relief

Tax relief on donations to parties should be introduced, capped at £500. It is more democratic that the parties should be supported by a large number of small donors than a small number of large ones. Parties will make greater efforts to attract this level of support.

Financing political parties in Parliament

There should be an increase in Short money. In 1997, the Tories received £986,762 and the Liberal Democrats £371,997, with smaller amounts going to minor parties. This was not enough to allow the opposition parties to do their job properly. Each party should be given three times the amount it now received, taking the total cost to £4.8 million. There should be extra money to fund the leader of the opposition's office and more money for the opposition parties in the Lords.

Limits on campaign expenditure

There should be a cap of £20 million on spending by each party at general elections, to end the 'escalating arms race' to raise cash. Although Labour and the Liberal Democrats supported the suggestion, the Tories were less enthusiastic, fearing it would restrict free speech. The Committee did not agree. The report stated that it was difficult to prove whether high spending bought elections. However, limits on spending are necessary to prevent undue concentration on fund-raising. There should be no change to the limitations placed on spending by individual candidates. There should be similar caps for elections in Scotland and Wales and to the European Parliament, as well as for the London mayor.

Third-party groups such as trade unions or single-issue pressure groups would be able to spend a maximum of £1 million on influencing the outcome of elections.

Electoral Commission

There should be an independent and impartial Election Commission to monitor the new regulations and to investigate abuses. The five commissioners should publish a report on the conduct of each election within six months. The Commission would keep lists of all donors, keep all party accounts and would take legal action if overspending or other abuses were discovered. It would lay down rules for elections and referendums and advise the government on any changes to election law. Cash would be forfeited from parties which exceed the spending limits, and staff handling the money could go to gaol. Parties breaking the new limits could be fined up to ten times the amount overspent. Party officials who commit 'deliberate and reckless' acts could even face gaol.

Referendums

There should be new rules to ensure that both sides have a fair opportunity to put its case. The Committee was concerned that the 'no' campaign in Wales was seriously underfunded, and that a fairer campaign might well have resulted in a different result. A total of between £1.2 million and £2 million is suggested.

The rules for referendums mean that it may be harder for the government to get its way over the single European currency and over proportional representation. Government will be required to be formally neutral and thus unable to call on taxpayers' money to promote its cause. While there would be no ban on ministers campaigning, it would have to be organised by the party not the government. Partisan material should not be sent out as government information.

Media and advertising

The ban on political advertising on television and radio should remain and should be extended to new forms of communication.

Honours

Nominations for an honour of CBE or above should be scrutinised if the recipient has donated £5,000 or more to a party within the last five years.

The changing pattern of party finance

The report highlighted the extent to which the two main parties had become dependent on large donations from wealthy individuals or organisations. While Labour received 134 gifts of £5,000 or more during 1997, including twenty-one in excess of £50,000, the Tories received 375 and

119 respectively in the same period. This has given rise to a widespread perception that money can buy access and even influence. The report commented 'While we have no evidence that such influence has been bought, we believe that the widespread assumption among the public that it can be bought is extremely damaging.'

Evidence printed in the report shows that the Tories received seventeen donations of over £1 million during 1992–7. The Liberal Democrats raised £15 million in the same period, including six cheques for over £100,000. Labour and the Conservatives raised that much almost every year. At least six of the Tories' £1 million cheques came from abroad; overseas donors contributed over £14 million.

Labour's pattern of fund-raising has changed. Subscription income from Party members remained almost static over 1992–7 (from £1.6 million to £1.9 million) and affiliation fees fell from £8.7 million to £6.4 million; donations from individuals, corporations and the unions rose from £3.5 million in 1992 to around £14.5 million in 1997. In 1992 there were twenty-six donations of £5,000 to £10,000 and only one at £90,000 to £100,000. In the two years of John Smith's leadership no cheque for more than £70,000 was received. However, in 1995 there were two gifts of between £100,000 and £250,000 and in 1996 seven, plus five even larger, one for over £1 million. In 1997 there were four £1 million gifts, and Lord Sainsbury is thought to have given over £2 million.

Conclusion

Party funding needs reform because the political conditions have changed. The links between Labour and the unions have declined and seem set to weaken even further, while those between business and the Tories have become more attenuated since Labour managed to convince much of the business community of its trustworthiness. The trend towards a more multiparty system has caused many to question the fairness of a system which favours the two main parties; the system of party funding is no longer in tune with electoral feeling. Reform would improve rather than weaken the internal health of the political parties, as well as extending the opportunities for political participation. The present system of party finance in Britain is 'market based'. This, it is alleged, distorts representative democracy by allowing some interests effectively to 'buy' influence. It also means that there is an ever-present danger that parties will run into financial problems which will endanger their capacity to perform their functions. It is clear that in the 1990s there is considerable cynicism about politicians and the political parties. Protestations of integrity by the politicians themselves will no longer be as acceptable as in the past. The demand for more information about the affairs of the political parties is part of an increasing demand for greater openness. The suspicion that politicians are manipulating the political system either to ensure a hold on power or in their individual self-interest is corrosive of faith in the democratic system. The demand for 'more light' will grow.

Reading

Blackburn, R. (1995) *The Electoral System in Britain*, Macmillan, ch. 7.

Bogdanor, V. (1997) *Power and the People*, Gollancz, ch. 6.

Fisher, J. (1994) 'Political donations to the Conservative Party', *Parliamentary Affairs*, Vol. 47 (1).

Fisher, J. (1996) *British Political Parties*, Prentice Hall.

Fisher, J. (1997a) 'Donations to political parties', *Parliamentary Affairs*, Vol. 50 (2).

Fisher, J. (1997b) 'Party finance', in P. Norton (ed.), *The Conservative Party*, Prentice Hall.

Garner, R. and Kelly, R. (1998) *British Political Parties Today* (2nd edn), Manchester University Press.

Hansard Society for Parliamentary Government (1991) *Paying For Politics*, Hansard Society.

House of Commons Home Affairs Select Committee (1994) *Funding of Political Parties*, HMSO.

Lemieux, S. (1995) 'The future funding of political parties', *Talking Politics*, Vol. 7 (3).

McConnell, A. (1994) 'The "crisis" of Conservative Party funding', *Talking Politics*, Vol. 7 (1).

Pinto-Duschinsky, M. (1988) 'Party finance. Funding of political parties since 1945', *Contemporary Record*, Vol. 2 (4).

Thomas, G. P. (1992) *Government and the Economy Today*, Manchester University Press, ch. 10.

17

The debate about the welfare state
Paul Wilding

Until the mid-1970s there was little real debate about the principle of the welfare state. Certainly, there had been sharp questions about it from the 1950s – for example from the Institute of Economic Affairs in its many publications – but there was little debate. Critics were seen as eccentrics, people who had failed to come to terms with the postwar world. Supporters of the welfare state felt sufficiently confident and assured not to engage in debate about fundamental issues.

In fact, supporters of the welfare state were its strongest critics through the 1950s, 1960s and 1970s – for example Richard Titmuss and Peter Townsend – but their criticisms were about the quantity and quality of provision. They wanted more, more quickly; they did not question the idea of the welfare state itself.

The consensus about the welfare state which existed from 1945 to 1975 can easily be overemphasised. There were differences between the main political parties about what should be done and how quickly, but there was near universal acceptance of the major role of the state in welfare which had emerged in the years between 1945 and 1950. There was little questioning of that principle.

The collapse of consensus

What has become quite clear is that consensus about the desirability of a major role for the state in welfare broke down in the 1970s. There are a number of reasons put forward for this change.

- The consensus was really never more than superficial. The welfare state in Britain has suffered from two damaging associations – with socialism and with austerity. Non-socialists in Britain have always had some doubts about a major role for the state in welfare – which has not always been the case in other countries. The association with austerity meant that prosperity raised further doubts about the need for a welfare state.

- The era of painless financing out of economic growth ended in the mid-1970s. As long as the economy was expanding, private consumption and welfare spending could expand simultaneously. In the 1970s for the first time it was much more either one or the other.
- Paying for the welfare state had come to rest more heavily on those with average and below-average incomes because the income at which people started paying tax had fallen. This gave greater credibility to politicians talking about 'the burden of taxation' caused by the welfare state and broadened concern about welfare expenditure.
- The welfare state was blamed for Britain's economic difficulties. The high taxes required to sustain it, it was alleged, fuelled inflation and reduced incentives, so weakening the economy. The welfare state was also charged with absorbing labour which would be better employed in productive enterprises rather than in the provision of social services.
- The welfare state also came under strong criticism for its ineffectiveness in achieving its aims. It had not, even its supporters agreed, abolished poverty, achieved equality of opportunity in education, or equality of access to health services. In many services, such as higher education, the middle classes were clearly the main beneficiaries.
- Public confidence in welfare state services had been weakened by the continuous deafening chorus of complaint about lack of resources and low standards of services which arose from those who worked in them. As Enoch Powell pointed out many years ago, to secure more resources, those in the services feel they have to denigrate them. People therefore came to think that services were substandard – and therefore not worth paying for or supporting.
- Welfare state policies depend on faith in experts, the belief that there are people who know how to solve the problems of poverty, ill health, bad housing, urban redevelopment, crime, and so on. The reputations of the key welfare professionals went down like skittles in the 1970s – and the welfare state suffered in consequence.
- The belief that public action is the appropriate way to deal with social problems was a basic building block in the consensus. This was weakened by the emergence of new and more complex problems which no one was confident they knew how to tackle – the problem of the inner city, the problem of law and order in society, the increasing numbers of very elderly people, for example.
- From all sides, the welfare state was attacked for what it was alleged to do to people and to society. The New Right talked of the 'nanny state' destroying independence, initiative and self-respect and fostering dependency. Feminists accused it of contributing to women's subordination.

Marxists saw it as propping up capitalism and disciplining the working class. The romantics talked of the 'schooled', 'medicalised' society.

- The essential underpinnings of the welfare state were provided by Keynesian economics. What Keynes did was to make legitimate high levels of government activity and spending. The eclipse of Keynesianism meant the removal of a basic philosophical prop to the welfare state.

Most of these points are contestable. They are clearly of varying degrees of importance but they make up the background to the debate about the welfare state which emerged in the 1970s and 1980s.

Positions in the debate

It is difficult briefly to characterise the various positions in the debate on the welfare state without seeming to caricature them. The sketches which follow can do no more than indicate the broad lines of the different perspectives which shaped the debate from the 1970s until the early 1990s. In the mid-1990s the democratic socialist perspective changes significantly and I explore those changes after reviewing the range of other perspectives.

The New Right position

The New Right critique of the welfare state proclaimed enthusiastically by Margaret Thatcher's governments in the 1980s, and pursued with some hints of pragmatic dilution by John Major in the 1990s, is the contemporary expression of anti-collectivism. It draws on the work of two distinguished academics, Milton Friedman and F. A. Hayek. It proclaims certain values – freedom, choice, individualism and inequality. It stresses the creative possibilities of the free market economy. It emphasises a range of doubts and anxieties about government action.

It makes a number of general and particular criticisms of welfare state policies.

- The welfare state is a threat to freedom because:
  - (a) it demands high rates of taxation which limit people's freedom to spend the money they earn as they wish;
  - (b) it gives people little or no choice about the type or quality of service which is provided;
  - (c) services are not subject to effective democratic control or direction;
  - (d) it puts people at the mercy of professionals such as doctors, teachers and social workers and of bureaucrats who have enormous power in a welfare state.
- State provision of welfare is fundamentally inefficient because it is monopolistic. There is no competition between providing bodies and

it is only through competition and market forces that efficiency is achieved.

- In a welfare state system what is provided is not what consumers want but what professionals and bureaucrats think they want. Public provision is therefore inevitably unresponsive to individual needs and wishes.
- Although designed to help, in fact the welfare state damages people. It creates dependency and weakens individuals' sense of responsibility for themselves and their families.
- A welfare state leads to the view that the state is the main source and provider of welfare services. Other sources and systems of welfare – the family, the community, the voluntary sector, the market – are neglected and weakened and, in time, perish.
- Welfare state policies weaken the economy because they depend on debilitating rates of taxation which fuel inflation, destroy incentives and damage investment. The real sources of welfare – a healthy economy and economic growth – are therefore undermined.
- As well as weakening the economy, welfare state policies also weaken the authority of government. Governments become the focus of interest-group activity as groups fight for the recognition and protection of what they see as their rights. Governments committed to particular welfare programmes all too easily become the creatures of particular groups.

Underlying the whole critique is one central belief – *private provision is nearly always better,*

- *economically* because it will be more efficient and because it is not damaging to the economy;
- *politically* because it does not make government the creature of particular interests;
- *socially* because it does not make people dependent, because it offers choice and makes providers accountable to consumers and so more responsive to them.

The Marxist position

What Marxists say about the welfare state is of no direct political importance. They are unlikely ever to have the opportunity to implement their ideas. It is also very difficult to talk about a Marxist critique because 'Marxist' is a loose category embracing a rich variety of opinions – as well, of course, as a simple term of political abuse. Nevertheless, the Marxist critique has been extremely important in the contribution it has made to the whole debate about the nature of the welfare state. Its critique has stimulated a broader questioning of the aims and functions of the welfare state. Bearing in mind the dangers of doing so, it is nevertheless possible to sketch the general features of a Marxist position.

Marxists see the welfare state as shaped essentially by two forces:

1 the needs of capitalism;
2 class conflict.

Capitalism needs healthy, educated and contented workers. It needs systems which maintain workers in times when the onward march of economic progress is temporarily checked. It needs a state whose authority is seen as legitimate, and the provision of welfare can contribute to such legitimacy. The capitalist state is characterised by the conflict which Marxists see as the inevitable element in the relationship between capital and labour. This conflict produces concessions by capital and/or victories for labour – and sometimes these take the form of welfare services. Marxists are therefore ambivalent about the welfare state. It is both a prop to capitalism and a symbol of victories won by the working class.

Marxists lay much stress on the social control functions of the welfare state, that is, its contributions to inculcating and reinforcing the values and patterns of behaviour required by the capitalist system. The social security system, for example, is seen as centrally concerned with maintaining labour discipline, the education system with producing a workforce which accepts failure, inequality and authority and which is properly 'socialised'.

An important strand in the Marxist critique is the argument that many of the problems with which the welfare state seeks to deal are the direct product of the very nature of the capitalist system. They are not therefore amenable to solution by social services – only by radical structural changes in society.

Marxists also stress the limited possibilities of social services. They are not, they argue, a tool for changing society. The most that can be achieved through welfare state policies is a certain humanisation of the existing order.

An anxiety which Marxists have is that, in providing tangible and immediate goals, welfare services will have a deradicalising effect on the working-class political movement. Workers will become content with the half loaf of the welfare state rather than striving for the whole loaf of socialism.

Marxists see the capitalist welfare state – like capitalism itself – as providing its own gravediggers. The argument is that capitalism needs the welfare state for purposes of legitimation but that capitalism cannot, at the same time, generate the resources required for a welfare state and for its own future development. The result is fiscal crisis – a shortfall in the tax revenues required for the welfare state.

Marxists cannot, therefore, be optimistic about the possibilities of welfare provided by a capitalist state. On the other hand, they recognise the real benefits accruing to the working class from such provision. They therefore contest the New Right arguments but they do not want to see welfare services become an alternative to radical social reconstruction.

The democratic socialist position

For many people in Britain, the welfare state is the historic symbol of democratic socialism. The welfare state is what socialism has come to be seen as being about. It represents gradualist social change. It is a strategy for the reduction of inequality and the promotion of equality. It aims at an extension of freedom and it both represents and promotes a sense of collective responsibility.

Democratic socialists have, therefore, always been fundamentally supportive of the welfare state. They see it – with pardonable historical inaccuracy – as their creation. Nevertheless, from this group has come a variety of criticisms of the welfare state which have been part of the raw material of the debate.

This group supported the welfare state as a means of reducing social inequality. Their researches, however, show that this has not happened. In health, housing and education, for example, there are still striking inequalities between class, gender, region and ethnic groups. This has reduced democratic socialists' faith in social services as a major mechanism for achieving social change. They have come to argue for a broader health or education *policy* rather than simple reliance on health and education *services.*

Democratic socialists have also contributed to the debate about the organisation of the welfare state. They have accepted the criticism that it is overcentralised. They have urged the decentralisation of many local government services so that they become more accessible – and hopefully more responsive – to users and would-be users.

Democratic socialists have also voiced anxieties about the role and power of professionals in the welfare state. Welfare states are – traditionally – professional states. They need – and depend on – the expertise of doctors, teachers, social workers, planners and so on. But the needs and demands of such groups can easily displace the needs of users as the crucial element in the organisation of services. The New Right has been more vocal in criticism of professionals but democratic socialists have shared some of these concerns.

Democratic socialists have moved on from simply calling for increased expenditure on the welfare state, which was what dominated their thinking in the 1950s and 1960s. They have also become increasingly willing to accept that awful mistakes have been made – for example, in some local-authority housing developments.

The democratic socialist critique has contributed to the dissatisfaction with the welfare state. The group saw criticism as the rational way to improvement. The New Right, however, has used their work as ammunition in the struggle to destroy the credibility of welfare state policies and to 'roll back' the state.

The feminist contribution

The first important point to make is that there is no one feminist contribution. Feminism is a movement with richly varied – and conflicting – elements. All there is space for here is a very crude general characterisation.

What feminists have done is to develop a powerful critique of the welfare state based on its implicit and explicit assumptions about the role of women and their impact on women's lives. Thus the welfare state is based on certain unstated value assumptions about sex roles. These shape policy and contribute directly and indirectly to the continuance of women's subordinate position in society. Community care, for example, is based on very clear assumptions about women's caring responsibilities. Those assumptions mean that public provision of caring services is scanty. This helps to shape women's opportunities at work. Again, education is seen as male dominated. History is a study of men's wars. Literature is dominated by men's books. Analysis of society by sociologists is constructed around men's position in the division of labour.

Feminists argue that much of life conventionally seen as *personal* – for example, the care of young children or elderly people – is in fact a *political* issue. It is political because of the implications of much supposedly personal activity for the whole of women's lives. In our society, the argument runs, paid employment is the key to citizenship. Anything which limits access to that is a political issue. Feminists, therefore, argue for an extension of the boundaries of the conventional welfare sate and more 'political' provision of services.

There has been much legislation aimed at promoting women's equality – for example by outlawing discrimination, laying down the principle of equal pay. Research has shown very clearly the limited results achieved by such approaches. Such failure, feminists argue, is inevitable in a state dominated by men and functioning in the interests of men. Just as Marxists categorise the state as capitalist and so limited in its possibilities of achieving reform, so feminists see the state as patriarchal and so similarly constrained. Social policy will – inevitably – be policy for men.

Feminists have also analysed the welfare state as a major source of work for women. It is, at the same time, a trap. It traps women into particular kinds of work – with low pay – which are an extension of women's traditional role and which reinforce it. Women are also concentrated in the lower ranks of such employment. There are few women hospital consultants, head teachers or directors of social services.

The feminist contribution to the debate is to raise questions about the outcomes of the welfare state for women. Too often, the argument runs, it confirms dependency and reinforces inequality. Feminists are not, in general, hostile to the principle of the welfare state. But they are keen to point out that good male intentions do not necessarily lead to desirable outcomes for women. Gender is a vital – if historically neglected – dimension of inequality and evaluation.

The anti-racist contribution

The anti-racist contribution to the debate about the welfare state has four main elements.

1   Like the feminist contribution, it opens up discussion about the values embedded in policies and services. It insists that their benevolence cannot be taken for granted but must be analysed for racist implications. What may, it is argued, seem entirely value free to white males may be far from value free for members of ethnic minorities, as for women.

2   It raises the specific issue of institutional racism – unquestioned values embedded deep in the assumptions of policy makers and planners which mean that services operate in ways which discriminate against people from ethnic minorities. In the 1960s and early 1970s, the concern was with the discriminatory behaviour of staff. That concern is still real but the focus of concern has moved on and taken this institutional focus.

3   There is an implicit and explicit call for the monitoring of outcomes – good intentions are no longer enough. The feminist and anti-racist positions have both pressed this point about the need to evaluate outcomes from particular perspectives.

4   The anti-racist position also insists that universalism is no longer enough, that the welfare state must advance from universalism to a considered pluralism. Providing the same services for everyone may, in fact, be discriminatory and promote inequality.

The green contribution

As with Marxism and feminism, there are many strands to the green movement and so generalisation about the green contribution is problematic. Though greens are beginning to be heard in academic debates and political speeches about the welfare state, their actual impact on policy is, as yet, insignificant. Five elements in the green critique are important.

1   Greens see the welfare state as part of the unsustainable society – for three reasons. It aims to soften some of the rough edges of industrial capitalism – and so to preserve it. Secondly, there is its focus on *people* whereas, for the greens, the centre of our models and plans should

be not people but the *earth*. Thirdly, and perhaps most importantly, the welfare state depends on – and therefore encourages – economic growth and it is the drive for growth which, in the green view, threatens the destruction of the planet.

2   The welfare state is – and encourages – a national response to problems which are essentially international. Welfare in one country is no longer possible. We must think globally even while we live locally. There is no hope, the greens argue, of tackling the big environmental issues, on which the future welfare of all of us depends, unless we tackle the inequalities between the developed and the developing countries. International redistribution is a precondition for an effective international approach to environmental issues.

3   The greens see the welfare state as inherently centralist and undemocratic. They see genuine social development as dependent on participation, which means that services must be local and democratic. As one of the former leaders of the Green Party, Jonathon Porritt, put it: 'nothing should be done at a higher level that cannot be done at a lower'.

4   The welfare state feeds faith in technological rationality – the notion that there is a technical fix for problems which are produced by the very nature of our way of life. The greens would see the National Health Service (NHS) in just this light. For them, our whole way of life is fundamentally unhealthy. The NHS simply looks at presenting problems of ill health and proclaims that they are solvable by the marvels of medical science. The greens think otherwise.

5   The greens see the welfare state as concerned with only the immediate and short term, as by its very nature unable to deal with anything beyond the immediate and the politically pressing. The really important issues do not, therefore, get attention because they never seem urgent.

The Labour Party's change in thinking

The positions which I have set out here are vital to an understanding of the debate about the welfare state which emerged in the 1970s and 1980s. In the mid-1990s, however, there was significant movement in the Labour Party's position – just as there was in the Conservative position in the 1970s and 1980s. The Labour Party moved from its traditional position as the great supporter of the 1945 settlement to a much more critical, questioning stance. That needs to be understood if debates in the mid-1990s are to be appreciated, but the older democratic socialist position needs to be grasped if the debates of the 1980s and early 1990s are to be understood.

I explore the new Labour position under three headings – why Labour's approach changed, how it changed and what the significance of the changes was.

Why did Labour's approach change?

Essentially, Labour's position changed for four main reasons. First, traditional approaches and policies did not seem to be working to solve the problems at which they were directed. Poverty and inequality, for example, survived. Secondly, there seemed to be a popular revolt against high-tax and high-spending policies. Political realism dictated a change from the Party's traditional stress on the value of high rates of public spending. Thirdly, concern about Britain's international competitiveness reinforced concern about labour costs and so, for example, about the impact of social security contributions. Finally, there was the undeniable influence of Conservative rule and political dominance since 1979. Conservative ideas had an immense impact on Labour thinking, particularly after the fourth election defeat in 1992.

How did Labour's approach change?

In what ways did Labour's thinking change?

Labour very clearly retreated from the belief that high levels of public spending were the way to combat social problems and build the good society. The Party committed itself in the 1997 election campaign to sticking to the existing very tight Conservative spending plans for its first two years in office. It committed itself, too, to not making any increase in the basic or the top rate of income tax.

Labour clearly adopted Conservative concern about welfare dependency. Labour's flagship policy became its Welfare to Work programme to get people off benefits and into work. Work, as Tony Blair argued, is the best form of welfare. Gordon Brown reinforced the particular slant of the message when he insisted that the best way to increase jobs is to increase people's employability. There is, too, a new disciplinary thrust to Labour's thinking – young people who refuse to take up jobs or training opportunities will lose all their benefits. What is disturbing about the Welfare to Work strategy is the way that it has focused attention on one relatively small part of social security spending. Certainly it is an important one, but the message conveyed by this flagship initiative serves to confirm the impression conveyed by eighteen years of Conservative policy that all social security expenditure is a problem and a burden.

Labour seems to have moved from its historic commitment to promote equality and attack poverty to a belief that the answer to both is the extension of opportunities rather than more direct action. The Party seems to have lost faith in the social security system as a tool for building a new society. It has made no attempt to increase social security benefits for those unable to work or even to begin to make good the sharp cuts in the real value of benefits in the previous eighteen years. There has been no attempt to use the social security system to attack poverty.

There is no longer talk of a return to full employment. There seems to be much more concern with the control of inflation and with reassuring the business world that Labour's priorities are similar to those of the outgoing Conservatives. Labour handed over control of monetary policy to a newly independent Bank of England, so divesting itself of a potentially crucial policy instrument. Key business people were recruited to a range of positions around the new administration to show its regard for business opinion.

There was a retreat from state provision and responsibility, from the notion of the state as the sole or the best provider for a range of needs – for example for pensions. There was discussion about a new, much more mixed economy of pension provision.

There was also a retreat from universalism. Means-testing was accepted as a rational way to use resources and as something which should be considered in relation to certain hitherto sacred heartland areas of the welfare state such as retirement pensions.

What was the significance of Labour's changes?

Essentially these changes show a major break with traditional thinking. Labour had always been the party of the welfare state as laid down in the years after 1945. If Labour was abandoning its traditional support, then the future of the welfare state was certainly going to be very different. It was not only that Labour was changing its views. It was changing them in a very clear direction and moving away from support for a major, dominant role for the state in welfare to giving individual responsibility and the market a much bigger role. Labour's change of heart is, in part at least, a tribute to the powerful influence of eighteen years of Conservative government.

Conclusion

The debate about the welfare state takes place in various arenas, but in the 1990s welfare has less political salience than it had in the 1960s. Parties can win elections even though the electorate has anxieties about their attitude towards the welfare state. The academic debate, however, continues. The risk is that the debate remains academic.

From the various positions which have been sketched here, it is possible, by way of conclusion, to list the issues which form the essential focus of the debate:

- There is debate about the very nature of a welfare state and the good society. Is individual welfare best achieved by facilitating individual enterprise and effort or by restraining and directing it in the interests of collective goals?

- What is the potential of state/political action for promoting welfare? The welfare state is an inherently political enterprise but how far can welfare be achieved or at least promoted by political action? Or is political action inevitably ineffective and inefficient? If there is a role for political action, is it actually to provide services or to enable other bodies to provide, and to regulate non-state provision?
- What is the potential of market systems – to promote welfare and to provide services more efficiently than traditional, public systems of provision?
- The ultimate test is outcomes. What are the outcomes of welfare state policies, for example for women, ethnic minorities, the environment?
- To what extent is economic growth the best – or indeed the only – way to increase welfare?
- What is the proper relationship between the various welfare-providing institutions in our society – public authorities, the private market, the family, the voluntary sector, the community? What is the nature of the so-called 'mixed economy of welfare'?
- What values can provide a firm foundation for the welfare state? Can a refurbished idea of citizenship supply what is needed? Or justice? Or sustainability? Do charity and altruism still have a part to play?
- What is the relationship between national and international welfare in a more global economy? Is it possible to have welfare – like socialism – in one country? If welfare demands an international perspective, where does that leave national welfare states?
- How is state welfare to be organised? What is the appropriate mix of central, local-authority and neighbourhood provision? What is the proper mix of professional and user power? How can users best be empowered – for example with charters, complaints systems and rights of redress – without damaging their relationships with service providers?
- What is the appropriate balance in the good society between rights and responsibilities?

The debate about the welfare state is important because it is about the kind of society we want. It is real because it raises fundamental questions about individual and social responsibility. It is about economic and political issues, about the more effective and efficient organisation, administration and financing of particular services in particular places.

The debate is confused. Therefore it can be unhelpful. But if policy makers listen attentively there is much to be learned.

Reading

Dobson, A. (1995) *Green Political Thought* (2nd edn), Routledge.
George, V. and Wilding, P. (1994) *Welfare and Ideology*, Harvester Wheatsheaf.

Pascall, G. (1997) *Social Policy: A New Feminist Analysis*, Routledge.
Social Justice Commission (1994) *Social Justice*, Vintage.
Walker, A. and Walker, C. (1997) *Britain Divided*, Child Poverty Action Group.
Willetts, D. (1992) *Modern Conservatism*, Penguin.

18

Placing New Labour

David Coates

Our whole understanding of British politics in the 1990s has been transformed by the election victory of the Labour Party in May 1997. Before it occurred, the dominant issue – on the left and beyond – was whether Labour could ever return to power again; and how, as part of that search for electoral credibility, the Labour leadership could relate to a dominant set of non-socialist ideas (broadly labelled Thatcherism) which seemed to sweep all before them. The lens through which even left-wing critics of the Labour Party approached issues of ideological change in the 1980s was one preoccupied with neo-liberalism. After the 1997 election victory, however, and particularly because of its scale, the question put to New Labour by such critics has become slightly different. It is New Labour who now set the political and ideological agenda: and it is the integrity, origin and thrust of their understandings which now become centre stage. The issue now is not how New Labour relates to Thatcherism, but rather how, in orchestrating its electoral defeat of the Conservatives, New Labour speaks to its own party's ideological past. The issue now is whether, and in what sense, New Labour is really new, and whether, in its newness, it has any connection at all to what historically/contemporarily can properly be understood as socialism.

Socialism and social democracy

Socialism has been a contested concept for the entirety of the twentieth century and the political forces pursuing it have, in consequence, fought each other with as much ferocity as they have fought capitalism. The oldest and deepest twentieth-century division on the left, certainly between 1917 and 1990, was that between communism and social democracy. The communist understanding of socialism was that it was simply a stage on the way to a fully communist society, in which the guiding principle of social organisation would eventually become 'from each according to their ability, to each according to their need'. The task of political parties in the socialist stage was to remove all vestiges of the earlier capitalist one, primarily by abolishing all forms of private ownership of the means of production, thereby disposing of capitalism's owning class (the bourgeoisie). It was also to install a period of party rule (the dictatorship of the proletariat) which would have no truck with the niceties of parliamentary democracy (which was understood in the communist tradition as being merely one form of capitalist class rule).

Needless to say, so stark and radical a view of the gap between capitalist and socialist democracy was too much for many on the left. In consequence, a revitalised social democracy quickly established itself as communism's major left-wing alternative: one with a different view of economic organis-ation, class relations and political power to those prevalent in Marxist circles. In the post-1917 social democratic tradition (in which the Labour Party was from its inception a major European player) the property relations of a capitalist economy were not so much to be rescinded as controlled. Post-1917 social democratic theoreticians and parties sought to subject capitalist firms to state control, including where appropriate public ownership; and to soften class divisions by socially egalitarian policies of progressive taxation, welfare provision, educational reform and the encouragement of individual social mobility. Social democratic politicians saw the democratic state not as a mask for the class rule of capital, but as *the* key mechanism through which a socialist society could be created: one in which the anarchic market forces of an unregulated capitalist economy could be controlled by state power and harnessed to the common good in a society characterised by fairness, social justice and equality of treatment.

Within social democracy itself, currents of radicalism then diverged. Left-wing social democracy always brought to the debate about economy and society some elements of the communist case. Such politicians were always conscious of the economic and political power of capital, the tenacity of social privilege and the vulnerability of radical political forces to orchestrated attempts by dominant classes to incorporate and subordinate them. Social democracy, in each of its generations thus far, has always produced a left-wing current which remains committed – no matter where the centre of gravity of party policy shifts – to a programme of extensive public ownership and economic controls (to break the power of private capital), to steeply progressive direct taxation and extensive welfare provision (to erode class privilege) and to the strengthening of democratic institutions both in the workplace (through trade union rights and industrial democracy) and in the wider society.

But left-wing social democracy has never been without challenge within the parties of the parliamentary left. Parliamentary socialists of a Marxist persuasion have always cohabited there with socialists whose radicalism has been rooted in ethical and Christian value systems and commitments. They have also cohabited with strands of left-wing liberalism: with political forces, that is, which were reluctant to form separate parties of the working class and which preferred instead to press within existing parties for state regulation of the market and welfare rights for the poor. From more moderate political currents of these kinds, revisionist currents have periodically emerged, arguing for a different understanding of how best to create a more egalitarian and prosperous society. Characteristically, revisionists have put less emphasis than their more radical parliamentary colleagues on the control of capital per se, arguing instead for a partnership between a democratic state and a socially responsible business community. The main focus of revisionist radicalism has invariably been civil society – theirs has characteristically been a social rather than an economic agenda – arguing in particular for educational reform and the freeing of personal relationships to create a more egalitarian and tolerant society. Revisionist social democrats have often been less enthusiastic than their left-wing compatriots about trade union rights. They have often seen trade unionism as a conservative force inimical to the modernised and meritocratic world they sought to create; but they have shared with the rest of the parliamentary left a strong sense of the democratic state as a key agency for the creation of a genuinely socialist society.

This clash of communism and social democracy, and within social democracy this struggle of left and right, has been the main stuff of left-wing politics in all the major western European democracies since 1917, with the relative weight of the various political forces involved varying between different labour movements and differing over time. In comparative terms, the political centre of gravity of the British labour movement has always been on the moderate end of this left-wing spectrum. The Communist Party was always weak in Britain; and within the dominant Labour Party itself, left-wing forces have invariably occupied a minority position (and have often played an oppositional role to their own party leadership). Only very occasionally has left-wing ascendancy occurred in the British Labour Party; and when it has, it has always stimulated a powerful backlash from more revisionist Labour forces. The major (and, with the possible exception of the years of opposition after 1970, in many ways the only) period of left-wing ascendancy in the twentieth-century history of British Labour was that between 1979 and 1983: one which stimulated, in its turn, first the defections to the Social Democratic Party (SDP) and then the rise of New Labour. Indeed, as we shall see, it is impossible properly to understand the ideological thrust of New Labour without placing the Blairite party historically in this way: as a reaction to the unprecedented impact on the Labour Party of a generation of left-wing forces associated in particular with the policies and personality of Tony Benn.[1]

1   At last this period of left-wing Labour ascendancy has been properly chronicled (Panitch and Leys, 1997).

Within the Labour Party itself, however, New Labour (as we shall see in more detail in the next section) has two historical reference points, not just one. New Labour certainly defines itself against Old Labour understood as the Bennite Left; but it also defines itself against Old Labour understood as the governmental practices of the postwar Labour administrations led by Attlee, Wilson and Callaghan. For socialism before New Labour was not just a socialism of ideas (as laid out by particular wings of left-wing political parties, or by whole parties of varying kinds): it was also a set of governmental experiences, a set of dominant policy packages and associated modes of implementation. Socialism in Britain to the generation who fought the Second World War meant the main policy lines of the Attlee government: public ownership of basic industries, direct state controls over private economic activity and the creation of an extensive welfare state. By the time first Wilson and then Callaghan led Labour governments a generation later, the policy package had shifted slightly. Welfare provision remained at the core of what both politicians and their electorate understood as socialism; but public ownership was less central to the project by then (though in fact the 1970s saw a second wave of extensive nationalisations), having been replaced in the socialist canon by the idea of extensive state aid to industry and the creation of national champions in each leading industrial sector. The tight administrative controls inherited by the Attlee government from the wartime coalition had also long gone, replaced in policy dominance by a commitment to Keynesian demand management (in the 1950s), to indicative state planning (in the 1960s) and to extensive tripartite economic management a decade later. By the 1970s socialism and corporatism had become synonymous in the public mind: as had both with the provision of an extensive welfare network that left the state as a major employer and provider of educational, health and social services. New Labour inherited as the popular understanding of socialism not just competing ideas about the proper relationship of capital, labour and the state, but also a tradition of governing in which public institutions took precedence over private ones and in which the working of the capitalist market was hedged about by high levels of state regulation and policy-making networks.[2]

New Labour: messages and policies

What divides the modern Labour Party from even the latest manifestations of Old Labour government and left-wing ascendancy is the great political trench of Thatcherism. The Wilson and Callaghan governments stand on one side of nearly two decades of Conservative ascendancy in Britain; the

2   The rise of New Labour has made the history of Old Labour politically important again. See Miliband (1973), Coates (1975) and Elliott (1993).

new Blairite government stands on the other. Between them lie four general election defeats for a Labour Party in transition (to use Blairite language for the moment) from 'old' to 'new': the defeats of 1979, 1983, 1987 and 1992. The width and depth of that trench has been the great legitimating backcloth for the whole Blairite project, silencing critics as much as inspiring adherents. Tony Blair led the Labour Party back to power at the end of a period in which – for many years – such a possibility looked literally beyond the capacity of any Labour leader to deliver. In 1983 the Labour Party stood on the brink of the electoral abyss, with only 27.6 per cent of the popular vote (a lower percentage than that attained by the Labour Party at any general election since 1918) and, perhaps more significantly, with only 2.2 per cent more of the vote than the SDP–Liberal Alliance. In 1983 the Labour Party came within a whisker of slipping down into third place in the hierarchy of British political parties. Yet by 1997 the Party had recovered from that election trauma to hold 43.2 per cent of the vote and – more significantly – to enjoy a parliamentary majority of 179: one bigger by far even than those of Attlee and Wilson at their peaks. Left-wing Labour took the Party to the edge of electoral obscurity. The Blairites brought the Party back to probably a decade or more of power. That at least is how New Labour sees the Party's recent past and immediate future.

So what was (and is) New Labour? By its own reckoning it is definitely not Old Labour. New Labour presents itself as being everything that the Party of 1983 was not. It also presents itself, less stridently but with equal determination, as qualitatively different from the Party of 1974–9 (Blair, 1996, pp. 123–4). New Labour has been keen to create in the public mind a sharp set of distinctions between what it now offers and what both Labour governments in the 1970s and the Labour Party in 1983 offered and represented. Indeed, it has seen in the establishment of those distinctions its only route back to power. As Tony Wright MP put it: 'it's clear from our recent electoral history [that] a lot of people have simply walked away from the Labour Party, walked away emotionally from it, and something had to be done about that'.[3] For that reason, if for no other, New Labour has been keen to heed 'the messages that the voters have been trying during the 1980s to send to Labour' (Wright, 1997, p. 23), messages which collectively constitute a clear guide to New Labour's understanding of the gap between itself and its Party's immediate past.

> There was an assortment of messages.... That a party agenda that seemed to revolve only around more state control and higher taxes was out of tune

---

3   Tony Wright MP in conversation with the author for the BBC/OU television programme *The 1997 Election: Traditions, Failures and Futures* (interview, 20 October 1997).

with the times. That it was not enough to be a caring party if the caring could not be paid for or priorities clearly established. That a party that seemed to be the prisoner of outside interests could not pursue the public interest. That a party that represented producer interests could not properly represent consumer interests, not least in the public sector. That a party that seemed more interested in defending yesterday's economy than in creating the conditions for tomorrow's was on the wrong track. That a party whose instincts on so many fronts appeared defensive and conservative was unlikely to be a source of radical ideas. That a party that seemed to be on an ideological trip from somewhere in the past ... was increasingly irrelevant to a changed world. (Wright, 1997, pp. 23–4)

So, initially, New Labour can best be placed by comparing its underlying strategies and immediate policy concerns with those of the Labour Party in 1983 (when the Bennite Left was in its ascendancy) and with those of the Labour governments led by Wilson and Callaghan in the 1970s (when corporatism and trade union power were very much the order of the day).

New Labour is not the Party of 1983. The 1983 Labour Party was a party of state ownership and control, in possession of an Alternative Economic Strategy which committed it to what it termed in its 1983 election manifesto an extensive programme of 'socialist reconstruction' based on an 'emergency programme of action'. That emergency programme was to have included a major increase in public investment, in house building, in job subsidies and in training allowances. The manifesto committed the Party to a five-year national plan negotiated primarily with the trade unions, to the renationalisation of all the firms and industries privatised by the Conservatives and to the withdrawal of the British economy from the European Community. It also committed the Party to exchange controls and to selective import quotas. New Labour's economic policy is light years away from any of that. Instead of controlling private industry and regulating market forces in the Bennite manner, New Labour is committed to the creation of 'a new partnership between government and industry, workers and managers – not to abolish the market, but to make it dynamic and work in the public interest, so that it provides opportunities for all' (Blair, 1996, p. 32). New Labour's economic policy is built around the consolidation of a close working relationship between government and progressive employers, one in which trade union power hardly figures at all, and in which a 'partnership with the trade unions' certainly does not, as was the case in the 1983 manifesto, 'stand at the heart of our programme'.

New Labour's economic policy is also built upon the explicit recognition and endorsement of the importance of market competition and the desirability of private enterprise. New Labour's leader certainly believes in markets. As he told the *Financial Times* as early as 1994, 'we want a dynamic market economy. It is not merely that I, as it were, with hesitation, acknowledge that this is the way we have to go, I say that it is positively in the public interest to have a dynamic market economy' (11–12 June, p. 8). Tony Blair also believes in private enterprise. As he put it in an important policy speech to the City just before the general election:

> I certainly believe that where there is no over-riding reason for preferring the public provision of goods and services – particularly where those services operate in a competitive market – then the presumption should be that economic activity is best left to the private sector with market forces being fully encouraged to operate. (*The Guardian*, 8 April 1997, p. 1)

Contrast that with the Labour Party's intention in 1983 to 'use agreed development plans ... negotiat[ed] with the large companies that dominate our economy, so as to influence their purchasing and development policies'; and to create a Foreign Investment Unit to 'monitor closely the activities of multinational corporations' to ensure that they operated within 'clearly laid down guidelines'.

However, New Labour's commitment to a concordat with business must not be understood as a Blairite creation alone. It is best seen as the culmination of a steady and incremental policy shift by successive Labour leaderships after 1983 from what they came to see as that year's 'far left excesses' (Mandleson and Liddle, 1996, p. 213): a policy shift that took both them and the Party from the 1983 position (the renationalisation of all privatised firms), to merely the social ownership of stakes in privatised companies (in 1987), to the stronger regulation of privatised utilities (1992) and finally to the advocacy of joint public–private partnerships (in 1997).[4] It was a policy shift, moreover, that brought with it an explicit acceptance, by the Blairite leadership, of the broad legacy of the Thatcher years, an explicit willingness on their part to leave 'intact the main changes of the 1980s in industrial relations and enterprise' in return for a 'new partnership with business for the future' built around a 'new agenda ... education, welfare reform, infrastructure, leadership in Europe' (Tony Blair, quoted in Anderson and Mann, 1997, pp. 40–1). By 1997, as the new Prime Minister told the Party conference, 'partnership between public and private sectors was the only language this New Labour government will respect'. New Labour sees its route to economic growth through the harnessing of the self-interest of what earlier generations of socialists would have called 'the national bourgeoisie'. 'For business', as Blair put it, 'this will be a government on your side, not in your way' (*Financial Times*, 1 October 1997, p. 1).

The 1983 Party was also heavily committed to the redistribution of wealth and power, and to the provision of an extensive and largely unreformed set of welfare services. New Labour is not. In 1983 the Party proposed to increase public spending (and to borrow extensively to finance

---

4   For the stages in that story, see Heffernan and Marquesee (1992); the epilogue to Wickham Jones (1996); and Thompson (1996b).

its investment programme), to tax the rich, to raise child benefit, to tie pensions to inflation or average earnings (whichever was growing fastest), to phase out health charges and to develop a range of disability benefits. But both before and after the 1997 election, New Labour articulated a quite different attitude to taxation, public spending and social equality. The New Labour message has been (and remains) that the Party is now determined – as Tony Blair put it when launching Labour's 1997 manifesto – to put 'the final nail in the coffin of the old tax-and-spend agenda' (*The Guardian*, 4 April 1997, p. 13). As if to underscore the point, the incoming Labour government adopted the spending ceilings inherited from its Conservative predecessor, and blocked off or postponed a range of initially radical welfare commitments because of the resulting non-availability of state finance. Indeed, New Labour in power has quickly made a virtue of 'thinking the unthinkable', taking what it calls 'hard decisions' and making 'hard choices' (invariably choices – it should be noted – which erode the options for the poorest sections of the community rather than the rich – hitting the rich is clearly not tough enough for New Labour); and Tony Blair has spoken with enthusiasm of his government's intention to create a society characterised by 'compassion with a hard edge'. He told the first Labour Party conference after the election:

> A strong society cannot be built on soft choices. It means fundamental reform of our welfare state, of the deal between citizen and society. It means getting money out of social breakdown and into schools and hospitals where we want to see it. The new welfare state must encourage work, not dependency. (*The Guardian*, 1 October 1997, p. 8)

So, in the world of New Labour, unlike that of the Labour Party in 1983, wealth creation is not to be taxed. Equality of opportunity, not equality of outcome, is the new watchword; and though major commitments remain from the 1980s, to welfare provision, to an improved National Health Service and to enhanced educational provision – indeed, 'education, education, education' was Blair's chosen mantra as he entered the election campaign – it is clear that New Labour's understanding of their welfare agenda is as much driven by their economic concerns as their social values. Equipped with the fashionable intellectual equipment of 'post neo-classical endogenous growth theory' (with its emphasis on the importance of investment in human capital as the key to economic growth and international competitiveness) (see Crafts, 1996), and influenced too from the USA by the arguments of people like Robert Reich (1992) (that the key to attracting overseas investment in an age of global capital lies in the level of skills in the labour force), New Labour has adopted with enthusiasm the strategy of 'welfare to work'. The whole thrust of New Labour's planned reform of the welfare state is to create the opportunity (and significantly, or ominously, depending on your politics, also the *responsibility*) for all those who can engage in paid work to do so: and this enthusiasm for moving people off welfare sits perilously close to the earlier Thatcherite hostility to welfare recipients as victims of a dependency culture.

Of course, New Labour does not see itself as Thatcherite in its welfare policies and is irritated by any accusation of such a similarity. Rather it sees 'welfare reform' as part of its general modernising strategy: a strategy of bringing old values up to date in a world which is now different from that which surrounded the early architects of the modern welfare state. 'The world has changed since Beveridge,' Tony Blair told the Fabians in 1995, and, because it has, 'we need a new settlement on welfare for a new age, where opportunity and responsibility go together' (Blair, 1996, p. 19). Part of what makes that new age new, for those supporting New Labour's welfare reforms, is that the world of work has changed dramatically since the 1940s: not least with the reappearance of long-term unemployment and the unprecedented entry of women into paid labour. But part of what establishes the novelty of the new age is the diminished willingness of those in work to finance those who are not. It is New Labour's view that 'we have reached the limits of the public's willingness simply to fund an unreformed welfare system through ever higher taxes and spending'.[5] This is not to say that the attitude of New Labour to welfare reform is exactly that of its Conservative predecessors. It is not. At the very least, the language of New Labour in relation to welfare reform is not the language of Thatcherism. It is still the language of opportunity, empowerment and hope: but it is also a language (as was that of its predecessors in power) which possesses great electoral appeal to those in work, whose tax receipts fund the meagre incomes of those excluded (by age, illness, disability or family responsibilities) from participation in capitalist labour markets. Labour's welfare reforms have yet to shake out, but it is at least possible that, when they do, we will see that, to its governmental alliance with the progressive bourgeoisie, New Labour has explicitly added an electoral alliance with the tax-paying middle classes.

If New Labour's understanding of its tasks and options is light years removed from the 1980s Labour Party at its most radical, New Labour has also been keen to establish its distance from the policies and predilections of the Wilson and Callaghan governments to which that Bennite radicalism was so powerful an initial response. For the 1974–9 Labour governments were ultimately corporatist in thought and intention (Coates, 1980). New Labour is not. The Wilson and Callaghan governments were committed to the building of a strong national manufacturing base via heavy state action in industry. New Labour is not. Labour governments before 1979 were committed to the consolidation of a close working relationship with national

5   Tony Blair, to the Commons, on the occasion of the Labour government's first
     Queen's speech (*The Guardian*, 14 May 1997, p. 1).

trade union leaders. New Labour is not. Instead, New Labour is a powerful advocate of the desirability of globalisation and of the need for flexible labour markets. It is adamant that there should 'be no going back to nationalisation or to corporatist management of the economy in which the state created industrial strategies designed to "pick winners"' (Tony Blair quoted in *The Guardian*, 8 April 1997, p. 1). It is also extremely wary of any close relationship with the trade union movement that might smack of old-style corporatism. New Labour had 'no proposals to return to tripartite institutions or beer and sandwiches at No. 10' (*ibid.*). It is not that New Labour is explicitly anti-trade union, in a Thatcherite fashion. On the contrary, the Blair government has promised (and no doubt will deliver) a modest degree of new legislative rights for workers and their representatives. It is also committed to the introduction of a minimum wage and has signed up to the European Union's Social Chapter. But in each case, the moves made (or planned) are extremely modest in content (and are invariably more symbolic than real in their labour market effects); and they fall within a determined commitment by New Labour to sustain the degree of labour market flexibility inherited from the Conservatives.

Time and again before the 1997 election, New Labour advocates conceded the general validity and desirability of Conservative trade union legislation after 1979 (e.g. Blair, 1996, p. 123; Mandelson and Liddle, 1996, pp. 12–13). Time and again after the election, New Labour ministers have proclaimed both the virtue and the necessity of keeping wages down and labour productivity up. As Tony Blair told his predominantly business audience at the launch of the IPPR's report *Promoting Prosperity: A Business Agenda* in January 1997, 'we want to keep more flexible labour markets. Our proposals for change would amount to less labour market regulation than in the USA' (Anderson and Mann, 1997, p. 41). It is not that New Labour wishes to shut the unions out in the pursuit of such a labour market vision. On the contrary, Tony Blair remains committed to the view that harmonious industrial relationships, based on mutual trust and respect, both explain the phenomenal growth stories of the Asian tigers and are needed in Britain, too. It is simply that New Labour ministers will deal sympathetically only with those trade unions which share this vision, and which cooperate in its attainment. As Tony Blair told his audience at the 1997 conference of the Trades Union Congress (TUC), the key modern fight facing the incoming Labour government is to create and sustain a competitive economy, and he 'want[ed] the unions to be part of that fight'. But New Labour would not go back to 'the days of industrial warfare, strikes without ballots, mass and flying pickets, secondary action and the rest'. New Labour, he told his audience, 'will keep the flexibility of the present labour market. It may make some shiver, but I tell you in the end it's warmer in the real world'.[6]

6 Speech to the TUC, Brighton, 9 September 1997, p. 8

The third way

That real world needs a new politics, according to New Labour; and New Labour sees itself as the new party for the new age. The very title adopted by the Blair leadership – that their party was the party of *New* Labour – signalled very clearly their belief in the qualitative transformation of the world in which the Labour Party must govern, and of the associated necessity for party transformation. Commentators and critics alike have been quick to record New Labour's verbal assertion of its modernity and newness. The term 'new' appeared 107 times, apparently, in the Party's 1996 *Road to the Manifesto* document (*The Guardian*, 5 July 1996, p. 13); and Tony Blair reportedly used the term 'new' thirty-seven times in a single hour-long speech to the 1995 party conference (Harrison, 1996, p. 2). This intensity of usage was not, of course, in any way accidental. It was, as Neil Kinnock later observed, *the* way in which:

> Tony Blair and the modern [*sic*] leadership of the Labour Party put a huge distance in reality and in public perception between the party that is now in government with a huge majority and the party that looked, for a period, 17, 18 years ago, as if it was never, ever going to be interested in government again.[7]

In policy terms, New Labour likes to present itself as a 'third way' between Old Labour and Thatcherism (Tony Blair, quoted in *The Guardian*, 8 April 1997, p. 1): one that combines the strengths of each while avoiding weaknesses rooted in the one-sidedness (in Blairite terms) of each of those previous political projects. As far as New Labour is concerned, Old Labour was excessively statist. Thatcherism was overly committed to market solutions. The Blairite third way involves a combination of both. It is a combination well laid out in Mandelson and Liddle's *The Blair Revolution* (1996), but even better captured by Tony Wright:

> in the past the Left believed that its job was to broadly embrace the state and to attack markets, and the Right on the whole believed it was its job to embrace markets and attack the state. I think we've reached a politics which understands the limitations of both those analyses, that it's possible to see what the state might do and possible to see what the market might do. That's where politics is at now, trying to find a way in which states and markets can be constructed for the public interest. But that's very different from the old way we used to talk about the mixed economy ... the Keynesian mixed economy, which simply said there shall be a market sector and there

---

7 Neil Kinnock in conversation with the author for the BBC/OU Television programme *The 1997 Election: Traditions, Failures and Futures* (interview, 23 October 1997).

shall be a state sector, and there shall be co-habitation between the two. Not that – well how can it be when we've seen so much of the public sector go into the market sector. What it is though, I think, is a way of saying 'given the fact that we on the Centre-Left have said we believe in certain things, how can those things be advanced by using the state and by using the market in different ways?' Now once you say that, you do get into quite new territory in thinking about how you regulate markets, how you organise the state, how these things come together. I think this is generally uncharted territory.[8]

At the core of New Labour's self-confidence in the viability (and radicalism) of its third way is a belief that markets, properly harnessed, can produce both economic growth and social justice. That self-confidence is partly a product of its adoption of what we earlier referred to as 'new growth theory', what Noel Thompson has called 'supply-side socialism': one which 'aims to increase the flow, enhance the quality and improve the use of factor inputs; the primary objective being to increase productive efficiency, reduce unit costs and crucially, enhance Britain's international competitiveness' (Thompson, 1996a, p. 39). The route to that competitiveness, according to the new growth theorists, is a set of government policies which aim to reskill and re-educate the labour force, encourage long-term investment, create flexible labour markets and retune 'the welfare state to reduce dependency and encourage self reliance' (Dunleavy, 1997, p. 13). Underpinning New Labour's confidence in its third way too is a more general faith in the ability of an economy to grow best when trust relationships prevail in the workplace. The Blairites entirely buy into the argument that trust-based capitalisms work better than purely market-based ones and that capital and labour must therefore work together to produce necessary technical change. They also buy fully into the wider social argument of communitarian thinkers like Etzioni, that economies (and societies) flourish best when the social bonds within them are firmly rooted in notions of mutual responsibility and duty.[9] New Labour, that is, has its own new language to set against Thatcherism's litany of market, choice and freedom. New Labour's language is 'one of community, solidarity, inclusiveness, fairness'.[10] It is the language of 'stake-holding'.

8 Tony Wright MP in conversation with the author for the BBC/OU television programme *The 1997 Election: Traditions, Failures and Futures* (interview, 20 October 1997).
9 This is very clear in the texts of both the Blair speeches made on his Far East tour in January 1996: those in Singapore and Tokyo.
10 Tony Wright MP in conversation with the author for the BBC/OU television programme *The 1997 Election: Traditions, Failures and Futures* (interview, 20 October 1997).

The concept of stake-holding is currently very fashionable on the British centre-left, where it has been much popularised by Will Hutton and where it has attracted the attention (and advocacy) of a string of influential intellectuals, not least David Marquand, John Kay, John Gray, John Plender and even Frank Field.[11] The academics attracted to stake-holding have offered it both as the key to economic revival (with trust-based stake-holder capitalisms outperforming market-based non-stake-holder ones) and as the guarantor of social harmony (with socially inclusive stake-holder societies free of the poverty and criminality characteristic of the socially divided market-based capitalist systems). Stake-holding is offered by them as 'the key to the high trust and willing co-operation between executives and workers, government and citizens, that is the secret of enduring success and survival in post-industrial society' (Perkin, 1997, p. 41), and is projected as the cornerstone of a coherent new politics for the entire centre-left. As Will Hutton put it:

> what underpins the fundamental idea of stake-holding is that social and economic inclusion, rather than equality, should be the over-riding objective for the contemporary left. Inclusion implies membership: you cannot be included if you are not a member. But membership entails obligations as well as rights. So a stakeholder society and a stakeholder economy exist where there is a mutuality of rights and obligations constructed around the notion of economic, social and political inclusion. What stakeholder capitalism does is to apply those principles to the operation of free market capitalism and by doing so it places limits on the operation of unfettered markets. (Hutton, 1994, p. 3)

By arguing in this way, and by developing so extensive a critique of Thatcherite Britain in the process, the advocates of stake-holding provided New Labour with two critical things which had visibly been missing from Labour politics in the early years of the Thatcherite ascendancy. It gave New Labour the start of a much-needed conceptual armoury with which to resist neo-liberal advocacy of unregulated capitalism; and in consequence it offered a powerful benchmark against which to set a systemic, wide-ranging and convincing critique of Conservative Britain. When all that Thatcherism faced was a discredited Keynesianism, the centre-left could make no progress: programmatically, electorally or hegemonically. Once the notion of stake-holding had been developed, the centre-left possessed again its 'big idea', its 'much needed intellectual glue for New Labour's policies (Leadbeater and Mulgan, 1996, p. 16), its 'theoretical spine around which detailed policies can cohere' (Marquand, 1995, p. 15). Stake-holding was

---

11 The key text here is Will Hutton's *The State We're In* (1994). See also Kelly *et al.* (1997).

both too limited and ambiguous a concept to do the entirety of New Labour's job for it: but it did at least contain 'the seeds of a post-Thatcher, post-Labourist project for the left which has a strong individualist dimension with its emphasis upon autonomy, rights and obligations, as well as a radical critique of the institutional obstacles to the creation of a more meritocratic and just society and an efficient economy' (Kelly *et al.*, 1997, p. 239). The concept of stake-holding offered New Labour, that is, the chance of establishing a hegemonic project again.

There have been moments when it looked as though New Labour intended to use the notion of stake-holding in this fashion, as the cornerstone of its new politics and indeed (since the New Labour project is still in formation) it could yet. Mandleson and Liddle (1996), when launching New Labour's broad agenda before the 1997 general election, certainly used stake-holding in this way, arguing that an incoming Labour government 'must do whatever it can to promote a stakeholder culture in industry and the City, and must tackle long-term unemployment to ensure that everyone should have a stake in society and no one should be excluded from it' (pp. 19, 87–8). In similar fashion, when Tony Wright (1997, p. 42) explained 'why [we should] vote Labour', 'a new language of stake-holding, community, inclusiveness and responsibility' figured prominently in his arguments. And well it might, because Tony Blair had embraced the idea explicitly in a widely cited speech given in Singapore in January 1996, when he argued that:

> the implications of creating a stake-holder economy are profound. They mean a commitment by government to tackle long term and structural un-employment ... a stake-holder welfare system ... [an] education system guaranteed to serve all our people, not an elite .... the right relationship of trust between business and government ... [and the encouragement of the] self-employed and small business.... Working as a team is an effective way of working; or playing a sport; or running an organisation. My point is that a successful country must be run the same way. That cannot happen unless everyone feels part of the same team, trusts it and has a stake in its success and future.[12]

But significantly for our purposes here, Blair was then quick to put a moderate gloss on his understanding of this stake-holder revolution, as later also was his Financial Secretary to the Treasury, Alistair Darling. Blair told the Frost programme that stake-holding was simply a 'unifying theme or slogan ... an umbrella concept under which a multitude of more specific policy initiatives will comfortably sit' (Thompson, 1996a, p. 38). Dearing told the Sheffield stake-holder conference that 'creating a stake-holder

12 Tony Blair, speech to the Singapore Business Community, 8 January 1996.

economy is very much about creating a change of culture in the country. It does not rely on new rules or regulations or new Acts of Parliament. These are not the essence of achieving real change' (Kelly *et al.*, 1997, p. 16). As the organisers of that conference then pointed out, stake-holding lends itself to both an individualistic and a collectivist interpretation. A stake-holder society can be one in which 'individuals hold stakes in the form of jobs, skills, capacities and property' or it can be one in which those stakes are held 'in the form of representation in collective entities like companies and nation-states'. In the hands of radicals like Will Hutton, 'the focus is on structures and economy-wide institutions'. But significantly, it is 'the individualist approach, by contrast, which is an increasingly important strand of New Labour thinking', where the priority is seen 'not as changing institutions but as helping individuals' (Kelly *et al.*, 1997, pp. 240–1). In Hutton's hands, stake-holding is a new form of society, one which empowers consumers, communities, long-term suppliers and workers against the dispro-portionate influence on economic decision-making of bankers, shareholders and owners. In Blair's hands, stake-holding is a much blander affair – one in which everyone has a stake (whatever that means) but in which pre-existing power relationships (particularly in private industry) remain largely unaltered. Blair has been quite explicit on that: 'this vision is quite simple. Everyone should have a stake in the economy. The stakeholder economy is not about giving power to corporations or unions or interest groups. It is about giving power to ... the individual' (Webb, 1996, p. 20).

So, the notion of stake-holding in the hands of New Labour seems unlikely to trigger a major resetting of the distribution of rights and responsibilities in the modern *economy*.[13] What seems more certain is that the notion of stake-holding in the hands of New Labour will be used to respecify the distribution of rights and responsibilities in a modern *society*. At times the language of New Labour on stake-holding is a language of new rights – for consumers, communities, parents, patients, even workers – rights to proper information, to high school standards, to hospital care, to retraining, to union recognition. But more normally the emphasis in New Labour's treatment of stake-holding is on duties and responsibilities and in particular on the responsibility of parents to control delinquent children and on the obligation of welfare recipients to move back into paid employ-ment. In a party committed to being 'tough on crime, tough on the causes of crime' (the sound bite on which, after all, Tony Blair began his meteoric rise to power) the notion of stake-holding quickly allows New Labour to place responsibility for reducing the incidence of delinquency and criminality on to those closest to the delinquents and criminals, for the Blairite vision of a stake-holder society is one based on strong communities, conventional families and a widespread respect for law and order. 'Duty', as Tony Blair

13 For the Blairite retreat from 'the big idea', see Thompson (1996a, p. 38).

understands it, 'is the cornerstone of a decent society' (1996, p. 237) and it is one that New Labour intends to foster by tough policies on youth crime, school truancy and inadequate parenting. Well might Tony Wright observe that 'some people may feel uneasy about Labour's emphasis on community and responsibility, thinking that at best it is irrelevantly nostalgic and at worst dangerously authoritarian'. In his view it is neither, but it does 'involve a challenge both to the possessive individualism of the New Right and to the thin rights-based liberalism of some of the Old Left' (1997, p. 78). It certainly does!

The reality of New Labour

The question therefore remains of how new, how radical and how socialist is the reality of New Labour. Its leading figures are keen to assert both its novelty and its radicalism, and to present it as a reconstitution of well established centre-left political traditions. In doing so, its adherents character-istically place New Labour in three ways: as a qualitative break from Thatcherism; as a politics firmly rooted in the basic and persistent values of the Labour tradition; and as a fusion of that tradition with an equally indigenous left-wing liberalism. Each of those placings is highly contested elsewhere on the British left and therefore needs to be considered in detail and in turn.

The supporters of New Labour are adamant that 1997 *was* a watershed election, marking a sharp break with the previous Thatcherite project; and they quickly become irritated by claims that it is not. Tony Wright, for example, put it this way:

> There is a fundamental difference of approach and belief between the New Conservatives and New Labour ... there might only be an inch of difference between a Labour Government and a Government of the right, [but] it [is] an inch worth living in.... There are moments and places when an inch can feel like a mile and this is one of them.... That inch matters, and it may be more than an inch, it may be an inch and a half, maybe two inches.... Anything that says this doesn't really matter is a kind of corrosive approach to politics that has served the Left very ill in the past. I fight furiously for the fact that we're into difference territory here.[14]

The advocates of New Labour are also prone to emphasise a basic continuity between their politics and those of Labour's distant past, and to do so particularly when they are engaged in the downplaying/discarding of previous Party policies or shibboleths. It is the recent past from which New Labour is keen to distance itself, while insisting that 'it has a moral outlook

14 Tony Wright MP in conversation with the author for the BBC/OU television programme *The 1997 Election: Traditions, Failures and Futures* (interview, 20 October 1997).

that Keir Hardie and Clement Attlee would fully have shared' (Mandleson and Liddle, 1996, p. 18). 'In renewing and modernizing itself', so the claim runs, New Labour 'has not repudiated its past' so much as 'rediscovered it' – applying 'traditional values to a modern setting' (Wright, 1997, p. 25). Tony Blair likes to present New Labour as the heir of the Party of Attlee – doing a similar job of national unification and renewal, but doing it in new circumstances and facing new challenges. The Blairite claim, made most explicitly in the process of resetting Clause 4 of the Party's constitution, was that in making such a move:

> our values do not change. Our commitment to a different vision of society stands intact. But the ways of achieving that vision must change. The programme we are in the process of constructing entirely reflects our values. Its objectives would be instantly recognisable to our founders. (Blair, 1996, p. 18)

The problem with this strident insistence on long-term continuity is that it has to live with an equally insistent assertion that New Labour is repositioning the Party, moving it into what the Blairites like to call the 'radical centre' of British politics. Tony Blair has spoken of New Labour as a 'party of the Centre as well as of the Centre-Left' (1996, p. 30). He has repeatedly made clear his own enthusiasm for early-twentieth-century 'new liberalism' and he has acknowledged his (and the whole Labour Party's) debt to such figures as Lloyd George, Keynes and Beveridge (p. 7). Indeed, New Labour under his leadership seems set on reconfiguring the entire political landscape of late-twentieth-century Britain, with an eye to making the next century a period of centre-left dominance. That may well involve (after changes in electoral laws) coalition politics between New Labour and the modern Liberal Democrats. It certainly involves the articulation of a political philosophy that is 'new liberal' (and not simply social democratic) in inspiration.

But Tony Blair does not see in this fusion of Labourist values with those of early-twentieth-century new liberalism any abandonment of the Labour Party's identification with the politics of socialism. On the contrary, for him such an infusion of ideas from the left wing of liberal politics is fully in the British socialist tradition. It is not, of course, in the socialist tradition that stretches back to Marx; but then Tony Blair explicitly rejects the relevance and desirability of that socialist tradition. He sees 'the socialism of Marx, of centralised state control of industry and production, [as] dead' (Blair, 1994, p. 3). New Labour traces its brand of socialism back to earlier Christian and ethical systems of belief. Socialism, for New Labour, is not a matter of changing ownership structures, altering class power, or triggering collective empowerment. It is rather a question of resetting the complex relationship between the individual and society. When Tony Blair talks of socialism he actually means a set of very practical things – jobs, training, social unity, national pride (e.g. Blair, 1996, pp. 29–30) – or, more generally, 'the need of society to act together to achieve what the individual cannot do alone' (Blair, 1991, p. 32). Socialism understood in this way, as a resetting of the interplay between the individual and the wider society, is fully in the tradition of radical/left liberalism that has come down to us through Hobhouse from the later John Stuart Mill. It is an understanding of socialism, moreover, which enables New Labour to assert the importance of 'the social' against the rampant individualism of the Thatcherite project, while using the language of individual rights and responsibilities against older, and more Marxist, conceptions of socialism.

From the many Blair speeches treating socialism in this way, two will suffice to illustrate the point: the first from his Fabian pamphlet on 'socialism' from 1994, the second from his 1945 commemoration address (to the Fabians again) in 1995.

> Social-ism [as Blair preferred to spell it in 1994] contains an ethical and subjective judgement that individuals owe a duty to one another and to a broader society – the Left view of citizenship. And it believes, objectively, that it is only through recognising that interdependence and by society as a whole acting upon it – the collective power of all used for the individual good of each – that the individual's interests can be advanced. It does not set apart individual interests and the interests of society as the Tories do. It takes an enlightened view of self-interest and regards it, broadly, as inextricably linked to the interests of society. (Blair, 1994, p. 4)

> Socialism is based on a moral assertion that individuals are interdependent, that they owe duties to one another as well as to themselves, that the good society backs up the efforts of the individuals within it, and that common humanity demands that everyone be given a platform on which to stand. It has an objective basis too, rooted in the belief that only by recognising their interdependence will individuals flourish, because the good of each does depend on the good of all. This conception of socialism requires both a form of politics in which we share responsibility both to fight poverty, prejudice and unemployment, and to create the conditions in which we can truly build one nation – tolerant, fair, enterprising, inclusive. (Blair, 1996, p. 15)

It is not difficult to see here a coherent line of radical thought linking the Blair understanding of socialism back to earlier advocates of ethical socialism such as R. H. Tawney and Alfred Marshall (see Dennis and Halsey, 1988) and Blair himself is convinced that the socialism he describes and advocates 'fundamentally was Attlee's kind of socialism' too (1996, p. 16); but that has not prevented others on the left finding his (and New Labour's) claims for radicalism and socialism vacuous, overdrawn or specious. An early and somewhat surprising critic from within Labour's own ranks has been Roy Hattersley, the deputy leader of the Party under Neil Kinnock and the man who nominated Tony Blair as Party leader in 1994. Roy

Hattersley sees himself very much as the keeper of the Croslandite legacy, the representative in the age of New Labour revisionism of the values and policies of an earlier Gaitskellite revisionism. For him, the current Labour Party is no longer loyal to the Croslandite democratic socialist view that 'the extension of liberty [is] impossible without the promotion of equality' (*The Guardian*, 4 September 1996, p. 15). Rather it has fallen into the hands of more moderate politicians – social democrats rather than democratic socialists, according to Hattersley – with the result that it is now 'hard to describe New Labour as a democratic socialist party' or as 'a force for a more equal society'. Because it is, he for one is 'no longer [prepared to be] loyal to Labour' (*The Guardian*, 26 July 1997, p. 21).[15]

Roy Hattersley is not alone in his unease with the policy drift of New Labour in power. Many academic and journalistic commentators (e.g. Crouch, 1997; Hay, 1997) are already noting the strong continuities linking New Labour to its Conservative predecessors in government. The advocates of radical stake-holding have been particularly vocal about what they see as the conservatism of the social and economic agenda of the Blair government and about the 'tension between economic conservatism and political radicalism' in the entire New Labour project (Marquand, 1997). When Will Hutton was asked whether he thought 1997 would eventually be seen as a watershed election of the 1945 variety, or be understood more like the election of 1951, it is significant that – on balance – he plumped for 1951, saying:

> The Tories won in 1951 promising to govern as nicer social democrats than the outgoing Labour Government; and they left in place the entire settlement that the Labour Party put in place between 1945 and 1951. Mr Blair is going to leave in place the economic and social settlement struck by Major and Thatcher. There will be no re-nationalisation. Privatisation will stand. Almost the entire panoply of labour and trade union reforms that took place in the Thatcher and Major years will stand. The attitude to public expenditure will stand.... British society will be more unequal at the end of this period of office than it was when they took power. In a sense Blair – in economic and social policies – is governing in the shadow of his Conservative predecessors even while he re-configures the political map of the country so that the Tories are out of office. The Tories are governing in a sense through their surrogates, New Labour.[16]

15 Hattersley and David Blunkett (the Secretary of State for Education) clashed again in the columns of *The Guardian*, 26–28 November 1997, on New Labour's retreat on the issue of selection in secondary schools – a topic dear to the Croslandite heart.
16 Will Hutton in conversation with the author for the BBC/OU television programme *The 1997 Election: Traditions, Failures and Futures* (interview, 20 October 1997).

And, of course, the old Labour Left just do not see any socialism (or indeed radicalism) in New Labour at all. In the same series of interviews, this was Tony Benn's initial judgement on New Labour in power:

> My understanding of New Labour has been put very clearly by the Prime Minister: it is a new political party. I'm not a member of New Labour. I'm a member of the Labour Party. It is a new political party ... trying to build a national coalition.... New Labour wants to distance itself completely from the unions rather like the Democrats in America, and wants to get very close relations with business.... So to that extent it is different [from Old Labour], but it's more than that, because the repudiation of what it calls Old Labour is a repudiation of the whole history of the party; and the removal of Clause 4, with its commitment to securing for the workers by hand and brain the full fruits of their industry, is a repudiation of the vision for the future. So when you get a group of political leaders who cut themselves off from the past, and cut themselves off from the future, they are in a fundamentally different position, and they lose their cultural strength. Put in another way, the Labour Party is in the middle of a big identity crisis.[17]

Conclusion

New Labour is certainly a new politics, one that holds the prospect of a prolonged period of centre-left government. The signs are already there, however, that in the fusion of left-wing liberal ideas and more radical social democratic/socialist ones, the new balance to be struck is further to the right – is more conservative and moderate – than at any previous time in Labour's history. New Labour may still be socialist in its own terms; but those terms self-consciously exclude the majority of the analysis and policy adopted by socialists in all their previous twentieth-century forms. That is fine if New Labour is right in its belief that new times require new politics. But it is not fine if they are wrong. If, contrary to New Labour's view, it transpires that the old beast of capitalism remains alive and well into the next century, then New Labour may yet come to regret throwing out the socialist baby with the Bennite bath water. Because then, as New Labour in power necessarily alienates the very electorate it so wooed in opposition, it will inexorably fall to new parties of the left to reconstitute a recognisable and effective socialist politics capable of dealing with capitalism in its twenty-first-century form. New Labour controls the political agenda now and claims the moral high ground. There is no space now on the British left for anything but the Blairite party. Time alone will show if New Labour's monopoly of political space will be long lasting or (as many of us suspect)

17 Tony Benn in conversation with the author for the BBC/OU television programme *The 1997 Election: Traditions, Failures and Futures* (interview, 20 October 1997).

merely transitory. And if it is transitory, of course, later generations of the British left may place New Labour as a sad ending to one millennium and not, as its adherents now do, as a bright and exciting bridge to the next.

Reading

Anderson, P. and Mann, N. (1997) *Safety First: The Making of New Labour*, Granta.
Blair, T. (1991) 'The fundamental principle of socialism', *Marxism Today*, October.
Blair, T. (1994) *Socialism*, Fabian Society, pamphlet no. 565.
Blair, T. (1996) *New Britain: My Vision of a Young Country*, Fourth Estate.
Coates, D. (1975) *The Labour Party and the Struggle for Socialism*, Cambridge University Press.
Coates, D. (1980) *Labour in Power? A Study of the Labour Government 1974–79*, Longman.
Crafts, N. (1996) 'Post-neoclassical endogenous growth theory: what are its policy implications?', *Oxford Review of Economic Policy*, Vol. 12 (2), pp. 30–47.
Crouch, C. (1997) 'The terms of the neo-liberal consensus', *Political Quarterly*, Vol. 68 (4), pp. 352–60.
Dennis, N. and Halsey, A. H. (1988) *English Ethical Socialism*, Clarendon Press.
Dunleavy, P. (1997) 'New times in British politics', in P. Dunleavy *et al.* (eds), *Developments in British Politics 5*, Macmillan.
Elliott, G. (1993) *Labourism and the English Genius*, Verso.
Harrison, R. (1996) *New Labour as Past History*, European Labour Forum, pamphlet no. 8.
Hay, C. (1997) 'Blaijorism: towards a one-vision polity', *Political Quarterly*, Vol. 68 (4), pp. 372–8.
Heffernan, R. and Marquesee, M. (1992) *Defeats from the Jaws of Victory: Inside Kinnock's Labour Party*, Verso.
Hutton, W. (1994) *The State We're In*, Cape
Kelly, G., *et al.* (eds) (1997) *Stakeholder Capitalism*, Macmillan.
Leadbeater, C. and Mulgan, G. (1996) 'Labour's forgotten idea', *Financial Times*, 2 October, p. 16.
Mandleson, P. and Liddle, B. (1996) *The Blair Revolution*, Faber and Faber.
Marquand, D. (1995) 'Escape to the future', *The Guardian*, 1 May, p. 15.
Marquand, D. (1997) 'Blair's split personality', *The Guardian*, 16 July, p. 15.
Miliband, R. (1973) *Parliamentary Socialism*, Merlin.
Panitch, L. and Leys, C. (1997) *The End of Parliamentary Socialism: From New Left to New Labour*, Verso.
Perkin, H. (1997) 'The third revolution', in G. Kelly *et al.* (eds), *Stakeholder Capitalism*, Macmillan, pp. 35–48.
Reich, R. (1992) *The Work of Nations*, Vintage.
Thompson, N. (1996a) 'Supply-side socialism: the political economy of New Labour', *New Left Review*, Vol. 216.
Thompson, N. (1996b) *Political Economy and the Labour Party*, UCL Press.
Webb, B. (1996) 'Stakeholding: the big idea?', *New Statesman and Society*, 29 March.
Wickham Jones, M. (1996) *Economic Strategy and the Labour Party*, Macmillan.
Wright, T. (1997) *Why Vote Labour*, Penguin.

19

Conservatism after Major

Martin Durham

This chapter examines the electoral defeat of the Conservative Party in May 1997 and explores the nature of post-Thatcher Conservatism and the possibilities of the Party's revival.

Defeat

On 1 May 1997, after eighteen years in power, the Conservative Party was evicted from office. In 1979 Margaret Thatcher had been elected with 43.9 per cent of the vote, a success which was repeated first in 1983, when she gained 42.4 per cent, and then in 1987, when she gained 42.3 per cent. In 1990 it would not be the electorate but Tory MPs who would bring the Prime Minister down and initially it was far from clear whether her successor would continue either with her policies or with her record of victory. But in 1992, while the former was still uncertain, the latter was not and the Conservatives were re-elected on 41.9 per cent of the vote. The Party's grip on power, however, was becoming increasingly weaker and in 1997 its vote fell to 30.7 per cent, its lowest share of the vote since 1832. In terms of seats, the situation was even worse. Compared with its 1992 result, the Party had lost 178 seats, and only 165 remained, the lowest figure since 1906. No Conservative MPs survived in Scotland or Wales. None remained in Bristol or Leeds or Plymouth and only one in Birmingham.

The withdrawal of Britain from the Exchange Rate Mechanism (ERM) in September 1992 had struck a profound blow to the Conservative advantage of a reputation for economic competence. The Party entered the 1997 election with what it could have been forgiven as seeing as favourable economic indicators. Not only was inflation low but unemployment was falling and the housing market was healthy. But even while only a minority of voters thought that the economy was weaker than it had been at the last election, the electorate no longer had faith in the government and in many cases believed that their own quality of life had worsened. The two main parties were almost neck and neck when voters were asked which they thought might take the right decisions on the economy and Labour had even overtaken the Conservatives when electors were asked which party they preferred on income tax. Labour's pledge not to raise the rate of income tax had neutralised a key Tory advantage while another Conservative weapon, party unity (and Labour disunity), had been broken by New Labour's formidable appearance of agreement and the Tories' spiralling quarrel over Europe (Kellner, 1997; Norris, 1997; *The Observer*, 4 May 1997).

Division

In so decisively losing the 1997 election, the Conservative Party was suffering the consequences of its economic misjudgements. But even without the debacle over the ERM, the Major government had been remarkably ill-fated. On key issues, particularly privatisation, John Major had continued with Margaret Thatcher's agenda. But, having originally supported him, his predecessor had turned against him, convinced that he was not really 'one of us' either on Europe or on the central importance of reducing taxation. Nor had Major been able to stamp his own imprint on post-Thatcher Conservatism. At the Party's 1993 conference, seeking to restore the government's fortunes, he had called upon Conservatives to lead the country 'back to basics'. The speech had referred to a range of concerns, from sound money and traditional teaching to respect for the family and for the law. Coming as it did after a spate of attacks on single motherhood by Michael Howard, Peter Lilley and John Redwood, Major's words were widely seen as part of a government onslaught against sexual permissiveness. Some ministers, among them Kenneth Clarke, sought to resist such a move and the Prime Minister himself cast doubt on such an intention. In the event, however, a wave of scandals, sexual and otherwise (see Chapter 15), were to make Conservative MPs and ministers look more in need of moral lessons than fit to teach them to others, and rather than having positioned itself as the champion of high standards, the Major government instead appeared both confused and hypocritical (Durham, 1994a).

A subsequent round of scandals was to deal yet further blows to the government's standing and gave accusations of sleaze and corruption ever greater credibility. But it was Europe that was to prove the greatest problem for post-Thatcher Conservatism. Thatcher had taken Britain further into Europe but had protected her patriotic reputation through an abrasive defence of Britain's national interest in confrontation with the country's partners in the European Union (EU). Ultimately, her doubts over the direction that Britain was taking were to cost her first her Chancellor of the Exchequer, Nigel Lawson, then her Foreign Secretary, Geoffrey Howe, and finally the leadership itself. John Major's declaration soon after coming to power that he intended to put Britain at 'the heart of Europe' was to appal the Euro-sceptics of the Tory right and increasingly polarise the Party until, as Baker *et al.* (1993) have argued, Conservatives were to find themselves potentially facing their most far-reaching crisis since the Tariff Reform dispute of the early twentieth century and the furore over the Corn Laws seventy years before that. Where the row over Tariff Reform had severely damaged the Party's electoral chances, the dispute over the Corn Laws had led to it actually splitting. Issues that had far-reaching implications both for the Party's domestic policies and the nation's standing in the world had already demonstrated their ability to harm the Party, and now the issue of European union threatened to plunge it into chaos once again. Claims that a looming Euro-federalism endangered both Britain's parliamentary sovereignty and Thatcherite free market policies divided the Party into two warring camps, with Major seeking to court first one side, then the other. Eventually, he was to disappoint both. Many Euro-sceptics found it hard to vote for him in 1997. (Over 900,000 people voted for the pro-withdrawal UK Independence Party or the less sceptic but considerably more well resourced Referendum Party.) Conversely, the less numerous Euro-enthusiasts, unless they defected to Labour or the Liberal Democrats, had little choice but to remain with a party from which they felt increasingly alienated, led by a man they saw as the prisoner of their foes. Margaret Thatcher had pulled Conservatism to the right, marginalised her critics within the Party (the so-called 'wets' of the Tory left) and still managed to keep the Party united and in power. Ultimately, however, the very issue that had brought her leadership to an end proved no more controllable by John Major and would end not only his leadership but the Conservative Party's protracted period of office.

Decline

Although the Conservatives' percentage of votes had fallen with each general election since 1979, they had nonetheless been re-elected each time. Beneath the surface, however, the Party's organisation deteriorated through the years Conservatism was in power. In 1979 the Party had 1.5 million members. By 1992, membership had fallen to 500,000. Five years later, it had declined yet further to as low as 300,000. According to a survey conducted in the run-up to the 1992 election, only 16 per cent of members were under forty-five in a party whose average age was sixty-two. The Conservative Students organisation had 5,000 members, the Young Conservatives less than 3,000. And if the number of MPs suddenly collapsed in 1997, support had long been waning at local government level. In 1979 there were 12,100 Conservative councillors. In 1992 this had fallen to 8,300 and by 1997 to 4,400. (The Liberal Democrats had 300 more councillors at this point and controlled twenty-six councils to the Conservatives' twenty-three – and Labour's 205.) If there were scarcely enough active members able to go out to persuade voters to support the Party, the decline of a Conservative presence in the council chamber meant that, in the words of the former director of research at Conservative Central Office, the Party 'often lost the principal character who mobilises the whole team' (*The Observer*, 25 May 1997; Whiteley *et al.*, 1994, pp. 43, 225, 240; and *The Guardian*, 8 and 23 October 1997).

Revival or rout?

If, at local level, a swathe of leading figures had been lost, now that had happened at national level too. The response of John Major to such a cataclysmic landslide was to announce that he would resign as leader. A number of candidates emerged. One, Stephen Dorrell, withdrew quickly but five remained when the first round of the contest took place in early June 1997. The former Chancellor of the Exchequer, Kenneth Clarke, came first, with forty-nine votes, narrowly in front of the former Secretary for Wales, William Hague. Behind them, clustered closely together, had been John Redwood, Peter Lilley and Michael Howard. The last two withdrew and in the second round, a week later, Clarke again came first, with Hague immediately behind. Where Clarke appealed to pro-Europeans and those said to be on the left of the Party, the other candidates all appealed to the right. Redwood, who had unsuccessfully challenged Major for the leadership in 1995, appeared the most right wing, yet, after his withdrawal, he gave his support to Clarke. But the right-wing vote could not be delivered to the figure it had hitherto condemned and on 19 June Hague gained a decisive victory, gaining ninety-two votes to Clarke's seventy.

During the contest, Hague had moved decisively in a Euro-sceptic direction, declaring that the Party should oppose the single European currency for the duration of both the new Parliament and the next. Such a pledge, while disappointing to those who wanted membership to be ruled out altogether, was enough to ensure that the more pro-European figures in the Party would feel, to say the least, uncomfortable with his leadership. There were, indeed, some defections under both Major and his successor. The bulk of those who opposed the right, however, remained within the Party and, worryingly for the new leadership, the earlier Tory left parliamentary grouping, the Macleod group, was dissolved in order to focus energies on a new body, Conservative Mainstream, with Michael Heseltine and Kenneth Clarke prominent among its number (*The Independent*, 31 October 1997).

Running for the Party leadership, Hague had argued that it was vital to rebuild its organisation, modernise its use of the media and review policy so that it expressed the hopes of the country's electorate. Such a review, he declared, would mean adjusting 'some cherished ideas in the light of new social realities'. On the organisational front, Hague moved quickly. Faced both with demands from activists for a greater say in the Party and with the pressing urgency of improving its organisation, he decided upon a postal ballot of the membership to ask whether or not they supported his leadership election and the need for an overhaul of the Party's structure. Nearly 400,000 ballot papers were sent out. A little over 140,000 voted in favour of Hague's leadership and the need to reform the Party, with a little under 35,000 against.

The reform document itself, *Blueprint for Change*, argued that the Party was suffering not from cyclical problems but from a structural decline and that, in order at least to double its present size, it needed both to involve its members and to avoid the appearance of perpetual division. Organisational confusion between the voluntary wing of the Party, the parliamentary party and Conservative Central Office would be ended by the creation of a single governing body and the leader would be elected by an electoral college involving Party members, MPs, MEPs and peers. (Crucially, however, the proportion of each had not yet been decided.) The Conservative Political Centre would be revitalised to allow members to play a role in policy making, a Women's Network would 'encourage talented women' (only thirteen of the Party's 165 MPs were women) and a new youth organisation, Conservative Future, would be established. Conservative council leaders would be brought together in an annual conference as part of a revival of Conservatism in local government, a national shortlist would be drawn up for by-election candidates and consideration would be given to a quota of places for women on constituency selection lists. (This notion was to be quickly abandoned, not least as a result of objections by some women in the Party, offended by the suggestion that they were a grouping needing special help.) Finally, an Ethics and Integrity Committee would be established to deal with cases 'where the reputation of our party may be threatened' (*The Spectator*, 10 May 1997; *The Independent* and *The Guardian*, 8 October 1997; *Daily Mail*, 3 December 1997).

In the first of two speeches to the 1997 conference, Hague declared that it was vital that the Party change its attitudes, its organisation and its culture. It had lost the general election because it had been seen as 'arrogant, selfish' and 'out of touch' and in five years, he promised, 'our party will not look, or sound, or feel the same – but its enduring values will be as powerful as ever'. But it was his speech at the end of the conference that would be the most important. He had already in his opening speech called for a more inclusive party, bringing in more black people, more Asians and more of the young. In the run-up to his closing speech, the press reported that he would be calling for a Conservatism that was compassionate and tolerant, determined 'to show it cares'. Already in a surprising move, the former standard bearer of the right, Michael Portillo, who had lost his parliamentary seat to an openly gay Labour candidate, had spoken in a conference fringe meeting in support of tolerance for single mothers and Hague himself had indicated his sympathy for this view in a Channel 4 interview (see below – 'Conservatism and the family'). (It would later be revealed that the two had coordinated their plans to speak on the issue.) On the last day of the conference, apparent concern over alienating more traditionalist Conservatives muted Hague's views on single parenthood and he declared instead that his personal belief was that it was 'best for children to be brought up in a traditional family'. But the speech made it very clear that Hague did indeed want to present the Party as not only inclusive but caring, with 'compassion ... at its very core' (*Daily Mail*, 8 October 1997; *The Times*, 10 October 1997; *The Guardian*, 11 October 1997; *Sunday Times*, 12 October 1997).

Repositioning the Party, difficult as it would be, was only part of the new leadership's task. There remained organisational problems. The Party had opposed the creation of a Scottish Parliament, just as it opposed a Welsh Assembly, and the victory of the devolutionists in both the referendums in September had placed the Party in an even worse situation than after the defeat of 1 May. Hague had argued that if the results were to go against the Party's view then it would 'respect' the decision, but he had been unwilling to promise that a future Conservative government would not seek to reverse it. A commission set up to examine the structure of the Scottish Conservative and Unionist Party, however, reported that many of those who gave evidence held that the Party was seen as out of touch with ordinary Scots and that it would be best to abandon the old name for something clearly indicating a new identity (*The World This Weekend*, Radio 4, 27 July 1997; *Sunday Telegraph*, 8 December 1997).

Hague had also managed to alienate leading figures in the House of Lords by appearing to suggest that he agreed with Labour on the removal of voting rights from hereditary peers, something from which he quickly retreated. Perhaps most importantly, proposals for reform of the election of the Party leader had also alarmed MPs and, in the weeks that followed the conference, a number of them fought to assure the minimum possible say for ordinary members and the greatest possible portion of an electoral college for the parliamentary party. Ultimately, however, it was decided that while MPs would retain the power to remove the Party leader and select candidates for the leadership, the actual vote for any new leader would be a matter for Party members as a whole (*Daily Mail*, 1 October 1997; *The Times*, 13 October 1997; *Sunday Telegraph*, 23 November 1997; *The Guardian*, 17 February and 30 March 1998). It would not, plainly, be an easy task to restructure the Party and renew its appeal. As a moderniser, Hague looked to a future when Conservatism would once more be a highly efficient political vehicle. But could the Party, as befits Conservatives, also gain from past experience?

Learning from the past

It was not, of course, the first time that Conservatives had found themselves in opposition. The reform document discussed at the 1997 conference had emphasised that the Party's problems should not be seen as the result of temporary unpopularity. Instead, it argued, a fundamental restructuring was urgently needed. Reflecting on the Party's return to office after its defeats of 1964 and 1966 or 1945 and 1950 was understandably a comfort for some of those plunged so harshly into obscurity, and one reading of the latter experience was to prove particularly attractive. Hague's suggestion that in office 'Somehow ... the message of freedom' had 'got lost' fitted neatly with an interpretation of New Labour as committed to much of Conservatism's economics but retaining Old Labour's urge to regulate and interfere. In this argument, the Conservative Party was the libertarian party, Labour the authoritarian, and thus for the deputy director of the party's policy review, David Willetts, there was an encouraging lesson in the Party's recovery from its 1945 defeat. When Labour gained its landslide victory in the mid-1940s, he argued, it was 'supposedly in tune with the instincts of the British people'. By the end of the decade, however, it 'had got out of tune with those instincts' and the Conservatives had proved able to regain the initiative among an electorate increasingly irritated by Labour 'bossiness'. In arguing this, he was reiterating an argument he had already made in his 1992 book, *Modern Conservatism*. The Party, he had argued, had revived in the late 1940s by appealing to voters as the party of freedom and prosperity. Freedom, indeed, was not only a good in itself but was the road to economic success.

Whether made in 1992, on the brink of Conservative victory, or in 1997, after his party's defeat, such an argument is somewhat strange. While it rightly points out how the Conservative opposition had been highly critical of the efforts at planning and the rationing and queuing which characterised the Attlee years, and reminds us that Conservatism has the proven ability to renew itself, it obscures one all-important aspect of that recovery. As numerous writers have noted, the Conservatism of 1951 was not solely about freedom versus compulsion. Instead, as Willetts partly acknowledges, it was about accepting much of what Labour advocated and implemented as part of a new political landscape that could not be redrawn. Willetts (1992) noted that a third element of postwar Conservatism, alongside freedom and prosperity, had been an acceptance of 'large parts of the welfare state' (pp. 33–5). But there was more to Conservatism's repositioning than that. Labour had fundamentally redrawn the boundaries of the politically possible and the Conservatism that came to power in 1951 was unable to reverse the nationalisation of major industries or reject the state's responsibility for full employment. The new Conservatism of the 1950s and '60s had been the Conservatism of the postwar consensus, and Thatcherism came in the late 1970s not as its heir but as its fundamental critic (*The Spectator*, 10 May 1997; *The Observer*, 17 August 1997; on the Conservative Party in the late 1940s see Gamble, 1974, ch. 3; Schwarz, 1991).

Conservatism and consensus

Certainly, then, it would be a mistake to equate the new Conservatism of the late 1940s with the New Right Conservatism of the late 1970s. Where the former used such slogans as 'Set the People Free' in criticising Labour's excesses and curbing its ambitions, it did not denote a fundamental rejection of the world that Labour had made. When Margaret Thatcher talked of freedom thirty years later, it was increasingly to mean the abandonment of that world, a minimisation of social responsibility, a maximisation of individual responsibility. This is not to say that Thatcherism succeeded in, for instance, uprooting the welfare state in the way that it drastically reshaped the economy or curbed the role of the unions. But it is to argue that it both partly did and even more intended to take the country away from the form of state and of economy that had prevailed since the war. Major, it is clear, shared many of the assumptions that had motivated Thatcher and those around her and so, it can fairly be said, does Blair (see Chapter 18). Here, it is particularly worth comparing the consensus established in the 1940s with more recent developments.

The Conservatives did not have to share Labour's reasons for pursuing certain policies or concur with the extent it would take them in order for the term 'consensus' to be useful. The parties agreed on key areas and it was an agreement that Labour dominated ideologically, even if it was the Conservatives who were to prove particularly adept in the 1950s and early '60s in combining it with some of its own themes and, most importantly, with its own occupancy of office. Privatisation, union reform and the other facets of Thatcherism not only represented a shift away from this but in time became the basis of a new consensus.

We are already familiar with the notion that Tony Blair accepts not only the constraints of Conservative spending limits but the priorities of the market, the irreversibility of privatisation and lower income tax and much else that Labour has inherited from its predecessor. Less frequently noted is the effect that Thatcherism had on the Conservative Party itself, in which the Tory left at the beginning of the 1980s believed that the state had responsibility for full employment and that the unions could not – and should not – be humbled. In the 1990s, however, the Tory left accepted the break with the postwar consensus on economics but doubted how far it could be extended within social provision and, above all, found itself in the anti-Thatcher camp on the new fault line that opened up in the Party, that around Europe. The creation of a post-Thatcher consensus on economic and, to a lesser degree, social policy is a mixed blessing for the Conservative Party itself. It opens up possibilities, seen around the furore over lone parent benefit, of cracking the facade of unity in the Labour Party. But it makes it impossible to argue that only the Conservatives can be trusted to preside over a modernised and marketised Britain. It has other problems, too. One is the degree to which Thatcherism could be said to have overemphasised economic freedom at the expense of the need for social cohesion – and social control.

Conservatism and community

During her period of greatest success, Margaret Thatcher had given an interview to a woman's magazine (*Woman's Own*, 31 October 1987) which would return to haunt her and the Conservative Party again and again. Lamenting that people were concerned too much to look to government for help rather than look after themselves, she declared that there was 'no such thing as society'. Instead, there were 'individual men and women, and there are families'. Her defenders found themselves in the unhappy state of trying to claim that she had been misrepresented and had not really denied the existence of obligations and responsibilities beyond the individual when plainly that is what she had come perilously close to saying. Only her reference to families had saved her from arguing for a simple individualism – one which not only disavowed the government responsibilities which many voters continued to believe in but also failed to recognise what Conservatives have always been supposed to have understood, that beyond the market there are 'ties of history, community and nationhood' (Willetts, 1992, pp. 47–8).

The best defence – and understanding – of Thatcher's remarks would be to see them as pointing to the tensions in Thatcherism, tensions between a narrow economic individualism and an older, social conservatism concerned with the transmission of values and the maintenance of order. Thatcherism was not a break with the Conservative tradition, abandoning its traditional concerns for an obsession with the balance sheet and the unthinking pursuit of wealth. As her controversial pronouncements on 'Victorian values' and on religion made clear, she was engaged in an attempt to create a market order in which individuals understood and operated within a moral framework. It was not, however, a successful project. Although in the early 1980s critics of free market Conservatism had proved ineffective, their arguments proved far more damaging as social problems escalated and by the early part of the following decade the argument that Thatcherism, and post-Thatcher Conservatism, rejected the importance of social bonds had become particularly effective.

This was evident when in 1994 a sympathetic think-tank, the Social Market Foundation, published two pamphlets on the future of Conservatism. One, by the Oxford Professor of Politics John Gray, argued that the Conservative Party's adoption of free market ideology was likely to lead to its political destruction. Initially, he argued, an uncompromising defence of markets had been victorious over the failings of corporatism in Britain and of planning in the eastern bloc. But now new problems had emerged, to which those who believed in indefinite economic growth and uncontrolled market forces had no answer. Indeed, left to its own devices, the market undermined social and political stability, destroying jobs and desolating communities. Elevating consumer choice above human wellbeing, he declared, would lead not only to social breakdown but would destroy Conservatism as a credible political project (Gray and Willetts, 1997, pp. 3–9).

It was not an argument that was likely to persuade a champion of Conservatism whom we have already encountered, the MP and former Director of Studies of the Thatcherite think-tank the Centre for Policy Studies, David Willetts. Conservatives, he acknowledged, had become uncertain in the face of relentless criticism of the supposed effects of their free market policies. What was needed, he went on, was a defence of the market while insisting that Conservatism was about more than just economic transactions. It was about supporting the nation state and the family, the two most important non-market institutions, and it was not to be confused with a free market liberalism which viewed the individual only as an economic agent. Instead, it sought to find how best to bring together market and community, understanding the importance of the values and the relationships that were both good in themselves and vital for economic success (Gray and Willetts, 1997, pp. 69–73, 97, 99).

The exchange was fascinating, not least because it took place before the downfall of the Major government. In 1997, the Foundation reprinted the two pamphlets in one volume, accompanied by new conclusions from each of the protagonists. For Willetts, the claims that free market ideology was destroying the nation while only social cohesion would bring about economic efficiency had proved to be 'Labour's double whammy'. The political success of twentieth-century Conservatism, he argued, had been because it had proved most able to combine freedom and opportunity with a sense of rootedness. Yet the Party had allowed Labour to claim Conservative territory as its own and Blair's success 'in seizing large chunks of the British political vocabulary' had proved crucial to 'his success in seizing large chunks of Parliamentary seats'. The answer was to demonstrate to all those who would soon find themselves suffering 'the depredations of New Labour' that Conservatism was on their side. For Gray, however, no such recovery was possible. Where before he had argued that the Conservative Party might be unelectable for a considerable time to come, he now suggested that it would cease to exist, even as an opposition party. Contrary to the protestations of its defenders, Gray declared, the free market did indeed undermine settled institutions. Indeed, the Conservative Party, he held, had itself fallen victim to its destructive power (Gray and Willetts, 1997, pp. 167–71, 180, 145–7, 158).

Conservatism and the family

If one problem for the Party is how to think about society, another, as we have seen, is how to think about the family. The back-to-basics campaign had turned out to be disastrous, but Conservatives could not escape the questions it had raised. John Redwood, for instance, had argued during his second challenge for the leadership that activists had abandoned the Party not only because of Europe but 'because we put up taxes, banned most handguns and made divorce easier – things they did not expect a Conservative government to do'. He had a wide-ranging critique of the Conservative record in office, attacking the government for putting VAT on fuel, cutting mortgage-interest tax relief and closing hospitals. But his mention of the Conservative government's controversial divorce reform was part of an overall stance on the family, which he well demonstrated by including support for marriage in his manifesto for the leadership and in declaring that it had been a mistake 'to allow Back to Basics to be pushed aside by a few tabloid private-lives stories' (*Daily Telegraph*, 29 May 1997; *The Independent*, 12 June 1997; *The Times*, 31 May 1997).

If Redwood represented what might be seen as a moralist line on the family, Portillo – and Hague – appeared to be leaning in the opposite direction. Portillo had declared during the Party conference that while children were best brought up in stable two-parent families, 'we admire those many people who are doing an excellent job raising children on their own'. Society had changed, he went on, and nowadays many people did not marry and yet had 'stable families with children. For a younger generation, in particular, old taboos have given way to less judgemental attitudes to the span of human relationships'. Hague had concurred, arguing that the Party did not hold that single parenthood was never right. 'We are saying', he continued, 'let's be alive to the 21st century, let's be tolerant at the way people wish to live'. The shadow Home Secretary, Sir Brian Mawhinney, likewise argued that the Party had in the past 'spent so much time defending the concept of Conservative values that ... we created the impression that if you weren't in a traditional nuclear family, we weren't interested in you' (*The Times*, 10 October 1997; *The Independent*, 11 October 1997).

But such a stance was inevitably to cause problems. Arguing that Portillo had always held 'broadly libertarian views about personal conduct', one sympathetic commentator suggested that the Party faced a division between those who wanted to 'marry' economic liberalism with 'a more tolerant social politics' and those, like the shadow Social Security Secretary, Iain Duncan-Smith, who believed that Conservatives were in danger of betraying their commitment to family values. For another observer, John Gray, Portillo's speech indicated the final defeat of traditional conservatism within the Party and the rise of a right-wing libertarianism. One of Hague's closest advisers, Alan Duncan, had long argued, Gray noted, that the state 'should be pared down to an irreducible minimum' and that individual choice should not be interfered with by government (*Sunday Telegraph*, 12 October 1997; *The Guardian*, 18 October 1997).

Yet while arguing that liberty was paramount, Duncan was not an advocate of neutrality between lifestyle choices. In the past he had passionately defended the 'traditional family', which he believed had been undermined by easier divorce and the rise of cohabitation and single parenthood. More importantly, regardless of Hague's or Portillo's or Duncan's personal inclinations, policy on the family was not only problematic because it posed a problem of Party management (what Gray had predicted would be the 'bloodily divisive task' of rescuing the Party from the prejudices of its activists). It was, as has been so evident in disputes over the issue in the 1990s, not solely a matter of morality. It was a question of finance, of the level of public spending on certain types of household, and whether benefits or taxation arrangements favoured some choices over others. In addition, as a controversial speech by Michael Howard had shown in the immediate prelude to Major's back-to-basics speech, at least some leading Conservatives were likely to be sympathetic to material published by the free market Institute of Economic Affairs declaring that children raised in single-parent households were more likely to underachieve in schools or come to the attention of the courts. Given this combination of factors, it would seem unlikely that the Conservative Party can shift to a thorough-going social liberalism. The Party is likely to continue to call for support for 'family values'. But this does not mean that it opposes abortion or the provision of contraception to young people or even a reduction in the gay age of consent. In practice, as in the Major years – and even the Thatcher ones – issues which are regarded more as matters of morality than of public finance may well be seen in a more liberal light than moral campaigners would wish, or libertarians would fear (*The Observer*, 12 October 1997; *The Guardian*, 18 October 1997; Durham, 1994a, 1994b).

Renewing Conservatism

The problems the Party faced were undeniably daunting. Where, during the Major years, traditionally sympathetic sections of the press had turned against it, now this was worsened by the problem of trying to get the media to show any interest at all. The Labour Party, while its remarkable honeymoon could not – and did not – last forever, had successfully occupied ground that had hitherto been the Conservatives' and, to make matters worse, had done so while still managing to paint their opponents as as greedy and damaging to the British economy as Old Labour had sought to do during the 1980s. Europe may not prove as damaging to the Conservatives as it has done if, as seems likely, the Tory left proves less of a problem for Hague than the Tory right did for Major. But it is far from clear that the Conservative Party will continue indefinitely with a stance on Europe so out of line with much of business, and if this is the case then the wrath of the Euro-sceptics will be unleashed once more. It is this, in part, that led to Hague's decision in September 1998 to poll the Party membership on his stance on the European single currency. The result, announced on the eve of the October annual conference, certainly appeared to vindicate the leader's approach, with 170,558 members supporting his policy and only 31,492 opposing it. But, as critics pointed out, this 84.4 per cent vote for a qualified Euro-scepticism needs to be seen in the context not only of the failure of over 40 per cent of the membership to vote, but also of the continued difficulty of either silencing Conservative Euro-philes or winning sufficient support outside the Party (*The Guardian*, 10 September 1998; *Daily Telegraph* and *The Times*, 6 October 1998).

Organisationally, too, it is far from assured that the Party can be rebuilt in the way the leadership hopes. The projected increase in membership, when the Party's average age is so high and membership of any party attracts so few people, seems likely to be highly optimistic. The demands of greater participation from members clashes with the concerns of MPs over a dilution of their control over the election of Party leader, and it clashes too with those aspects of the recent reform proposals that seek to centralise the Party rather than democratise it. In the late 1940s, a reorganisation of the Party was followed by a massive increase in membership. It is unlikely to recur at the end of the 1990s.

Electorally, the road back from such a cataclysmic defeat as the Party suffered in 1997 will prove to be especially difficult. While the Party – at least in England – will not change its name, it will be forced to change its methods and its appeal. If the Labour government, with the help of the Liberal Democrats, were to introduce proportional representation (see Chapter 3), then the situation could worsen yet further, but even under first past the post, revival will be much more a matter of the long haul than the short term. Nor does the gain of 255 seats in the 1998 local elections, in Lord Parkinson's words a 'modest recovery', indicate a significant improvement in fortunes (*The Guardian*, 9 May 1998).

.Ideologically, the Party has still to find a secure and attractive identity for a post-Thatcher Conservatism. Compassion still appears to be a difficult characteristic for voters to associate with Conservatism, and claims that the Party can successfully combine the championing of the market with a concern for community, while not inherently implausible, still need to be demonstrated to a sceptical public. The Party must at one and the same time claim to stand for its core principles while being open to change. It cannot lean too far in the latter direction. But, as Hague has recently warned, many voters will not listen to a party until it is seen to listen to them. In a radio interview shortly after his election as leader, he declared that by 1999 he wanted 'to be able to show that the Conservative Party is an extremely effective fighting force ... in tune with the arrival of a new century' (*The Times*, 15 July 1998; *The World This Weekend*, Radio 4, 27 July 1997). In many ways, it is more likely to be the new century before we can tell whether the Party has, once again, returned from the depths of defeat.

Reading

Baker, D., Gamble, A. and Ludlam, S. (1993) '1846 ... 1906 ... 1996? Conservative splits and European unity', *Political Quarterly*, Vol. 64 (4), 420–34.

Durham, M. (1994a) 'Major and morals: back to basics and the crisis of Conservatism', *Talking Politics*, Vol. 7 (1), 12–16.

Durham, M. (1994b) 'The Conservative Party and the family', *Talking Politics*, Vol. 6 (2), 66–70.

Gamble, A. (1974) *The Conservative Nation*, Routledge and Kegan Paul.

Gray, J. and Willetts, D. (1997) *Is Conservatism Dead?*, Profile Books.

Kellner, P. (1997) 'Why the Tories were trounced', *Parliamentary Affairs*, Vol. 50 (4), 616–30.

Norris, P. (1997) 'Anatomy of a Labour landslide', *Parliamentary Affairs*, Vol. 50 (4), 509–32.

Schwarz, B. (1991) 'The tide of history: the reconstruction of Conservatism, 1945–51', in N. Tiratsoo (ed.), *The Attlee Years*, Pinter.

Whiteley, P., Seyd, P. and Richardon, J. (1994) *True Blues. The Politics of Conservative Party Membership*, Clarendon Press.

Willetts, D. (1992) *Modern Conservatism*, Penguin.

20

Britain and the European Union

Neill Nugent

It is not possible to understand the nature of modern British politics without having some comprehension of the international context in which they are set and in which they are conducted. For, in all sorts of ways, the British political system is increasingly shaped and conditioned by international forces and circumstances.

In many respects the most important aspect of this international dimension of British politics is the European Union (EU). As a result of EU membership, many of the policies which are pursued and the laws which apply in Britain are now no longer determined by national decision-makers but are the outcome of EU decision-making processes. Britain has an important input into these processes, but not always a decisive one. Indeed, many decisions at EU level can be, and are, taken by a qualified majority vote of the Union's fifteen member states, with the consequence that policies and laws which the British government opposes are sometimes adopted.

The implications for Britain of EU membership are thus profound. As this has been increasingly realised, and as too the pace of integration within the EU has increased in recent years, so has 'Europe' become a central issue in British politics. This chapter examines some of the key aspects of this issue. It does so by focusing on five crucial questions. How have Britain's relations with the EU evolved? How does the EU work? What does the EU do? In what ways has EU membership undermined British sovereignty? And to what extent are attitudes towards the EU a source of division between the main political parties in Britain?

The historical evolution: a troubled relationship

Three phases

The EU came into existence in November 1993 when the 1992 Treaty on European Union (TEU) – the so-called Maastricht Treaty – entered into force. However, the EU was largely based on the European Community (EC), which had been established in the 1950s and which had over the years come to assume responsibility for a wide range of policies and laws.

Britain's relations with the EC/EU fall into three broad phases:

- In the 1950s, when the foundations of the EC were being laid, Britain decided not to participate. A free trade area would have been acceptable, but not the more integrated arrangements the six founding EC states had in mind.
- In the 1960s, as the EC was increasingly seen to be a success, Britain twice tried to become a member. On both occasions the approach was rebuffed by the then French President, General de Gaulle.
- In 1973 Britain eventually became a member of the EC. Since then, reservations and objections by British governments to a wide range of proposals and practices have resulted in Britain being seen to be a somewhat reluctant and awkward member state.

Reasons for the troubled relations

The troubled and difficult relations between Britain and the EC/EU have reflected domestic suspicions and uncertainties about the benefits of membership. There have been four main sources of such suspicions and uncertainties:

1   Concern that close relations with Europe should not endanger long-established relations with the Commonwealth and the USA loomed large in the early years. These concerns have subsequently lost much of their force, but a continuing determination by British governments not to see any weakening of the Atlantic Alliance still makes for difficulties between Britain and its EU partners, most particularly in regard to the development of common foreign, security and defence policies.
2   Concern that membership threatens and undermines national sovereignty has consistently figured prominently in the continuing debate in Britain about the EC/EU. Although it has come to be generally recognised that no country can be completely sovereign and independent in what is an increasingly interdependent world, the belief persists that the EU has, and is always attempting to have, more powers in more policy areas than is either desirable or necessary. Evidence of the continuing potency of the sovereignty issue is seen in the way concern about loss of sovereignty featured almost as prominently in the 1991–3 debates in Parliament on the TEU as it had twenty years earlier when the Treaty of Accession was debated.
3   Concern that Britain has not had a very good financial deal from the EC/EU has been a commonly held view over the years, with politicians

of all parties voicing their dissatisfaction with the fact that although Britain has been one of the less prosperous member states it has been a major net contributor to the budget (to the tune, in recent years, of between £2 billion and £3 billion per annum). This, in turn, has led to widespread criticism of the Common Agricultural Policy (CAP), which accounts for almost half of EU expenditure and from which Britain – because of its relatively small agricultural sector – does not reap much benefit. Rows over the budget and the CAP were particularly acrimonious in the early 1980s, but have been less bitter in recent years following agreements in 1984 and 1988 which reduced the size of Britain's budgetary transfers.

4 Concern that the EC/EU has been ideologically unsound has long been expressed by important sections of political opinion. Until the mid to late 1980s such sentiments were especially prevalent in the Labour Party, with many taking the view that the EC was little more than a 'capitalists' club'. Since the mid-1980s, however, as ideological changes have occurred within the Conservative and Labour parties, and more importantly as the EU has been seen to be increasingly expansionist and interventionist in its approach to policy, Labour has become more European minded, while the Conservative Party – which for the most part tends to the view that the EU should be not much more than an integrated market – has become decidedly sceptical.

The Treaty on European Union

A mixture of the factors just outlined resulted in John Major's government adopting a very cautious and restrictive stance in the year-long negotiations which, at the Maastricht meeting of the European Council in December 1991, culminated in the member states agreeing to the highly controversial and much-debated TEU. Since the main purpose of negotiating the TEU was to provide a legal base for progression towards both political union and economic and monetary union (EMU), and since the British government was not convinced that these were desirable objectives, it naturally devoted much of its efforts in the negotiations to damage limitation. That is to say, it sought to limit new commitments of an integrationist nature by, for example, generally resisting policy expansion, trying to ensure that such policy expansion as could not be avoided would be based on inter-governmental cooperation rather than supranational integration, and seeking to ensure that the powers of the non-governmental institutions – notably the Commission, the European Parliament (EP) and the Court of Justice – were not greatly expanded. In the event, and as is customary in most important negotiations, the agreement eventually reached reflected a compromise in which none of the member states gained everything it wanted, but there was at least something on offer for all.

The main plus points of the TEU from the viewpoint of the British government were as follows:

- The EU was established on three pillars: the EC, a common foreign and security policy (CFSP) and cooperation in the spheres of justice and home affairs (JHA). The significance of the three pillars was that policy development in the highly sensitive areas covered by the second and third pillars would be, by virtue of being outside the institutional framework of the EC, not much subject to the influence of the Commission, the EP or the Court of Justice and would be based largely on voluntary and intergovernmental decision-making processes.
- Britain was not committed to entering the single currency provided for in the EMU provisions, which was planned to be established in the second half of the 1990s.
- Britain was not obliged to associate itself with legislation which was developed on the basis of the Social Chapter.
- A clause emphasising the importance of the so-called subsidiarity principle was included. Though open to different interpretations, subsidiarity was generally taken to imply that policy should be an EU responsibility only when it was quite clear that the policy in question could not be developed and conducted effectively at national, regional or local levels.

The main defects of the TEU in the eyes of the British government were:

- There were increases in the EU's policy competence, including aspects of the EMU programme, which it would be difficult to avoid. Furthermore, there were clear indications of policy pressures to come – not least with the first appearance of defence on the policy agenda, albeit in a very tentative manner.
- Provision was made for a significant increase in the number of policy areas where important decisions could be made by a qualified majority vote.
- Significant new powers were granted to the EP.

John Major claimed that the TEU demonstrated that Britain was at 'the heart of Europe'. The basis for this claim was not only that Britain did sign the Treaty, but also that there was much in it which reflected the British government's preference for an EU which was essentially intergovernmental and decentralised in its structure and limited in its responsibilities. However, this implied claim to have laid to rest Britain's traditionally difficult and troubled relations with 'Europe' rather overlooked the extent to which Britain's generally minimalist position in the negotiations frequently resulted in its being in a minority of one, and rather played down the significance of the opt-out of the Social Chapter and the lack of commitment to the single currency.

The Treaty of Amsterdam

Provision was made at Maastricht for a review of the operation of the TEU to be conducted in 1996. This duly took place within the framework of an intergovernmental conference (IGC) which began its deliberations in March 1996 and concluded its work at the Amsterdam European Council in June 1997.

The Conservative government's representatives in the IGC adopted their familiar minimalist position towards integrationist advance and made clear their opposition to proposals which would, for example, extend qualified majority voting and increase the powers of the EP. However, the other EU governments were well aware that a general election was due in Britain in the first half of 1997 and that there was a strong possibility that a more pro-European Labour government would be elected. Much of the work of the IGC was, therefore, in effect, virtually put on hold while fourteen of the fifteen EU states 'waited for Tony'.

The waiting proved to be worthwhile, in that Labour duly won the May 1997 general election and within days was signalling that it wished to be an active and cooperative EU player. In the IGC the new Labour government continued with the intergovernmentalist stance of its Conservative predecessor on particularly sensitive matters, but on a range of issues on which the Conservatives had been isolated Labour had little difficulty in reaching agreement with the other fourteen governments. In consequence, a new treaty – the Treaty of Amsterdam – was agreed.

The Treaty of Amsterdam was not as comprehensive or as wide ranging as the TEU. It did not contain any major new initiatives in the way that the TEU established the EU on a three-pillar structure and made arrangements for EMU. For the most part, the Amsterdam Treaty consisted of relatively modest amendments to the arrangements that were set in place at Maastricht. Some of these amendments were, however, of significance. In particular:

- There were further extensions of the policy areas in which decisions may be taken by qualified majority vote.
- The powers of the EP were further increased.
- Britain's opt-out from the Social Chapter was removed.
- Arrangements for joint policies and actions in the sphere of JHA were strengthened, though with some special provisions for Britain, including a recognition that it could retain border checks on people travelling from other EU countries.

How the European Union works

It is common in Britain for politicians and the media to make assertions along the lines of 'Brussels has decided that ...'. The use of this sort of shorthand to refer to EU decision-making rather suggests that EU decisions are made by people who cannot quite be identified, who are not accountable and who are certainly not British. As such, it seems probable that the use of such phrases contributes to the suspicion of the EU that public opinion polls show exists in Britain.

In fact, important EU decisions are not made by unidentifiable Eurocrats at all but are the consequence of well established, and often long and exhaustive, decision-making processes in which Britons and British representatives play a full part. Five main institutions are involved in these decision-making processes.

(1) *The Commission*

Europianized in that sense

The Commission is sometimes thought of as the civil service of the EU. In fact it is both more, and less, than a civil service. It is more in that many of its powers exceed those of national civil services: it has particular responsibilities for proposing EU policies and laws, for making secondary legislation, for acting as a watchdog to ensure laws are properly applied in all member states, and to act as the representative of the EU in many aspects of its external relations. It is less than a civil service in that it does not itself directly administer many EU policies, but rather delegates this responsibility to appropriate authorities and agencies in the member states.

At the summit of the Commission are twenty Commissioners, who are nominated by the governments of the member states. The five larger EU states (France, Germany, Italy, Spain and Britain) each have two Commissioners and the ten smaller states each have one. Below the Commissioners is the Commission bureaucracy, which has around 18,000 staff (tiny in size when compared with national bureaucracies). This bureaucracy is divided on a functional basis into twenty-five directorates general. A key requirement of all Commission employees, from the most senior to the most junior of levels, is that they represent the EU as a whole and not the countries of which they are citizens or from where they originate.

(2) *The Council of Ministers*

The Council is, in effect, the legislature or co-legislature of the EU, in the sense that virtually all important and controversial EU legislation is made in its name or in the name of itself and the EP. Proposals for such legislation must be drafted by the Commission but the Council or the Council and the EP is the final decision-maker.

The Council is composed of national representatives who meet at different levels of seniority. All decisions, however, have to be approved at the most senior level, which is ministerial level. At ministerial level the appropriate national ministers attend – agriculture ministers in the case of agriculture, energy ministers in the case of energy, and so on.

Decisions in the Council on proposals for EU legislation are subject in some particularly sensitive policy areas to a unanimity requirement, but in most policy areas qualified majority voting is possible. Where the latter is the case, states cannot veto proposals and must find allies if they are to stop proposals they do not like. (Under qualified majority rules, eighty-seven votes are distributed between the states: ten to France, Germany, Italy and Britain; eight to Spain; five to Belgium, Greece, the Netherlands and Portugal; four to Austria and Sweden; three to Denmark, Finland and Ireland; two to Luxembourg. A qualified majority requires a minimum of sixty-two votes.)

(3) *The European Council*

The European Council may be said to embody the highest level of political authority in the EU. This is because of the seniority of its membership, which comprises the fifteen heads of government, the fifteen foreign ministers, plus the President and one Vice-President of the Commission.

Although it meets only two or three times a year, the European Council takes many of the EU's key political decisions. It does so, for example, on accessions, on the general direction of policy and on institutional reforms. It is to be emphasised, however, that the decisions of the European Council – which are usually taken only by unanimity – are political, not legal. To be given legal effect, European Council decisions must be formally approved by the Council of Ministers.

(4) *The European Parliament*

The EP has traditionally been seen as a rather weak institution: a special sort of advisory body rather than a proper parliament. However, though its formal powers are not as strong as those of most national parliaments, they have been increased over the years, notably by the 1986 Single European Act (which gave it a second reading on certain categories of legislation), the TEU (which gave it, for the first time, a veto over some categories of legislation) and the Treaty of Amsterdam (which extended the categories of legislation over which it has a veto). Further to these 'constitutional reforms' which have increased its powers, the EP has also been adept at using such powers as it does have to the full: to such an extent that it exercises much more influence over the content of EU legislation than does the House of Commons over British legislation.

Elections to the EP are held every five years. There are 626 Members of the European Parliament (MEPs), with eighty-seven from the UK.

(5) *The Court of Justice*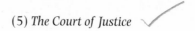

The Court acts as a sort of EU supreme court. (Strictly speaking, it would be more accurate to use EC rather than EU here, because the remit of the Court does not extend beyond the EC pillar of the TEU apart from in a few special circumstances. However, it has become common to use EU even when it is not completely accurate to do so in legal terms.) The Court deals with some types of cases directly and some only on referral from national courts, but in all cases that it hears it acts as the highest judicial authority in respect of EU law. Because so much of EU statute law is underdeveloped or is lacking in clarity, many Court judgements have the effect of making judicial law.

The Court consists of fifteen judges: one from each member state.

The making of legislation

The Commission, the Council of Ministers, the European Council, the EP and the Court of Justice are thus at the heart of EU decision-making. So, as regards EU legislation, the essence of the decision-making process is as follows: the Commission makes a proposal – perhaps within the framework of general policy guidelines which have been indicated by the European Council or the Council of Ministers; the EP offers its opinion on the proposal – on the basis of either a two-reading or a single-reading procedure, and with its potential for exercising influence varying according to the nature of the proposal; the Council of Ministers or the Council of Ministers and the EP takes final decisions – with the former acting on the basis of either unanimity or a qualified majority; the legislation is administered and applied at national level, but with disputes over interpretation being ultimately subject to rulings of the Court of Justice.

The most obvious distinctive features of EU decision-making processes as compared with British processes are their international character and the unique institutional system on which they are based. Two other characteristics should also be noted. First, the processes can be less efficient in the sense that because they inevitably involve a multiplicity of participants they are often protracted, cumbersome and very susceptible to the necessity of compromise. Second, they are less democratic in the sense that the European Council and the Council of Ministers are only indirectly elected (via national elections) while those who are directly elected (MEPs) do not have full decision-making powers.

EMU = economic + monetary union

What the European Union does

When the EC was established in the 1950s its policy aims were primarily economic in character: in essence, to construct a common market in the medium term and an economic union in the longer term. Much of the policy focus of the EU is still taken up with these aims. So, the much-discussed and highly publicised Single European Market (SEM) programme, upon which the EC/EU has been embarked since 1985, is concerned with dismantling all barriers to the free movement of goods, services, capital and labour between the member states. Going beyond the SEM programme, most EU states, though not Britain, are now participating fully in EMU, which involves a single currency and an increasing convergence of national economic and monetary policies (see Chapter 21).

However, the policy interests and responsibilities of the EU are by no means confined to economic integration. Indeed, such has been the increase in EU policy interests and responsibilities over the years that there are now few areas in which the EU is not involved in some way. The nature of this involvement differs between policy sectors in two particularly important respects: extent and status.

The extent of European Union policy involvement

The extent of EU involvement in particular policy areas can be thought of as being ranged along a spectrum. At one end are policy areas where most responsibilities have been transferred from the member states to the EU, while at the other end are policy areas which member states still largely control. On this spectrum agriculture and external commerce (trade) are the policy sectors most obviously placed at the 'extensive EU involvement' end; regional, competition, environmental, monetary and foreign policy sectors are among several located somewhere in the middle, where responsibilities are shared between the EU and the member states; and education, health, and law and order are among the policy sectors which are very much located at the 'limited EU involvement' end.

Two specific examples may be taken to illustrate the enormous variations between policy sectors as regards the extent of EU involvement.

1 *Commercial policy* is placed at the 'extensive involvement' end because virtually all decisions affecting national trade policies and conditions are now taken at EU level. That is to say, the British government can no longer decide the balance between protectionism and liberalisation in its external commercial relations and can no longer set the tariffs, the levies, or the quota restrictions that are to apply on goods entering the country. Such decisions are now taken by the fifteen member states

in common, by qualified majority vote if need be, and negotiations with non-EU trading partners about such matters are undertaken by the Commission on behalf of all the member states.

2   *Education policy* is at the 'minimal' end of the spectrum because virtually all key decisions about education – organisation, curriculum, funding and so on – are taken at member state level. EU education policy is limited to not much more than funding and coordinating a number of research, language and exchange programmes.

The status of European Union policy involvement

The EU's policy involvement and activity ranges in character from the very informal, loose and essentially voluntary, to the highly formal, regulatory and legally binding. Where policy involvement is of the former type, it is essentially intergovernmental in that no member state is obliged to do anything against its will and policy activity is focused primarily on encouraging exchanges of information, facilitating liaising and generally promoting cooperation. Where, however, policy involvement is of the latter type, it is much more supranational in that the status of decisions amount not just to understandings which it is hoped the member states will act upon, but laws which they are obliged to apply and uphold.

If policy sectors are spread along an intergovernmental–supranational spectrum, policy is normally seen to be conducted on an essentially intergovernmental basis in those sectors where EU policy involvement is limited, and to be conducted on an essentially supranational basis where the policy involvement is extensive. The two spectrums do not, however, match completely. Foreign policy, for example, is an important policy sector where there is a significant divergence: the EU is increasingly involving itself in foreign policy, to such an extent that it now issues declarations on just about every international political issue of any significance, but it does so mainly on the basis of non-binding agreements which are reached by common accord.

As well as demonstrating the lack of complete congruence between the nature and status of EU policy involvement, foreign policy also demonstrates that the intergovernmental/supranational distinction is by no means fixed. It does this by virtue of the fact that although EU foreign policy was established, and continues to be mainly conducted, on an intergovernmental basis, elements of supranationalism can be seen to be creeping in – for example, the provisions of the Maastricht and Amsterdam Treaties for some operational foreign policy decisions to be taken by qualified majority vote. Such creeping supranationalism is unquestionably a key characteristic of the evolution of the EU: policies which are initially loose and voluntary tend, over time, to become more structured and obligatory.

The sovereignty issue

The nature of sovereignty

There are two main aspects to the British conception of sovereignty. First, there is the question of the extent to which Britain as a nation can make decisions about its policies and laws without being subject to outside interference; this, the external aspect of sovereignty, is commonly called 'national sovereignty'. Secondly, there is the long-established tradition of parliamentary supremacy and the belief that no law or other instrument can prevent Parliament from doing whatever it wishes, by way of either making new laws or unmaking existing laws; this, the internal aspect of sovereignty, is commonly called 'parliamentary sovereignty'.

The debate on sovereignty

Whether British sovereignty has ever existed in a pure form, in either of the two senses of the word, is debatable. Certainly it has not existed in modern times, as international interdependence has weakened national sovereignty and as expanding executive powers have undermined parliamentary sovereignty. Because, however, this loss of sovereignty has tended to occur gradually, in a non-formalised manner, and has generally been seen to be unavoidable, it has not attracted too much attention from politicians or commentators.

Sometimes the signing of an important international treaty, such as on the control of nuclear weapons, or the implications of membership of an international organisation, such as the International Monetary Fund, have stimulated debate about sovereignty but few, other than constitutional purists, have regarded such treaties and organisations as constituting threats to sovereignty. This is because:

- the loss of sovereignty has been seen to be limited and subject to conditions;
- the loss has been only for specified purposes;
- it has not been possible for the loss to be extended without authorisation by the appropriate national authorities;
- there has always been the option of reclaiming the sovereignty that has been lost.

Membership of the EU, however, is seen to have undermined sovereignty in unique and dramatic ways. Most obviously, EU membership requires that certain decision-making responsibilities be transferred from national to Union institutions: transfers that in recent years have appeared to become almost uncontrollable as the EU has broadened the range of its policy interests.

This transference of powers has helped to ensure that even today, with Britain in its third decade of membership, the sovereignty issue looms large in political and public debate on Britain's relations with the EU. It has also helped to ensure that while British political elites recognise some loss of sovereignty has to be accepted as a price of EU membership, they resist – or, at least, present themselves as resisting – significant extensions of that loss when the furtherance of integration is placed on the EU agenda.

The loss of sovereignty

There are three principal dimensions to the loss of sovereignty (both national and parliamentary) which Britain has experienced as a result of EU membership.

(1) *The status of EU decisions.* As noted earlier, many of the EU's decisions have legal status. Should there be a conflict between EU law and national law, the former must prevail. In the event of a dispute that involves EU law – a dispute, perhaps, between the British government and the government of another member state, or between the British government and an EU institution – the final authority on interpretation rests not with a British court but with the European Court of Justice.

(2) *The EU's decision-making process.* Many EU laws can be adopted without the agreement of the British government and without the approval of the British Parliament. They can be adopted without the approval of the British government where qualified majority voting rules apply in the Council of Ministers. Until 1983/4, the EU took virtually all of its decisions by consensus, even when qualified majority voting was legally possible. Inevitably this made for, on the one hand, very slow decision-making and, on the other hand, decisions which were often little better than lowest common denominators. To rectify this unsatisfactory situation and increase the pace and dynamism of integration, qualified majority voting began increasingly to be used from the mid-1980s. At the same time, under the Single European Act, the policy areas in which qualified majority voting was permissible were extended – including, crucially, to most internal market legislation. Under the TEU and the Treaty of Amsterdam qualified majority voting was further extended – including to most aspects of environmental, regional and competition policy.

As for the ability of the British Parliament to exercise control over EU legislation, two main channels are available, both of which fall far short of embracing full control:

• Parliament can try to influence the negotiating position adopted by the government in the Council of Ministers. The main procedure for attempting this is via the House of Commons Select Committee on European Legislation, which scrutinises EU documents and recommends for debate – either in one of the House's two European Standing Committees or on the floor of the House – those documents which are considered to raise important issues and principles.

- EU legislation that is issued in the form of directives – which, in practice, includes most important legislation – is not directly applicable but must be transposed into national law by appropriate national authorities. In Britain, transposition procedures take a number of forms but they all give some limited opportunity for Parliament to express a view if it so wishes. However, it is not open to Parliament to reject the principles of a directive or to delay transposition beyond a specified date.

(3) *The range of EU policies.* When Britain first entered it in 1973, the policy and legal competence of the EC was limited; the main treaty was, after all, the Treaty of the European *Economic* Community, and the EC was commonly referred to as the *Common Market.* As was noted earlier, however, the EC's – now EU's – reach has expanded considerably over the years and it is now moving towards, in the words of the TEU and the Amsterdam Treaty, 'an ever closer union among the peoples of Europe'. EMU – with its single currency and its mixture of common and closely harmonised macroeconomic policies – was established in 1999, with most EU member states participating, and political union shows every sign of continuing to progress. As the EU thus becomes increasingly integrated, more and more policy decisions are taken at Union level, or at least have to be approved at that level. Britain and the other member states are, in other words, becoming ever more restricted in their ability to decide policies and laws for themselves.

The party political debate on the European Union

Of the three main political parties in Britain, only the Liberal Democrats and their predecessors in their various guises have never had a significant 'problem' with the EC/EU. Liberal Democrats have unfailingly argued the need for Britain to be a committed member of a more united European political system and they have consistently attacked the government of the day for being too cautious and timid on Europe. Their strong pro-EC position was clearly and forcefully expressed in their 1992 election manifesto:

> Liberal Democrats will take decisive steps towards a fully integrated, federal and democratic European Community. We believe that by sharing sovereignty and pooling power, Britain and its partners will be better able to achieve common goals for the economy, the environment, society and security than by acting alone.

These sentiments were echoed in the 1997 election manifesto, though more was made of the fact that the Europe the Liberal Democrats support is 'decentralised, democratic and diverse. A strong and united Europe, but one that respects cultural traditions and national and regional identities' (*Make the Difference*, p. 57).

The two main parties, by contrast, have both been troubled and divided over the years by the EC/EU. Traditionally, the Conservatives were the stronger advocates of the Community but since the late 1980s this situation has changed and Labour has been the more 'pro-European' of the two. This movement in party positions is largely accounted for by two factors.

First, ideological changes have occurred within both parties. In Labour's case, the dropping of the 1983 general election commitment to withdrawal from the EC was one of the first planks of the 'new realism' that was gradually introduced under Neil Kinnock's leadership. The increasingly moderate social and economic policies which were adopted first under Kinnock and then under John Smith and Tony Blair further eased the way to a more pro-EC/EU stance in that such policies were broadly in line with policies emanating from the EC/EU and from other member states. Many of the Party's earlier suspicions of the free market philosophy of the EC, and doubts about whether the EC would permit a Labour government to introduce interventionist, let alone socialist, policies and laws, thus came to be allayed. In the Conservatives' case, Margaret Thatcher increasingly linked her advocacy of political nationalism and laissez-faire economics on the one hand with the need to defend and safeguard sovereignty against EC encroachment on the other. The link was provided by the supposed federalist intentions of many in the EC and also by the alleged interventionist and bureaucratic nature of many of its policies and activities. As Thatcher said in a famous speech at Bruges in 1988: 'My first guideline [for the future of Europe] is this: willing and active co-operation between independent sovereign states is the best way to build a successful European Community'. With John Major, the tenor of the language moderated and a more pragmatic approach was adopted, but the underlying policy position was not fundamentally different: the British government continued to insist that the EU should concentrate on establishing the SEM and that it should involve itself in other policy areas only on a limited and intergovernmental basis. Under William Hague, an avowed Euro-sceptic who Conservative MPs chose in preference to Euro-friendly Kenneth Clarke to succeed Major as party leader after the 1997 election, these policy positions have been further reinforced.

Second, developments in the EU itself, and perceptions of their nature, have been important. The extension of EU influence into more and more policy spheres, and especially the development of the so-called social dimension, has done much to make Conservatives more uneasy, and Labour more comfortable, with the EU. Whereas in Conservative eyes the EU is interesting itself in policy spheres which should be none of its business, in Labour eyes its increasing interest in the likes of social, environmental, research and development and (very tentatively) industrial policy has done much to dispel the image of an unsympathetic free trade club. Indeed, in certain respects the EU has come to be seen by much of the Labour Party almost as an ideological ally.

The changed positions of the two parties on the EU was reflected in their 1992 and 1997 election manifestos, with Labour's tone being decidedly more positive. The more pro-EU attitude of Labour was seen, for example, in its commitment in 1997 to end the opt-out from the Social Chapter, its willingness to accept extensions to qualified majority voting in the Council in some policy areas and its more open attitude towards the single currency – though, on the latter, it followed the Conservatives and Liberal Democrats in promising that it would not take Britain into the single currency without first receiving the approval of the British people in a referendum.

One of the main features of the 1997 general election was that Labour sought not to be outflanked by the Conservatives on any issue which might be thought to have significant popular appeal. A consequence of this in terms of European policy was that Labour emphasised rather more than it had in 1992 its commitment to the nation state: 'Our vision of Europe is of an alliance of independent nations choosing to co-operate to achieve the goals they cannot achieve alone. We oppose a European federal superstate' (*Because Britain Deserves Better*, p. 37). This language was almost identical to that of the Conservatives' manifesto, where it was stated that 'A Conservative Government will seek a partnership of nation states.... A British Conservative Government will not allow Britain to be part of a federal European state' (*You Can Only Be Sure With the Conservatives*, p. 46).

Notwithstanding, however, such similarity of general rhetoric, the real and different positions of the parties was quickly confirmed after the election. The new Labour government agreed, as was noted above, to the Treaty of Amsterdam, which was concluded between the EU member states in June 1997. This was vehemently opposed by the Conservatives on the grounds that it advanced supranationalism too far and it ended the Social Chapter opt-out. The government then proceeded, in the winter of 1997, to announce that it was in favour of the single currency in principle but that it believed the economic conditions were not right for Britain to be a member of the currency when it was launched in January 1999. A clear signal was given that in all probability Labour would make a recommendation to the British people shortly after the next general election that Britain should become part of the single currency system. For the Conservatives, William Hague had hardly settled into his post as leader before announcing that his party would not consider any possibility of Britain joining the single currency system in the current or the next Parliament: thus, in effect, ruling out membership for at least ten years.

The gap between the Labour and Conservative parties on Europe is thus both significant and widening. It would be going too far to describe Labour as Euro-enthusiastic, but it does recognise the unavoidability of the European integration process and it is seeking to play an active and supportive role therein. It would similarly be going too far to describe the Conservative Party as anti-European – not least since it does contain within its ranks a sizeable pro-European body of opinion – but it takes a somewhat minimalist view of what the EU should be doing and what the nature of Britain's engagement with it should be.

Conclusion

As the EU has impinged increasingly on aspects of British political, economic and social life, so have Britain's relations with the EU come to be a central political issue. The relationship is extensively discussed and debated, with the focus of attention ranging from the specific, such as the need for EU food hygiene law and the desirability of Britain maintaining border checks on EU citizens, to the general, such as whether Britain should be in the mainstream of EMU and how much sovereignty should be transferred to the EU.

It can confidently be anticipated that in the years to come the EU, and Britain's relations with it, will continue to command considerable political attention. The nature and pace of political union and of EMU, the probable loosening of the EU into fast and slow integration streams, and the desire of many non-EU states to become members, are but some of the more obvious of the many key issues which will be on the EU's, and therefore also on Britain's, political agenda.

Reading

Archer, C. and Butler, F. (1996) *The European Community: Structure and Process* (2nd edn), Pinter.

Baker, D. and Seawright, D. (eds) (1998) *Britain for and Against Europe: British Politics and the Question of European Integration*, Clarendon Press.

Beloff, Lord (1996) *Britain and European Union*, Macmillan.

Buller, J. (1995) 'Britain as an awkward partner: reassessing Britain's relations with the EU', *Politics*, Vol. 15.

George, S. (ed.) (1992) *Britain and the European Community*, Clarendon Press.

George, S. (1998) *An Awkward Partner* (3rd edn), Oxford University Press.

Nugent, N. (1994) *The Government and Politics of the European Union* (3rd edn), Macmillan.

Nugent, N. (1996) 'Sovereignty and Britain's membership of the European Union', *Public Policy and Administration*, Vol. 11.

Wallace, H. (1997) 'At odds with Europe', *Political Studies*, Vol. 45.

21

Economic and monetary union

Andrew Scott

The decision to implement economic and monetary union (EMU) within the European Union (EU) was taken at the Maastricht summit in December 1991 and formed a central element in the Treaty on European Union (TEU), which entered into force on 1 November 1993. The commitment to EMU represents the most significant economic and political challenge to the EU in its history. If successful, the implementation of EMU will alter fundamentally the dynamics of European integration and will alter – probably irrevocably – the economic sovereignty of the participating countries. In this sense, it is right to view EMU as representing a major step along the road to European political union. The repercussions from EMU will be considerable. Once implemented, national currencies will cease to exist and will be replaced by a single, common currency, to be called the euro. This will have enormous symbolic importance to the process of European integration, eliminating as it does national currencies – one of the most durable emblems of west European nationhood. EMU will have even greater significance in economic terms, producing a fundamental change in the economic policy conditions prevailing within the single-currency area. With the disappearance of national currencies, governments in EMU member states will no longer be able to use monetary policy as an instrument of macro-economic policy in order to achieve domestic objectives – such as full employment or price control. Instead, exclusive competence over monetary policy will transferred to the EU level of governance and become the responsibility of a newly established European Central Bank (ECB), which, although being advised by national central banks, will be prohibited from taking instructions from the governments of the participating member states. Instead, it will be required to shape monetary policy with the principal aim of ensuring price stability. Consequently, member states will be unable to change interest rates or the exchange rate in order to influence domestic economic performance. Beyond this, EMU, as provided for in the TEU and subsequent agreements, also requires that participating countries

397

conform to specific (and legally binding) guidelines when conducting national fiscal policies.

In this chapter our principal focus will be on the economic consequences of EMU. It is important to appreciate at the outset that the economic arguments over EMU are finely balanced. Moreover, it is all too easy to become embroiled in an ideological dispute over the desirability or otherwise of closer political integration in Europe. In this chapter, we focus on the economic and governance issues pertaining to EMU and not on ideological matters. It makes little intellectual sense to be 'for' or 'against' EMU solely for ideological reasons. The industrial (and non-industrial) world is replete with examples of monetary unions which are essentially stable and beneficial arrangements. There is no inherent reason why EMU cannot be equally stable or economically beneficial as these other arrangements.

Rather, the questions raised here will focus on the operating arrangements of this monetary union, and our critique of EMU will be founded on criteria that illuminate the impact EMU is likely to have upon the economic – and so political – welfare of the EU. While accepting that EMU will lead to closer political integration in the EU, in large measure the politics of EMU will unfold as its economic consequences become clear. Particularly important, of course, will be the extent to which EMU affects – or is seen to affect – unemployment within member states. It is from the changes to the underlying relationship between national governance and domestic economic performance necessitated by EMU that the political consequences of a single currency will flow. It is on this that we will focus.

The evolution of European monetary cooperation

The TEU set out a timetable for the realisation, by 1 January 1999, of monetary union between the member states of the EU. Monetary union describes a situation in which the various national currencies of the EU member states are replaced by a single currency which, thereafter, will represent the common legal tender for the area as a whole. At that time, authority over monetary policy will pass from the central banks of individual member states to a new institution, the European System of Central Banks (ESCB), at the heart of which will be the ECB. The immediate and direct consequence of EMU, therefore, is the loss of control by national authorities over interest rates (which will now be determined by the new common monetary authority – the ESCB) and the exchange rate (by definition exchange rates will no longer exist in a single-currency area). Given that all EU countries have, over the years, used both interest rates and the exchange rate as instruments of national economic policy, we must ask why they have now decided to sacrifice these policy levers by opting to participate in a single currency. To answer this question requires that we consider the merits, first, of the exchange rate as a policy instrument.

A fixed exchange rate is one in which governments commit themselves to maintain the external value of their currency against other currencies at a specific rate of exchange (or parity). Of course, as the exchange rate is the price of one currency when expressed in another currency, no individual country may determine unilaterally what the exchange rate will be. Instead, this will be the outcome of the forces of supply and demand in the foreign exchange market, with the role of governments (or their agents in the form of central banks) being to influence – directly or indirectly – the relative trading conditions in that market. This they may accomplish either by intervening in the market to buy or sell the currency as necessary to stabilise the exchange rate around its pre-announced level, or by influencing the behaviour of private agents by raising (lowering) domestic interest rates to make the currency more (less) attractive to private investors.

There are limits to government action. Direct intervention in foreign exchange markets is possible only to the extent that centrally held reserves (of foreign currency) permit. Similarly, changes to domestic interest rates will usually be continued only as long as the effects on the domestic economy are acceptable. It is often the case that the change in interest rate required to stabilise the exchange rate will conflict with the needs of the domestic economy. In the final instance, however, a government might find that, regardless of the policy it follows, pressures in the foreign exchange market are so intense that the prevailing parity cannot be maintained. At that point an exchange rate realignment (devaluation or revaluation) is required. Necessarily, however, exchange rate realignments must be infrequent events. Otherwise those who hold national currencies as investment instruments – or who invest directly abroad – will lose confidence in the ability of a currency to maintain its value through time and will seek to sell it. Consequently, fixed exchange rate systems require governments to frame economic policies (particularly monetary policy) in a manner consistent with maintaining the value of a currency around the pre-announced exchange rate. The principal difficulty with this, as implied above, is that sometimes the policy required to achieve exchange rate stability will run counter to that required in the context of national economic developments.

By contrast, a 'flexible' exchange rate system is one in which governments are not committed to any specific parity for the currency and leave exchange rate determination entirely to market forces. The obvious attraction of this arrangement is that domestic economic policies (monetary and fiscal) are not tied to an exchange rate target and can instead be shaped solely by domestic economic considerations. However, there are two main problems with flexible exchange rates.

First, experience has shown that exchange rates tend to fluctuate considerably if left entirely to market forces. Exchange rate volatility inevitably creates uncertainties over the future value of the currency and this may adversely affect international trade and investment flows. In addition, actual changes in exchange rates often exceed those which would be justified by prevailing economic conditions. This problem (known as exchange rate 'overshooting') arises because, in markets for financial assets, the behaviour of economic agents is shaped largely by their expectations of the future value of the asset concerned and not solely by current conditions. This means that dealers will react to any 'news' that reaches the market insofar as this is expected to affect the future prices of the assets being traded. This will trigger price changes in the assets ahead of the events to which the news relates. Because all currencies are financial assets, in which individuals and companies often invest, currency markets similarly respond to 'news', and this explains the often large daily changes in exchange rates that we observe.

Second, experience has shown that exchange rate flexibility can lead to higher inflation rates. If the exchange rate between two countries is fixed, any tendency for prices in one country to rise faster than in the other country will result in falling production and rising unemployment in the high-inflation country. This is because consumers increasingly will prefer to buy products that originate in the low-inflation country, resulting in falling exports from, and rising imports to, the high-inflation country. Consequently, the commitment to participate in a fixed exchange rate arrangement effectively acts as a discipline upon an inflation-prone country to control its rate of inflation such that it does not exceed that in the lowest-inflation country in the arrangement. However, the measures needed to curtail domestic inflation may be politically unpopular and may lead to demands that the exchange rate commitment is sacrificed in preference to continuing with domestic anti-inflation policies. In such circumstances a devaluation of the currency will temporarily restore the foreign competitiveness of exports from the high-inflation country and will make imports more expensive, thereby curtailing domestic demand for foreign products. Should this occur, we can expect unemployment to begin to fall as domestic production picks up once more. However, the rate of inflation will now be higher, and the increase in the price of imported goods and services will fuel further the domestic rate of inflation. Unless accompanying measures are introduced to address the underlying causes of the high rate of inflation, it is likely that the country will have further bouts of inflation followed by further rounds of devaluation of its currency. Ultimately the country can become locked into an unsustainable circle of rising inflation and a depreciating currency. Adherence to a fixed exchange rate arrangement is generally regarded as precluding this essentially unstable process, and instead providing a framework for the long-term control of domestic inflationary forces.

By applying the foregoing analysis to the EU, we can understand why close cooperation over exchange rates has always been a central issue in European integration. Any tendency for exchange rates to become unstable would not only interfere with the growth of intra-EU trade and investment (the source of the economic gains from integration) but would also be likely to fuel inflation within the weaker economies. And, with the exception of a relatively brief spell in the second half of the 1970s, EU member states have operated under fixed exchange rates.

Until the early 1970s, exchange rate stability was maintained within the global framework of the Bretton Woods system, established in 1944. However, with the collapse of this system in 1973, and the floating of the US dollar, EU member states devised their own exchange rate arrangement known as the 'snake'. Within the 'snake', exchange rate stability would be maintained by the central banks of the participating countries cooperatively intervening in the foreign exchange markets to support, where necessary, another 'snake' currency. This would give the relevant government time to adjust domestic economic policies to the extent necessary to stabilise the underlying value of its currency.

Although the introduction of the 'snake' coincided with the collapse of the Bretton Woods system, and was thus timely, it had originally been devised with a much more ambitious objective in mind – to deliver European monetary union by 1980. This aim dates from the Hague summit of December 1969. The issue before that meeting was to give effect to the objective of 'deepening' integration, given that the initial priority of establishing a customs union had been secured. In the relatively optimistic environment of the late 1960s, monetary union seemed a logical next step. In 1970 a committee under the chair of Pierre Werner was convened to consider how monetary union might be achieved. The Werner report advocated a staged transition, in which there would be ever closer economic policy coordination between countries within the framework of a tightly constructed fixed exchange rate arrangement, coupled with the progressive establishment of common institutions which eventually would assume responsibility for delivering a single monetary policy. The first stage in the process began in April 1972 with the inauguration of the 'snake'.

Self-evidently, this initiative for monetary union of the 1970s did not succeed. The combined effects of the floating of the US dollar in 1973 and the recession triggered by the quadrupling of oil prices late in 1973 persuaded Britain, Ireland, France and Italy to abandon fixed exchange rates and pursue instead monetary and fiscal policies aimed at countering the rising level of domestic unemployment. The exchange rate would be left to find its own level in the currency market. Thus, by the mid-1970s, the 'snake' (as a vehicle for monetary union) had collapsed and all that remained was a Deutschmark zone, in which the currencies of Belgium, Luxembourg, the Netherlands and Denmark were tied to the Deutschmark.[1]

---

1   For a comprehensive review of this early phase of monetary cooperation in the EU, see Tsoukalis (1977) and Ludlow (1982). Steinherr (1994) provides an excellent source for many of the issues covered in this chapter.

By the late 1970s, however, the mood within European Community (EC) countries again had shifted. Four years of experience with exchange rate flexibility (or volatility) had produced no lasting benefit for the countries concerned. Not only had these countries failed to resolve their unemployment problems, but each had additionally become victim to higher rates of inflation, which now coexisted alongside low rates of economic growth.

The European Monetary System

It was against this background that the then President of the European Commission, Roy (now Lord) Jenkins, called for a return to exchange rate stability in Europe (Jenkins, 1977). Jenkins argued that not only would this produce lower inflation, it would also create the economic conditions required for a recovery in growth across the EC. The call was taken up in both Germany and France, where Chancellor Schmidt and President Giscard d'Estaing proceeded to construct what became the European Monetary System (EMS). At the heart of the EMS was a fixed exchange rate arrangement – the Exchange Rate Mechanism (ERM). Under the ERM, participating countries (not yet Britain) would declare a (fixed) 'central rate' for their currency against a composite currency, the European currency unit (ECU). This would establish a bilateral parity grid, indicating the exchange rates between the individual EC currencies. Each currency would be permitted to move 2.25 per cent either side of its ECU central rate, although a band of ±6 per cent was permitted for the weaker currencies. In the event, only Italy took advantage of this wider band. Central rates would be defended by central bank intervention, although it was presumed that a country would adjust domestic economic policy if this was required to restore market confidence in its currency. While exchange rate changes were possible, these were subject to negotiation between the EMS countries and would be sanctioned only if undertaken in conjunction with necessary changes in domestic economic policies.[2]

The EMS was launched in March 1979. Essentially it was a pragmatic response to Europe's economic problems. It was not an attempt to revive European monetary union. Its sole objective was to establish a 'zone of monetary stability' across the EC through a regime of fixed exchange rates supported by anti-inflationary domestic policies, and led by highly credible West German monetary policy. It is clear that the ERM achieved this aim. In the course of the 1980s inflation rates across the EC fell steadily towards German levels, as did interest rates. This success was underpinned by a significant (although incomplete) convergence of monetary policies within

---

2 For a comprehensive review of the operation of the EMS, see Gros and Thygesen (1992), especially ch. 2.

the ERM countries towards West German monetary policy. As a result, after an initial (1979–83) phase during which a number of exchange rate adjustments were made, the frequency of exchange rate changes within the ERM declined markedly and the ERM became the framework for price stability in almost all EC member states.[3]

From EMS to EMU

By the mid-1980s the relative success of the EMS was prompting further discussion concerning the viability of moving beyond a cooperative arrangement designed to bring exchange rate stability to the EC. By 1985 the ERM had settled down. Indeed, following a realignment in July 1985, there was only one further significant exchange rate change (in January 1987) until the exchange rate crisis of September 1992. By then, however, EMU had become a treaty-based objective of the EU.

Despite its initial objectives, by 1988 the ERM effectively had been transformed from its original purpose – a mechanism for establishing a zone of monetary stability in the EC – to a vehicle for delivering European monetary union. This was a direct consequence of the decision, embodied in the Single European Act of 1986, to complete the SEM by 31 December 1992.

The link between the single market and the single currency is both direct and compelling, and was most forcefully made in a report produced by a group of experts under the chair of Tomaso Padoa-Schioppa (1987). The essence of their argument was that prevailing exchange rate arrangements were incompatible with an EU internal market in which there were no obstacles to the free movement of goods, services, capital and persons. The immediate problem concerned national obstacles to the free movement of capital. Throughout the 1980s, both France and Italy had used controls on currency convertibility as a way of helping to stabilise the exchange rate. These capital controls were incompatible with a single market. Also, capital controls militated against free trade in financial services. An individual would not purchase a financial service denominated in a foreign currency if there was the slightest risk that the asset could not be converted into the home currency upon demand. As long as capital controls remained, this risk existed. More broadly, it was argued that multiple currencies obstructed trade, as the ever-present risk of exchange rate changes deterred cross-border trade. The Padoa-Schioppa report described the problem as being rooted in an 'inconsistent quartet' of policy aims, comprising:

---

3 For an appraisal of the EMS during the 1980s, see Gros and Thygesen (1992), De Grauwe (1997) and Barrell (1992).

1   free trade;
2   fixed exchange rates;
3   the elimination of capital controls;
4   national monetary policy autonomy.

These four aims cannot be attained simultaneously. For instance, should a high-inflation country eliminate capital controls as required by the single market programme, this would be bound to increase the volatility of its exchange rate unless accompanied by more restrictive monetary policy. Thus domestic monetary sovereignty will be eroded. If a country insists on retaining monetary autonomy, it will not be able to guarantee exchange rate stability unless it imposes capital controls or introduces alternative restrictive measures. It was the incompatibility with the prevailing arrangements in the context of the single market that propelled the EU towards reviving the question of monetary union.

It would, however, be misleading to suggest that EU politicians mechanically followed the logic of economic policy. There was no doubt that the politics of EMU would shape events, and not solely economic considerations. So why did member states agree to embark on such a momentous course of action? Undeniably, the success of the ERM in the 1980s implied that EMU was, by that stage, a realistic proposition. It would cement the internal market, in which much political capital had by then been invested. But there were other considerations, involving particular national interests. In France, EMU was seen as a way of diminishing the economic hegemony of West Germany. As the dominant economy, since the introduction of the EMS West Germany had dictated the course of monetary policy across the EC. Under EMU, on the other hand, EU monetary policy would be fashioned by all participating countries, with the result that it would reflect better the prevailing economic conditions in other countries and not just those in Germany.

If the motivation underlying French support for EMU is clear enough, it is more difficult to explain German support. Indeed, one might have expected German opposition to EMU for precisely those reasons that explain French enthusiasm. It is clear that broader political considerations came into German reckoning. In promoting EMU, Chancellor Kohl was in part simply continuing the tradition of successive West German leaders who saw ever-closer European integration as the essential architecture of a peaceful Europe. It was inevitable that EMU would promote European political integration, and this remained a fundamental objective for Germany. However, EMU would not be accepted unreservedly: Germany would accept EMU only under certain conditions – conditions which precluded any common monetary policy being less rigorous in countering inflation than was German monetary policy. The institutions and policies of EMU would have to be shaped in the image of German (rather than French) arrangements to be acceptable.[4]

4   For a review of the political debates surrounding EMU, see Dyson (1994).

Just as the Werner committee had been set up in 1970 to consider how to achieve EMU at that time, so in 1988 the EU heads of government and state established a committee chaired by the President of the European Commission, Jacques Delors, to advise as to how best EMU might be attained (Delors, 1989). The committee recommended that EMU be implemented through three stages, with each stage involving a combination of economic policy convergence along with the creation of an institutional structure which would implement the single monetary policy once the single currency was introduced. The Delors report proved to be very influential in the negotiations that culminated in the signing of the TEU.

Although the Governor of the Bank of England was a member of the Delors committee, the British government remained hostile towards EMU. Indeed, by the end of the 1980s, and despite giving undertakings since 1979 to take sterling into the ERM 'when the time was right', not only was Prime Minister Thatcher implacably opposed to EMU, but she had resisted repeated calls to take sterling into the ERM. Inevitably this brought Britain into conflict with the rest of the EU, where support for EMU was virtually solid. British opposition to EMU was in part technical, with many economists doubting its viability. But it was principally ideological. Within the governing Conservative Party there was by now deep-seated opposition to further European integration, on essentially political grounds. Although a number of senior Conservative politicians (including some cabinet ministers) clearly supported closer British attachment to the EMU initiative, the Euro-sceptic hard-liners, in whose number the Prime Minister seemed to be counted, dominated the debate. By the late 1980s the Euro-debate in Britain focused on the position of sterling with respect to the ERM. Not only were those politicians fearful of a diminution of British influence within the EU advocating participation in the ERM, but many of Britain's leading industrialists were by then campaigning for the same objective. The political stakes were high. If sterling did join the ERM, this would signal a victory for the pro-EU camp inside the government; if it remained outside, then the Euro-sceptics were in control of a large swathe of British foreign policy.

The outcome was a victory for the pro-EU group. In November 1990, the then Chancellor of the Exchequer – John Major – announced that sterling would join the ERM at a rate of 2.95 Deutschmarks, within a ±6 per cent band of fluctuation. Thatcher resigned as premier weeks later. In the event, the timing of British entry was particularly unfortunate. The Gulf crisis had pushed sterling's foreign exchange value upwards (due to its petro-currency status), resulting in an overvaluation from the perspective of domestic manufacturers, who now found exporting much more difficult. Moreover, by late 1991 the British economy was beginning to slide into recession, no doubt exacerbated by the high value of sterling. Simultaneously, the fiscal costs arising from German unification were pushing interest rates upwards throughout the EU, adding further to the recessionary forces afflicting the British economy. By 1992, it was clear that the combination of an overvalued sterling and high domestic interest rates was untenable in the prevailing economic situation. The economic and political pressure to take sterling out of the ERM intensified, fuelling speculation in the currency markets. Eventually, late in 1992, the pressures had become irresistible and sterling exited the ERM on 16 September. Thereafter, British interest rates fell quickly and, by the following January, sterling had depreciated some 15 per cent against the Deutschmark and an economic recovery was under way. The triple effects of German unification, the launching of EMU and the onset of the British recession were simply too much to contend with. And although the turmoil in the foreign exchange markets had not been confined to sterling, with the Italian lira and the Spanish peseta in particular coming under strong speculative attacks, it did serve to lessen the prospect of further British involvement in European monetary cooperation.[5]

Outside Britain, the currency turmoil of 1992 reflected growing doubts concerning the ratification of the TEU – particularly in France, where President Mitterrand had decided to hold a referendum to settle the issue. In the spring of 1993 the French franc came under sustained selling pressure as the markets increasingly came to doubt the economic and political viability of EMU. By the summer the pressure on the franc was intolerable. However, rather than devalue, on 2 August it was decided that the band within which a currency could fluctuate around its ERM central rate should be increased from ±2.25 per cent to ±15 per cent. By widening the band, the immediate pressure on governments to defend currency values was eliminated. Almost immediately the crisis abated and, despite the wider band, exchange rates soon returned close to their central rates. In effect, the decision to widen the ERM band succeeded in restoring stability to foreign exchange markets without jeopardising the EMU objective. Somewhat ironically, the 1992–3 ERM crisis was regarded as showing the importance of EMU. Only by moving to a single currency could the EU forever remove the threat of the damaging economic instability that resulted from the actions of speculators in the foreign exchange markets.

The nature of EMU

The precise format that EMU would take, and the timetable for its realisation, were set out in the TEU. EMU would be achieved over three stages, culminating with the introduction of a single currency no later than 1

---

5   See Cobham (1994) for a series of papers explaining the currency turmoil of 1992–3.

January 1999.[6] However, EU countries would not automatically be eligible to move to EMU. Instead, and resulting very much from German concerns discussed earlier, each country would need to meet specific criteria – the convergence criteria – designed to demonstrate that an applicant country could deliver economic policies consistent with price stability. The introduction of EMU as an objective of the EU required a fundamental overhaul of the founding Treaty of Rome. The revised Article B of the Common Provisions (TEU) set out the objectives of the EU as:

> to promote economic and social progress which is balanced and sustainable, in particular through the creation of an area without internal frontiers, through the strengthening of economic and social cohesion and through the establishment of economic and monetary union, ultimately including a single currency.

Elsewhere in the TEU new provisions and protocols were added which together provided a detailed blueprint for EMU.[7] These included articles specifying the objectives of, transition to, and operating arrangements for, the new ECB; the convergence criteria a member state had to satisfy before it would be permitted to join the single-currency area, and associated transitional measures; the contingent arrangements for member states which failed to qualify for EMU by the starting dates; and the legal bases of the British and Danish 'opt-outs'.

The 'opt-outs' refer to the provision that was made in the TEU to allow both Britain and Denmark to remain outside the single-currency area while not preventing the other member states proceeding to form a monetary union as they wished. Although the TEU defined EMU as a binding legal obligation of membership of the EU, that is as part of the *acquis communautaire*, two protocols attached to the TEU excluded Britain and Denmark from this obligation. While both countries would be free to join EMU subject to the normal provisions should they wish, neither was bound to do so. In effect, the opt-out reconciled the ambitions of the overwhelming majority of EU member states which wanted EMU with the fears of a minority for whom it represented an unacceptable (in political terms) erosion of national sovereignty. While the resultant TEU might be considered somewhat less than satisfactory when viewed as a constitutional document, the alternative would have been to trigger a major political crisis within the EU, with consequences that were difficult to foresee. It is inconceivable

6　The TEU did allow for EMU to begin on 1 January 1997, but only if the majority of member states were eligible for membership at that time; in the event this requirement was not met.

7　The EMU provisions are contained in a new Title VI, Articles 102–9m, of the TEU and in a number of protocols to the TEU. For an excellent discussion, see Kenen (1995).

that Britain would have ratified a TEU which bound it to participation in EMU.

For the remaining ten member states, the TEU provided a timetable for the staged transition to monetary union. The first stage, which was deemed to have begun in June 1990, required all EU currencies to be within the narrow ±2.25 per cent ERM band and capital controls to be removed. Stage 2 was to begin on 1 January 1994 – as it did – and would see the establishment of the European Monetary Institute (EMI), the precursor to the ECB, which would be created in stage 3. The EMI was charged with preparing the way for the introduction of the single currency and would attend to the many and varied technical issues involved. The EMI was also to monitor the progress member states made with respect to meeting the convergence criteria. Finally, stage 3 would see the introduction of the single currency, to replace the national currencies of the participating countries. Countries which failed to meet the convergence criteria at that time would be given a derogation from the relevant provisions of the TEU until they did meet them. The ECB would be created and, along with representatives from national central banks in the newly established ESCB, would be pivotal in setting monetary policy for the single-currency area as a whole.

The convergence criteria were central to the realisation of EMU. By meeting these criteria, a member state was deemed to have demonstrated that it could conduct domestic economic policy in a manner consistent with price stability. Consequently, the loss of national monetary policy would have no detrimental effect on that economy.[8] The four convergence criteria were:

1   that a country's inflation rate should be within 1.5 per cent of that recorded by the three best-performing countries;
2   that a country's long-term nominal interest rate should be within 2 per cent of that of the three lowest-inflation countries;
3   that a country's currency should have been within the narrow ERM band for at least two years and should not have been devalued during that time;
4   that the country avoided an excessive budget deficit, defined as a ratio of annual net public sector borrowing (the budget deficit) to gross domestic product (GDP) not exceeding 3 per cent and a ratio of the stock of outstanding public debt to GDP not exceeding 60 per cent.

That inflation rates should converge in the context of a single currency is clearly desirable as, once the single currency has been introduced, it will

8   For a discussion of the convergence criteria, see Kenen (1995), Bean (1992) and De Grauwe (1997).

no longer be possible for the inflation-prone country to counter the adverse effects of high inflation on levels of output and employment by an exchange rate adjustment. Instead, unemployment would simply continue to rise. Convergence in national long-term interest rates would demonstrate a convergence of expectations concerning future national rates of inflation. If market participants expect a country's rate of inflation to rise in the future, then it will demand higher interest rates as an inducement to hold debt instruments issued by the government of that country. The necessity for a currency to be within the narrow band of the ERM for at least two years without having devalued provided a test of whether inflation rate differentials within the EU had been eliminated to the extent consistent with the introduction of a single currency. In the event, the 1992–3 exchange rate turmoil effectively rendered redundant this criterion. Given that the 'narrow' band of fluctuation had been increased to ±15 per cent, this criterion no longer proved an adequate test for membership of the single-currency area. Nonetheless, it remained the case that an aspiring EMU participant must be inside the ERM for at least two years before it would be eligible to move to the third stage.

The fourth criterion relates to fiscal policy.[9] Of all the preconditions that a country must meet before being accepted into the single-currency area, the two fiscal conditions comprising the fourth criterion above have attracted the most attention. Two questions have been raised: first, why should national fiscal policy in EMU be restricted at all and, second, what is the economic rationale for setting these restrictions at 3 per cent and 60 per cent? That there should be restrictions on fiscal policy resulted from (principally German) concerns that, otherwise, governments would be able to engage in potentially inflationary expenditure programmes financed by borrowing (in ECU-denominated debt instruments) on international capital markets. This would cause a general rise in interest rates across the EMU area, thus transmitting inflationary forces to other countries. Moreover, the cost of servicing the national debt would rise as interest rates were pushed higher. As higher interest rates would be likely to depress the level of economic activity, and so trigger a decline in government revenue from taxation, yet further government borrowing would be necessary to service the national debt. Such a situation, if permitted to arise, would impart instability to all EMU economies. Consequently, aspirants to stage 3 must

9 In fact, the TEU provides some latitude in the interpretation of both ceilings such that even where the upper limits (of 3 per cent and 60 per cent) are breached, the country concerned nonetheless may be deemed to have met these so-called 'excessive deficit' criteria. This latitude has been utilised in determining who should move to stage 3.

demonstrate their ability to conduct 'sound' fiscal policy before joining the single-currency area.[10]

It is worth noting that of these four convergence criteria, the first three lose their relevance immediately upon a country moving to stage 3. National inflation rates become unified as only one inflation rate is possible inside a monetary union; differences in interest rates are eliminated as national central banks merge into a single entity; and exchange rate bands vanish as the single currency replaces its national counterparts. The excessive deficit criteria, on the other hand, retain their relevance beyond stage 3 because member states continue to have exclusive competence over national fiscal policies. Consequently, the considerations underlying the introduction of the fiscal criteria would be equally pertinent post-EMU as previously. It was therefore decided that governments would be required to observe the TEU 'excessive deficit' criteria after joining EMU, unless their economy was subject to an 'exceptional' economic disturbance. This agreement was formalised as the Stability and Growth Pact, negotiated at the Dublin summit in December 1996. An 'exceptional' disturbance was defined as an annual fall of 2 per cent in GDP, whereupon a government is permitted to incur an excessive deficit, although it *may* be authorised to do so should the annual fall in GDP be greater than 0.75 per cent.

EMU: the controversy

In the period since the ratification of the TEU, EMU has been subject to increasing rather than decreasing criticism. As the deadline for realising EMU has approached, the debate over the accompanying costs and benefits has intensified. In large measure this debate revolves around the likely consequences of EMU for the participating economies and, in particular, the extent to which the policy constraints implicit under EMU will restrict the capacity of member states to address problems of unemployment or to deal with unexpected economic shocks (see Hughes Hallett and Scott, 1993; Artis, 1997; Feldstein, 1997).

There is, however, broad agreement that EMU will bring certain economic benefits (Emerson and Huhne, 1991). In particular, three categories of economic gain have been identified, each of which should contribute to

---

10 While it is clear that countries suffering from chronic fiscal problems could pose problems should they be permitted to move to stage 3 prematurely, much less certainty surrounded the choice of 3 per cent and 60 per cent of GDP as the appropriate ratios for the annual deficit and the total stock of debt, respectively. It seems that these limits were selected simply because they conformed to the average situation prevailing in the main economies (i.e. France and Germany) during the period of negotiation of the Maastricht Treaty.

economic welfare across the EU. First, a single currency will eliminate costs that arise due to transactions involving different currencies – that is, the 'transaction costs' a company, or an individual, incurs when changing one currency into another to pay for foreign goods or services.[11] The European Commission estimated that lower transaction costs would benefit the EU by approximately one-half of 1 per cent of combined GDP. Second, a single currency means greater price transparency across national borders, with the result that producers will no longer be able to charge different prices for identical products in different national markets. This possibility exists not only because transaction costs deter some cross-border trade, but also because consumers have limited access to the information required to allow them to compare prices denominated in different currencies. Finally, proponents of EMU argue that the very elimination of exchange rate uncertainty with the introduction of a single currency will encourage more trade and investment, leading to an increase in output and employment in all EMU countries.

While not denying that benefits will accrue from EMU, critics argue that there are also costs which should not be ignored. These costs arise because EMU countries surrender monetary policy as an instrument of national economic management. Once EMU is established, differences in national interest rates will not be possible and a country will be unable to change its exchange rate with respect to the other EMU countries or, indeed, with respect to third countries. The loss of these instruments of economic policy means that a country will no longer be able to respond to an external economic shock – such as a decline in demand for its exports – by lowering domestic interest rates, or by devaluing its currency. To the extent that these measures permit a country to offset the initial decline in demand, and the unemployment that accompanies this, critics argue their loss means that EMU will lead to higher levels of unemployment in those countries than before. Clearly, the force of this argument rests on a view that the impact of an external shock is unevenly spread throughout the monetary union. If all economies are affected equally, then it would be appropriate for the ECB to lower interest rates for the area as a whole, in that there would be no danger of this triggering a rise in the rate of inflation. However, if only a few countries – or regions – within the monetary union are affected (i.e., if the shock is asymmetric), the ECB would be unlikely to adjust union-wide monetary conditions. Most economists would accept, at least in principle, that there is some force to this criticism of EMU. How then do the advocates of EMU respond? There are two principal responses.

The first is to argue that asymmetric external economic shocks are extremely rare. The implication of this argument is that the economies of

---

11 This 'cost' is equivalent to the commission that banks charge customers for exchanging currencies.

all EMU countries are highly uniform in their underlying structure. How valid is this assumption? While one might argue that the economies of France and Germany or Belgium and Denmark are similar, each having a highly diversified manufacturing and services base, it is much less clear that there are close similarities between the economies of, say, Germany and Spain, or of France and Portugal. In other words, while accepting that some parts of the EU may well comprise a coherent currency area from this perspective, implying that the loss of national monetary policy would not be problematic, it is quite a different matter to suggest that all countries do. And for those economies which do diverge from the 'norm', membership of EMU may be a costly exercise.

The second response is to argue that other instruments exist to accommodate asymmetric external shocks. Three such mechanisms are identified. The first is labour mobility – that people made unemployed as a result of any shock can move to areas of the monetary union where there are employment opportunities. This obviates the need for a change in economic policy. The second is nominal wage flexibility: by lowering their money wage demands, people made unemployed by an external shock would thereby price themselves into an alternative job. The third option is for central government to mitigate the impact of the economic shock through domestic fiscal policy. As output falls and unemployment rises in the 'shocked' region or country, the operation of national fiscal measures (i.e. unemployment and other transfer payments, regional policy, etc.) would automatically transfer resources towards those regions and this would counter the unemployment-inducing impact of the initial shock.

However, it is difficult to place much confidence in these adjustment mechanisms. First, labour mobility across national borders in the EU is low. This is because language and a host of other social and cultural factors militate against intra-EU labour mobility on any significant scale. Similarly, wage flexibility tends to be extremely weak across the EU. And while a greater measure of wage flexibility may follow from labour market reforms within individual member states, this is not an immediate prospect. Moreover, the evidence from the German experience with monetary union – when the eastern and western parts of the country were reunited – is that money wages tend to equalise around the higher end of the earnings scale once workers in previously different currency areas are able to compare directly the rates of pay being earned for ostensibly similar jobs. To the extent that this occurs, realising EMU may result in money wages in some areas being bid upwards after EMU, which, given prevailing divergences in labour productivity, will serve only to worsen the problem of unemployment. Consequently, many commentators doubt that greater wage flexibility can be relied upon as an adjustment mechanism. Finally, national fiscal policy will operate under tight limits after EMU, making it more difficult for governments to respond to local economic disturbances. At the same time, there is no prospect of the EU developing a fiscal policy capable of effecting cross-border resource transfer on the scale that would be required to stabilise incomes in regions subject to external shocks. The EU budget is very modest in comparison with its national counterparts. Typically member state budgets account for 35–45 per cent of national GDP. By contrast, the EU budget accounts for just over 1 per cent of the combined EU GDP, of which less than one-third is allocated to programmes which are regionally targeted – the so-called structural funds – and which therefore may have a role in assisting adjustment to regional shocks. Presently there is no prospect for the development of an EU-wide fiscal capacity on the scale many would argue is required if member states are to be compensated for the loss of national monetary policy autonomy.[12]

Current developments

Since the TEU was signed, three new countries have joined the EU – Austria, Sweden and Finland – bringing the total membership to fifteen countries. It has now been agreed that the launch of EMU on 1 January 1999 will include eleven of these fifteen member states – that is, all EU member states except Britain and Denmark (both of which have opted out), Greece (which did not meet the convergence criteria) and Sweden (which will not be seeking membership of EMU at that time). In March 1998, the European Commission presented a report which concluded that all eleven met the TEU convergence criteria and should proceed to EMU.[13] Despite this, however, considerable doubt remains regarding the wisdom of some countries proceeding to EMU according to the TEU schedule.

The concern is that while nominal convergence might be deemed to have been achieved, this is only because the relevant fiscal provisions of the TEU are being interpreted extremely generously, or because the fiscal data have been 'massaged' by individual governments with the sole purpose of meeting the EMU convergence criteria. In either case, this should not mask the underlying weakness of those countries with respect to the consequences of EMU membership. The concern is that premature membership of EMU will create difficult economic and political conditions in these countries, and that this will lead them to exert pressure on the institutions of EMU – particularly the ECB – to adopt a less restrictive monetary policy stance.

12 In 1977 the MacDougall report estimated that an EU budget of up to 5 per cent of combined GDP would be required to ensure that national unemployment levels did not rise as a consequence of a move to monetary union.
13 Although some member states failed to fulfil precisely the two excessive deficit criteria, the wording of Article 104c(2) of the TEU allows a degree of latitude to be applied when assessing individual cases.

As this would be wholly unacceptable to the rest of the EMU countries, it might have been better for those countries to postpone joining EMU until the economic situation had improved.

Particular worries surround the impact of EMU on unemployment. Currently, some 11 per cent of the EU labour force is unemployed, representing some 18–19 million citizens. If EMU is implemented in this environment, with the accompanying effect of this on national economic policy, it is difficult to see how member state governments can possibly devise macro-economic strategies that will reduce the level of unemployment over the short to medium term. And if they are unable to do this, some fear that membership of EMU will be seen as a cause of persistent unemployment. Indeed, over the course of the recession which began in 1992, EU member state governments found national fiscal policies (particularly annual budget deficits) being determined, in large part, by the need to conform to the TEU convergence criteria. Arguably, this forced governments to pursue a pro-cyclical macro-economic policy (i.e. reducing public expenditure during a recession to restrict the size of the budget deficit), which served only to exacerbate the severity of the recession. For instance, in France during 1996–7 there was considerable popular unrest over government public expenditure cuts, measures which were attributed to the need to observe the EMU convergence criteria. As a result, even EMU supporters have cautioned against the over-hasty implementation of the policy.

Notwithstanding the controversy over EMU membership in the first round, it is clear that four states will remain outside the single-currency area. What will be the relationship between these currencies and the euro? At the Amsterdam summit in June 1997, it was agreed that a reconstituted Exchange Rate Mechanism (ERM II) will be established from the start of EMU, to operate in the same manner as the original ERM. Currencies will fix a central rate against the euro and will be permitted to move up to 15 per cent either side of this central rate. Intervention arrangements conducted jointly by the new ECB and the relevant national central bank will ensure that non-EMU currencies are protected against any short-term speculation, although it is assumed that domestic economic policy will be adjusted if this is required to stabilise a currency. It is impossible to predict how long it will take these 'pre-in' countries to become full members of EMU, but the intention is that it should not be too long. Otherwise interest rates in these countries may be forced upwards to compensate foreign investors for the perceived risk that the currency may be devalued against the euro at some future date. Clearly, this would not be desirable, and it is the interests of the relevant governments to maintain an economic policy stance consistent with early EMU participation.

In both Britain and Denmark, membership of EMU raises deep-seated political, if not constitutional, questions. Denmark is bound to conduct a national referendum on the matter and the British government has stated that it, too, will put the question to a referendum before any decision to take Britain into EMU is made. Notwithstanding this debate, economic policy under successive Danish governments has been framed in the context of a fixed exchange rate between the krone and the Deutschmark, reflecting the high degree of economic integration between the two countries. Although Denmark will not participate in the first wave of EMU, there is no reason to anticipate a change in its exchange rate policy.

For Britain, however, the matter is considerably more complex. A powerful political lobby continues to oppose closer exchange rate links with the rest of the EU. Indeed, the government will not seek membership of ERM II. But there are vital economic issues at stake. Should Britain indicate that sterling is unlikely to participate in EMU over the long term (and keeping sterling out of ERM II might be interpreted in this way), this may cause a long-term increase in British interest rates, to insure sterling holders against the risk of holding a currency that may be subject to devaluation against the euro. At the same time, future foreign direct investment might be discouraged as non-EU companies opt to locate their production facilities within the euro area, thereby reducing their exposure to currency risks. On the other hand, moves to take sterling into ERM II could provoke a political outcry. All of the questions raised during the previous episode of sterling's ERM membership would be reopened – questions over the rate at which should sterling join; what the government should do if domestic considerations pointed to a lower British interest rate than that consistent with maintaining the prevailing parity; how the government should avoid external interference with economic policy, and so on.

The British position was clarified by the Chancellor of the Exchequer in a speech to the House of Commons on 27 October 1997. In that speech, Gordon Brown made it quite clear that while there was no constitutional obstacle to Britain participating in EMU, economic conditions at present ruled against this. Moreover, the Chancellor thought it highly unlikely that the decision to join EMU would be taken in the lifetime of the present Parliament – that is, before the year 2002. Chancellor Brown set out five criteria which he declared had to be assessed before Britain would consider joining EMU:

1 Are business cycles and economic structures in Britain and the EMU countries compatible, so that the monetary policy followed by the EMU group is also appropriate for the British economy?
2 Does the economy display sufficient labour market flexibility to ensure that the loss of monetary policy as a macro-economic lever does not result in higher unemployment?
3 Will joining EMU create better conditions for firms making long-term decisions to invest in Britain?

4   What impact will entry to EMU have on the financial services industry?
5   Will joining EMU be beneficial to employment and economic growth
    in Britain?

British policy will, therefore, be shaped by economic interests and not by political or constitutional matters. Finally, the Chancellor made it clear that British economic policy would continue to 'shadow' the monetary and fiscal criteria necessary for sterling to be eligible to join EMU at the appropriate juncture: 'We will ensure that our fiscal rules and our deficit reduction plan continue to be consistent with the terms of the stability pact, thus underlining our commitment to avoid an excessive deficit.'

Despite the comparatively constructive posture struck by the Labour government with respect to British relations with the EU, it remains the case that, as a non-member of EMU, British influence over monetary and fiscal policy in the EMU area will be minimal. However, decisions taken by these countries will affect the British economy, creating potential difficulties for British policy makers. In practice, this is a problem that is unlikely to be resolved unless, and until, Britain signs up for EMU.

Conclusions

Monetary union represents a profound and challenging step in the process of establishing an 'ever closer Union' between the peoples of Europe. If successful, it will propel the EU forward towards ever closer political integration; if unsuccessful, it will represent the most serious political crisis in the EU's history. Opinions are sharply divided over the viability of EMU at this juncture. The critics argue that – even if desirable in the long run – it is premature to move to EMU at the present time, with the current EU circumstances of high unemployment and slow economic growth being those least likely to secure a successful launch for EMU. Beyond this, many oppose EMU from a variety of other perspectives, including considerations of constitutional sovereignty, the fear of weakening the historical basis of domestic economic successes and the absence of a sufficient degree of EU political integration to ensure that EMU will work.

Despite the critics, however, EMU will happen. Calls for its postponement or abandonment have failed to influence a generation of politicians who have invested heavily in delivering EMU and for whom it will represent their crowning achievement. In short, the politics of EMU are seemingly irresistible. Moreover, those who criticise EMU from the economic perspective must also consider the viability of the alternative – namely, a return to a system of fixed, though periodically adjustable, exchange rates. Given the degree and the scale of capital mobility that is such a defining feature of late-twentieth-century global capitalism, can governments – even powerful ones like those of Germany, France and Britain – effectively stabilise conditions in foreign exchange markets once speculative fever takes hold? And if not, then what are the implications of the resultant exchange rate volatility for trade flows across national boundaries? While one might point to a number of economic – and political – problems that will arise under EMU, the real question that has to be addressed by the critics is whether the alternative to a single currency is any longer a viable option from the perspective of European integration (Eichengreen, 1994, ch. 7).

Reading

Artis, M. (1997) 'European Monetary Union', in M. Artis and N. Lee (eds), *The Economics of the European Union*, Oxford University Press.

Barrell, R. (ed.) (1992) *Economic Convergence and Monetary Union in Europe*, Sage.

Bean, C. (1992) 'Economic and Monetary Union in Europe', *Journal of Economic Perspectives*, fall, pp. 31–52.

Cobham, D. (ed.) (1994) *European Monetary Upheavals*, Manchester University Press.

De Grauwe, P. (1997) *The Economics of Monetary Integration* (3rd edn), Oxford University Press.

Delors, J. (1989) *Report on Economic and Monetary Union in the European Community*, European Commission.

Dyson, K. (1994) *Elusive Union: The Process of Economic and Monetary Union in Europe*, Longman.

Eichengreen, B. (1994) *International Monetary Arrangements for the 21st Century*, Brookings Institute.

Emerson, M. and Huhne, C. (1991) *The ECU Report*, Pan Books.

Feldstein, M. (1997) 'The political economy of the European Economic and Monetary Union: political sources of an economic instability', *Journal of Economic Perspectives*, fall, pp. 23–42.

Gros, D. and Thygesen, N. (1992) *European Monetary Integration: From the European Monetary System to European Monetary Union*, Longman.

Hughes Hallett, A. and Scott, A. (1993) 'The fiscal policy dilemmas of monetary union', in P. Coffey (ed.), *Main Economic Policy Areas of the EC – After 1992*, Kluwer.

Jenkins, R. (1977) *Europe's Present Challenge and Future Opportunity* (Jean Monnet Lecture), EUI.

Kenen, P. (1995) *Economic and Monetary Union in Europe*, Cambridge University Press.

Ludlow, P. (1982) *The Making of the European Monetary System*, Butterworth.

Padoa-Schioppa, T. (1987) *Efficiency, Stability and Equity*, Oxford University Press.

Steinherr, A. (ed.) (1994) *European Monetary Integration: From the Werner Plan to EMU*, Longman.

Tsoukalis, L. (1977) *The Politics and Economics of European Monetary Integration*, Allen and Unwin.

Index

Political issues
in Britain today

7

MANCHESTER
UNIVERSITY PRESS

Politics Today

Series editor: Bill Jones